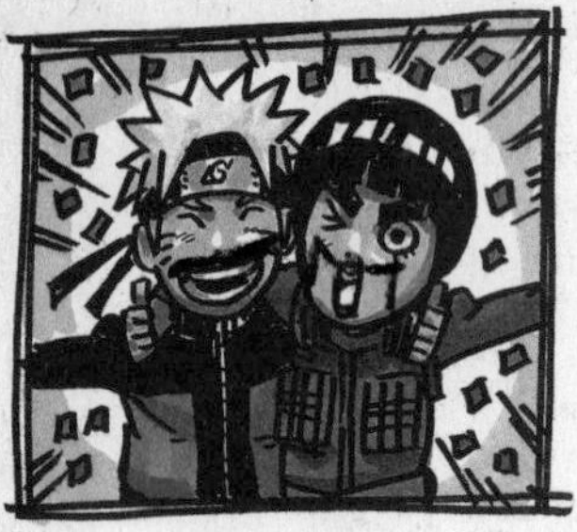

岸本斉史

Can you believe it?! Rock Lee has become a main character! *Rock Lee & His Ninja Pals!!!* (by Kenji Taira) is being simultaneously released with this volume*!! *Rock Lee* is fundamentally a youthful gag manga that revolves around Lee, but we're also aiming for a comedic touch and to dig further where all of you *Naruto* fans wished we'd gone before... A-ha ha!! In any case, congrats, Lee!!

—Masashi Kishimoto, 2012

You can watch the anime, *Naruto* Spin-Off: *Rock Lee & His Ninja Pals* now at vizanime.com!

Author/artist Masashi Kishimoto was born in 1974 in rural Okayama Prefecture, Japan. After spending time in art college, he won the Hop Step Award for new manga artists with his manga **Karakuri** (Mechanism). Kishimoto decided to base his next story on traditional Japanese culture. His first version of **Naruto**, drawn in 1997, was a one-shot story about fox spirits; his final version, which debuted in **Weekly Shonen Jump** in 1999, quickly became the most popular ninja manga in Japan.

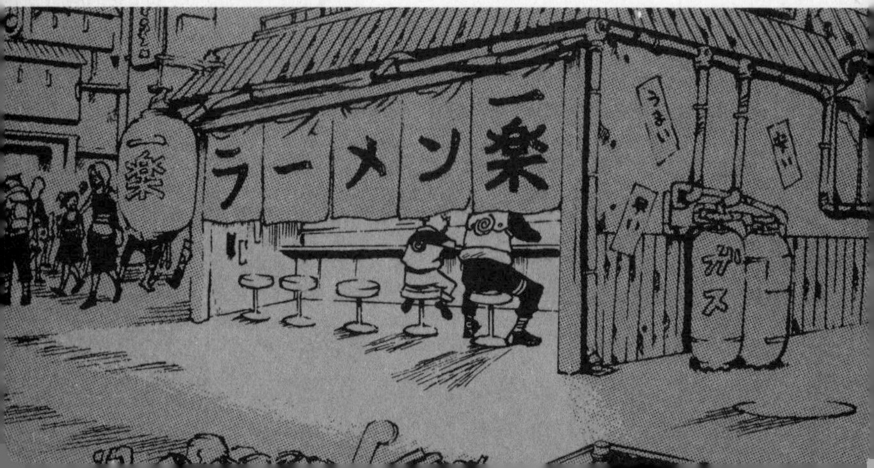
一楽
ラーメン一楽
うまい

NARUTO VOL. 59
SHONEN JUMP Manga Edition

STORY AND ART BY MASASHI KISHIMOTO

Translation/Alexis Kirsch, Mari Morimoto
English Adaptation/Joel Enos
Touch-up Art & Lettering/Sabrina Heep
Design/Sam Elzway
Editor/Joel Enos

Published by VIZ Media, LLC
P.O. Box 77010
San Francisco, CA 94107

10 9 8 7 6 5 4 3 2 1
First printing, November 2012

PARENTAL ADVISORY
NARUTO is rated T for Teen and is recommended
for ages 13 and up. This volume contains realistic
and fantasy violence.
ratings.viz.com

www.viz.com

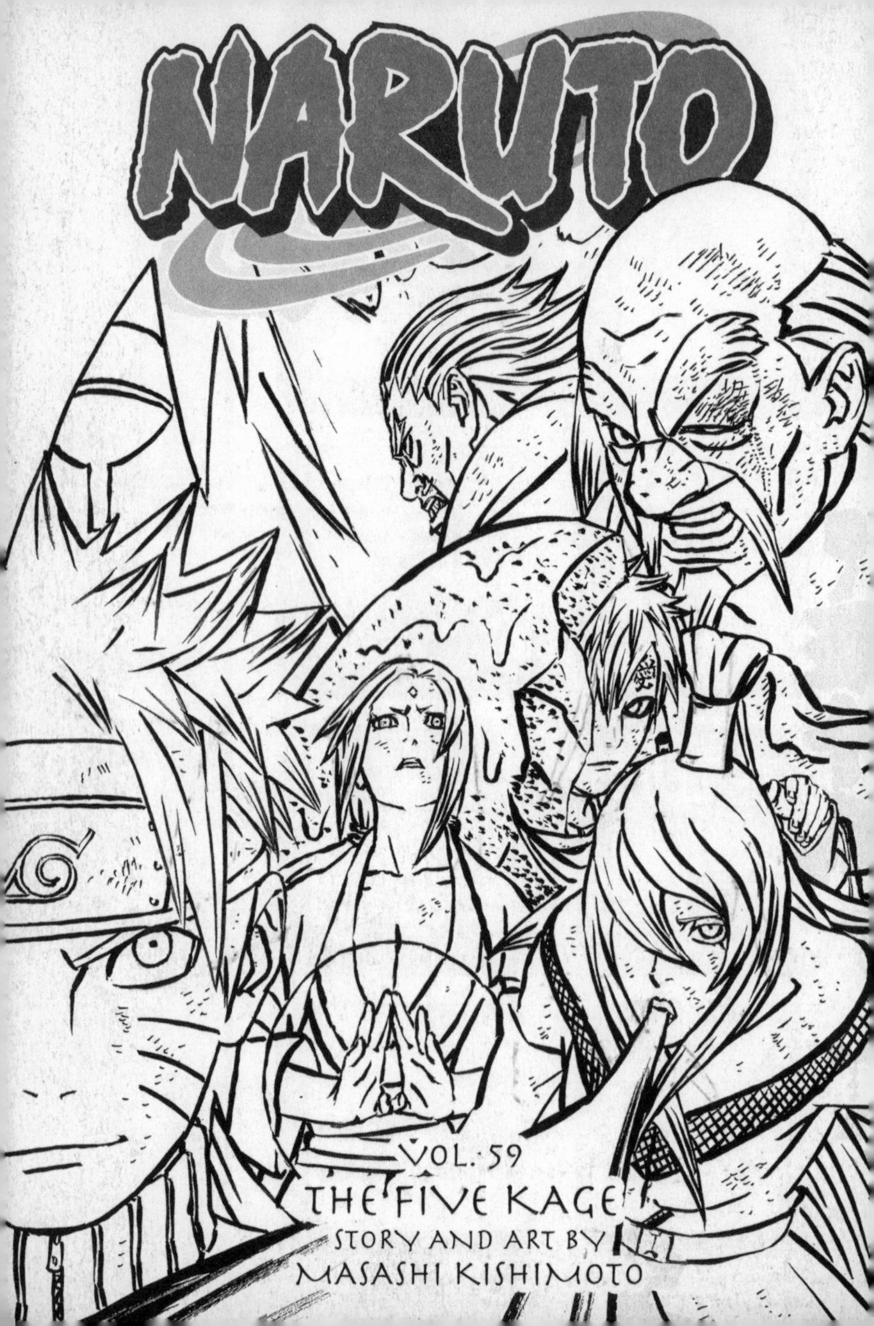
NARUTO
VOL. 59
THE FIVE KAGE
STORY AND ART BY
MASASHI KISHIMOTO

CHARACTERS

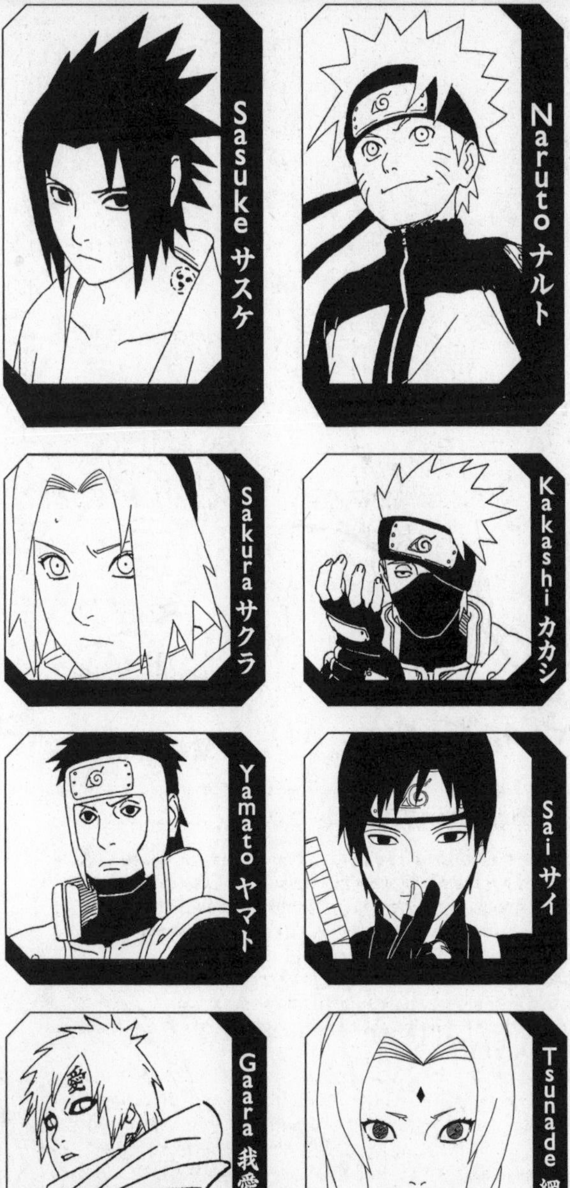
Naruto ナルト
Sasuke サスケ
Kakashi カカシ
Sakura サクラ
Sai サイ
Yamato ヤマト
Tsunade 綱手
Gaara 我愛羅

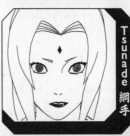

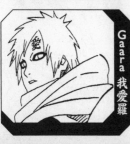

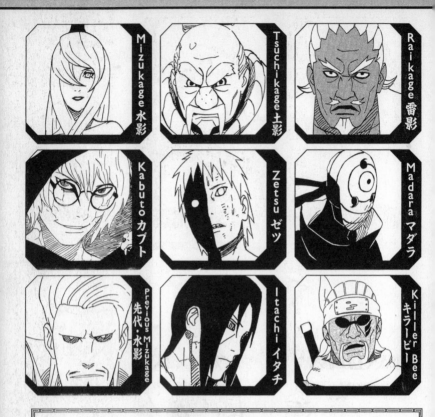

Mizukage 水影

Tsuchikage 土影

Raikage 雷影

Kabuto カブト

Zetsu ゼツ

Madara マダラ

Previous Mizukage 先代・水影

Itachi イタチ

Killer Bee キラービー

—— THE STORY SO FAR... ——

Naruto, the biggest troublemaker at the Ninja Academy in the Village of Kono-hagakure, finally becomes a ninja along with his classmates Sasuke and Sakura. They grow and mature through countless trials and battles. However, Sasuke, unable to give up his quest for vengeance, leaves Konohagakure to seek Orochimaru and his power.

Two years pass. Naruto grows up and engages in fierce battles against the Tailed Beast-targeting Akatsuki. Elsewhere, after winning the heroic battle against Itachi and learning his older brother's true intentions, Sasuke allies with the Akatsuki and sets out to destroy Konoha.

Upon Madara of the Akatsuki's declaration of war against the Ninja Alliances, the Five Kage put together an Allied Shinobi Force. The Fourth Great Ninja War against the Akatsuki begins. Upon breaking out of the training grounds and rushing forth to each battleground, Naruto helps his comrades successfully seal away the previous Raikage, who had been called up through Edotensei, a method of using dead ninja, reanimated as soldiers. Now Gaara, leader of the Sand Village, and Ohnoki, leader of the Stone Village, battle the previous Mizukage, former leaders of the Mist Village!

NARUTO

VOL. 59
THE FIVE KAGE

CONTENTS

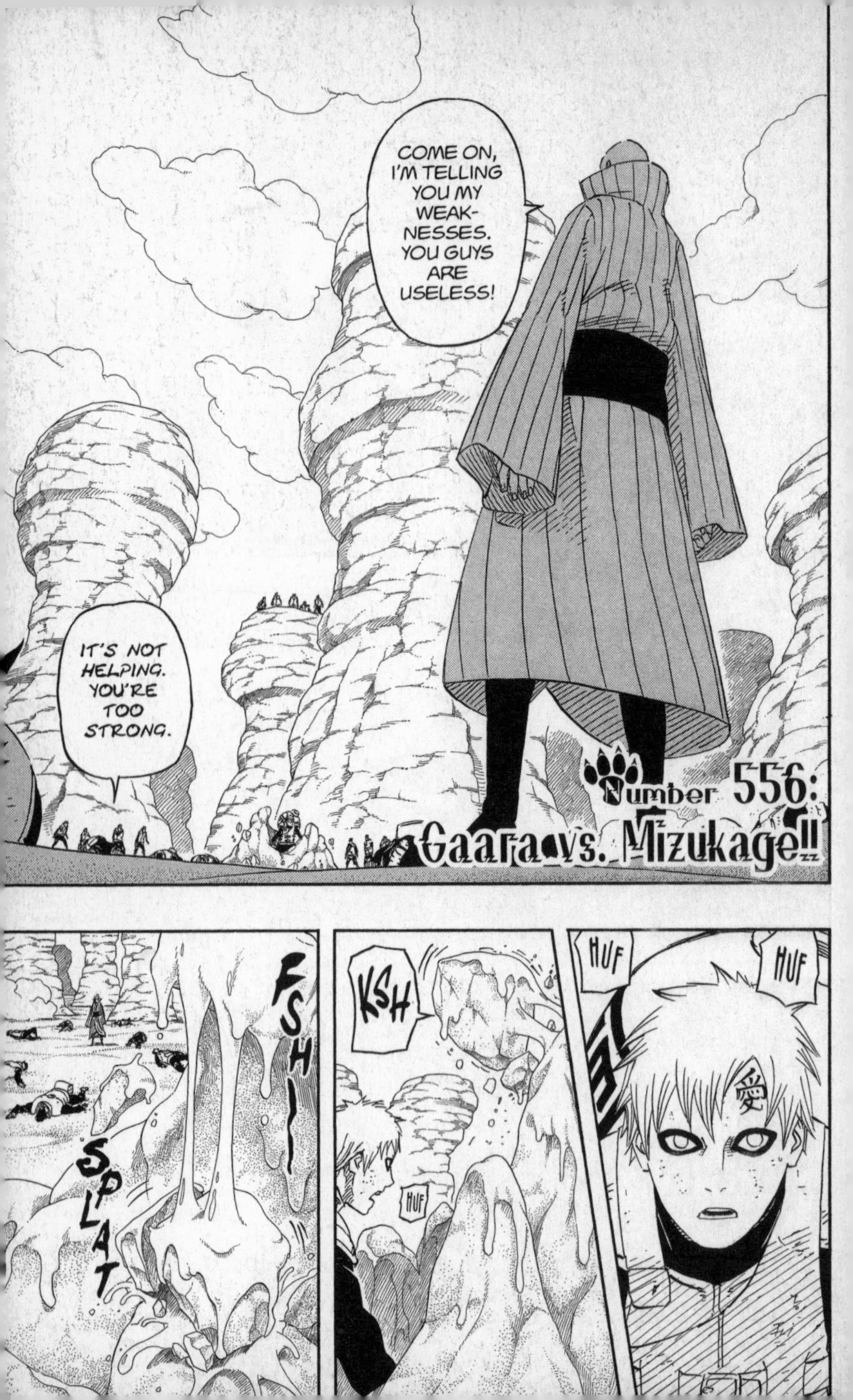
COME ON, I'M TELLING YOU MY WEAK-NESSES. YOU GUYS ARE USELESS!
IT'S NOT HELPING. YOU'RE TOO STRONG.
Number 556: Gaara vs. Mizukage!!
HUF
HUF
KSH
HUF
FSHH
SPLAT

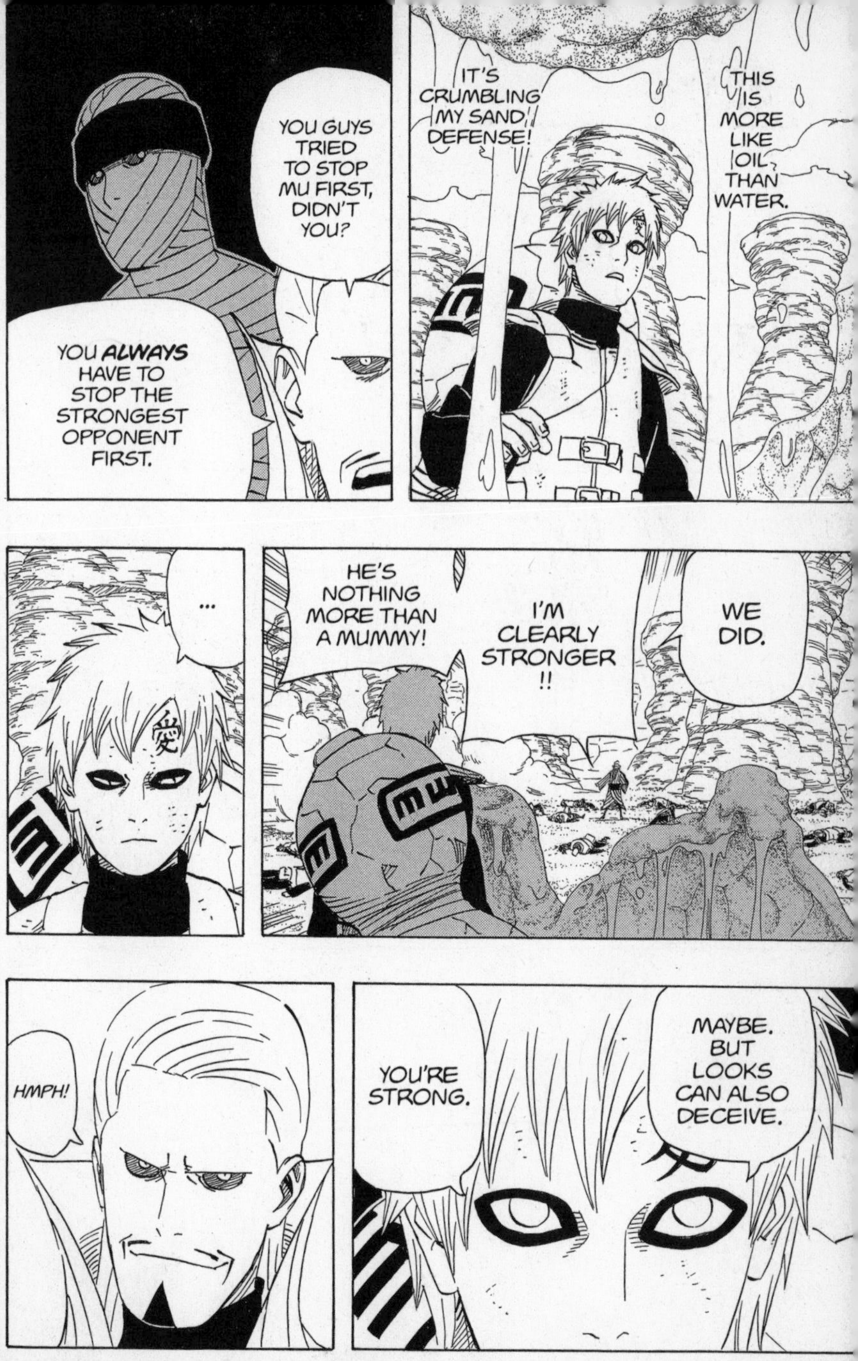
THIS IS MORE LIKE OIL THAN WATER.
IT'S CRUMBLING MY SAND DEFENSE!
YOU GUYS TRIED TO STOP MU FIRST, DIDN'T YOU?
YOU **ALWAYS** HAVE TO STOP THE STRONGEST OPPONENT FIRST.
WE DID.
I'M CLEARLY STRONGER !!
HE'S NOTHING MORE THAN A MUMMY!
...
MAYBE. BUT LOOKS CAN ALSO DECEIVE.
YOU'RE STRONG.
HMPH!

READ THIS WAY

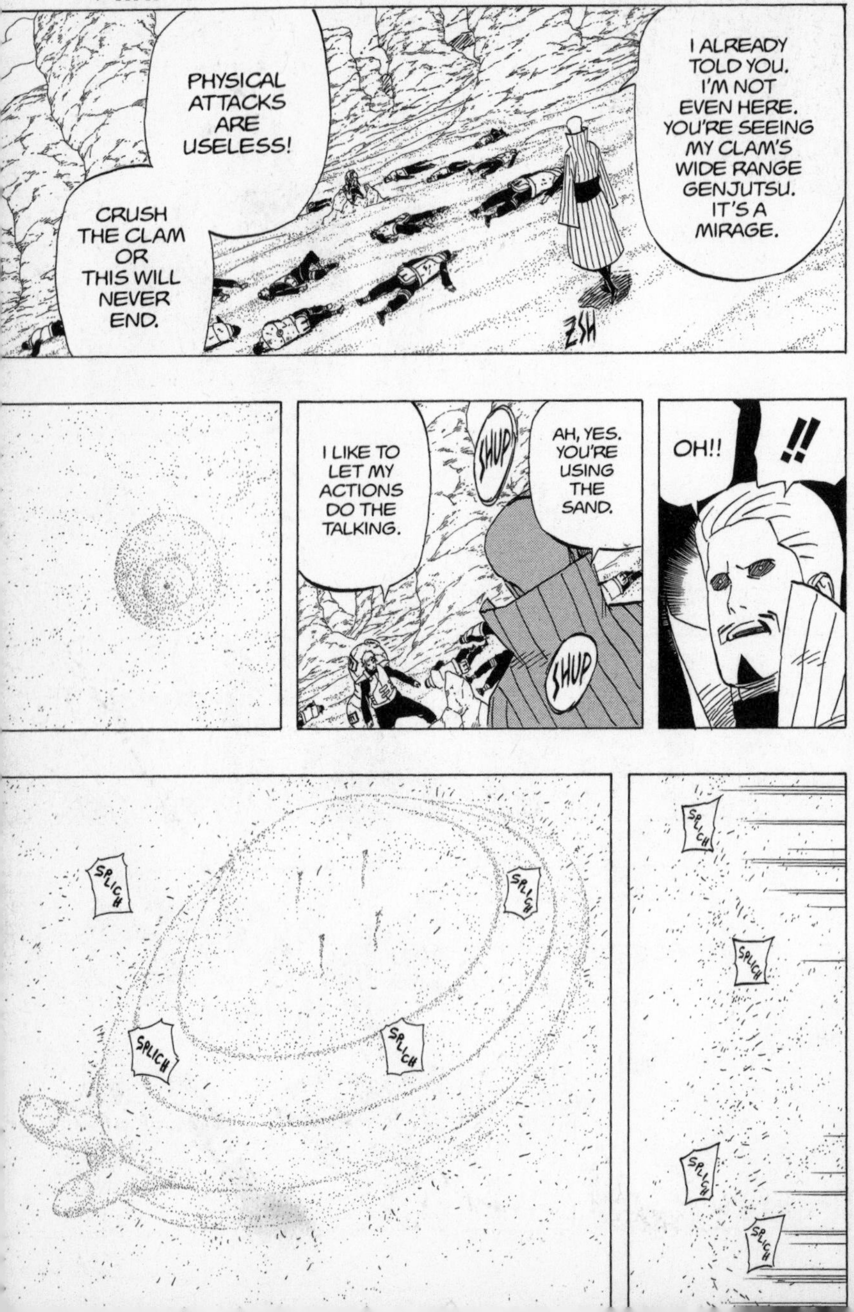
I ALREADY TOLD YOU. I'M NOT EVEN HERE. YOU'RE SEEING MY CLAM'S WIDE RANGE GENJUTSU. IT'S A MIRAGE.
PHYSICAL ATTACKS ARE USELESS!
ZSH
CRUSH THE CLAM OR THIS WILL NEVER END.
OH!!
!!
AH, YES. YOU'RE USING THE SAND.
SHUP
I LIKE TO LET MY ACTIONS DO THE TALKING.
SHUP
SPLICH
SPLICH
SPLICH
SPLICH
SPLICH
SPLICH
SPLICH
SPLICH

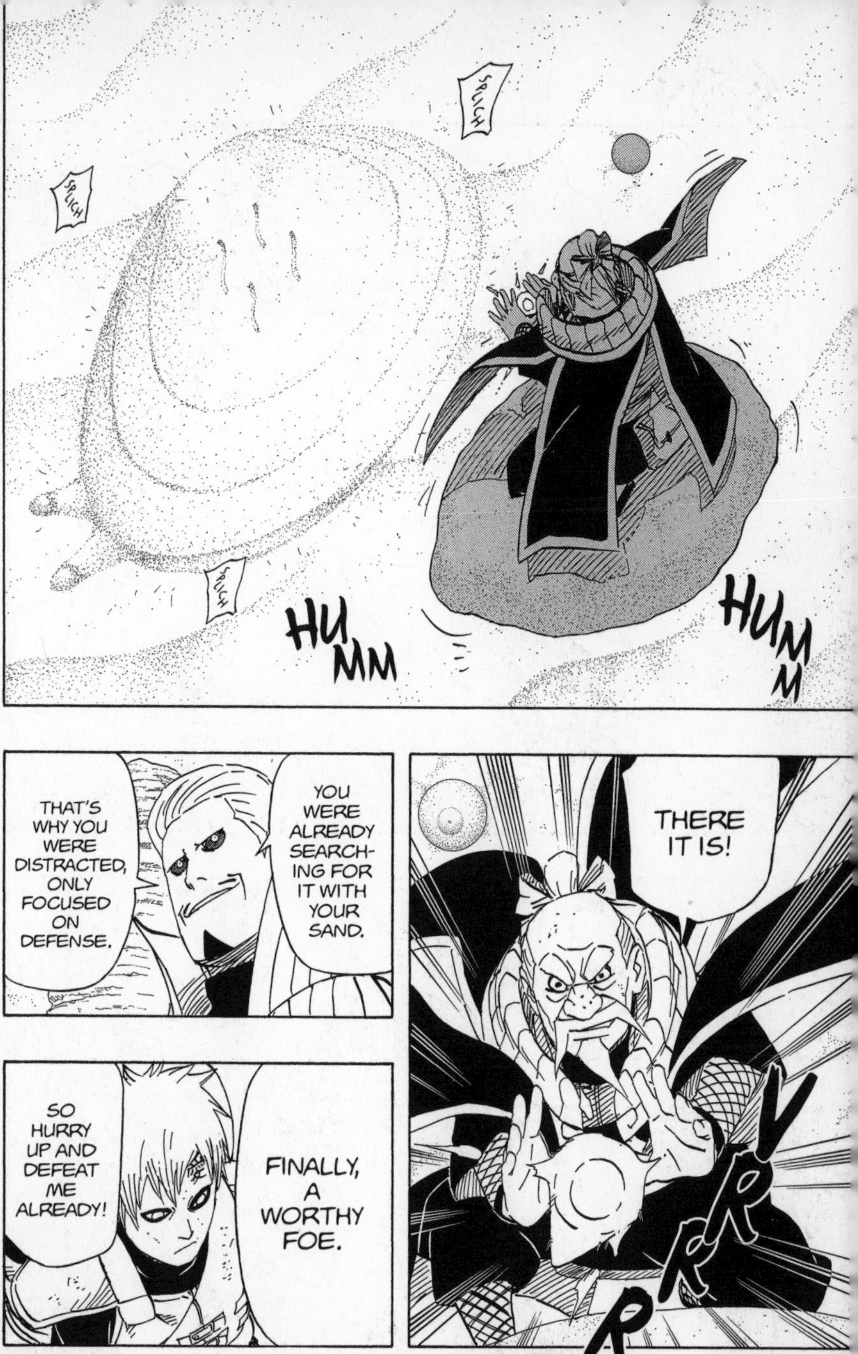
SPLICH
SPLICH
SPLICH
HUMM
HUMM
THERE IT IS!
RRRR
YOU WERE ALREADY SEARCHING FOR IT WITH YOUR SAND.
THAT'S WHY YOU WERE DISTRACTED, ONLY FOCUSED ON DEFENSE.
FINALLY, A WORTHY FOE.
SO HURRY UP AND DEFEAT ME ALREADY!

READ THIS WAY

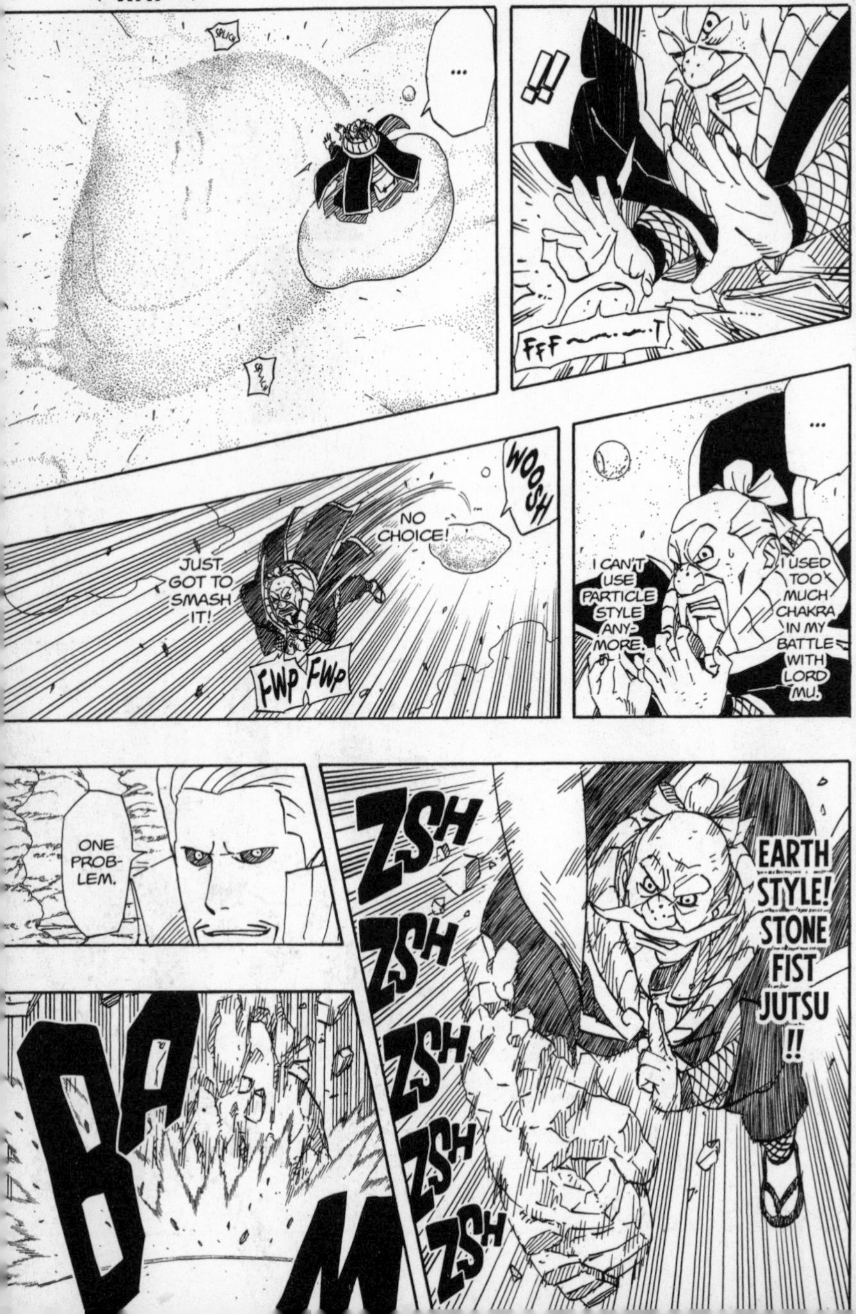
!!
FFF~~~T
SPLICH
...
SPLICH
...
I USED TOO MUCH CHAKRA IN MY BATTLE WITH LORD MU.
I CAN'T USE PARTICLE STYLE ANYMORE.
WOOSH
NO CHOICE!
JUST GOT TO SMASH IT!
FWP FWP
EARTH STYLE! STONE FIST JUTSU!!
ZSH ZSH ZSH ZSH ZSH
ONE PROBLEM.
BAM

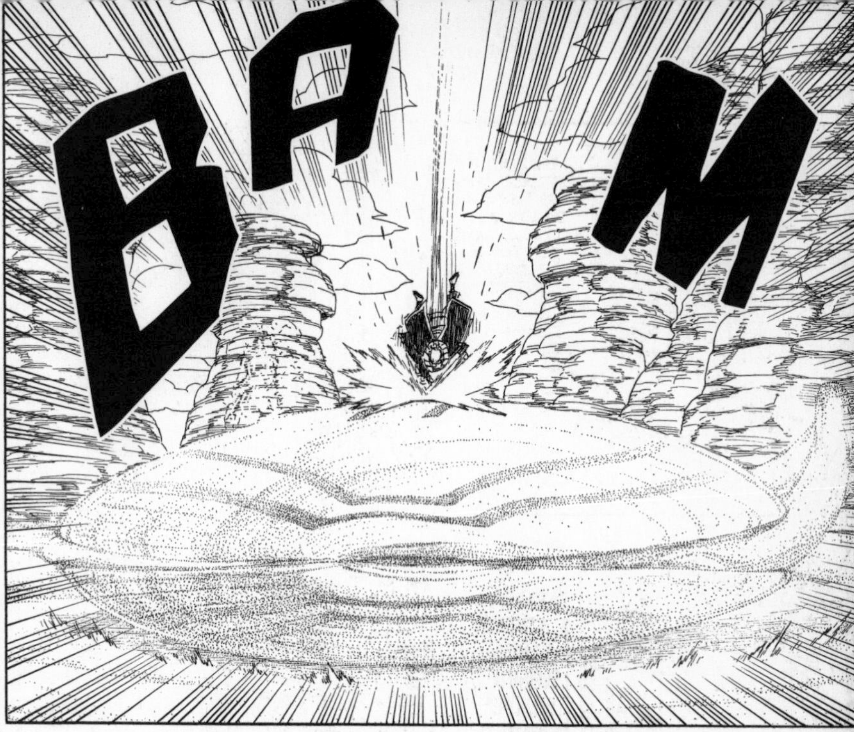
BAM

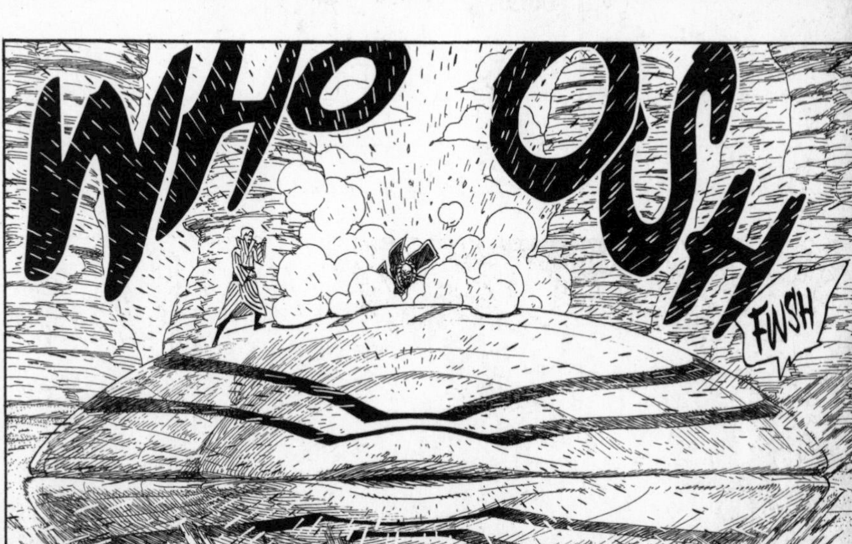
WHOOSH
FWSH

READ THIS WAY

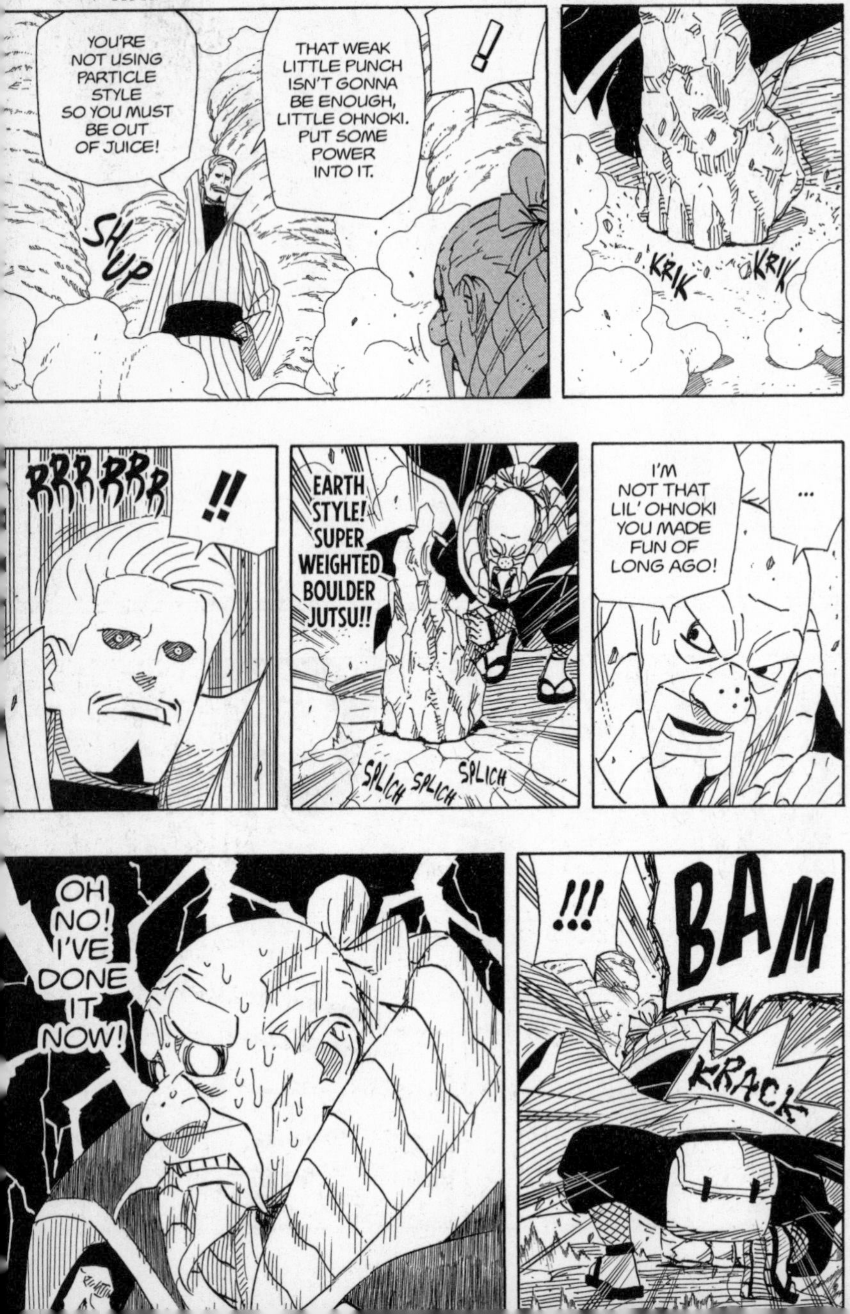
KRIK
KRIK
!
THAT WEAK LITTLE PUNCH ISN'T GONNA BE ENOUGH, LITTLE OHNOKI. PUT SOME POWER INTO IT.
YOU'RE NOT USING PARTICLE STYLE SO YOU MUST BE OUT OF JUICE!
SHUP
...
I'M NOT THAT LIL' OHNOKI YOU MADE FUN OF LONG AGO!
EARTH STYLE! SUPER WEIGHTED BOULDER JUTSU!!
SPLICH
SPLICH
SPLICH
!!
RRRRRR
BAM
!!!
KRACK
OH NO! I'VE DONE IT NOW!

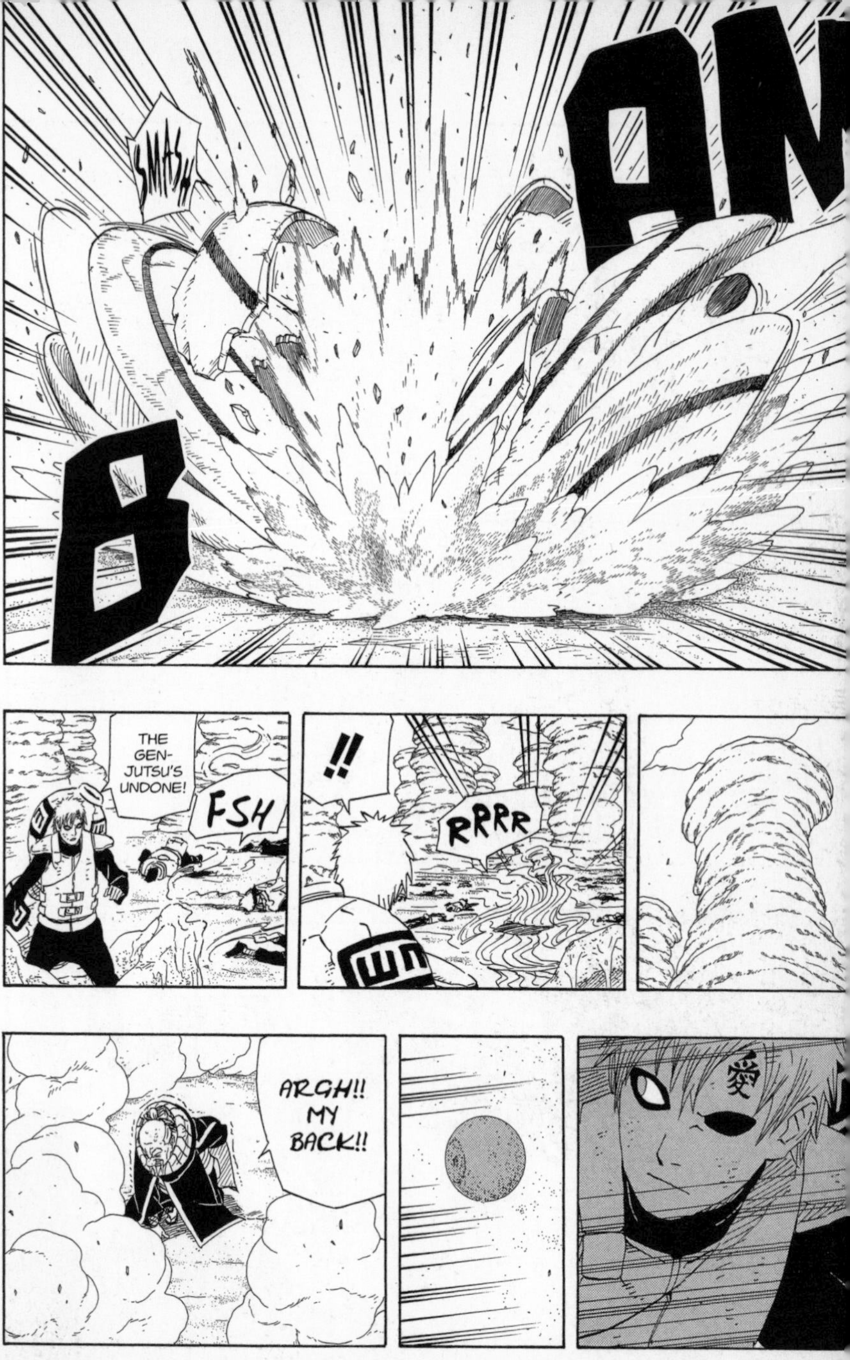
BAM
SMASH
!!
RRRR
THE GEN-JUTSU'S UNDONE!
FSH
ARGH!! MY BACK!!

READ THIS WAY

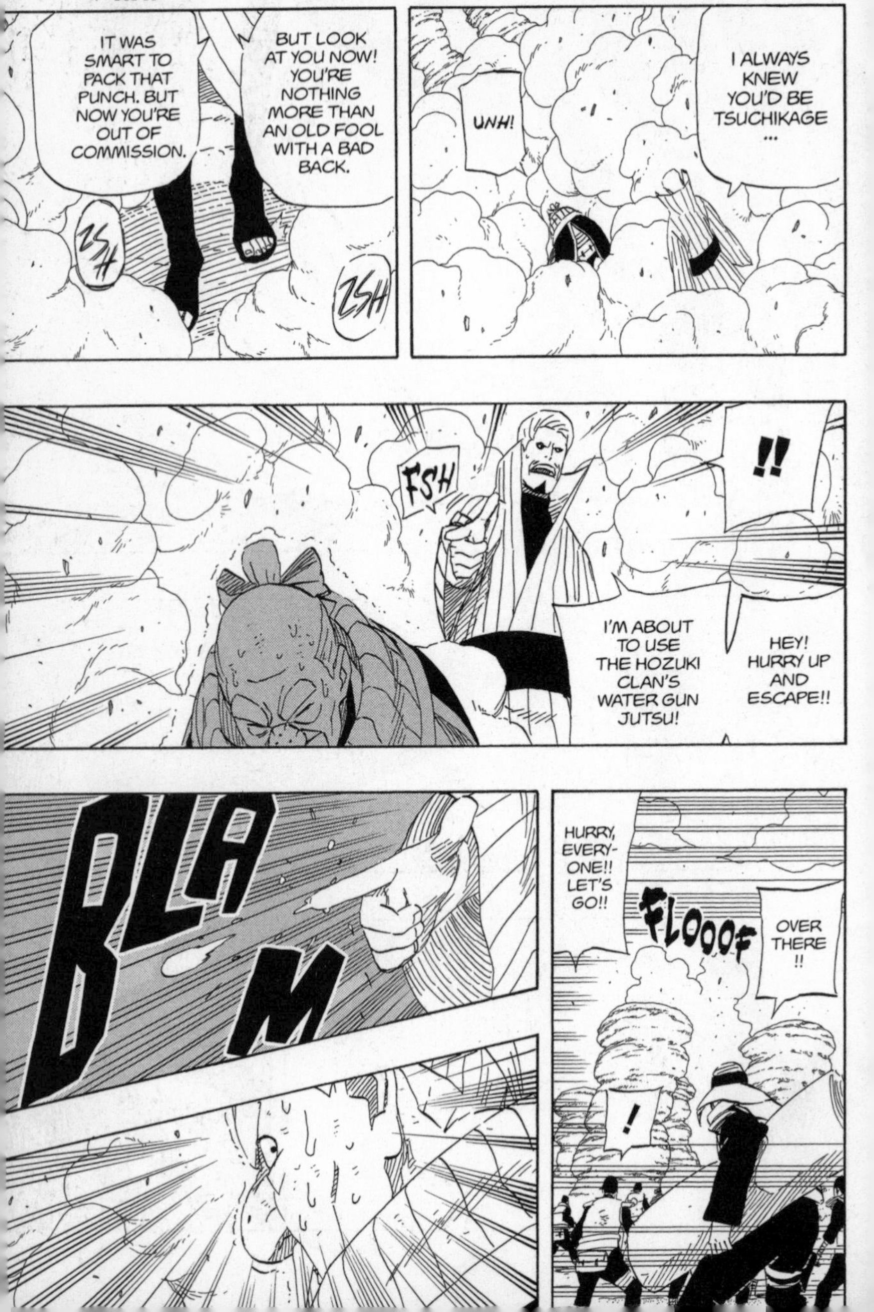
I ALWAYS KNEW YOU'D BE TSUCHIKAGE ...
UNH!
BUT LOOK AT YOU NOW! YOU'RE NOTHING MORE THAN AN OLD FOOL WITH A BAD BACK.
IT WAS SMART TO PACK THAT PUNCH. BUT NOW YOU'RE OUT OF COMMISSION.
ZSH
ZSH
!!
FSH
HEY! HURRY UP AND ESCAPE!!
I'M ABOUT TO USE THE HOZUKI CLAN'S WATER GUN JUTSU!
OVER THERE !!
HURRY, EVERY-ONE!! LET'S GO!!
FLOOOF
!
BLAM

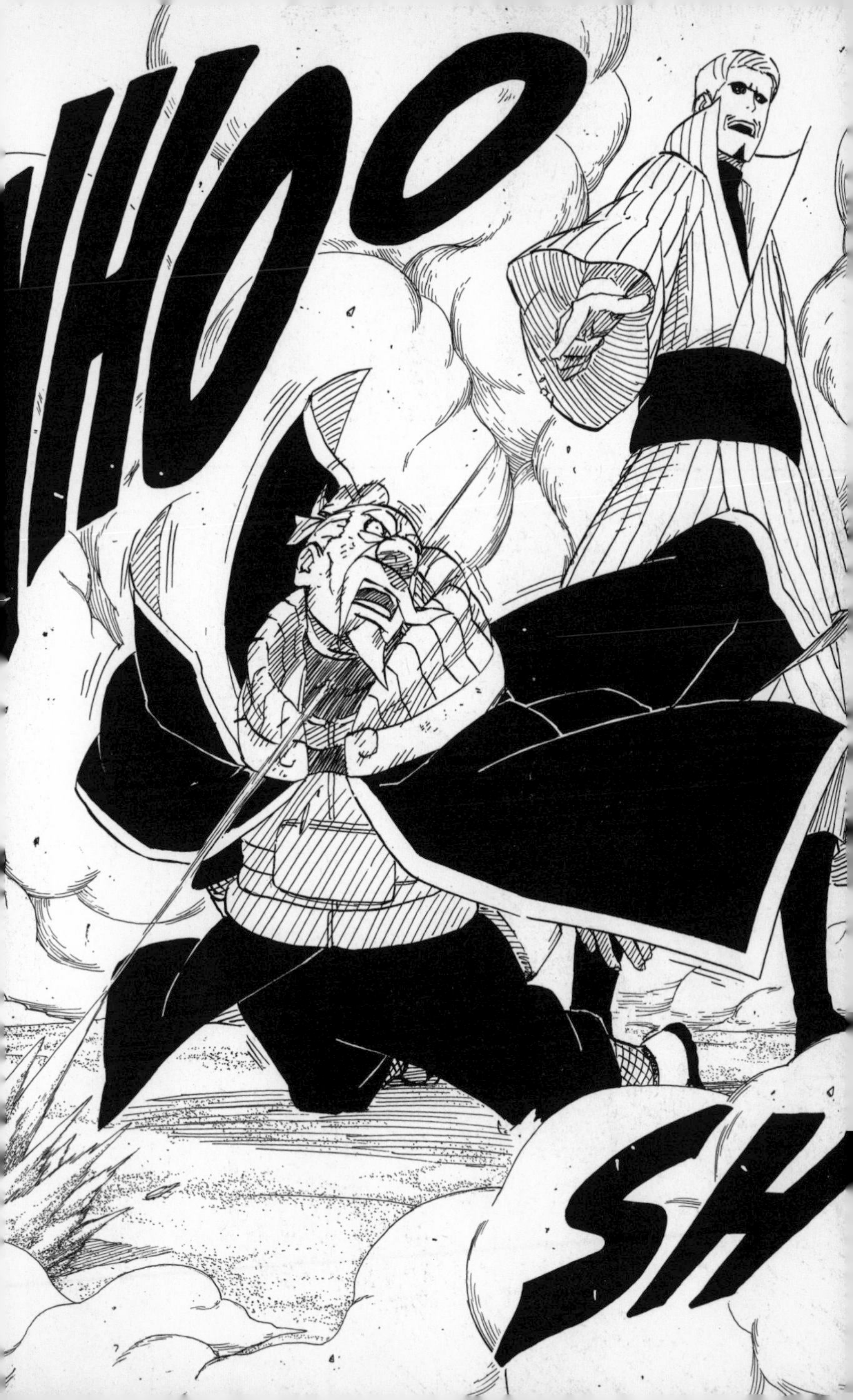
HOO
SH

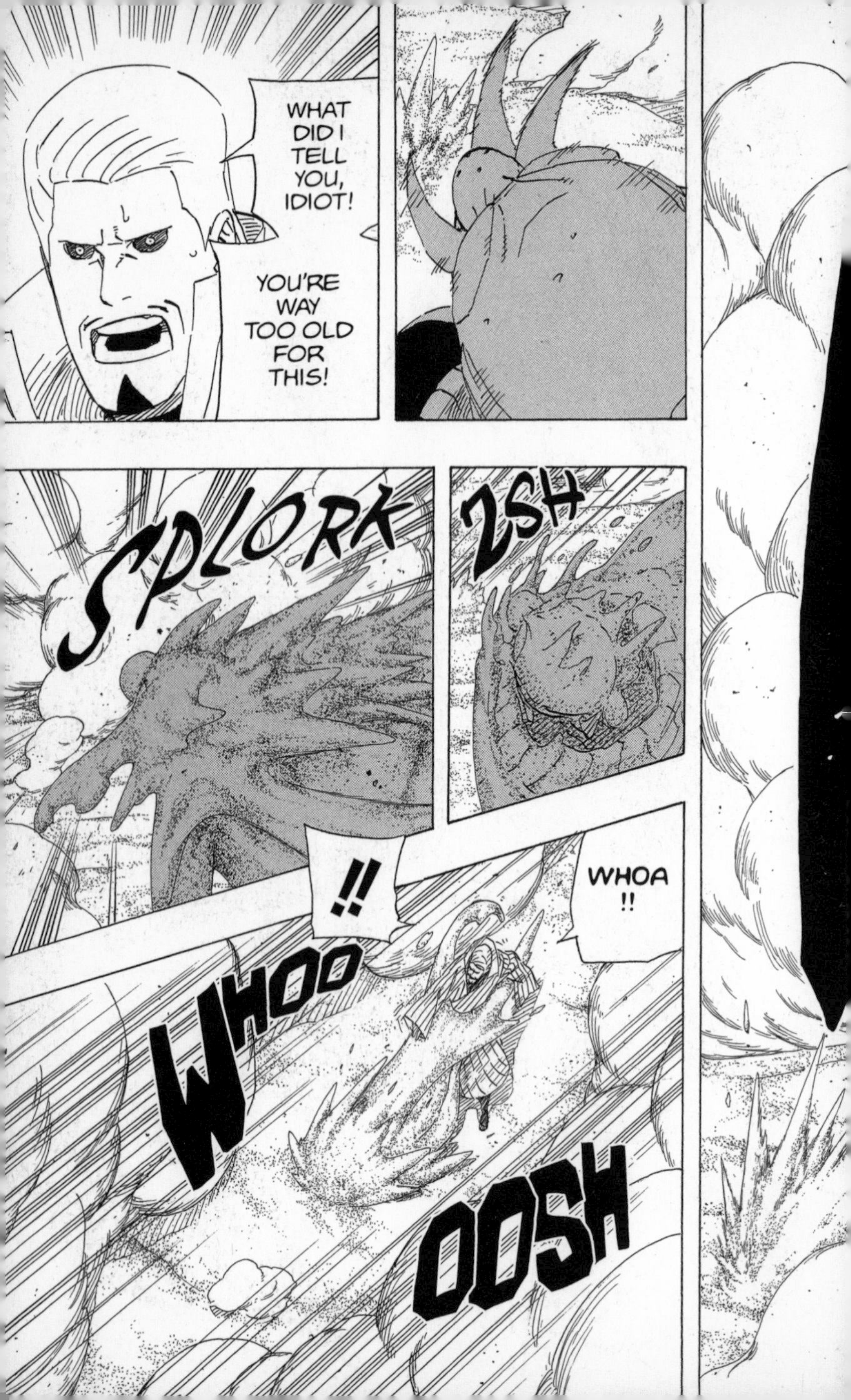
WHAT DID I TELL YOU, IDIOT!
YOU'RE WAY TOO OLD FOR THIS!
ZSH
SPLORK
WHOA !!
!!
WHOOOSH

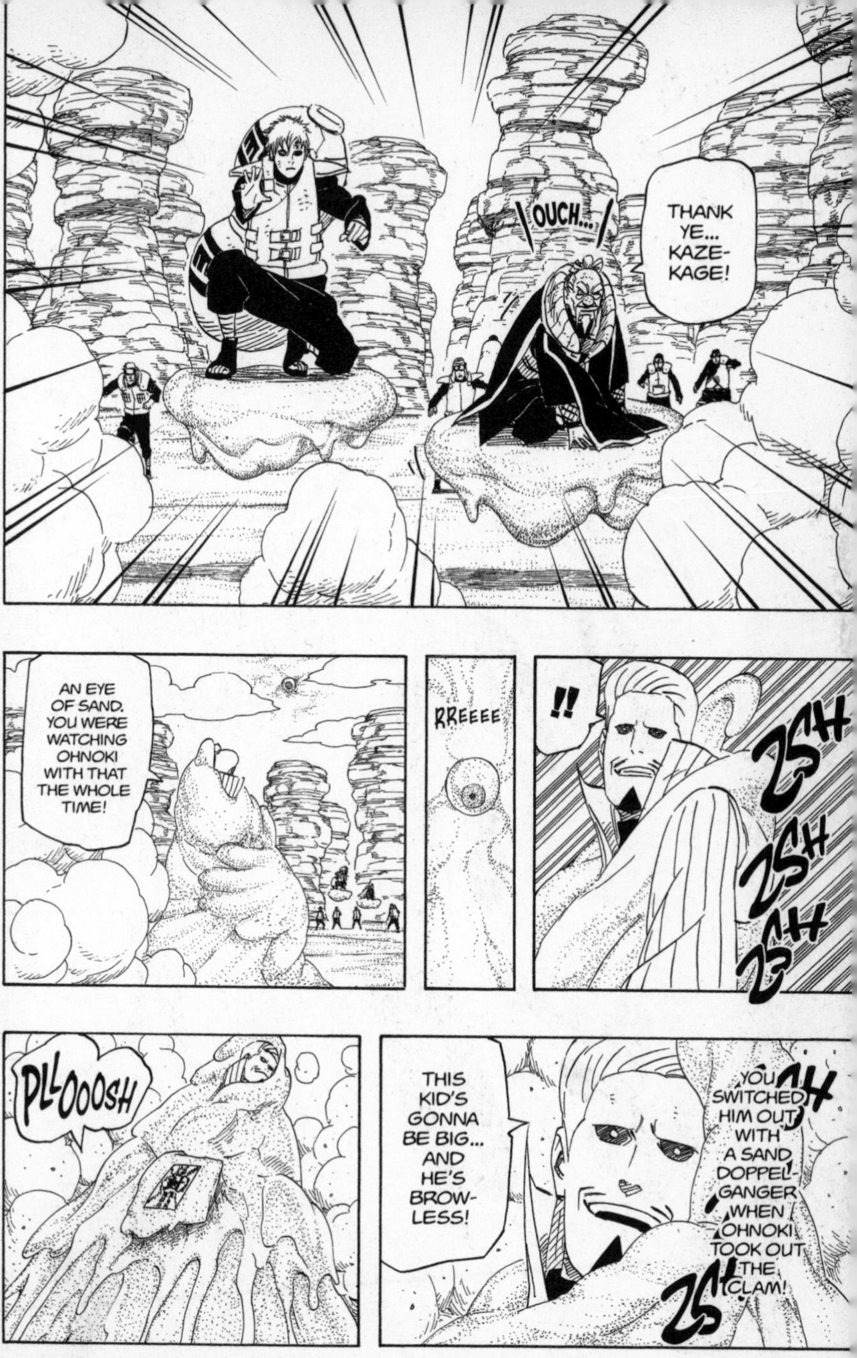

THANK YE... KAZE-KAGE!
OUCH...
!!
ZSH
ZSH
ZSH
RREEEE
AN EYE OF SAND. YOU WERE WATCHING OHNOKI WITH THAT THE WHOLE TIME!
ZSH
YOU SWITCHED HIM OUT WITH A SAND DOPPEL-GANGER WHEN OHNOKI TOOK OUT THE CLAM!
THIS KID'S GONNA BE BIG... AND HE'S BROW-LESS!
ZS
PLLOOOSH

READ THIS WAY

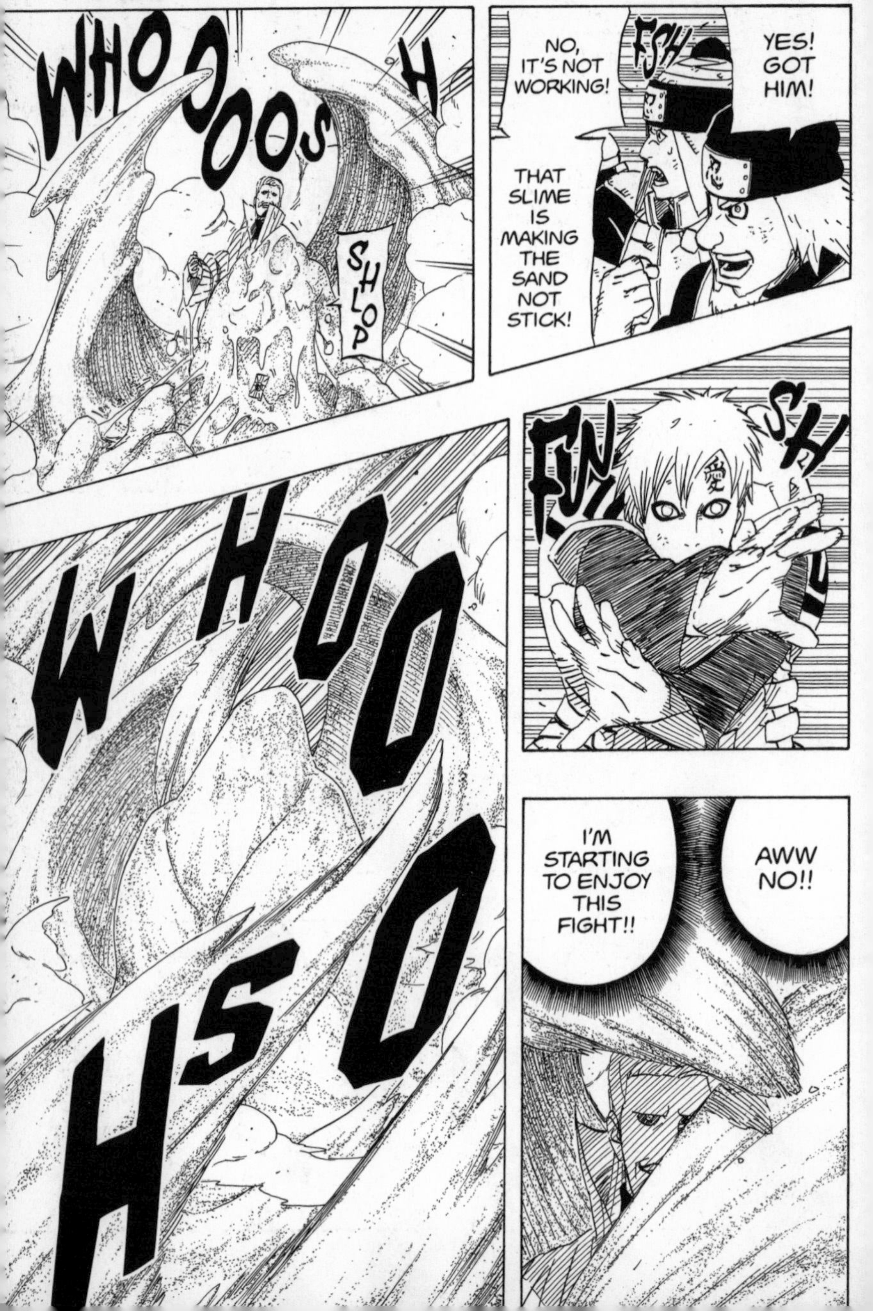

YES! GOT HIM!
FSH
NO, IT'S NOT WORKING!
THAT SLIME IS MAKING THE SAND NOT STICK!
WHOOOOSH
SHLOP
SH
WHOOOOSH
AWW NO!!
I'M STARTING TO ENJOY THIS FIGHT!!

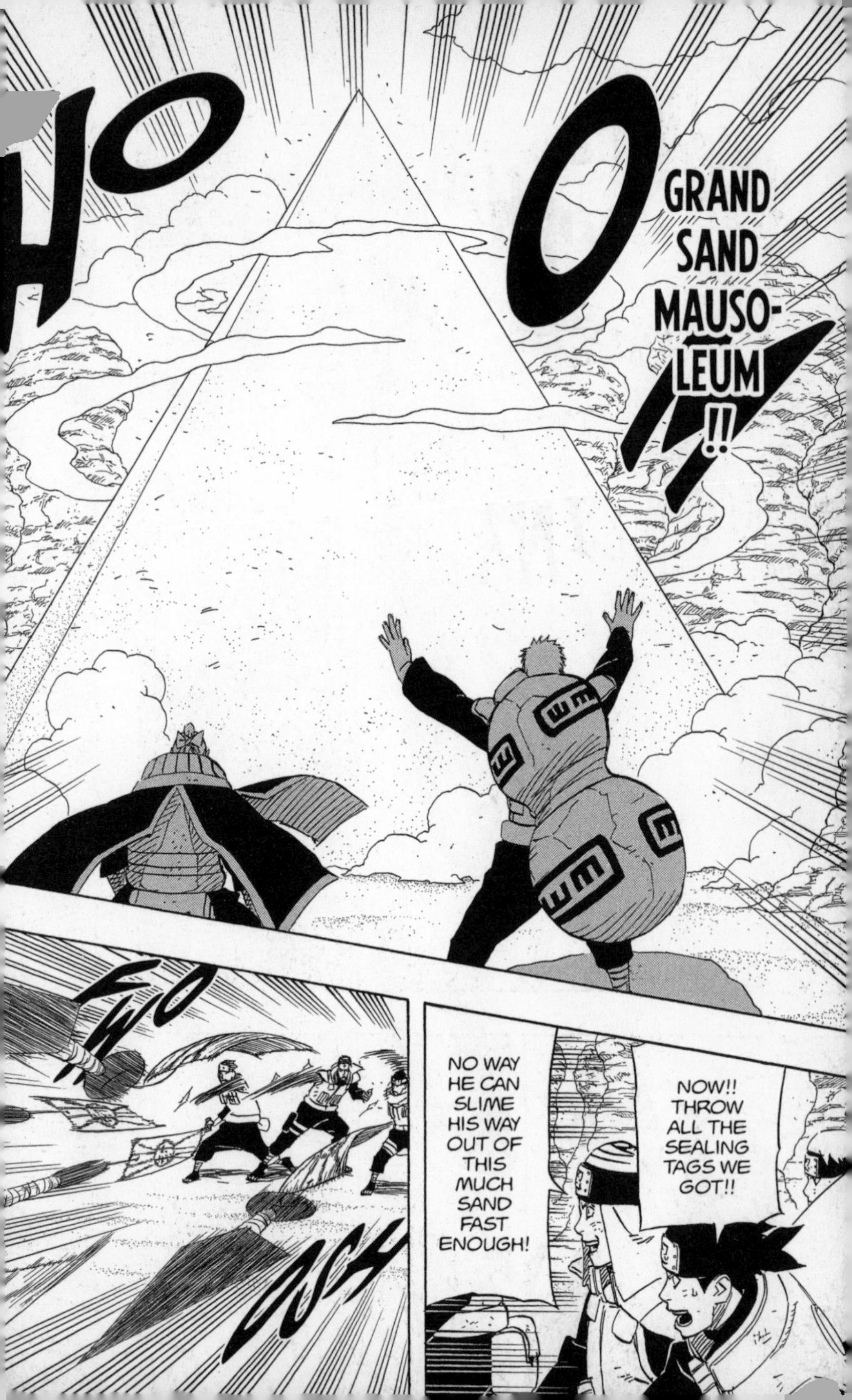
GRAND SAND MAUSO-LEUM!!
NOW!! THROW ALL THE SEALING TAGS WE GOT!!
NO WAY HE CAN SLIME HIS WAY OUT OF THIS MUCH SAND FAST ENOUGH!

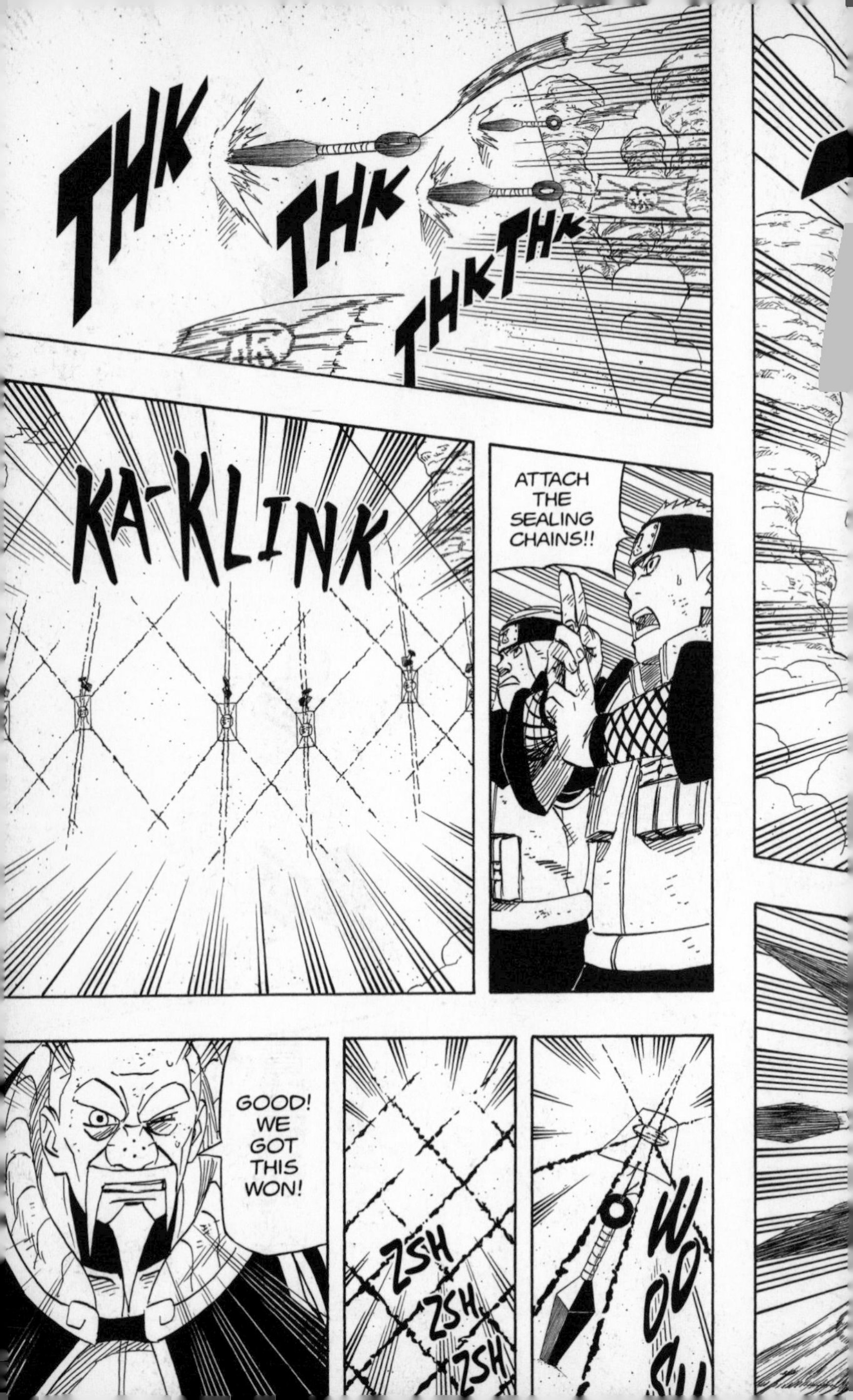
THK
THK
THKTHK
ATTACH THE SEALING CHAINS!!
KA-KLINK
WOOS
ZSH
ZSH
ZSH
GOOD! WE GOT THIS WON!

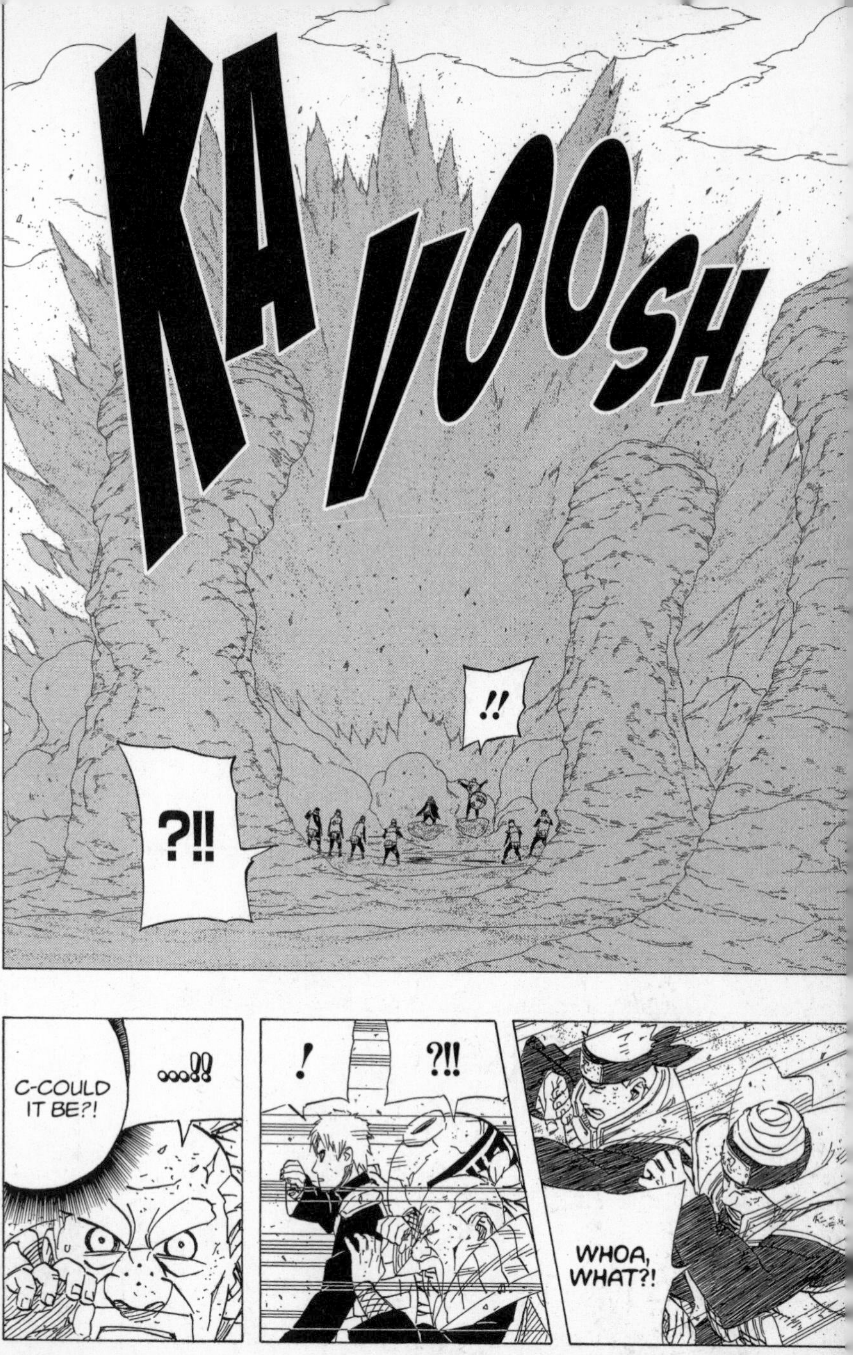
KA VOOSH
!!
?!!
WHOA, WHAT?!
?!!
!
...!!
C-COULD IT BE?!

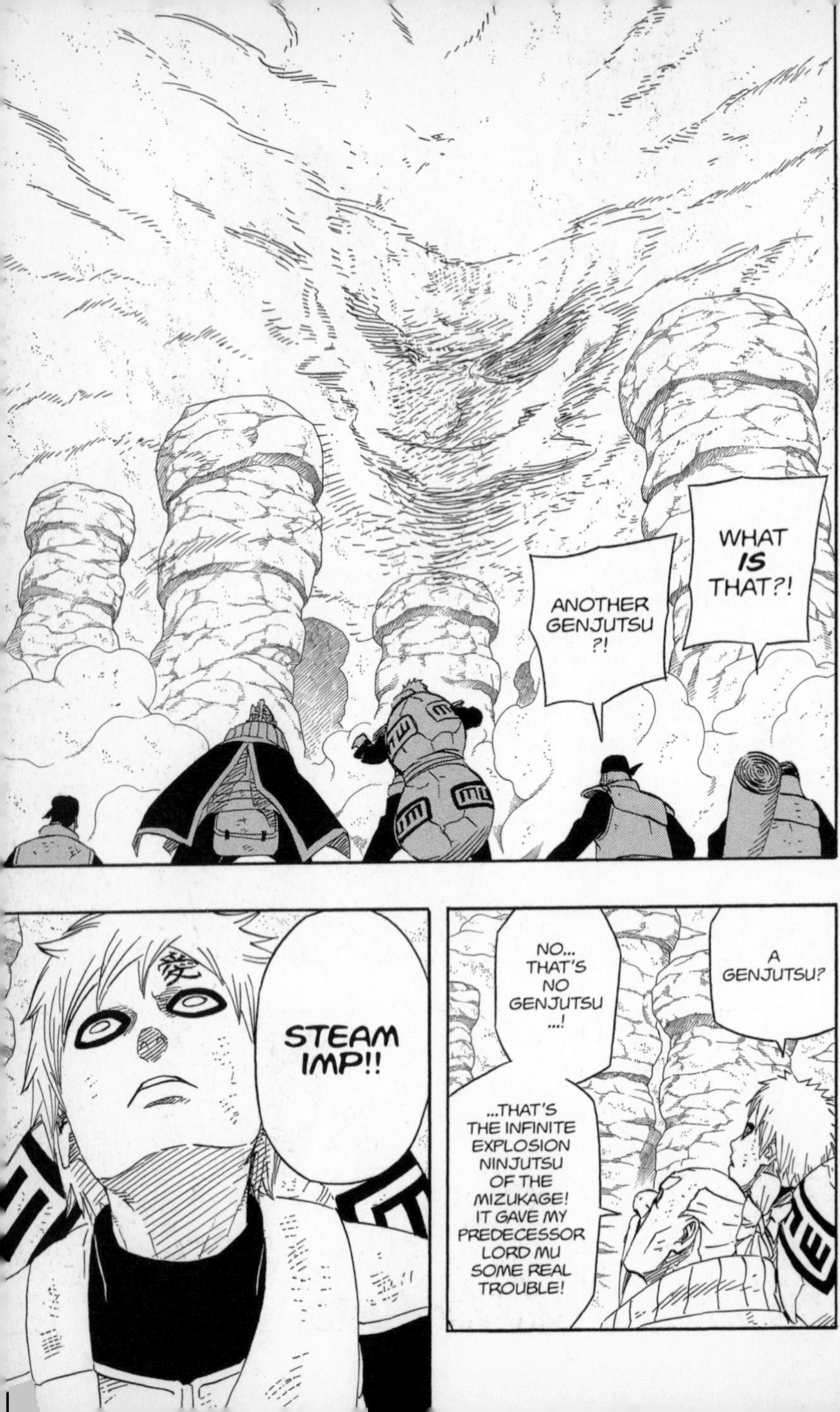
WHAT IS THAT?!
ANOTHER GENJUTSU ?!
A GENJUTSU?
NO... THAT'S NO GENJUTSU ...!
...THAT'S THE INFINITE EXPLOSION NINJUTSU OF THE MIZUKAGE! IT GAVE MY PREDECESSOR LORD MU SOME REAL TROUBLE!
STEAM IMP!!

NARUTO

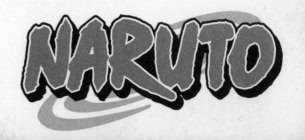

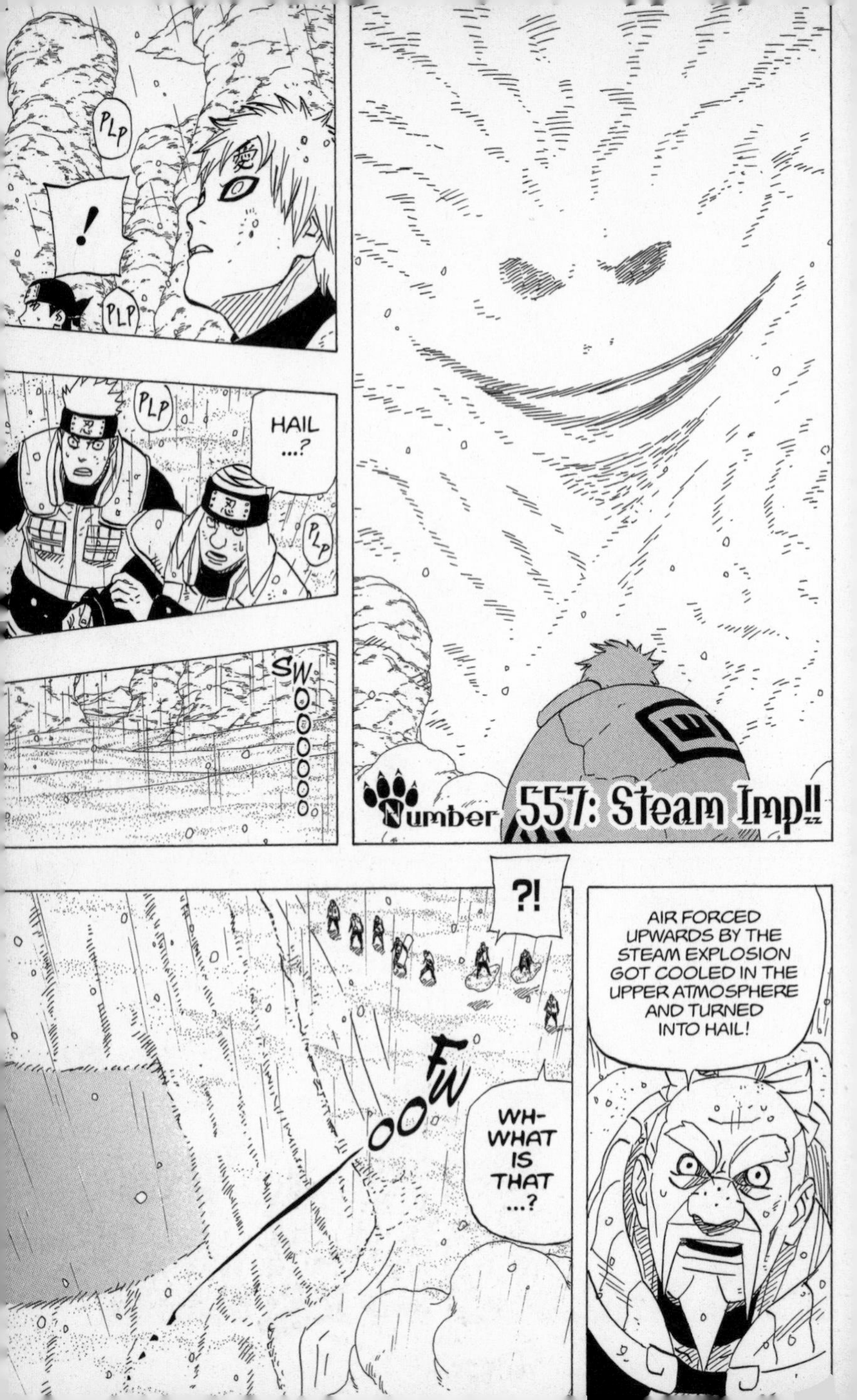
Number 557: Steam Imp!!
PLP
!
PLP
PLP
HAIL ...?
PLP
SWOOOOOOOOO
AIR FORCED UPWARDS BY THE STEAM EXPLOSION GOT COOLED IN THE UPPER ATMOSPHERE AND TURNED INTO HAIL!
?!
WH-WHAT IS THAT ...?
FWOOO

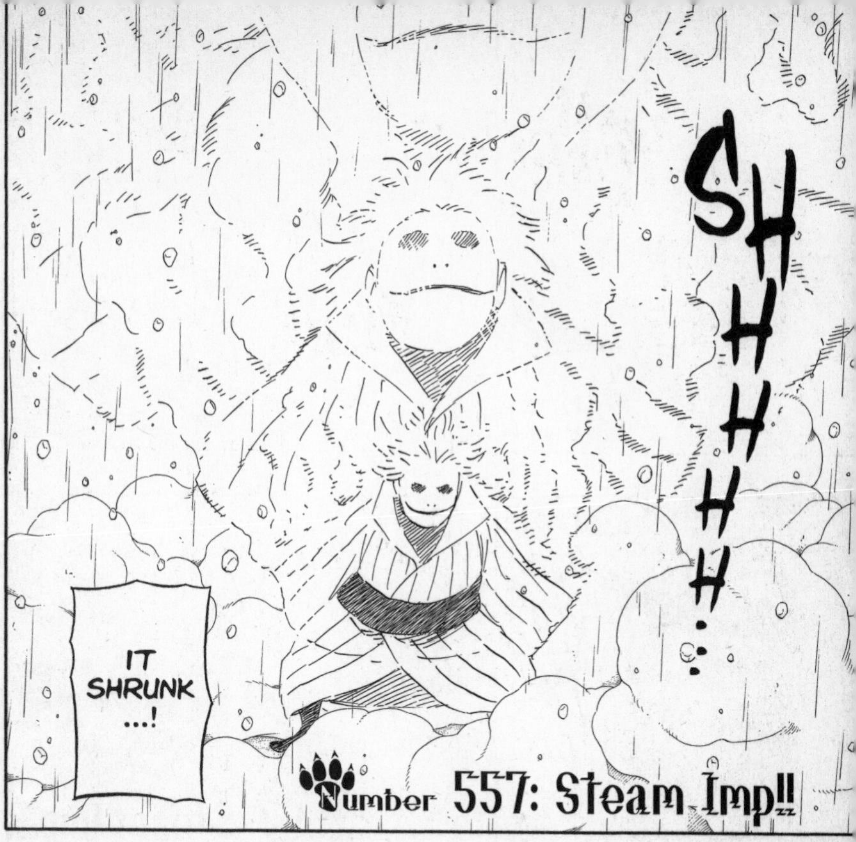
SHHHHHH...!!
IT SHRUNK ...!

Number 557: Steam Imp!!

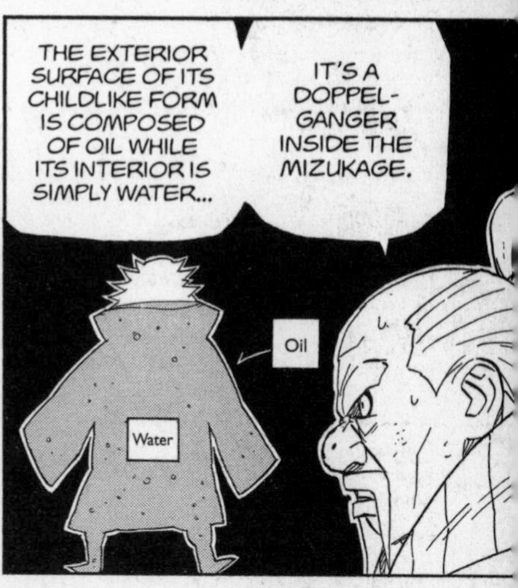
IT'S A DOPPEL-GANGER INSIDE THE MIZUKAGE.
THE EXTERIOR SURFACE OF ITS CHILDLIKE FORM IS COMPOSED OF OIL WHILE ITS INTERIOR IS SIMPLY WATER...
Oil
Water

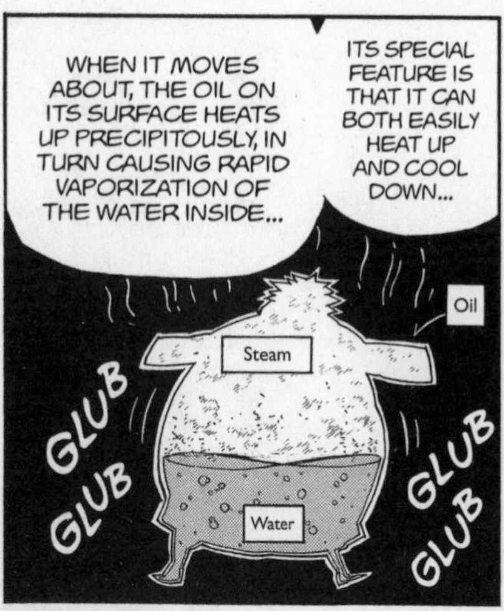
ITS SPECIAL FEATURE IS THAT IT CAN BOTH EASILY HEAT UP AND COOL DOWN...
WHEN IT MOVES ABOUT, THE OIL ON ITS SURFACE HEATS UP PRECIPITOUSLY, IN TURN CAUSING RAPID VAPORIZATION OF THE WATER INSIDE...
Oil
Steam
GLUB GLUB
GLUB GLUB
Water

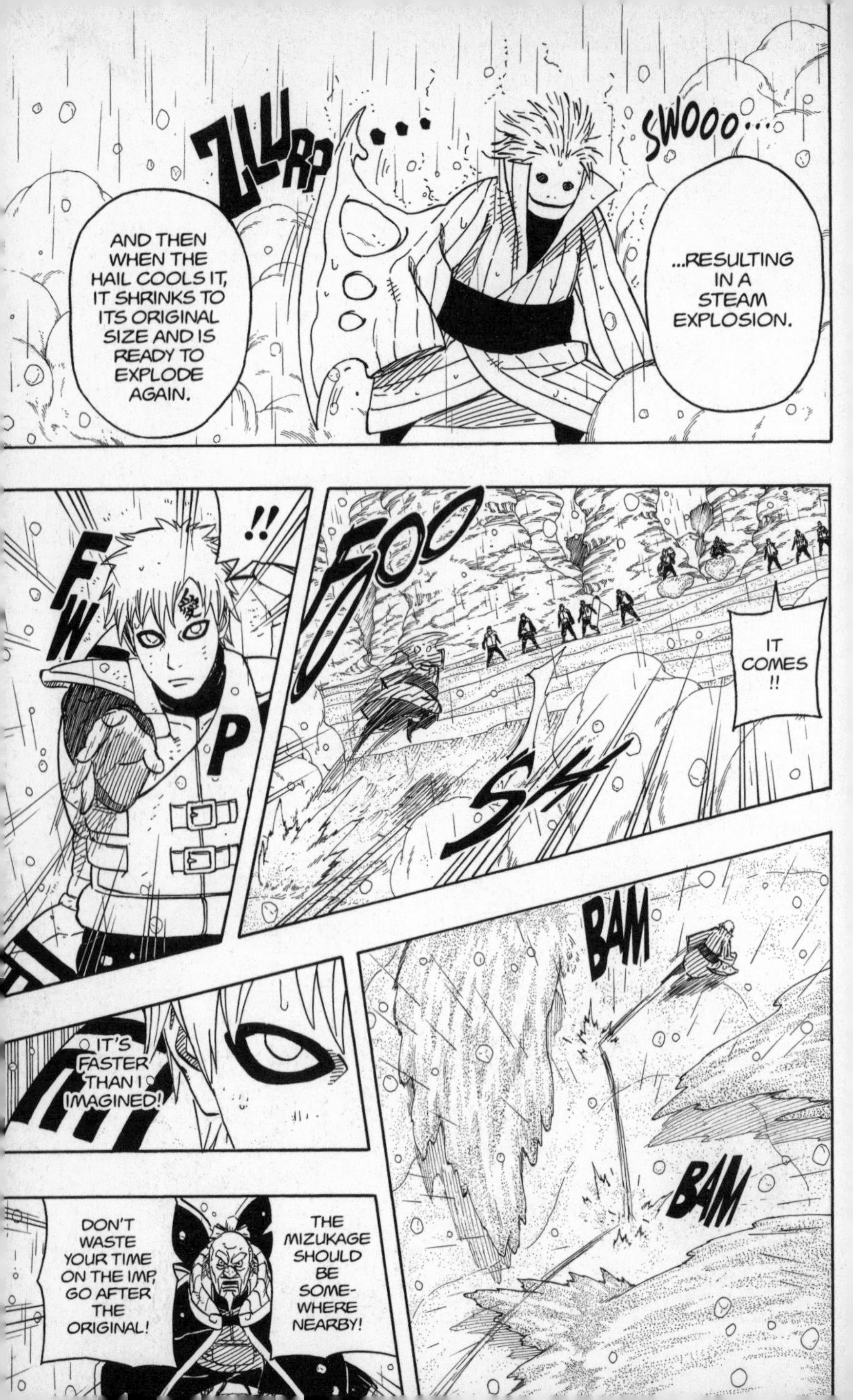
SWOOO...
...RESULTING IN A STEAM EXPLOSION.
ZLURP
...
AND THEN WHEN THE HAIL COOLS IT, IT SHRINKS TO ITS ORIGINAL SIZE AND IS READY TO EXPLODE AGAIN.
FOOO
IT COMES!!
SH
!!
FWP
BAM
BAM
IT'S FASTER THAN I IMAGINED!
THE MIZUKAGE SHOULD BE SOMEWHERE NEARBY!
DON'T WASTE YOUR TIME ON THE IMP, GO AFTER THE ORIGINAL!

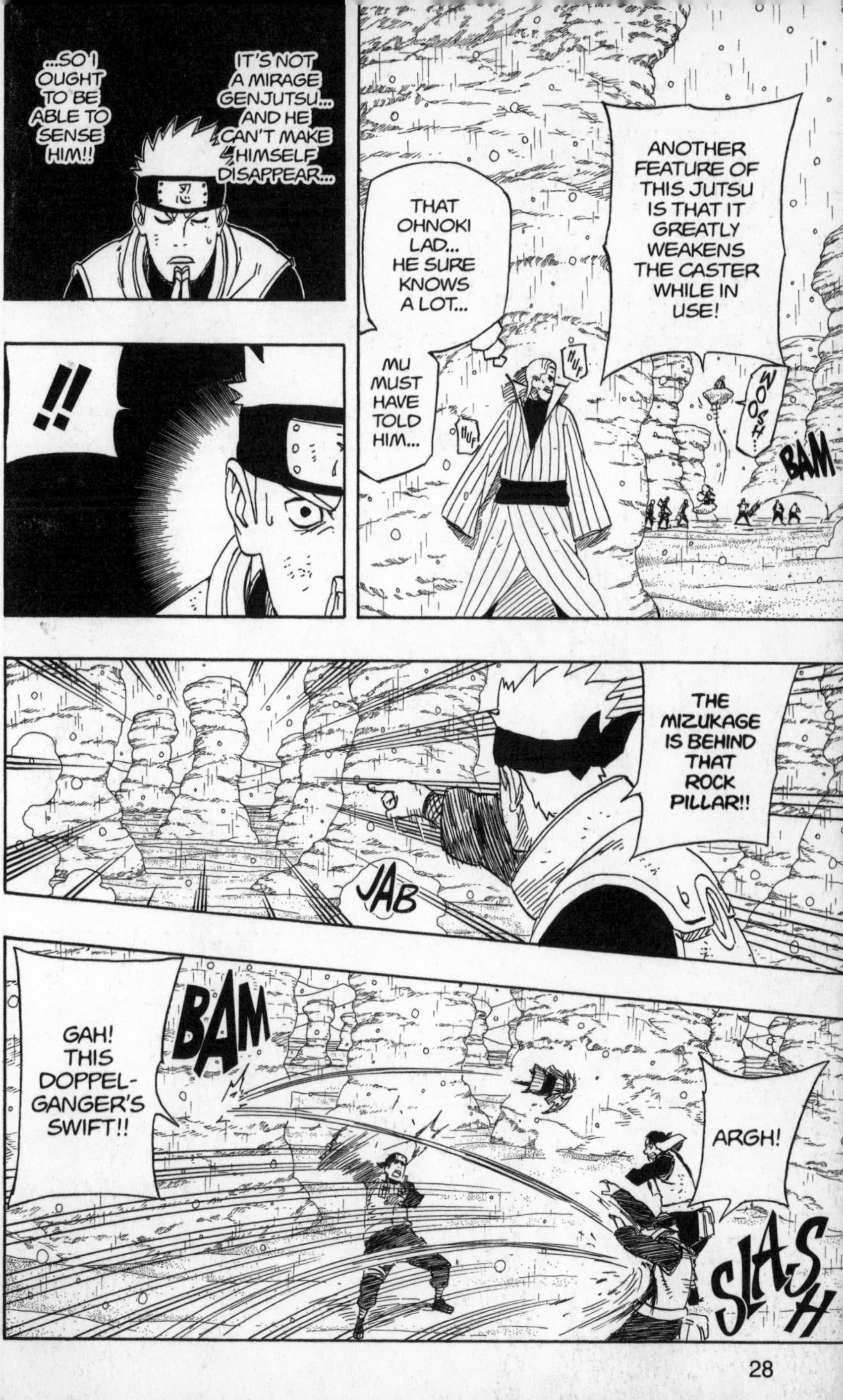
ANOTHER FEATURE OF THIS JUTSU IS THAT IT GREATLY WEAKENS THE CASTER WHILE IN USE!
THAT OHNOKI LAD... HE SURE KNOWS A LOT...
HUF
MU MUST HAVE TOLD HIM...
HUF
WOOSH...
BAM
IT'S NOT A MIRAGE GENJUTSU... AND HE CAN'T MAKE HIMSELF DISAPPEAR...
...SO I OUGHT TO BE ABLE TO SENSE HIM!!
!!
THE MIZUKAGE IS BEHIND THAT ROCK PILLAR!!
JAB
ARGH!
SLASH
BAM
GAH! THIS DOPPEL-GANGER'S SWIFT!!

READ THIS WAY

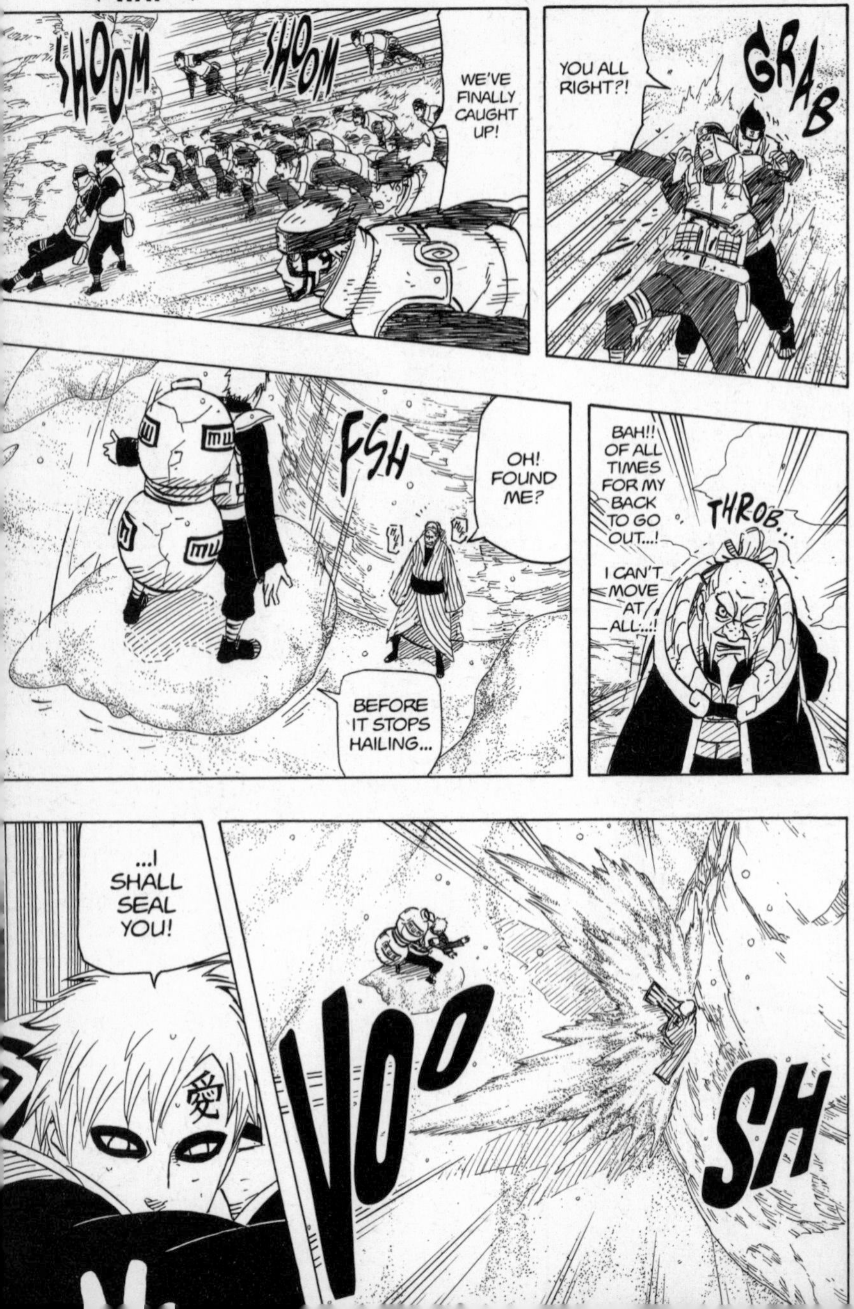
YOU ALL RIGHT?!
GRAB
SHOOM
SHOOM
WE'VE FINALLY CAUGHT UP!
BAH!! OF ALL TIMES FOR MY BACK TO GO OUT...!
I CAN'T MOVE AT ALL...!
THROB...
FSH
OH! FOUND ME?
BEFORE IT STOPS HAILING...
VOOOSH
...I SHALL SEAL YOU!

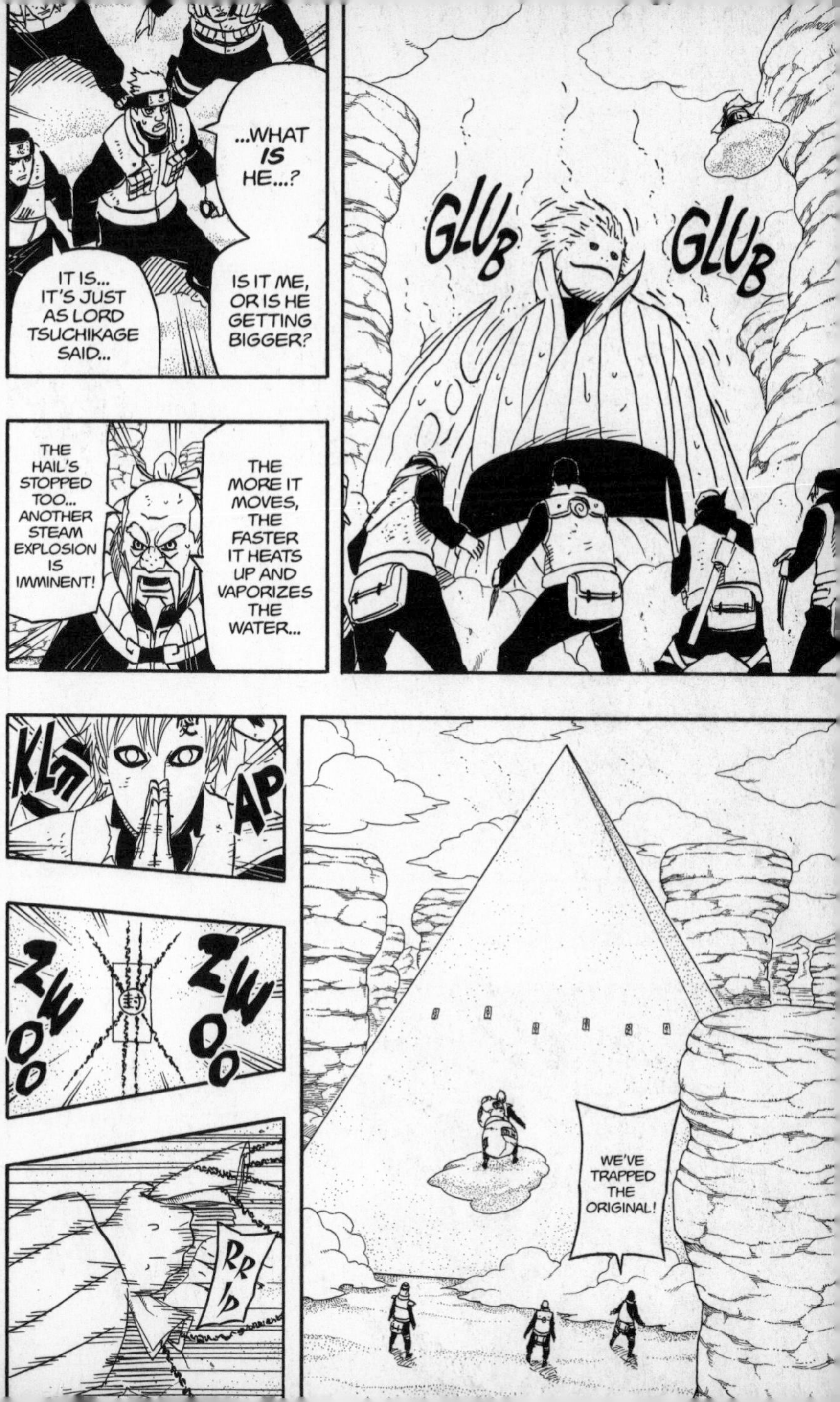
GLUB GLUB
...WHAT IS HE...?
IS IT ME, OR IS HE GETTING BIGGER?
IT IS... IT'S JUST AS LORD TSUCHIKAGE SAID...
THE MORE IT MOVES, THE FASTER IT HEATS UP AND VAPORIZES THE WATER...
THE HAIL'S STOPPED TOO... ANOTHER STEAM EXPLOSION IS IMMINENT!
WE'VE TRAPPED THE ORIGINAL!
KLAP
ZWOO ZWOO
RRIP

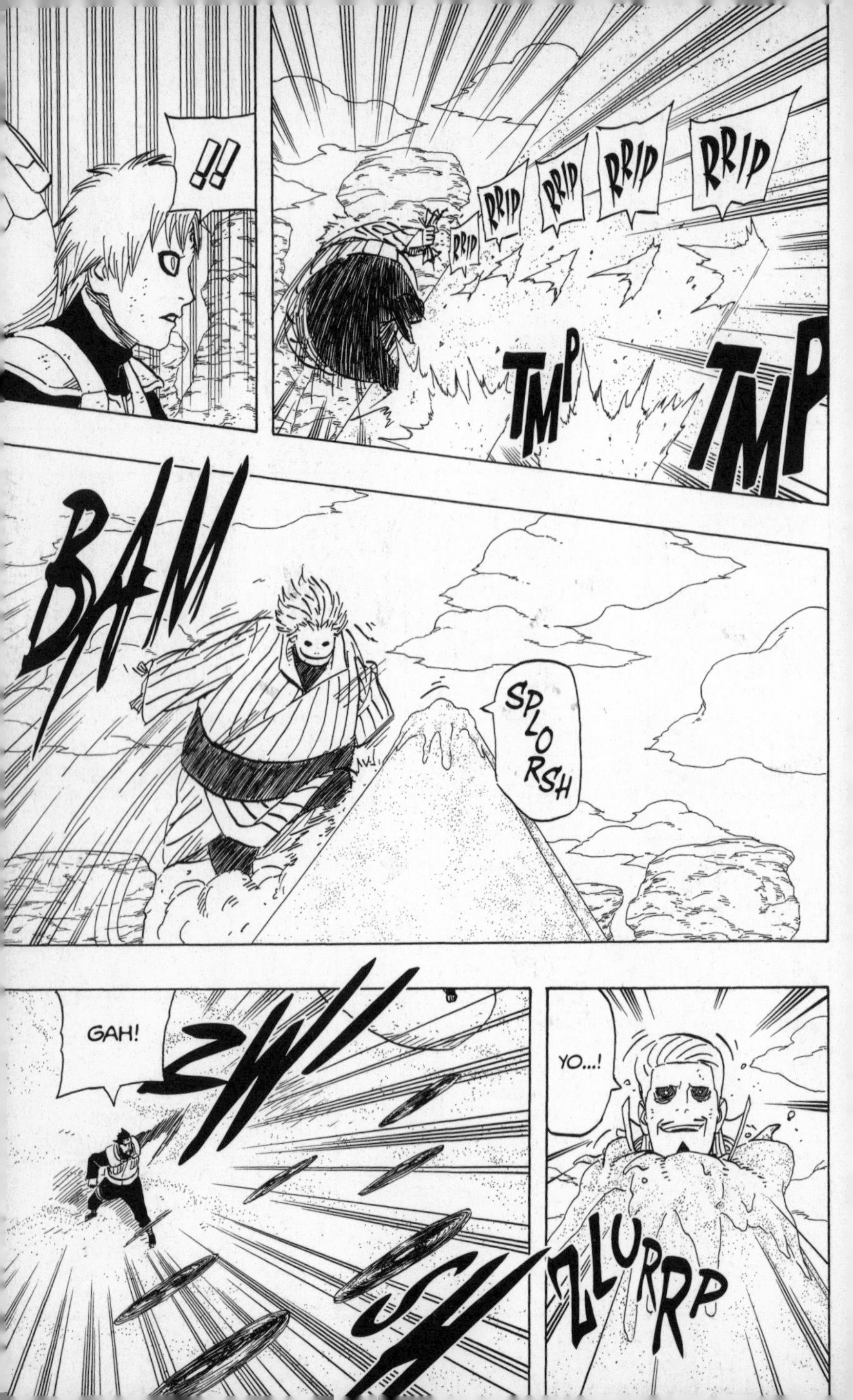
RRIP
RRIP
RRIP
RRIP
RRIP
TMP
TMP
!!
BAM
SPLORSH
YO...!
ZLLURRP
GAH!
ZW
SH

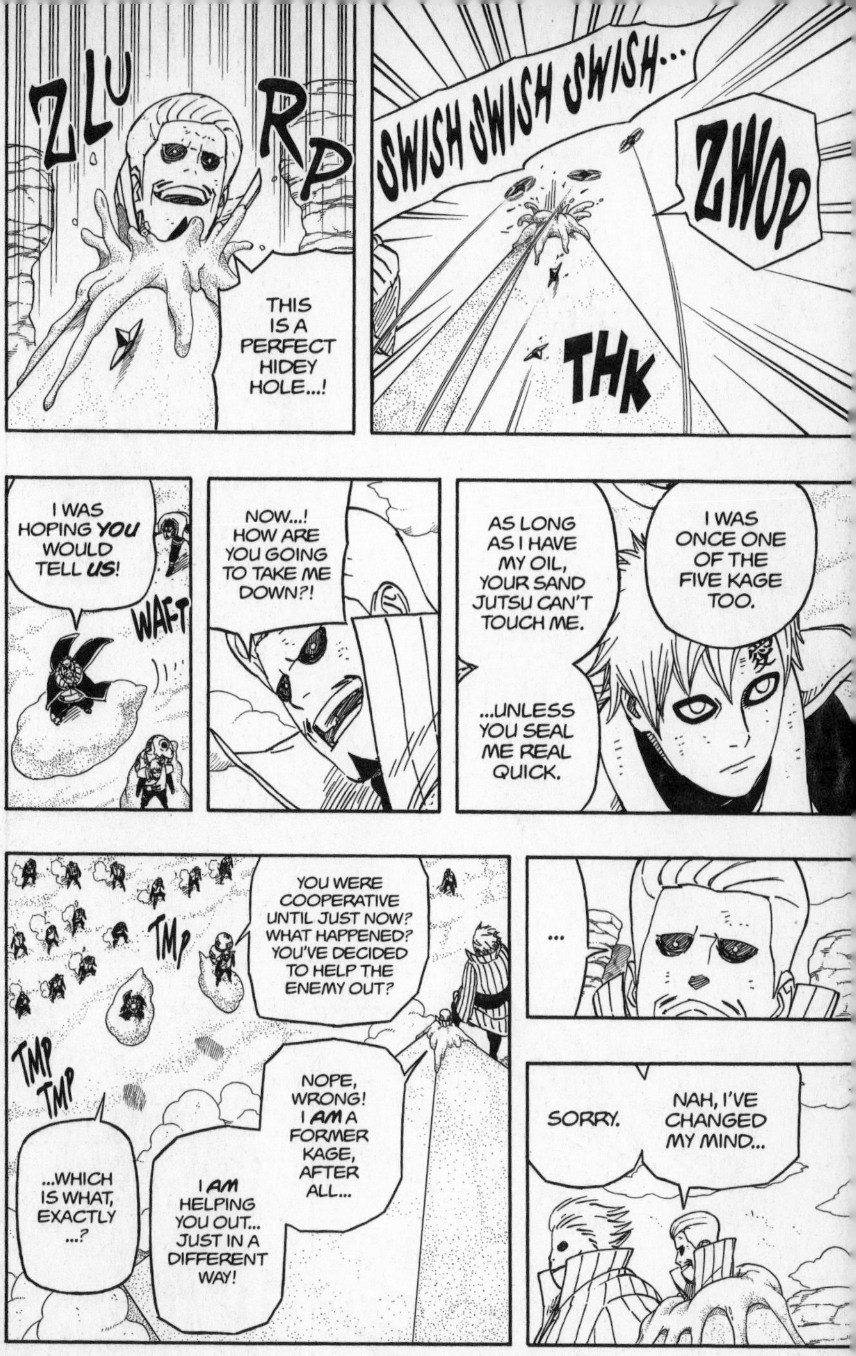
SWISH SWISH SWISH...
ZWOP
THK
ZLURP
THIS IS A PERFECT HIDEY HOLE...!
I WAS ONCE ONE OF THE FIVE KAGE TOO.
AS LONG AS I HAVE MY OIL, YOUR SAND JUTSU CAN'T TOUCH ME.
...UNLESS YOU SEAL ME REAL QUICK.
NOW...! HOW ARE YOU GOING TO TAKE ME DOWN?!
I WAS HOPING **YOU** WOULD TELL **US**!
WAFT
...
NAH, I'VE CHANGED MY MIND...
SORRY.
TMP
YOU WERE COOPERATIVE UNTIL JUST NOW? WHAT HAPPENED? YOU'VE DECIDED TO HELP THE ENEMY OUT?
NOPE, WRONG! I ***AM*** A FORMER KAGE, AFTER ALL...
I ***AM*** HELPING YOU OUT... JUST IN A DIFFERENT WAY!
TMP TMP
...WHICH IS WHAT, EXACTLY ...?

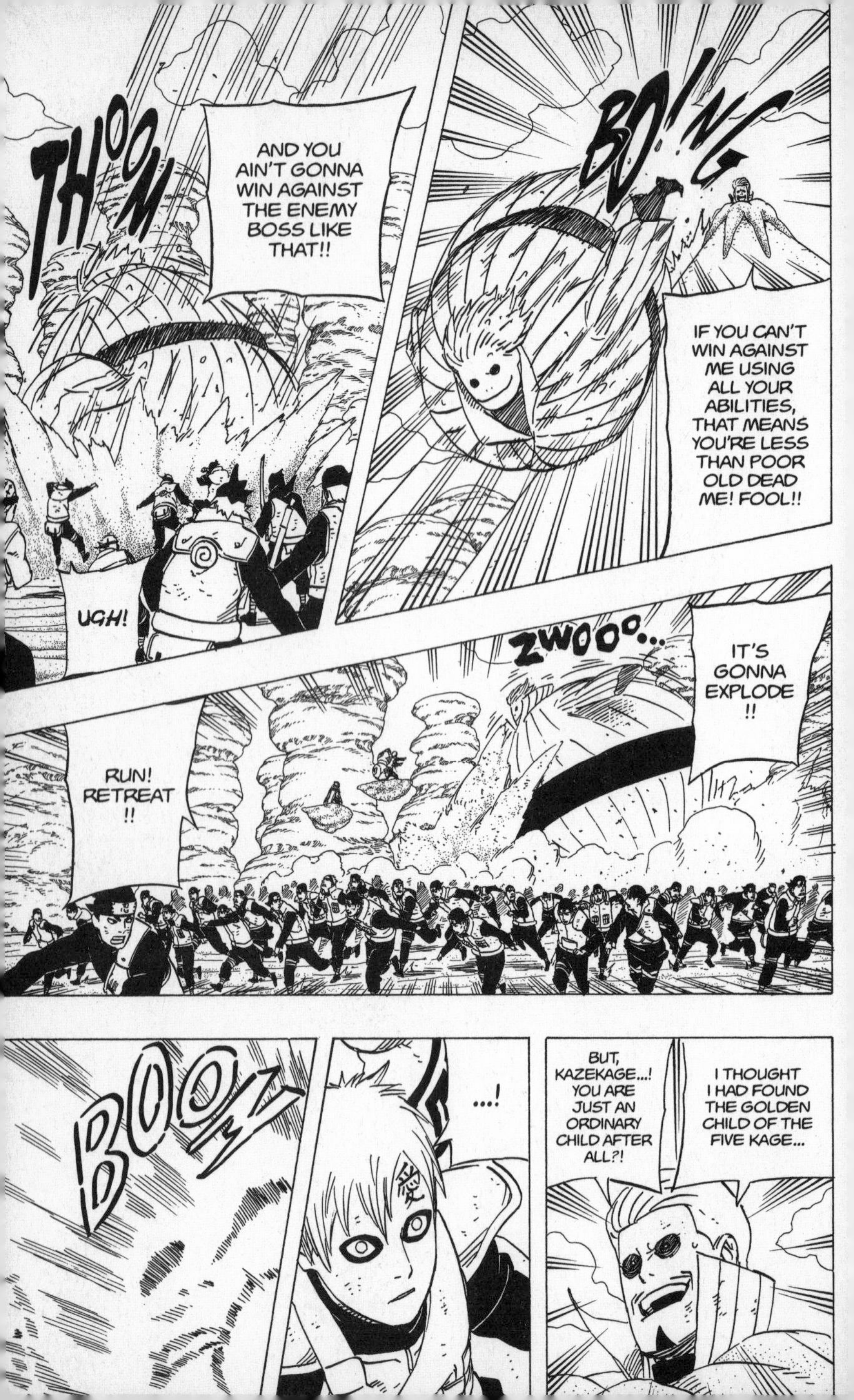
BOING
IF YOU CAN'T WIN AGAINST ME USING ALL YOUR ABILITIES, THAT MEANS YOU'RE LESS THAN POOR OLD DEAD ME! FOOL!!
THOOM
AND YOU AIN'T GONNA WIN AGAINST THE ENEMY BOSS LIKE THAT!!
UGH!
IT'S GONNA EXPLODE!!
ZWOOO...
RUN! RETREAT!!
I THOUGHT I HAD FOUND THE GOLDEN CHILD OF THE FIVE KAGE...
BUT, KAZEKAGE...! YOU ARE JUST AN ORDINARY CHILD AFTER ALL?!
...!
BOOM

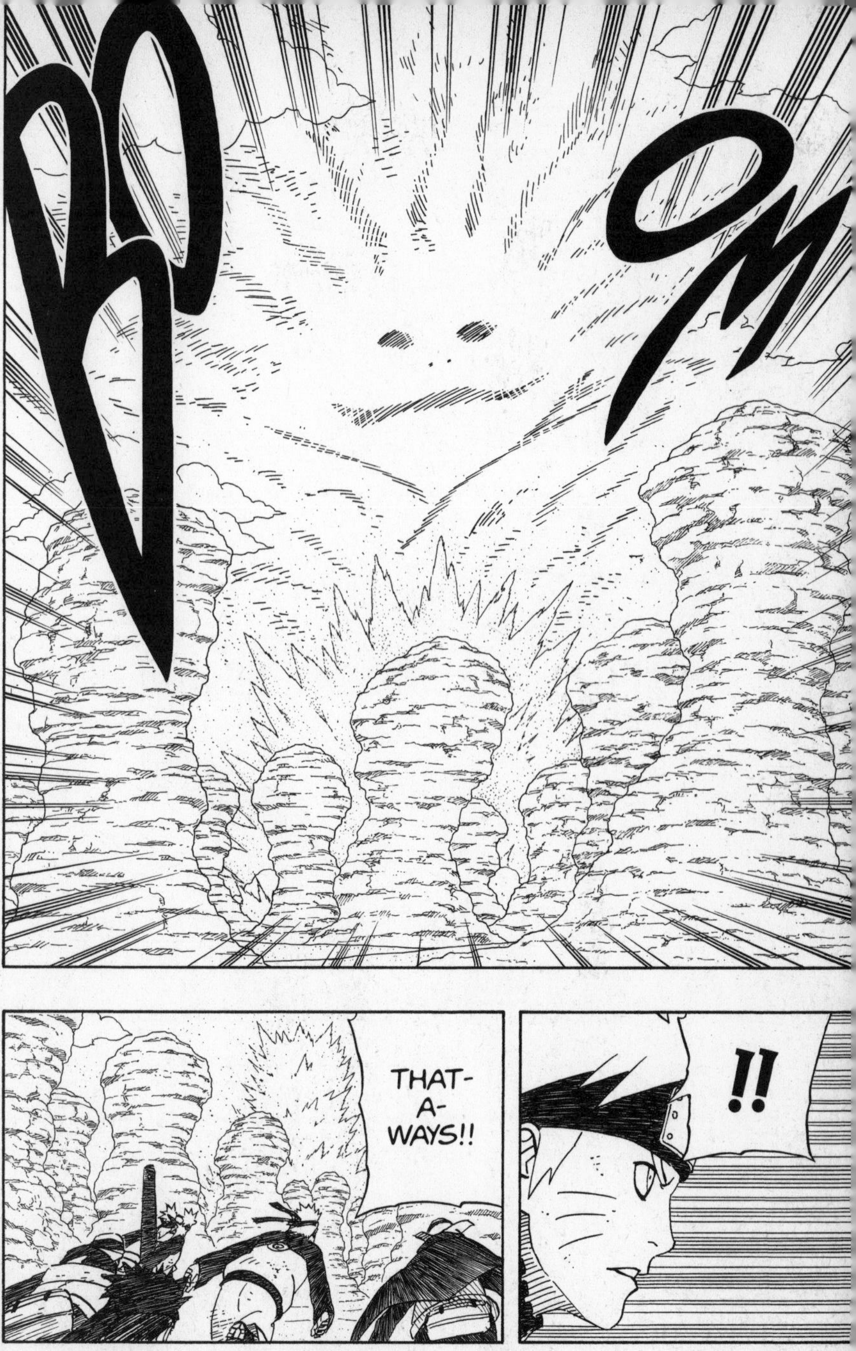
BOOM
!!
THAT-A-WAYS!!

READ THIS WAY

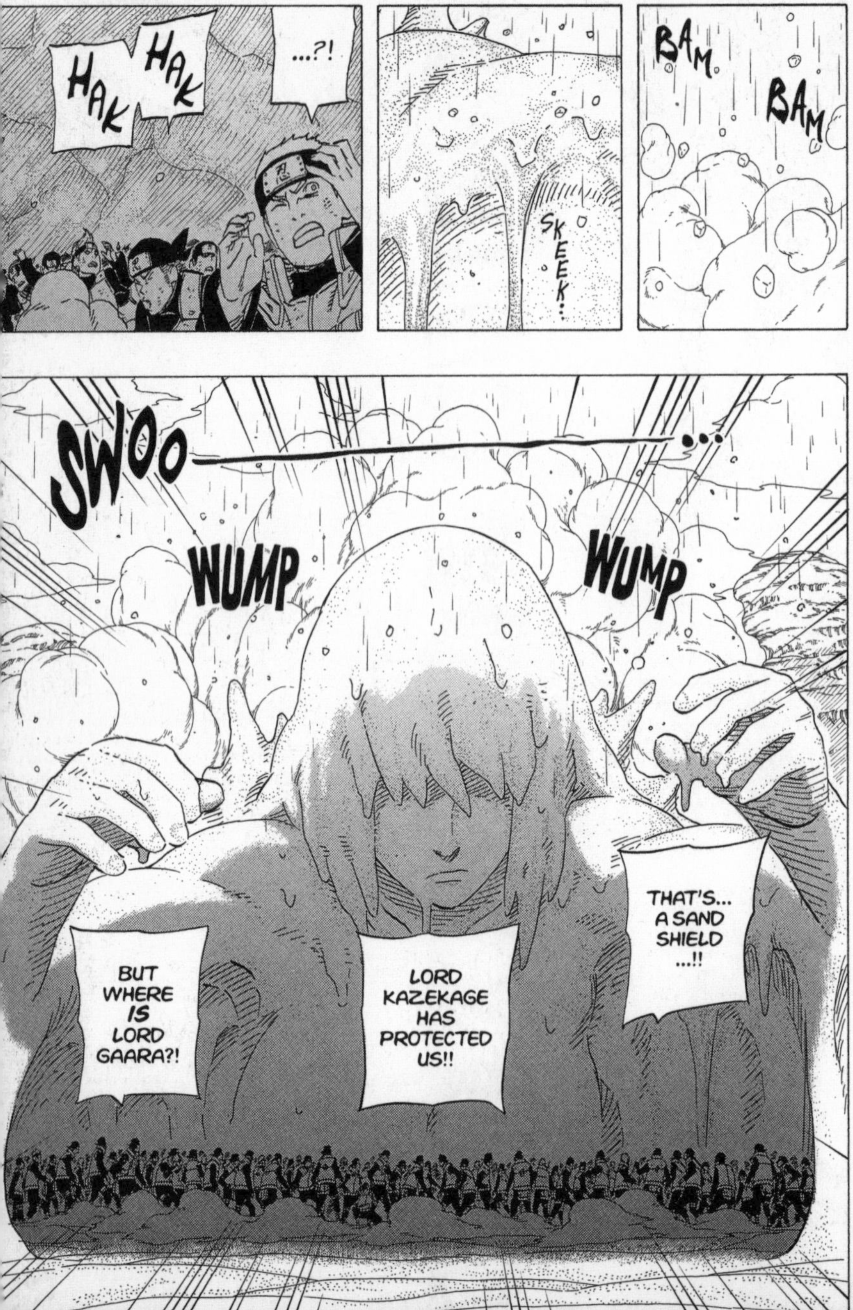
BAM
BAM
SKEEK...
...?!
HAK
HAK
SWOO———...
WUMP
WUMP
THAT'S... A SAND SHIELD ...!!
LORD KAZEKAGE HAS PROTECTED US!!
BUT WHERE *IS* LORD GAARA?!

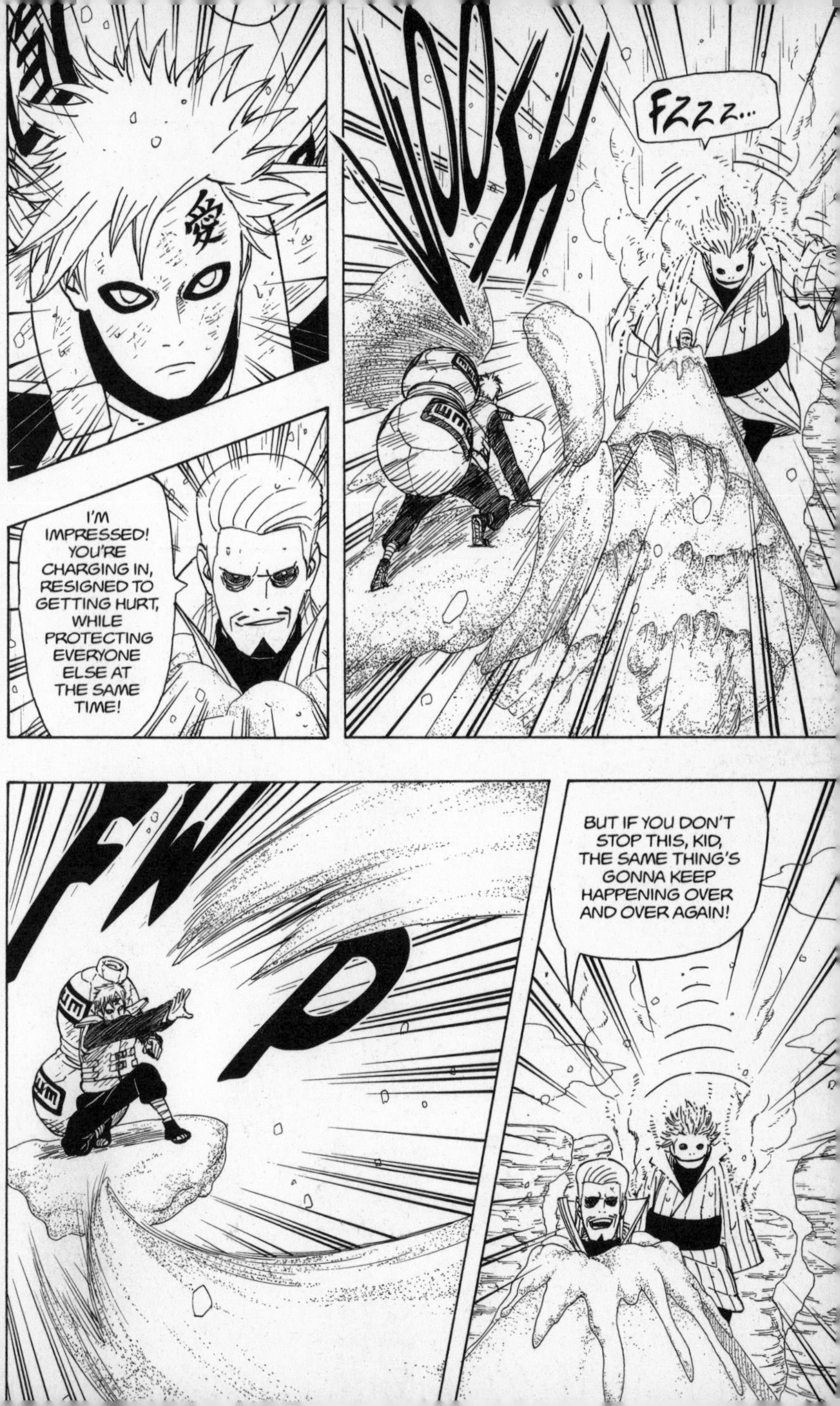
FZZZ...
WOOSH
I'M IMPRESSED! YOU'RE CHARGING IN, RESIGNED TO GETTING HURT, WHILE PROTECTING EVERYONE ELSE AT THE SAME TIME!
BUT IF YOU DON'T STOP THIS, KID, THE SAME THING'S GONNA KEEP HAPPENING OVER AND OVER AGAIN!
FWP

READ THIS WAY

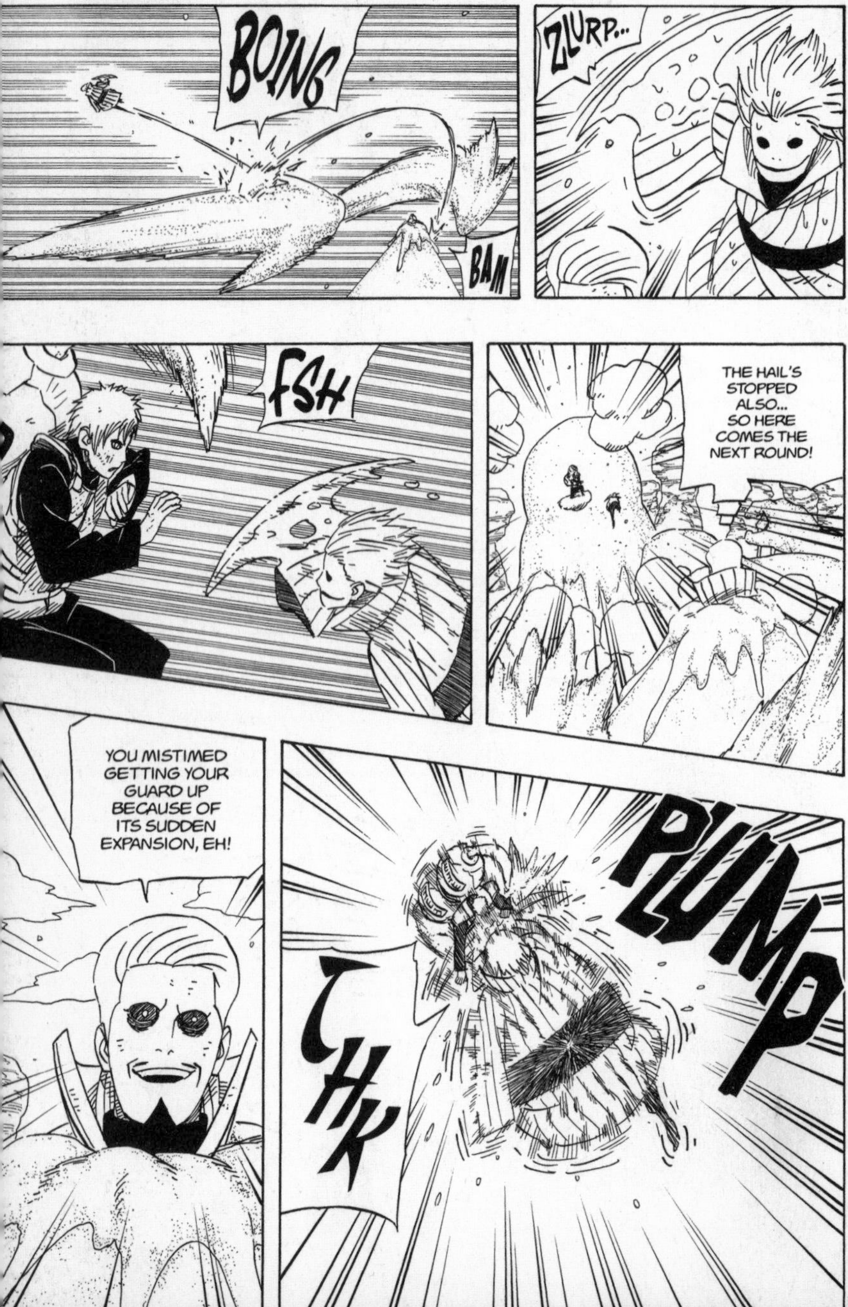
ZLURP...
BOING
BAM
THE HAIL'S STOPPED ALSO... SO HERE COMES THE NEXT ROUND!
FSH
PLUMP
CHK
YOU MISTIMED GETTING YOUR GUARD UP BECAUSE OF ITS SUDDEN EXPANSION, EH!

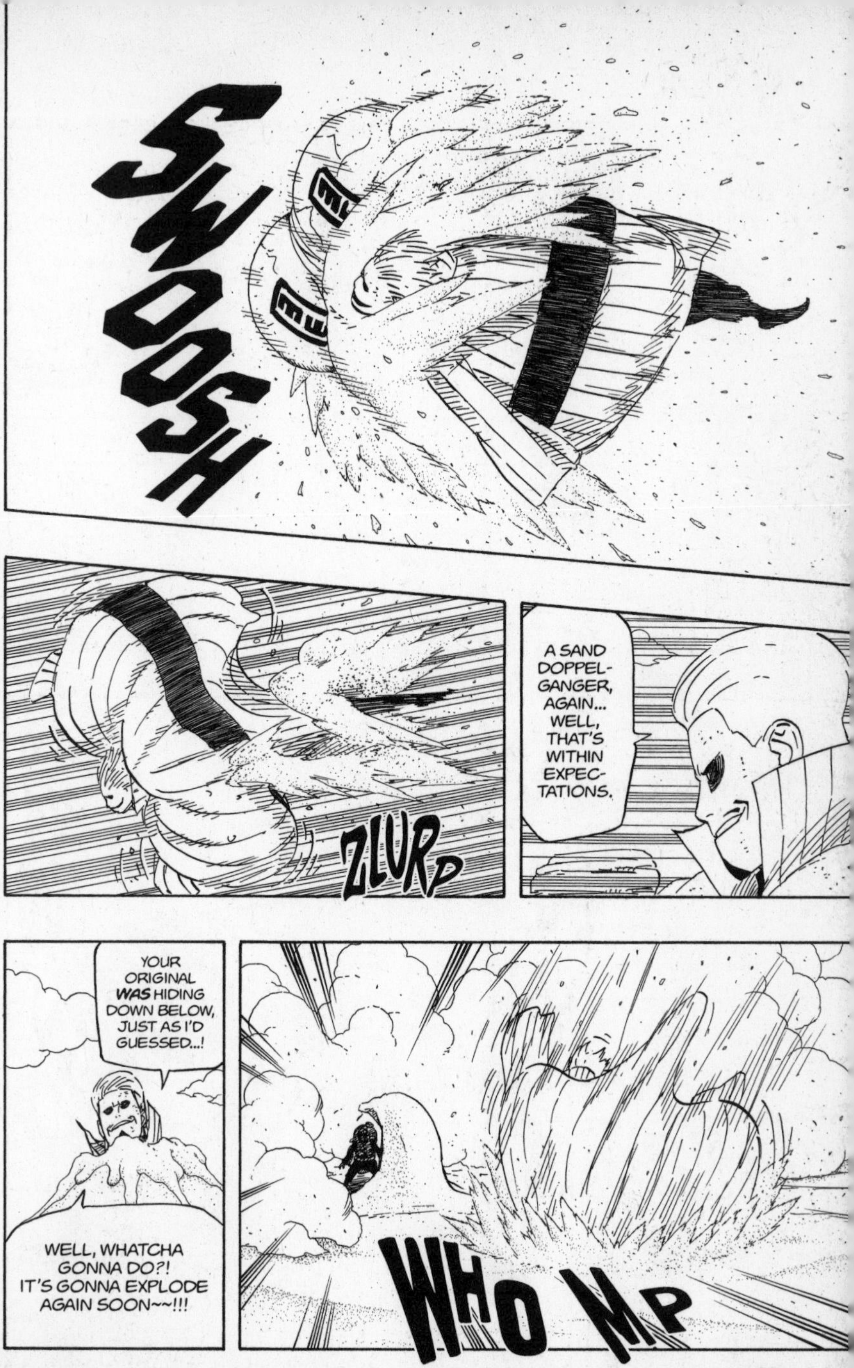
SWOOSH
A SAND DOPPELGANGER, AGAIN... WELL, THAT'S WITHIN EXPECTATIONS.
ZLURP
WHOMP
YOUR ORIGINAL ***WAS*** HIDING DOWN BELOW, JUST AS I'D GUESSED...!
WELL, WHATCHA GONNA DO?! IT'S GONNA EXPLODE AGAIN SOON~~!!!

READ THIS WAY

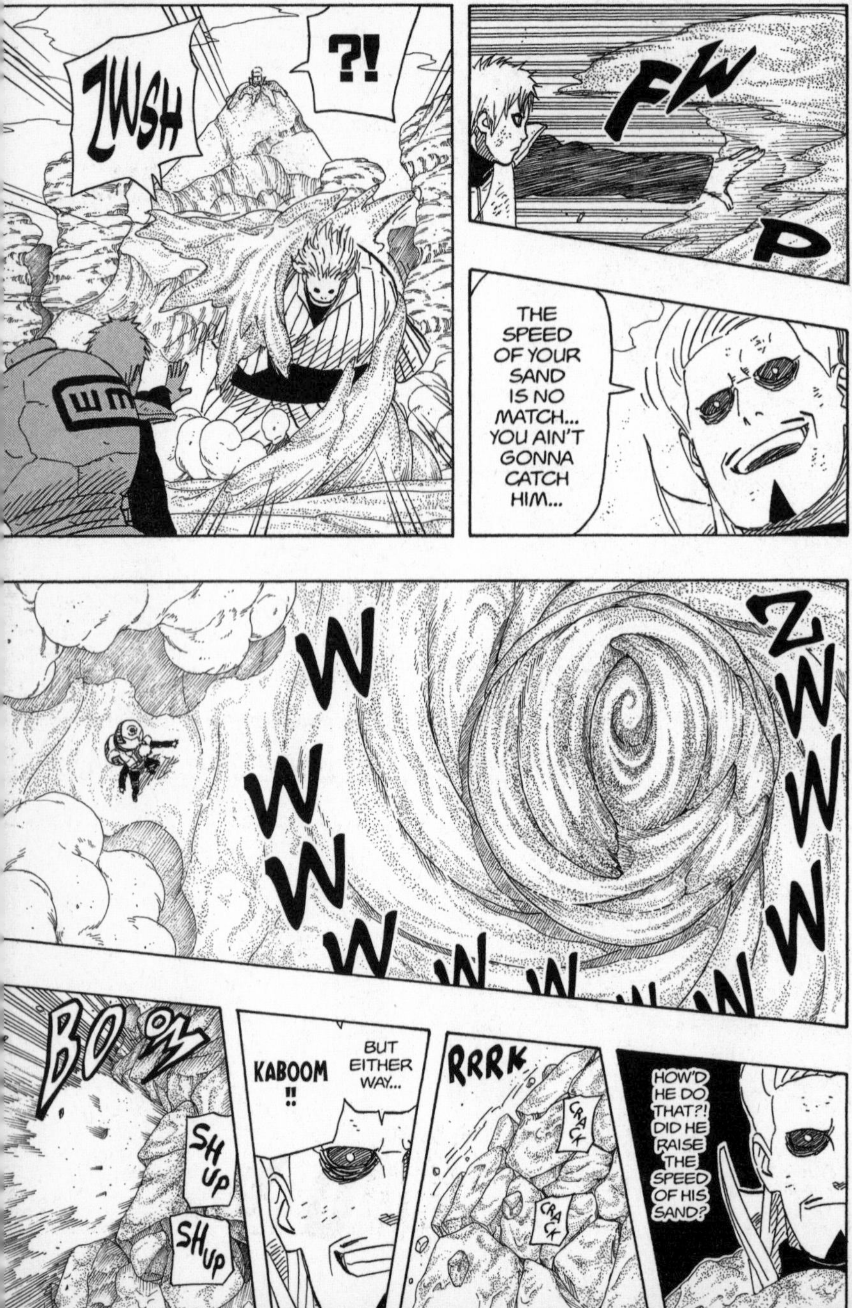
FWP
THE SPEED OF YOUR SAND IS NO MATCH... YOU AIN'T GONNA CATCH HIM...
?!
ZWSH
ZWWWWWW
WWWWW
WWWWWW
HOW'D HE DO THAT?! DID HE RAISE THE SPEED OF HIS SAND?
RRRK
CRACK
CRACK
BUT EITHER WAY...
KABOOM!!
BOOM
SHUP
SHUP

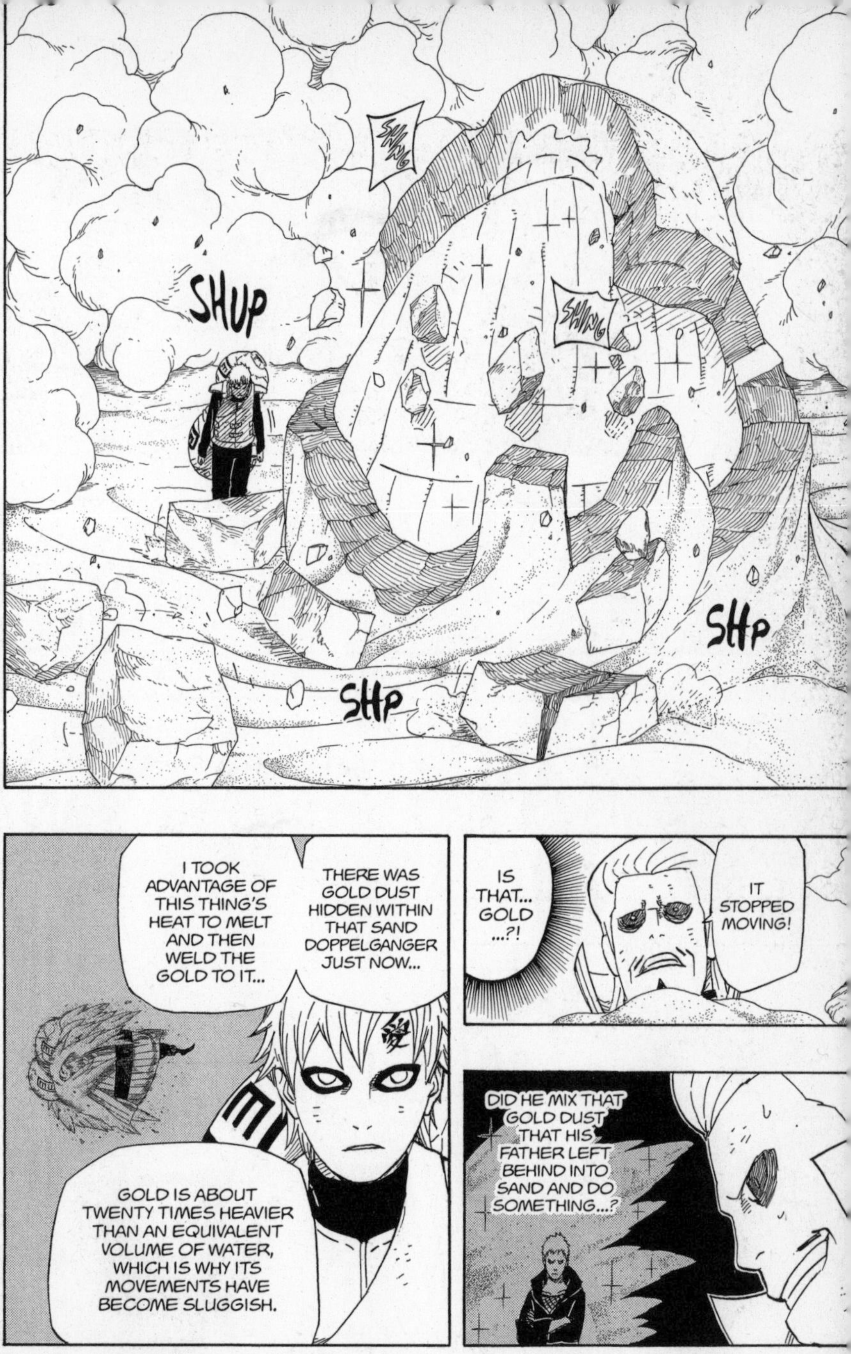
SHING
SHING
SHUP
SHP
SHP
IT STOPPED MOVING!
IS THAT... GOLD ...?!
DID HE MIX THAT GOLD DUST THAT HIS FATHER LEFT BEHIND INTO SAND AND DO SOMETHING...?
THERE WAS GOLD DUST HIDDEN WITHIN THAT SAND DOPPELGANGER JUST NOW...
I TOOK ADVANTAGE OF THIS THING'S HEAT TO MELT AND THEN WELD THE GOLD TO IT...
GOLD IS ABOUT TWENTY TIMES HEAVIER THAN AN EQUIVALENT VOLUME OF WATER, WHICH IS WHY ITS MOVEMENTS HAVE BECOME SLUGGISH.

READ THIS WAY

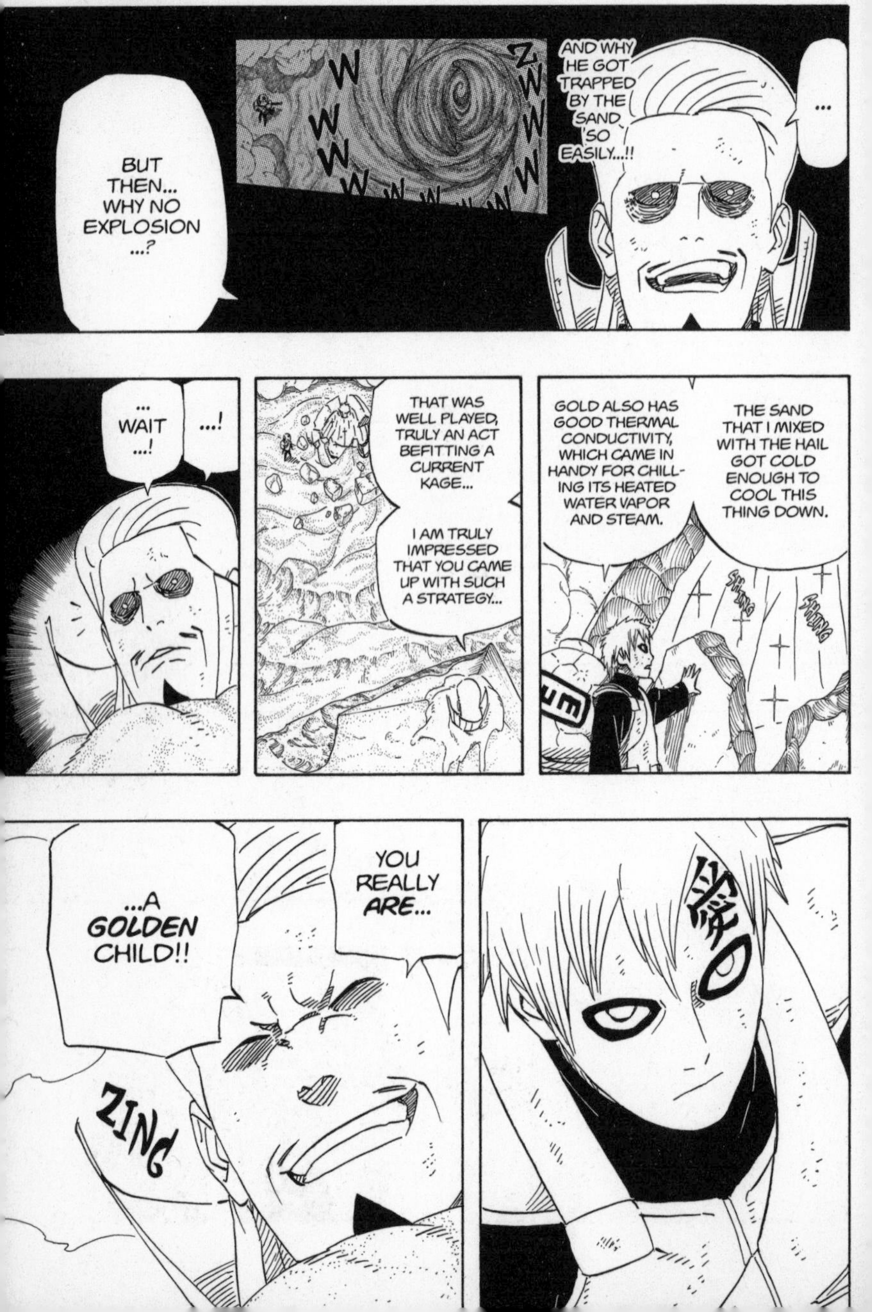
...
AND WHY HE GOT TRAPPED BY THE SAND SO EASILY...!!
ZZWWWWWWWWWWW
BUT THEN... WHY NO EXPLOSION ...?
THE SAND THAT I MIXED WITH THE HAIL GOT COLD ENOUGH TO COOL THIS THING DOWN.
GOLD ALSO HAS GOOD THERMAL CONDUCTIVITY, WHICH CAME IN HANDY FOR CHILLING ITS HEATED WATER VAPOR AND STEAM.
SHING
SHING
THAT WAS WELL PLAYED, TRULY AN ACT BEFITTING A CURRENT KAGE...
I AM TRULY IMPRESSED THAT YOU CAME UP WITH SUCH A STRATEGY...
...!
... WAIT ...!
YOU REALLY ARE...
...A GOLDEN CHILD!!
ZING

NARUTO

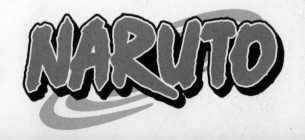

Number 558: Kabuto's Trump Card...!!

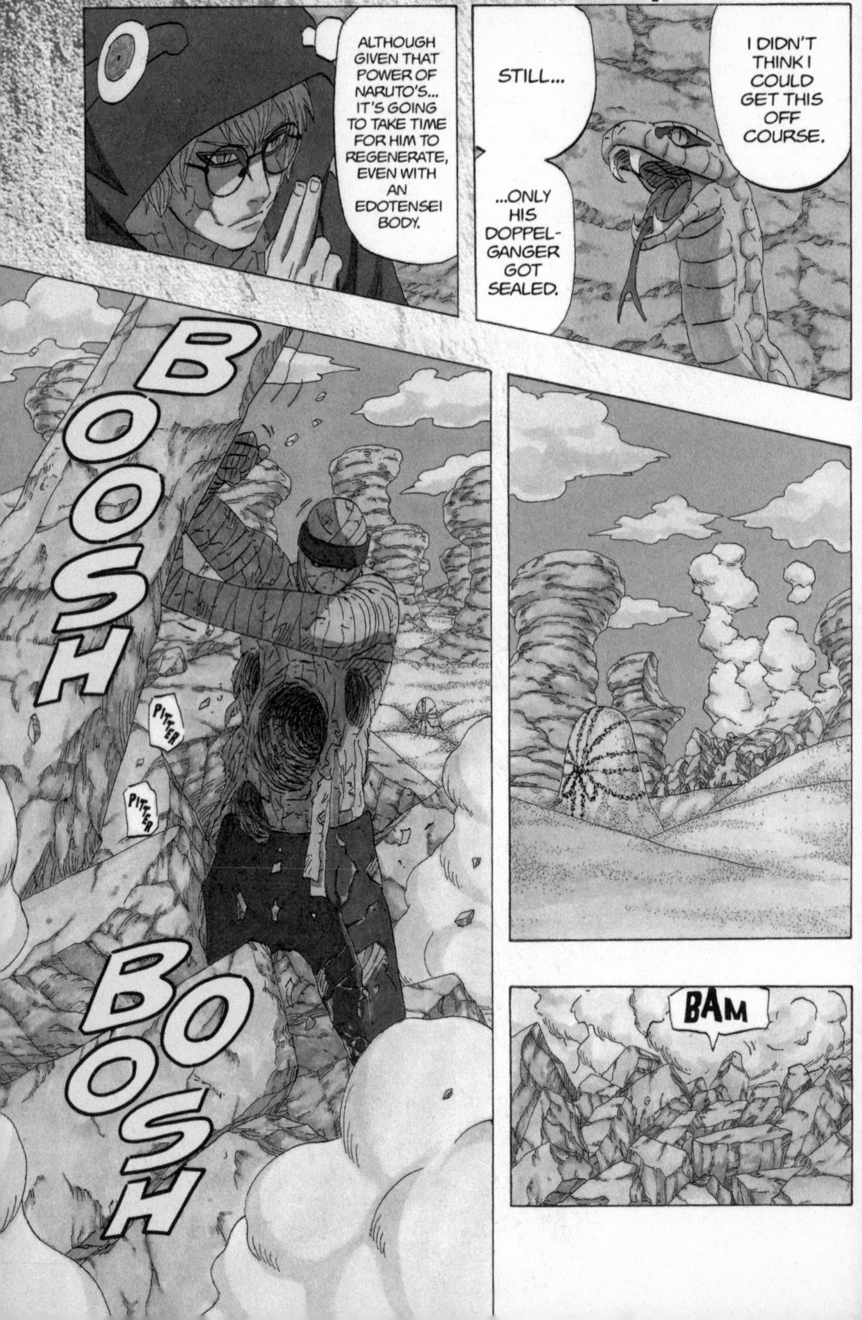

I DIDN'T THINK I COULD GET THIS OFF COURSE.
STILL...
...ONLY HIS DOPPEL-GANGER GOT SEALED.
ALTHOUGH GIVEN THAT POWER OF NARUTO'S... IT'S GOING TO TAKE TIME FOR HIM TO REGENERATE, EVEN WITH AN EDOTENSEI BODY.
BAM
BOOSH
PITTER
PITTER
BOOSH
BOOSH

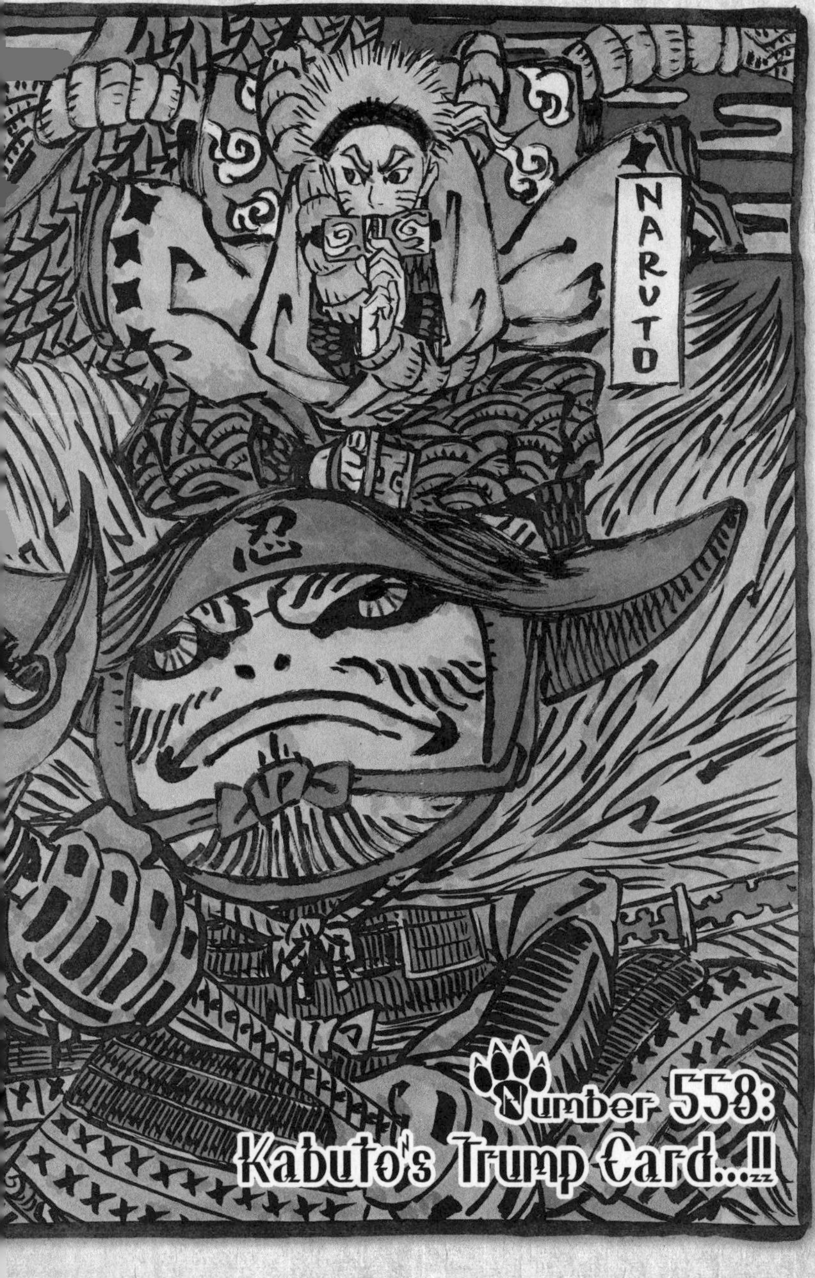
NARUTO
Number 558:
Kabuto's Trump Card...!!

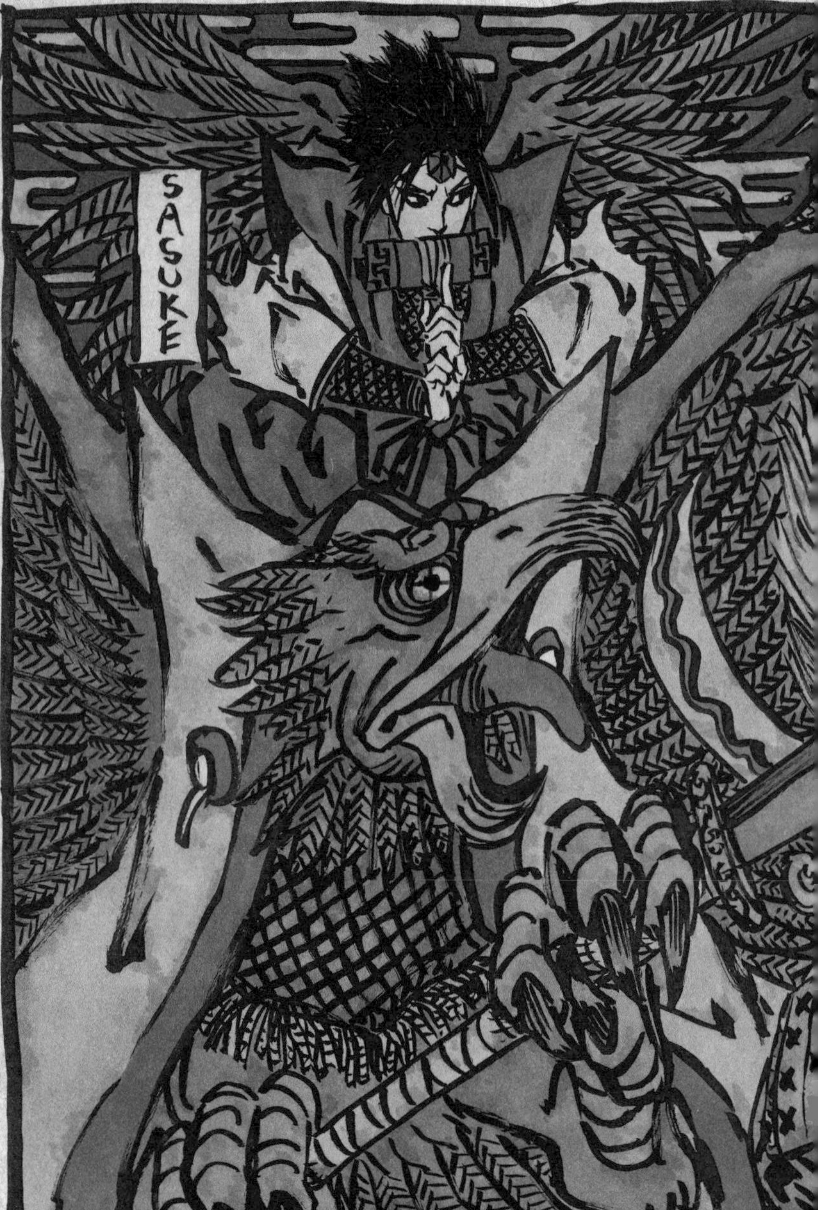
SASUKE

NARUTO

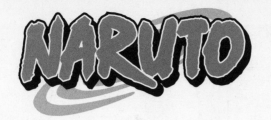

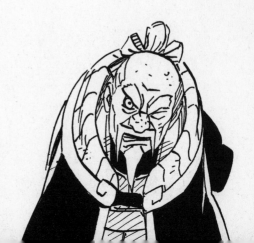

HOW NAÏVE OF YOU, OHNOKI... YOU WERE MY DISCIPLE...
THOOM
YOU COMPLETELY MISSED ME FRAGMENTING...
G-G-
GWEEEN
ZWOP...
SHOOM

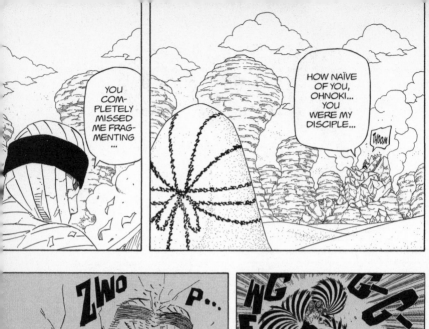

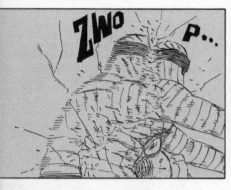

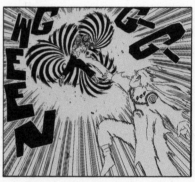

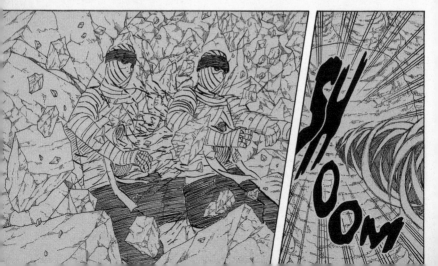

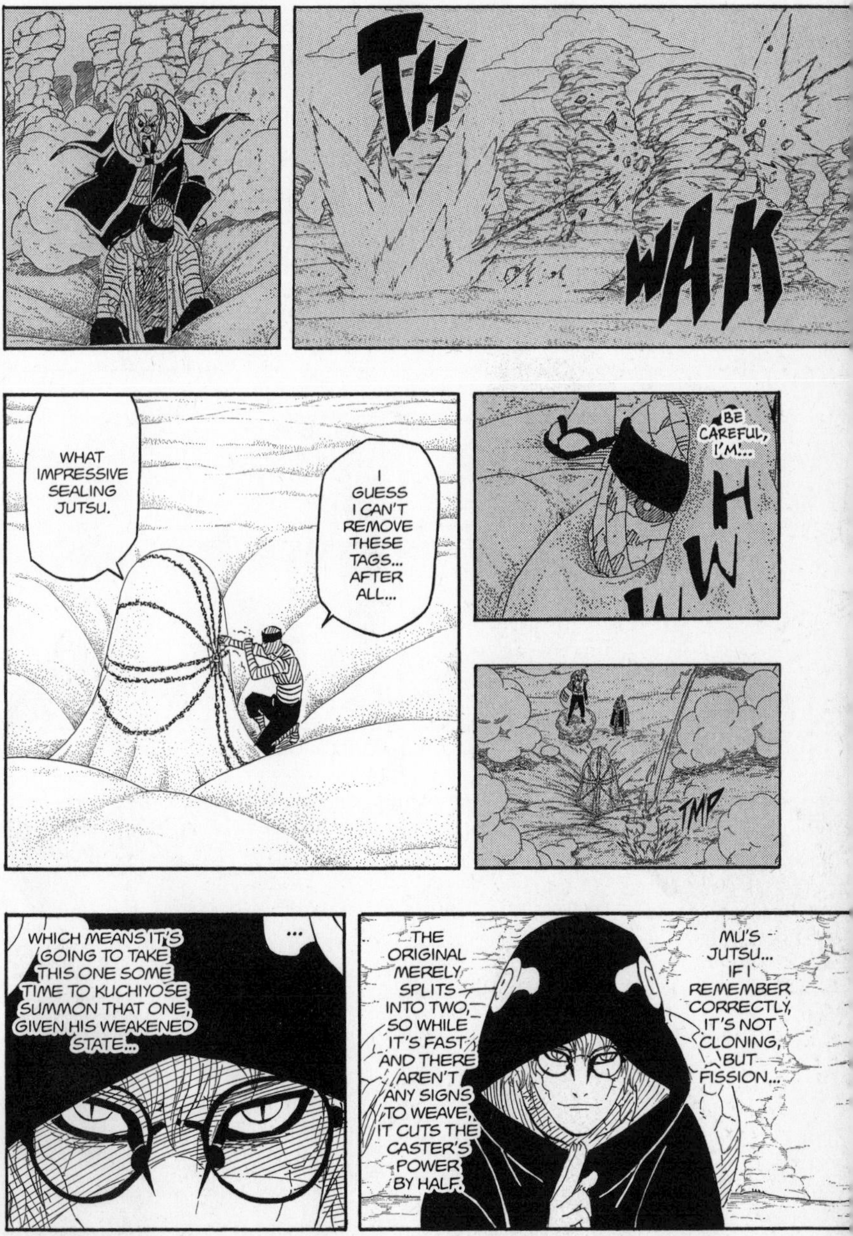
THWAK
BE CAREFUL, I'M...
HWW
TMP
WHAT IMPRESSIVE SEALING JUTSU.
I GUESS I CAN'T REMOVE THESE TAGS... AFTER ALL...
MU'S JUTSU... IF I REMEMBER CORRECTLY, IT'S NOT CLONING, BUT FISSION...
THE ORIGINAL MERELY SPLITS INTO TWO, SO WHILE IT'S FAST AND THERE AREN'T ANY SIGNS TO WEAVE, IT CUTS THE CASTER'S POWER BY HALF.
...
WHICH MEANS IT'S GOING TO TAKE THIS ONE SOME TIME TO KUCHIYOSE SUMMON THAT ONE, GIVEN HIS WEAKENED STATE...

READ THIS WAY

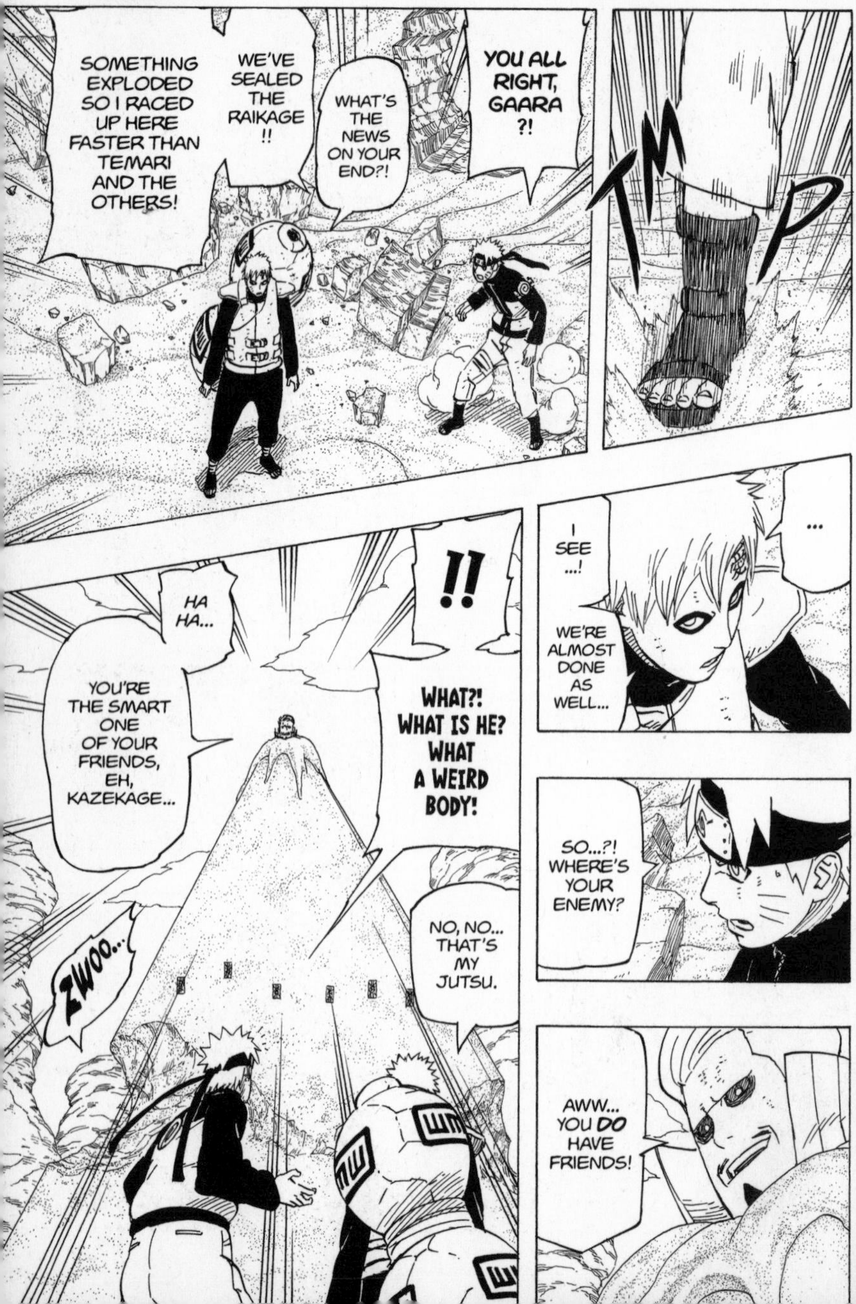
TMP
YOU ALL RIGHT, GAARA?!
WHAT'S THE NEWS ON YOUR END?!
WE'VE SEALED THE RAIKAGE!!
SOMETHING EXPLODED SO I RACED UP HERE FASTER THAN TEMARI AND THE OTHERS!
...
I SEE...!
WE'RE ALMOST DONE AS WELL...
SO...?! WHERE'S YOUR ENEMY?
AWW... YOU DO HAVE FRIENDS!
!!
HA HA...
YOU'RE THE SMART ONE OF YOUR FRIENDS, EH, KAZEKAGE...
WHAT?! WHAT IS HE? WHAT A WEIRD BODY!
NO, NO... THAT'S MY JUTSU.
ZWOO...

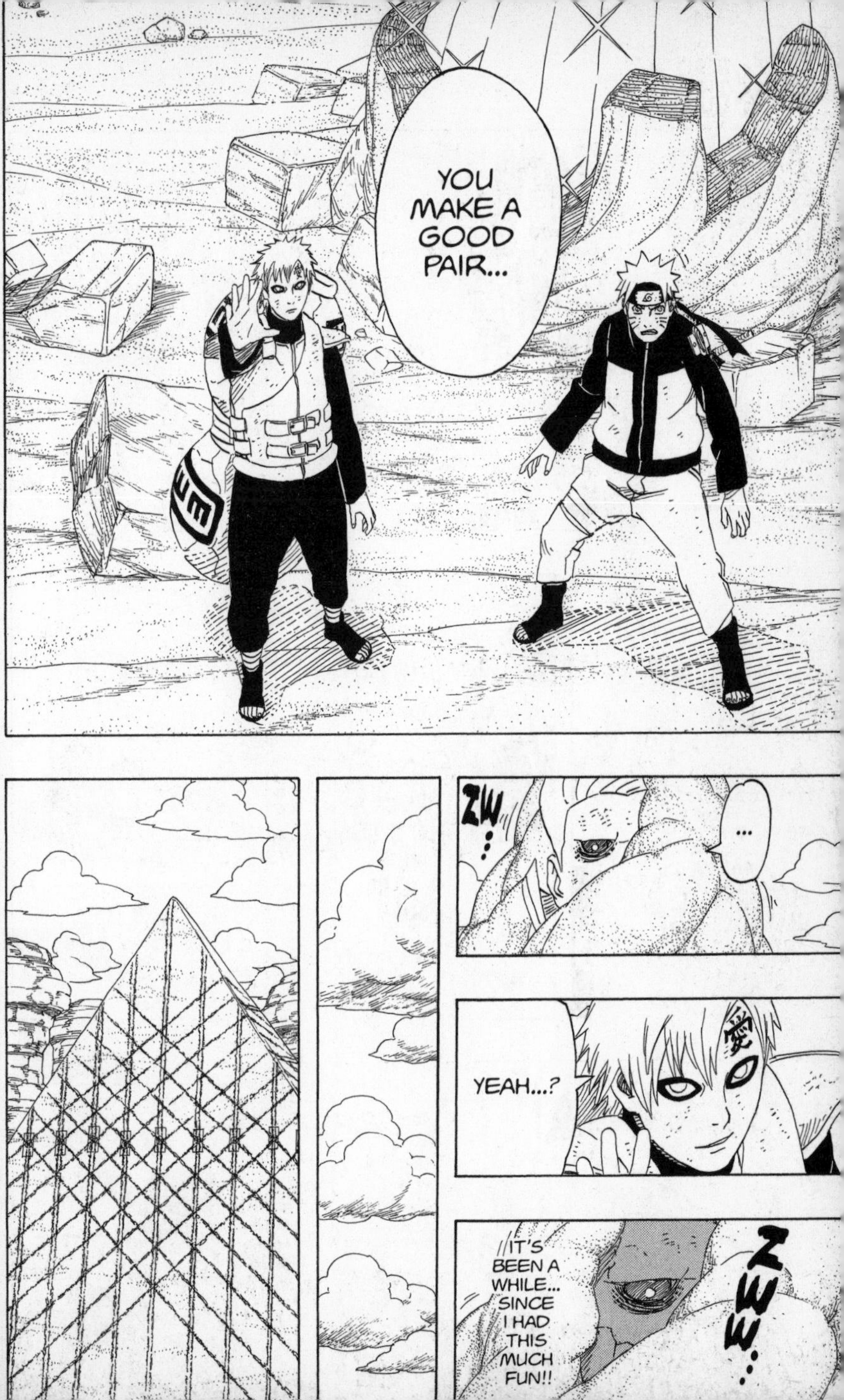
YOU MAKE A GOOD PAIR...
ZW...
...
YEAH...?
IT'S BEEN A WHILE... SINCE I HAD THIS MUCH FUN!!
ZWW...

READ THIS WAY

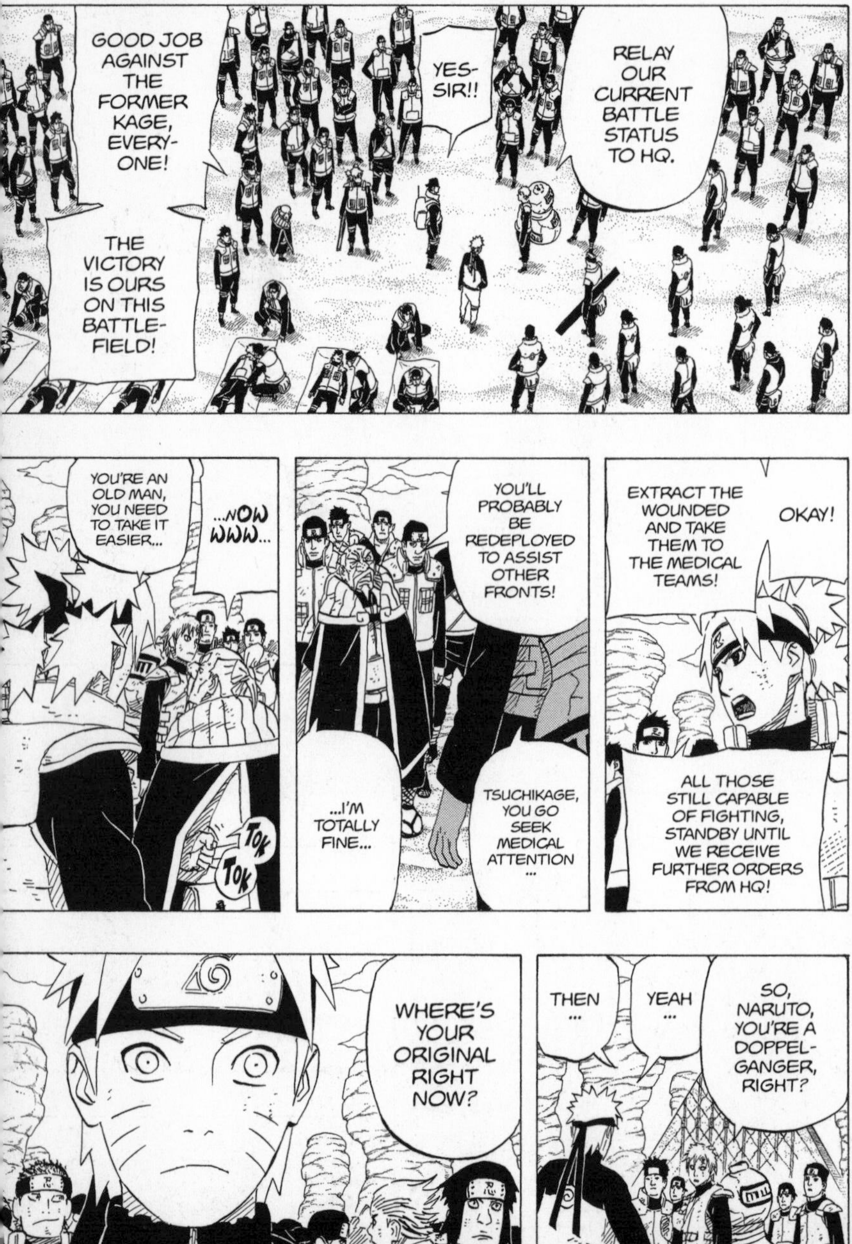
RELAY OUR CURRENT BATTLE STATUS TO HQ.
YES-SIR!!
GOOD JOB AGAINST THE FORMER KAGE, EVERYONE!
THE VICTORY IS OURS ON THIS BATTLEFIELD!
EXTRACT THE WOUNDED AND TAKE THEM TO THE MEDICAL TEAMS!
OKAY!
ALL THOSE STILL CAPABLE OF FIGHTING, STANDBY UNTIL WE RECEIVE FURTHER ORDERS FROM HQ!
YOU'LL PROBABLY BE REDEPLOYED TO ASSIST OTHER FRONTS!
TSUCHIKAGE, YOU GO SEEK MEDICAL ATTENTION ...
...I'M TOTALLY FINE...
...NOW WWW...
YOU'RE AN OLD MAN, YOU NEED TO TAKE IT EASIER...
TOK TOK
SO, NARUTO, YOU'RE A DOPPEL-GANGER, RIGHT?
YEAH ...
THEN ...
WHERE'S YOUR ORIGINAL RIGHT NOW?

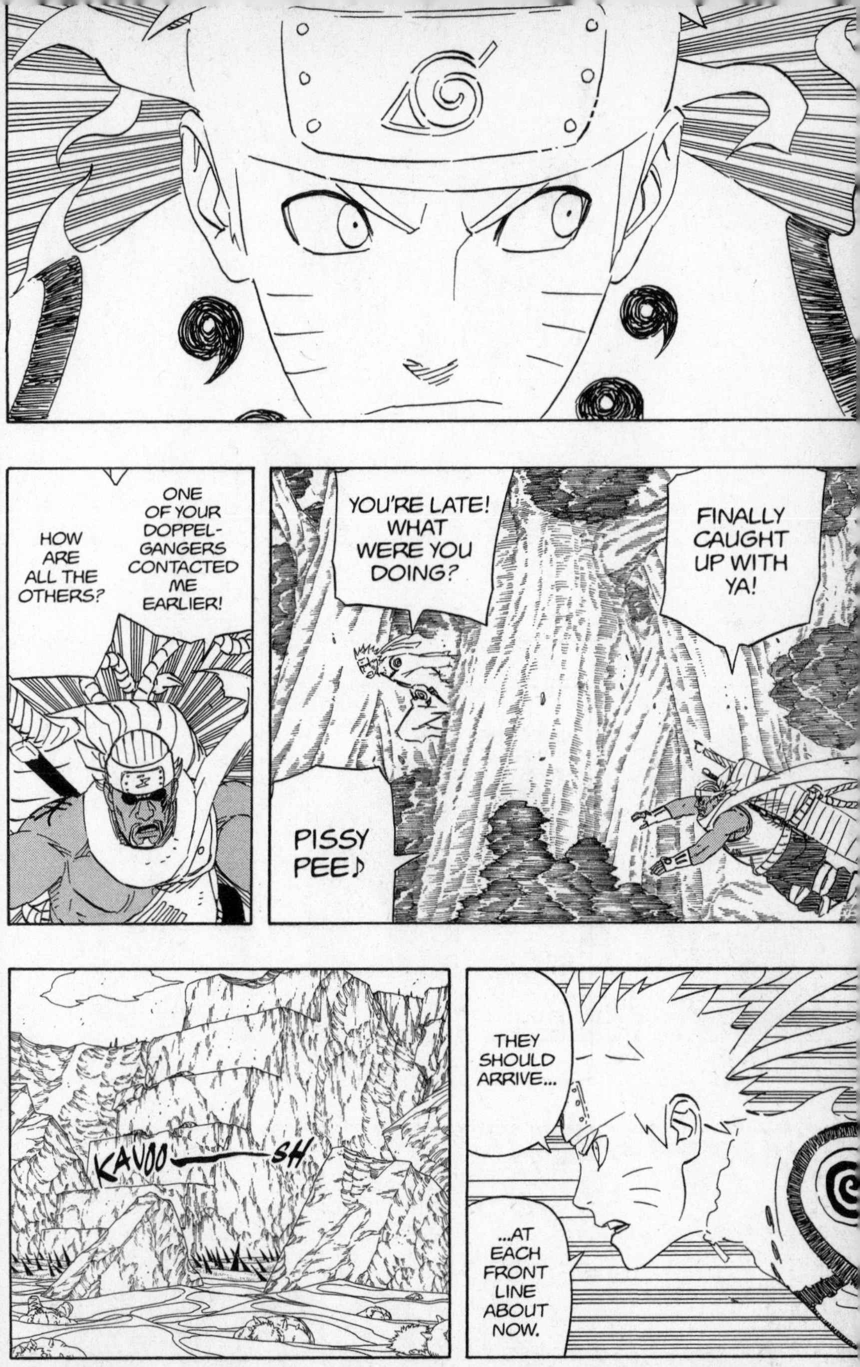
FINALLY CAUGHT UP WITH YA!
YOU'RE LATE! WHAT WERE YOU DOING?
PISSY PEE♪
ONE OF YOUR DOPPEL-GANGERS CONTACTED ME EARLIER!
HOW ARE ALL THE OTHERS?
THEY SHOULD ARRIVE...
...AT EACH FRONT LINE ABOUT NOW.
KAVOO——SH

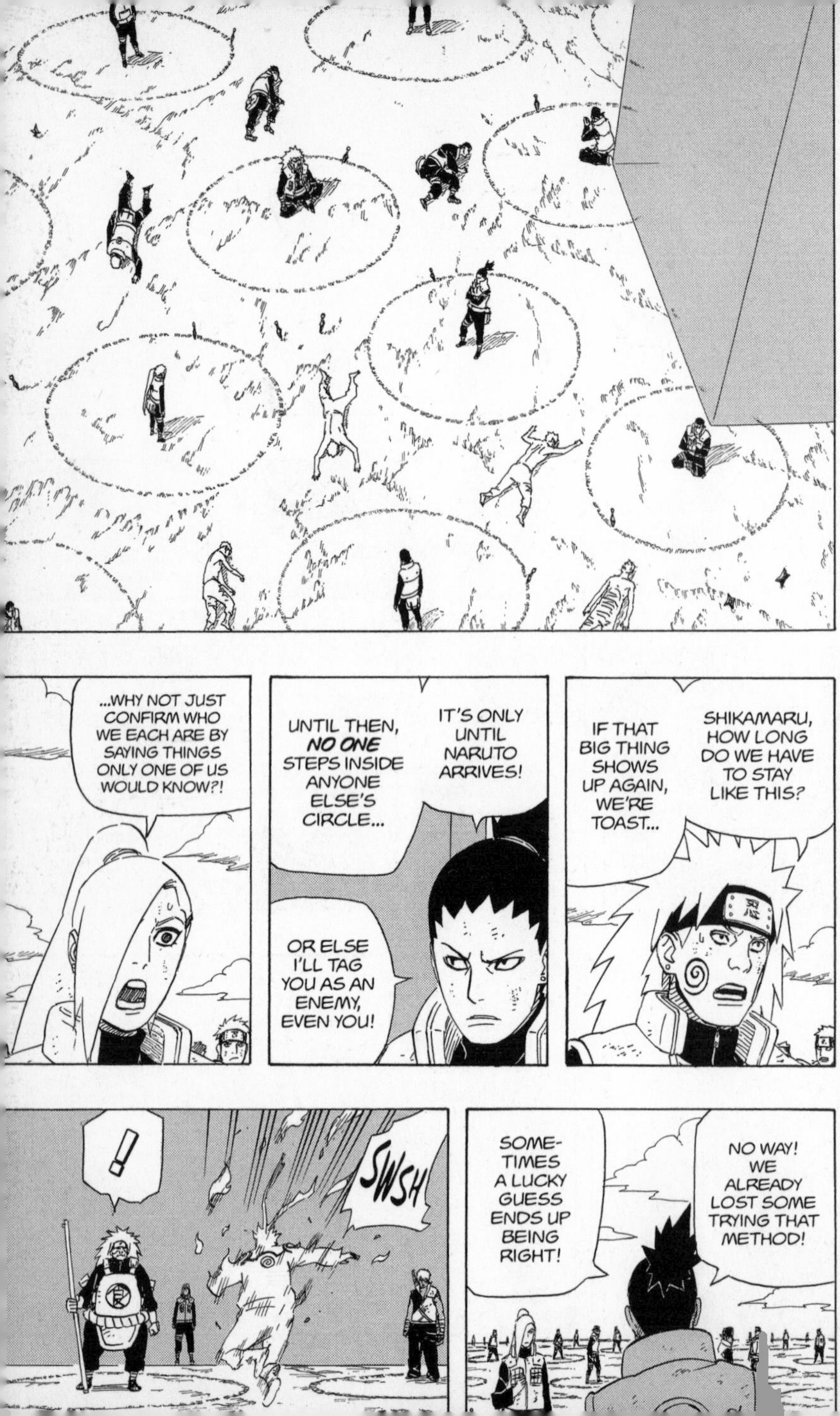
SHIKAMARU, HOW LONG DO WE HAVE TO STAY LIKE THIS?
IF THAT BIG THING SHOWS UP AGAIN, WE'RE TOAST...
IT'S ONLY UNTIL NARUTO ARRIVES!
UNTIL THEN, ***NO ONE*** STEPS INSIDE ANYONE ELSE'S CIRCLE...
OR ELSE I'LL TAG YOU AS AN ENEMY, EVEN YOU!
...WHY NOT JUST CONFIRM WHO WE EACH ARE BY SAYING THINGS ONLY ONE OF US WOULD KNOW?!
NO WAY! WE ALREADY LOST SOME TRYING THAT METHOD!
SOME-TIMES A LUCKY GUESS ENDS UP BEING RIGHT!
SWSH
!

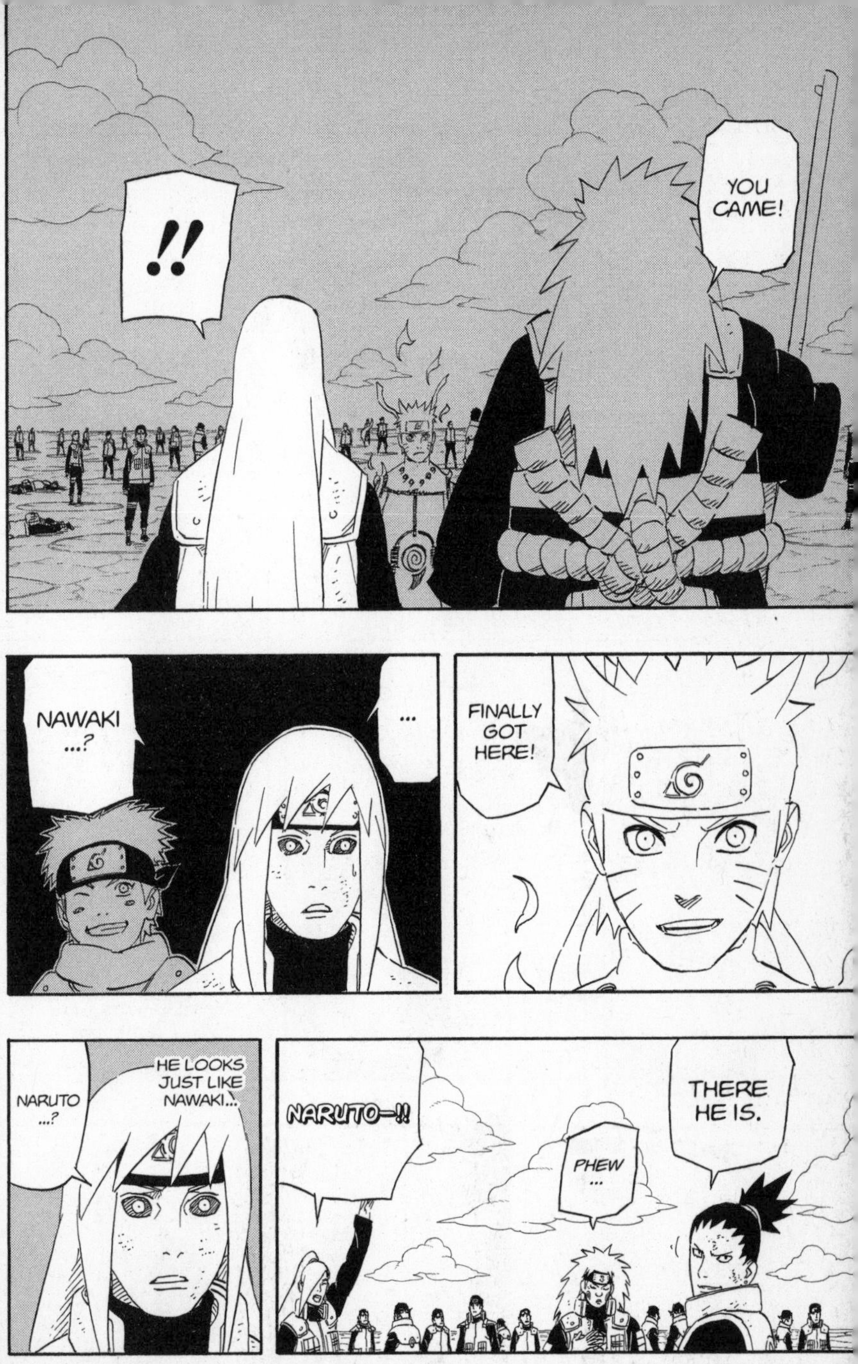
YOU CAME!
!!
FINALLY GOT HERE!
...
NAWAKI ...?
THERE HE IS.
PHEW ...
NARUTO—!!
HE LOOKS JUST LIKE NAWAKI...
NARUTO ...?

READ THIS WAY

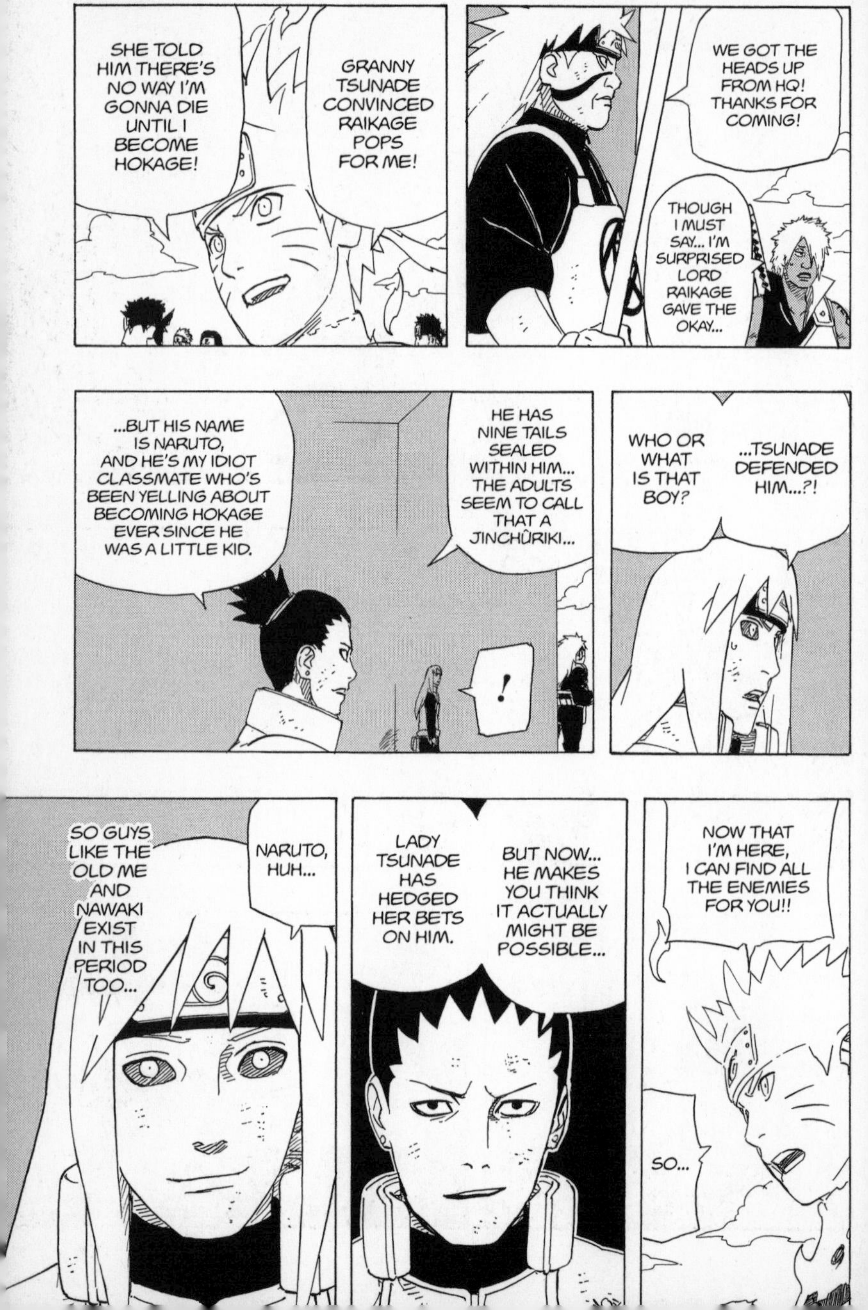
WE GOT THE HEADS UP FROM HQ! THANKS FOR COMING!
THOUGH I MUST SAY... I'M SURPRISED LORD RAIKAGE GAVE THE OKAY...
GRANNY TSUNADE CONVINCED RAIKAGE POPS FOR ME!
SHE TOLD HIM THERE'S NO WAY I'M GONNA DIE UNTIL I BECOME HOKAGE!
...TSUNADE DEFENDED HIM...?!
WHO OR WHAT IS THAT BOY?
HE HAS NINE TAILS SEALED WITHIN HIM... THE ADULTS SEEM TO CALL THAT A JINCHŪRIKI...
...BUT HIS NAME IS NARUTO, AND HE'S MY IDIOT CLASSMATE WHO'S BEEN YELLING ABOUT BECOMING HOKAGE EVER SINCE HE WAS A LITTLE KID.
!
NOW THAT I'M HERE, I CAN FIND ALL THE ENEMIES FOR YOU!!
SO...
LADY TSUNADE HAS HEDGED HER BETS ON HIM.
BUT NOW... HE MAKES YOU THINK IT ACTUALLY MIGHT BE POSSIBLE...
NARUTO, HUH...
SO GUYS LIKE THE OLD ME AND NAWAKI EXIST IN THIS PERIOD TOO...

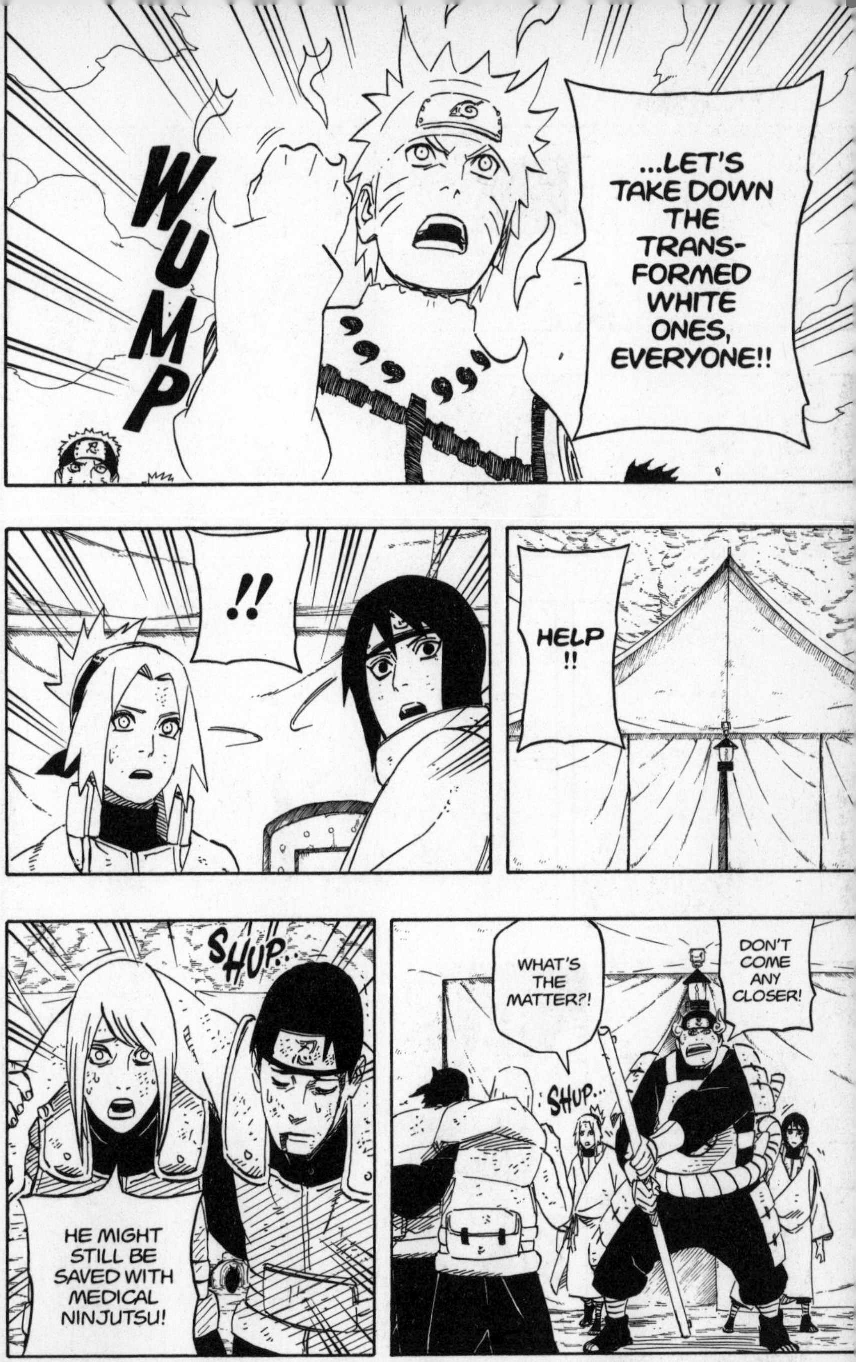
...LET'S TAKE DOWN THE TRANS-FORMED WHITE ONES, EVERYONE!!
WUMP
HELP!!
!!
DON'T COME ANY CLOSER!
WHAT'S THE MATTER?!
SHUP...
SHUP...
HE MIGHT STILL BE SAVED WITH MEDICAL NINJUTSU!

READ THIS WAY

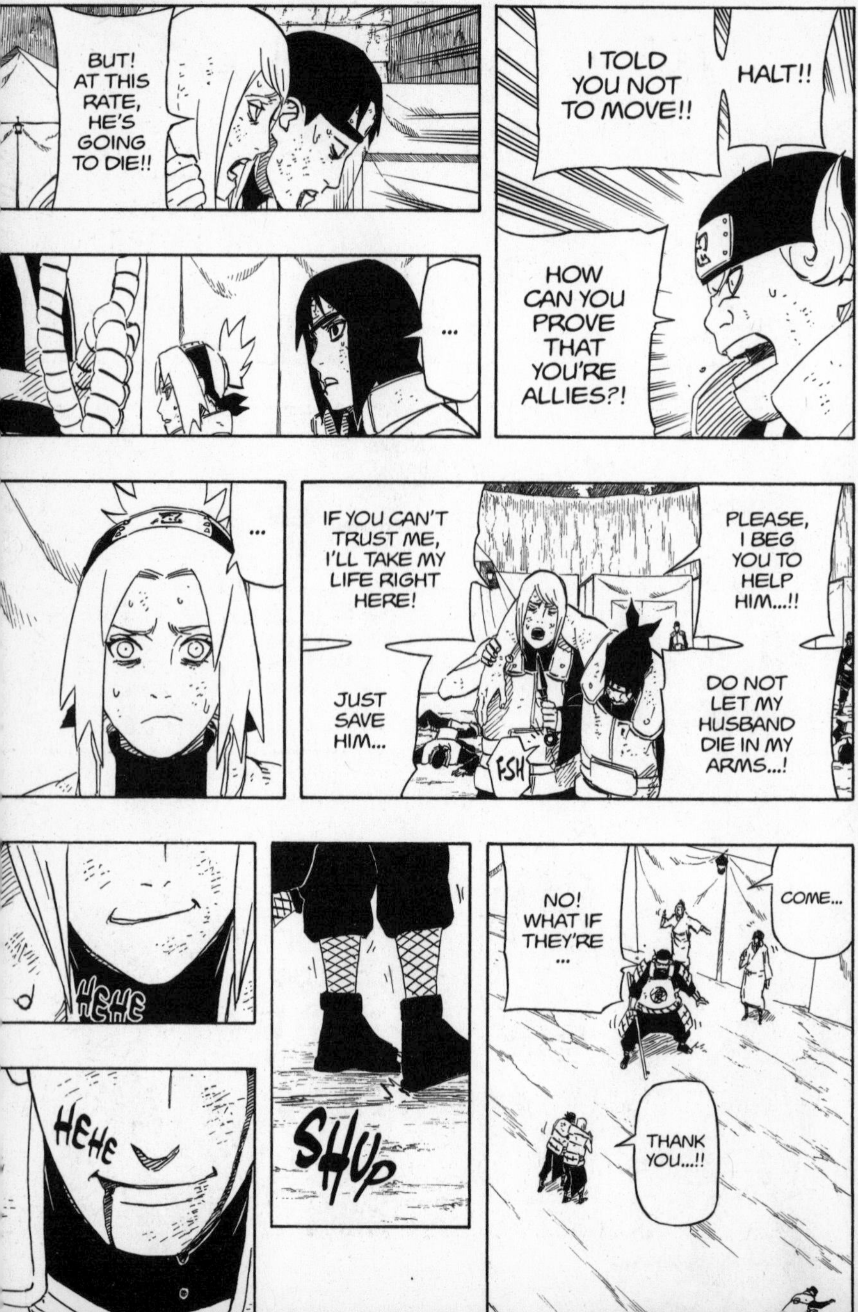
HALT!!
I TOLD YOU NOT TO MOVE!!
HOW CAN YOU PROVE THAT YOU'RE ALLIES?!
BUT! AT THIS RATE, HE'S GOING TO DIE!!
...
PLEASE, I BEG YOU TO HELP HIM...!!
IF YOU CAN'T TRUST ME, I'LL TAKE MY LIFE RIGHT HERE!
DO NOT LET MY HUSBAND DIE IN MY ARMS...!
JUST SAVE HIM...
FSH
...
COME...
NO! WHAT IF THEY'RE ...
THANK YOU...!!
SHUP
HEHE
HEHE

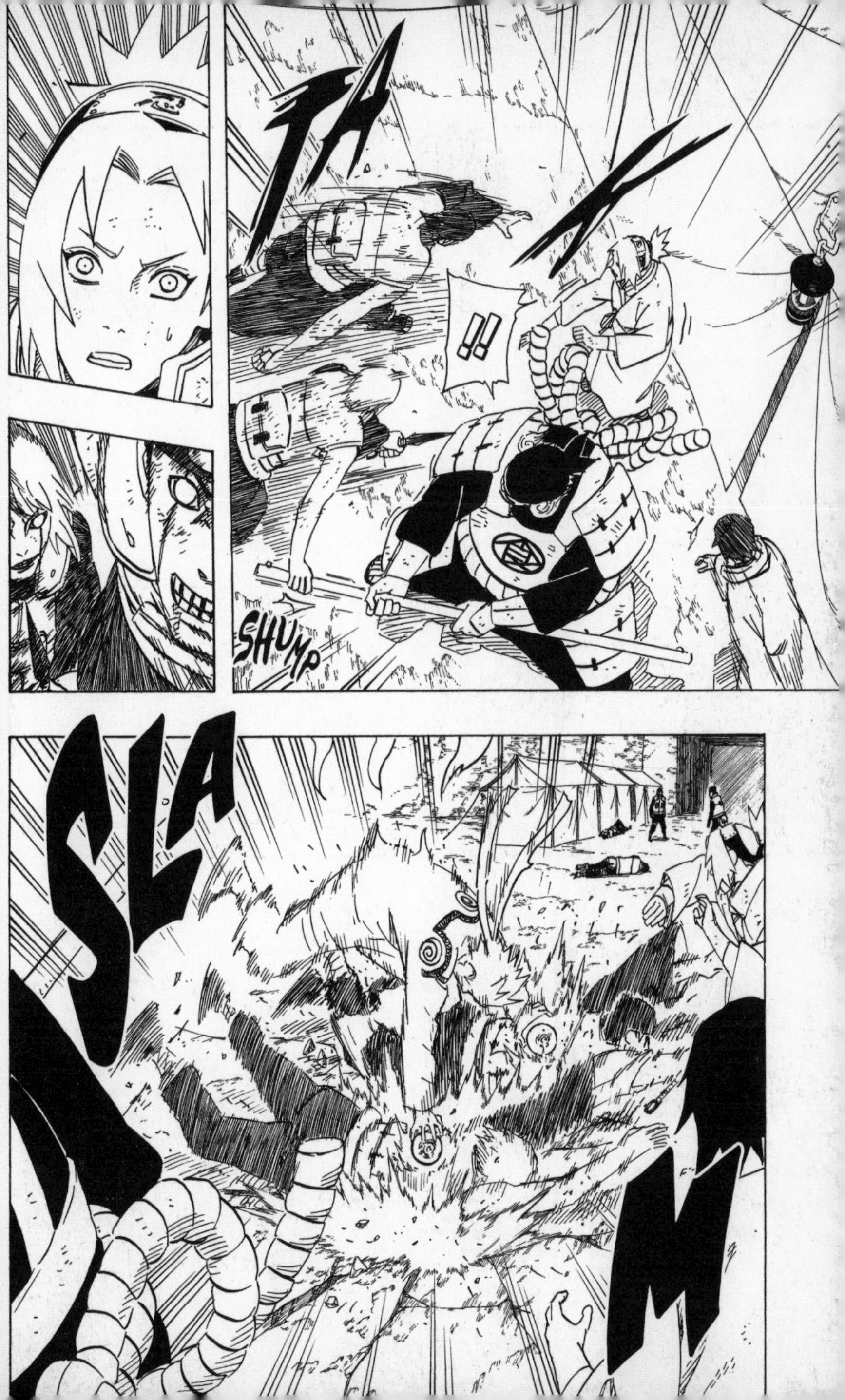
TAK
!!
SHUMP
SLAM

READ THIS WAY

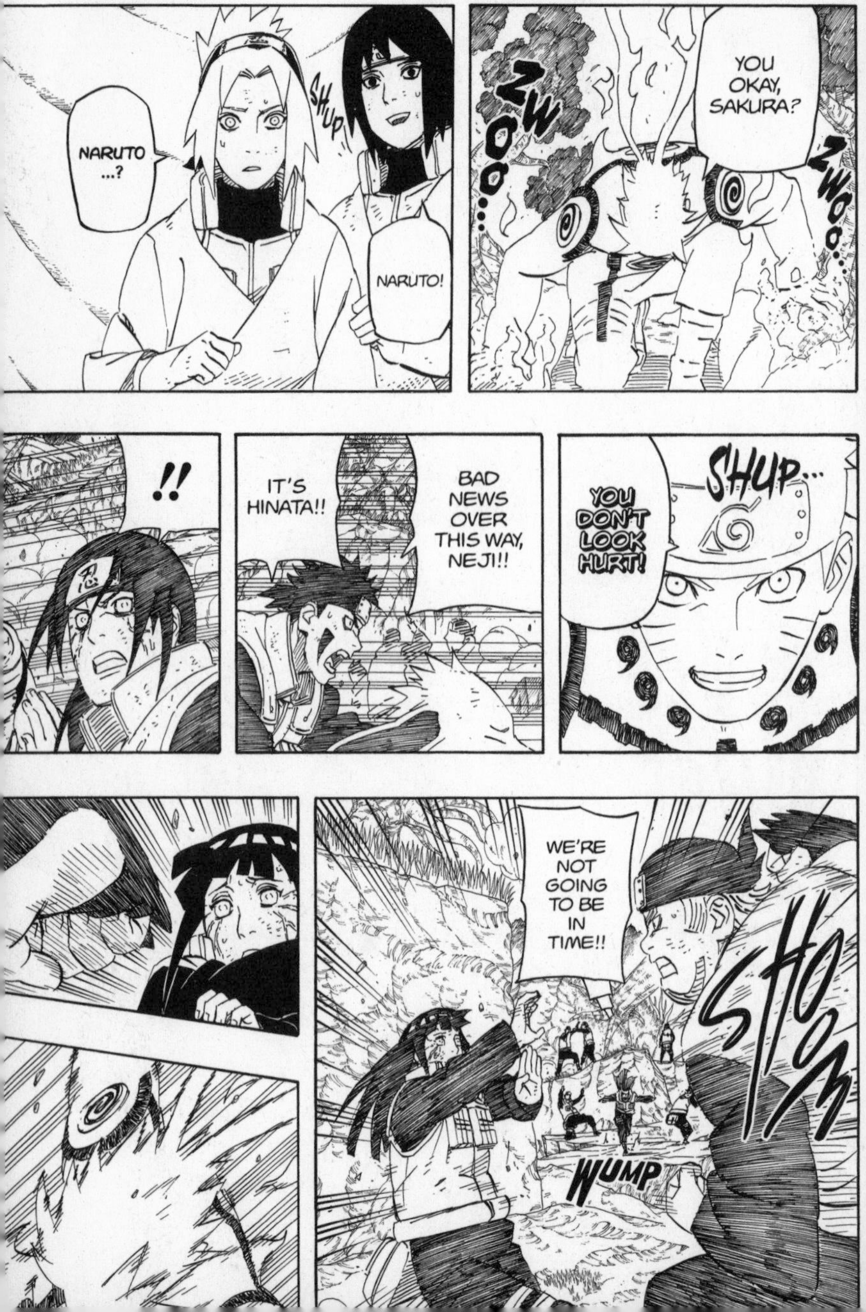
YOU OKAY, SAKURA?
ZWOOO...
ZWOO...
SHUP
NARUTO ...?
NARUTO!
SHUP...
YOU DON'T LOOK HURT!
BAD NEWS OVER THIS WAY, NEJI!!
IT'S HINATA!!
!!
WE'RE NOT GOING TO BE IN TIME!!
SHOOM
WUMP

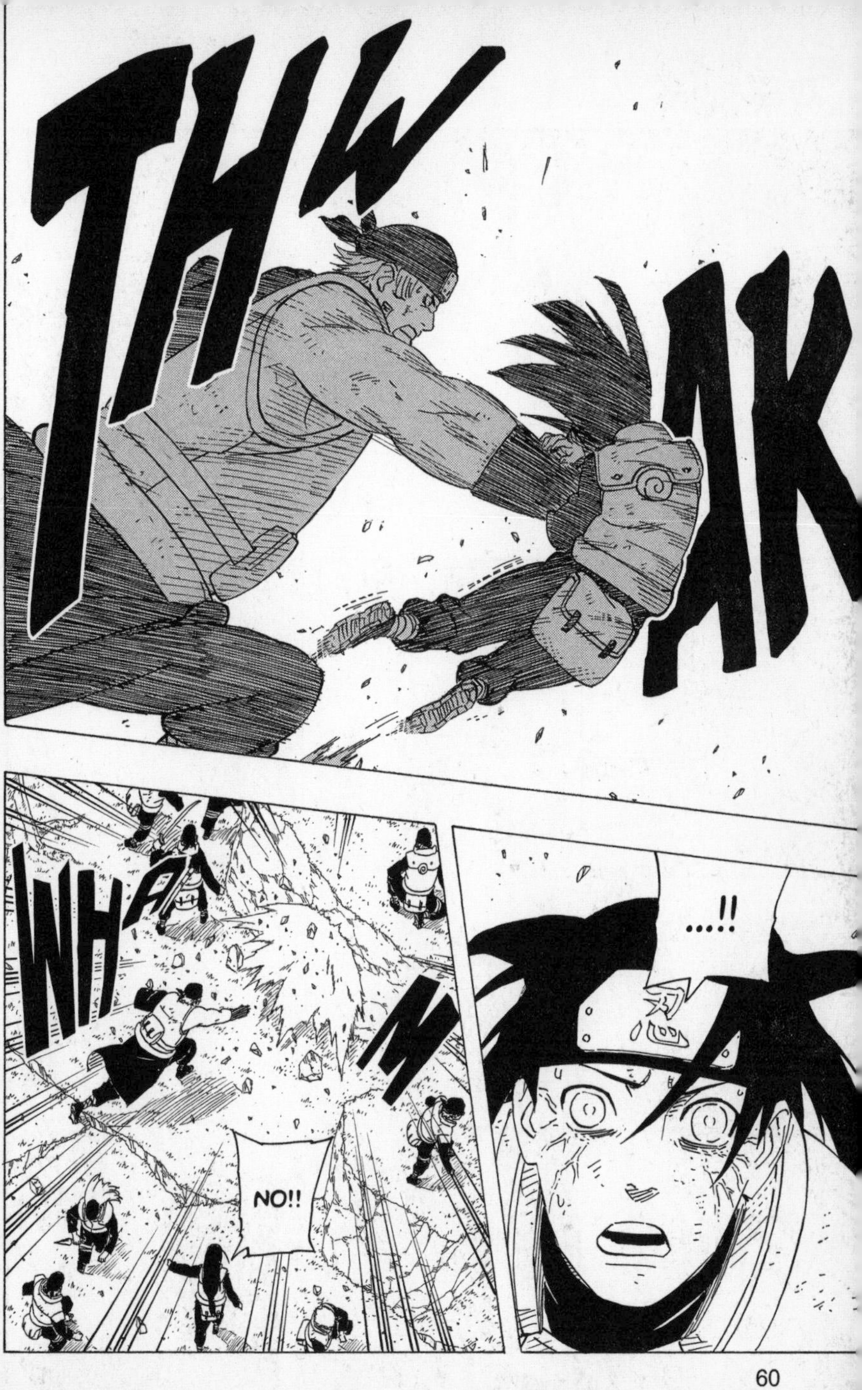
THWAK
...!!
WHAM
NO!!

READ THIS WAY

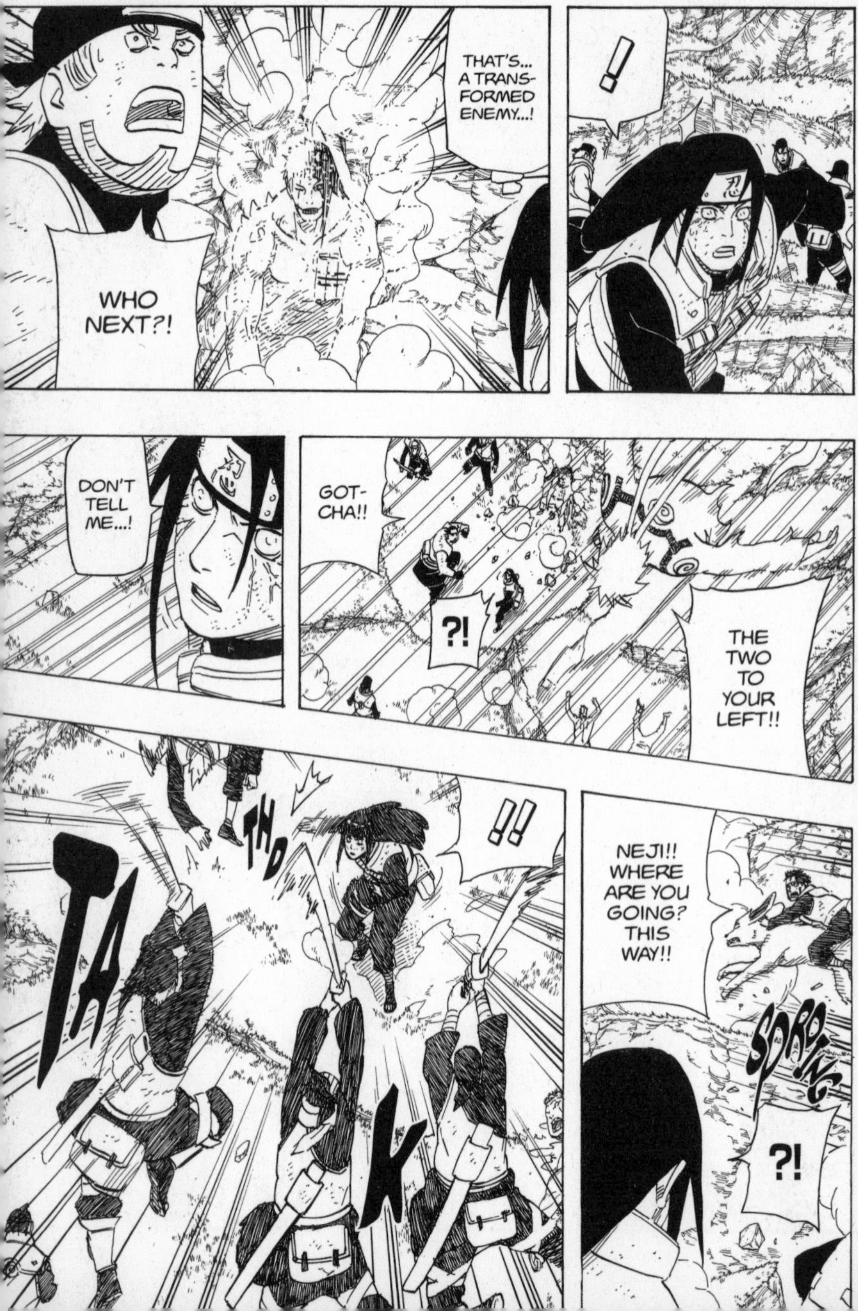
!
THAT'S... A TRANS-FORMED ENEMY...!
WHO NEXT?!
GOT-CHA!!
?!
THE TWO TO YOUR LEFT!!
DON'T TELL ME...!
NEJI!! WHERE ARE YOU GOING? THIS WAY!!
SPROING
?!
!!
THD
TAK

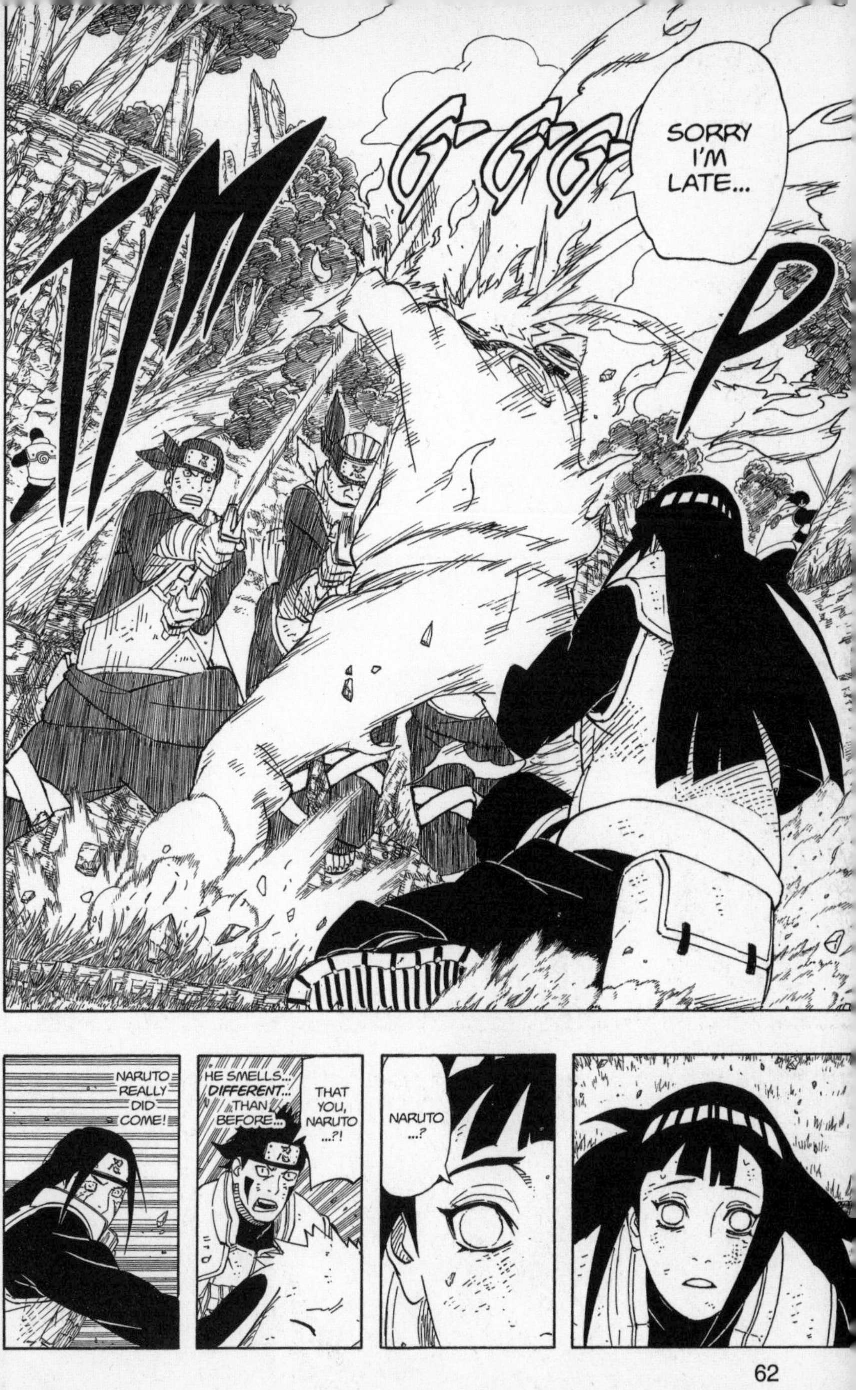
SORRY I'M LATE...
G-G-G
TMP
NARUTO ...?
THAT YOU, NARUTO ...?!
HE SMELLS... **DIFFERENT**... THAN BEFORE...
NARUTO REALLY DID COME!

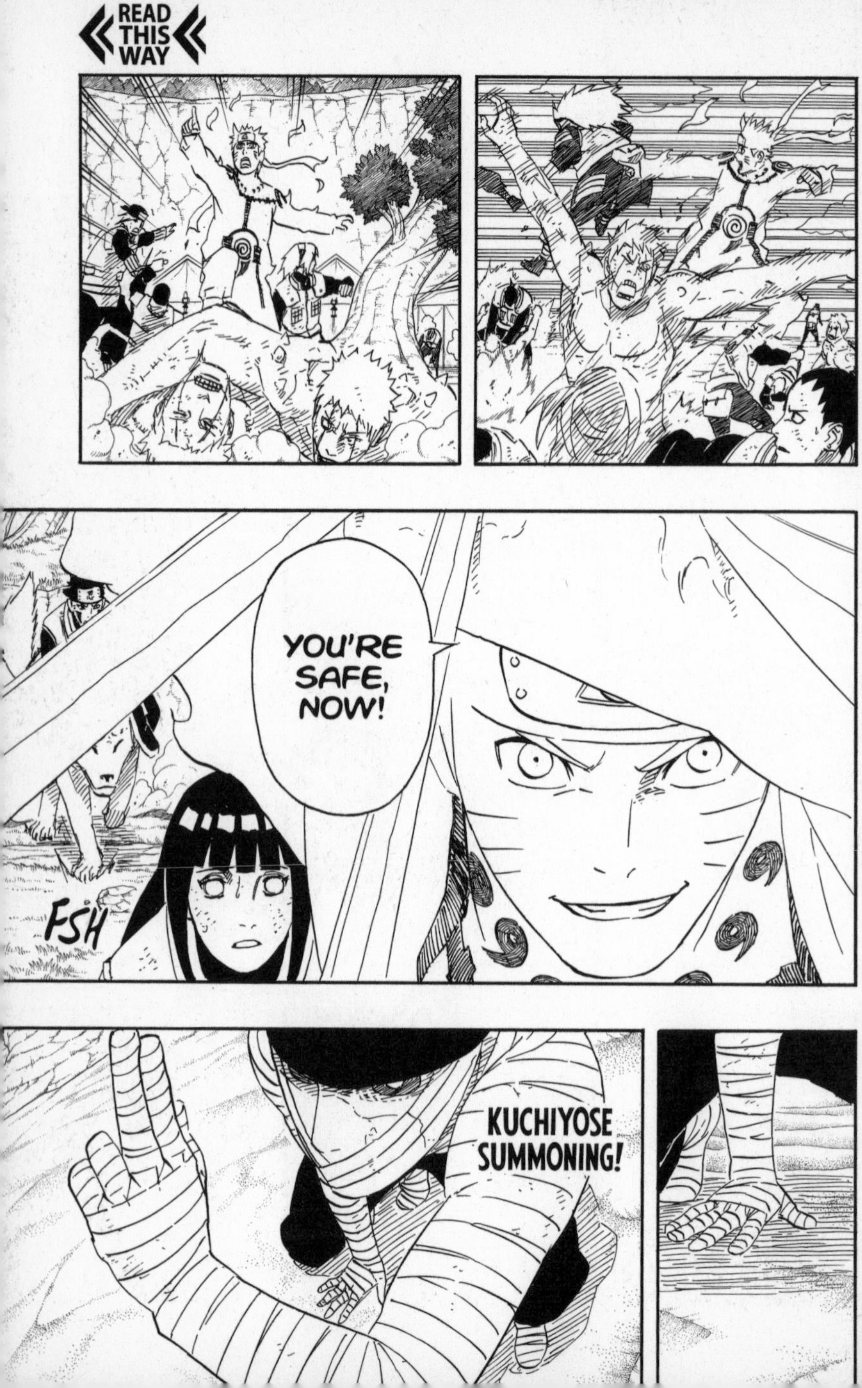
READ THIS WAY
YOU'RE SAFE, NOW!
FSH
KUCHIYOSE SUMMONING!

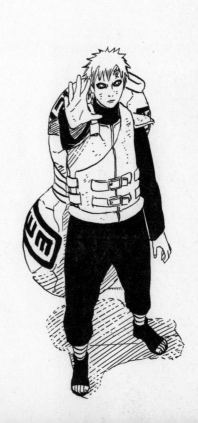

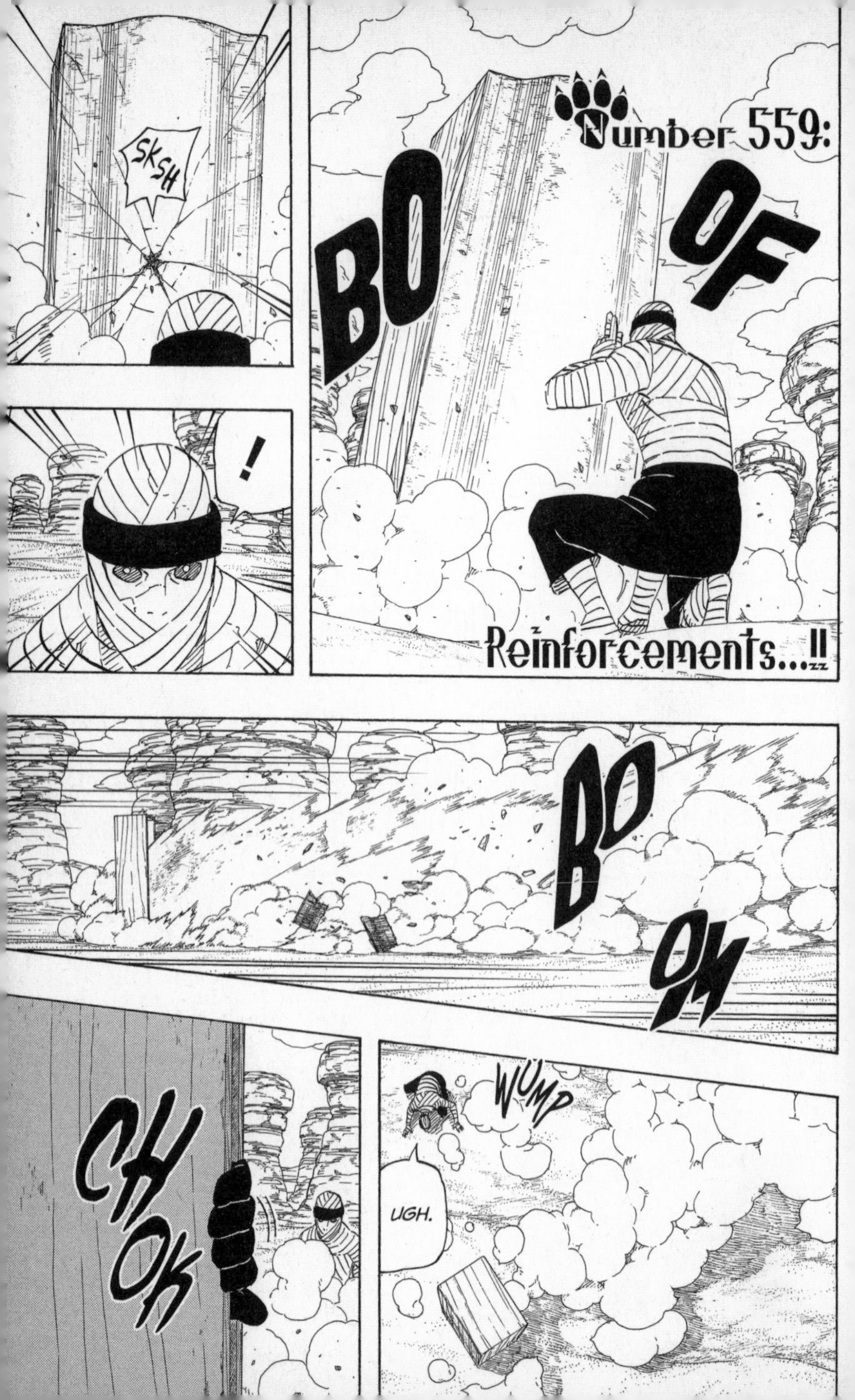
Number 559:
Reinforcements...!!
BOOF
SKSH
!
BOOOM
WUMP
UGH.
CHOK

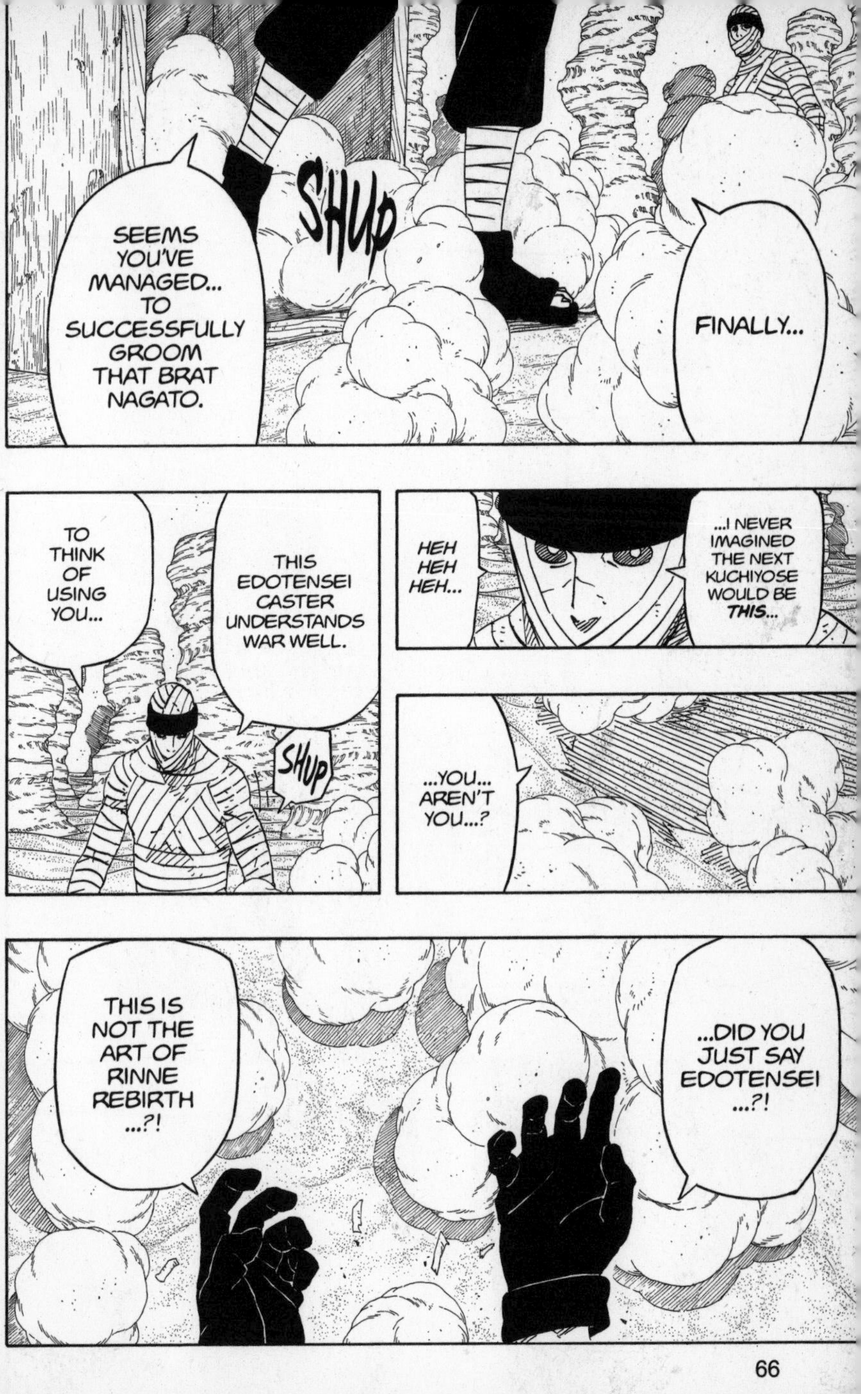
FINALLY...
SHUP
SEEMS YOU'VE MANAGED... TO SUCCESSFULLY GROOM THAT BRAT NAGATO.
...I NEVER IMAGINED THE NEXT KUCHIYOSE WOULD BE *THIS*...
HEH HEH HEH...
...YOU... AREN'T YOU...?
THIS EDOTENSEI CASTER UNDERSTANDS WAR WELL.
TO THINK OF USING YOU...
SHUP
...DID YOU JUST SAY EDOTENSEI ...?!
THIS IS NOT THE ART OF RINNE REBIRTH ...?!

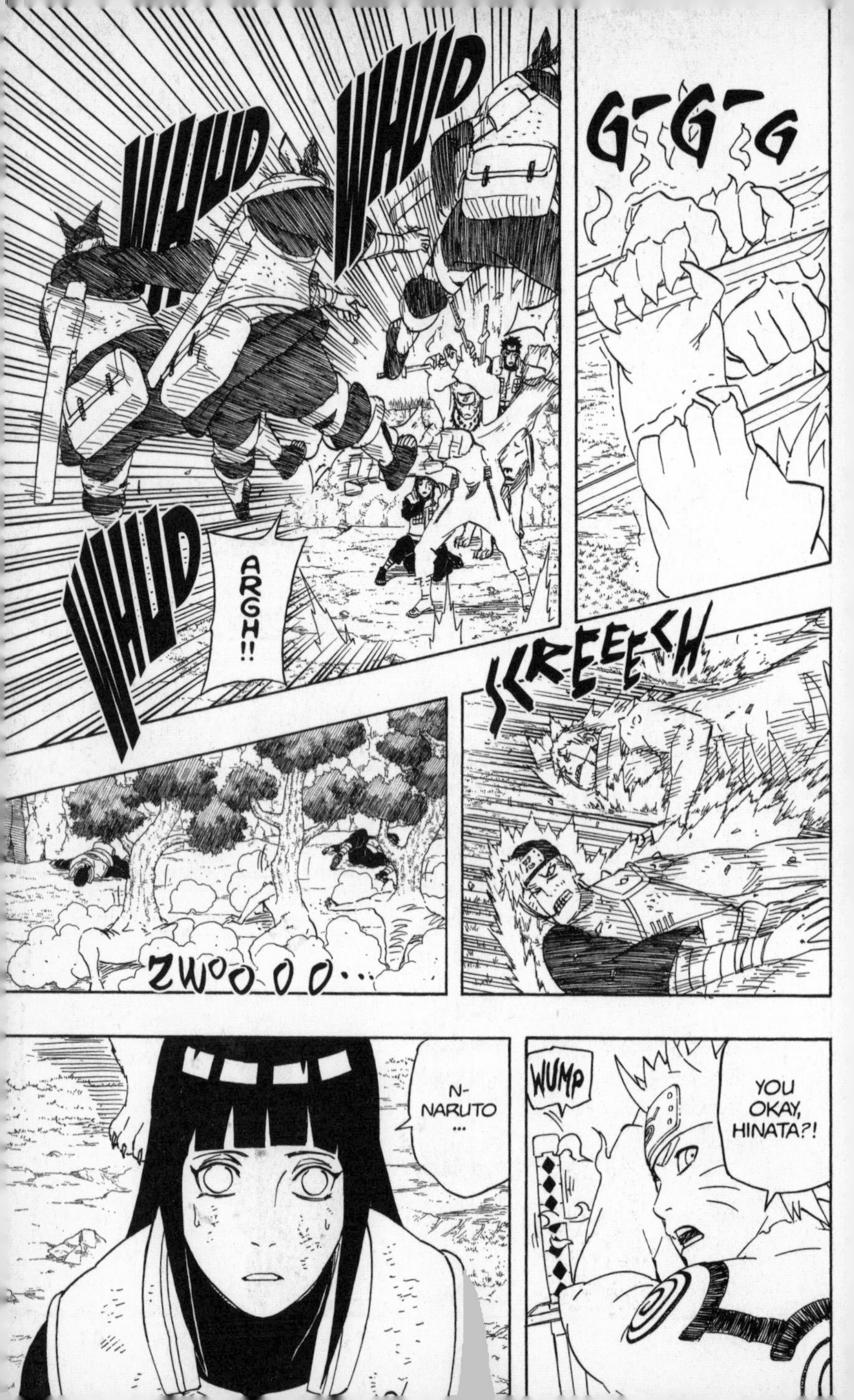
G-G-G
WHUD
WHUD
WHUD
ARGH!!
SCREEECH
ZWOO O O...
YOU OKAY, HINATA?!
WUMP
N-NARUTO...

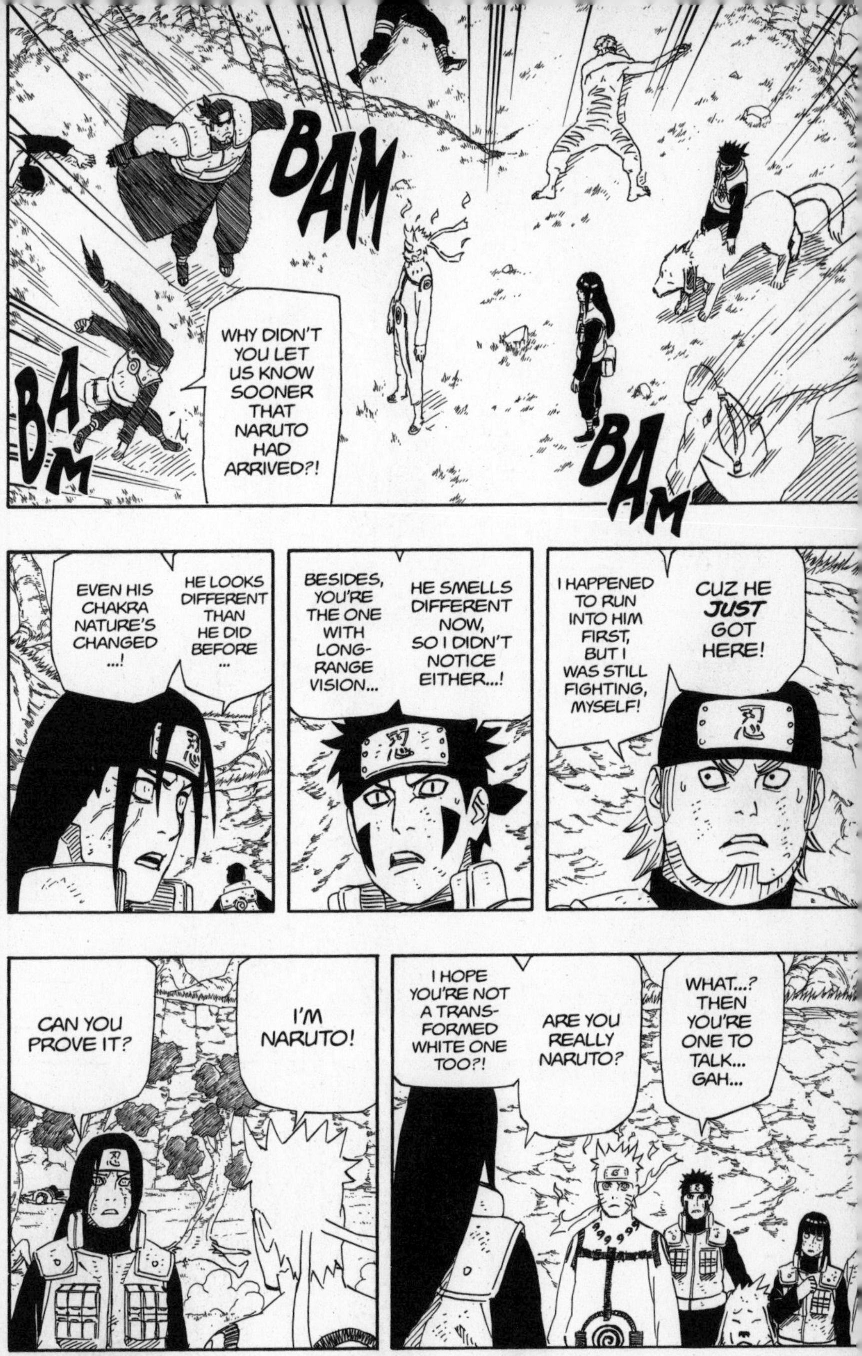
BAM
WHY DIDN'T YOU LET US KNOW SOONER THAT NARUTO HAD ARRIVED?!
BADOM
BAM
CUZ HE **JUST** GOT HERE!
I HAPPENED TO RUN INTO HIM FIRST, BUT I WAS STILL FIGHTING, MYSELF!
HE SMELLS DIFFERENT NOW, SO I DIDN'T NOTICE EITHER...!
BESIDES, YOU'RE THE ONE WITH LONG-RANGE VISION...
HE LOOKS DIFFERENT THAN HE DID BEFORE...
EVEN HIS CHAKRA NATURE'S CHANGED...!
WHAT...? THEN YOU'RE ONE TO TALK... GAH...
ARE YOU REALLY NARUTO?
I HOPE YOU'RE NOT A TRANSFORMED WHITE ONE TOO?!
I'M NARUTO!
CAN YOU PROVE IT?

READ THIS WAY

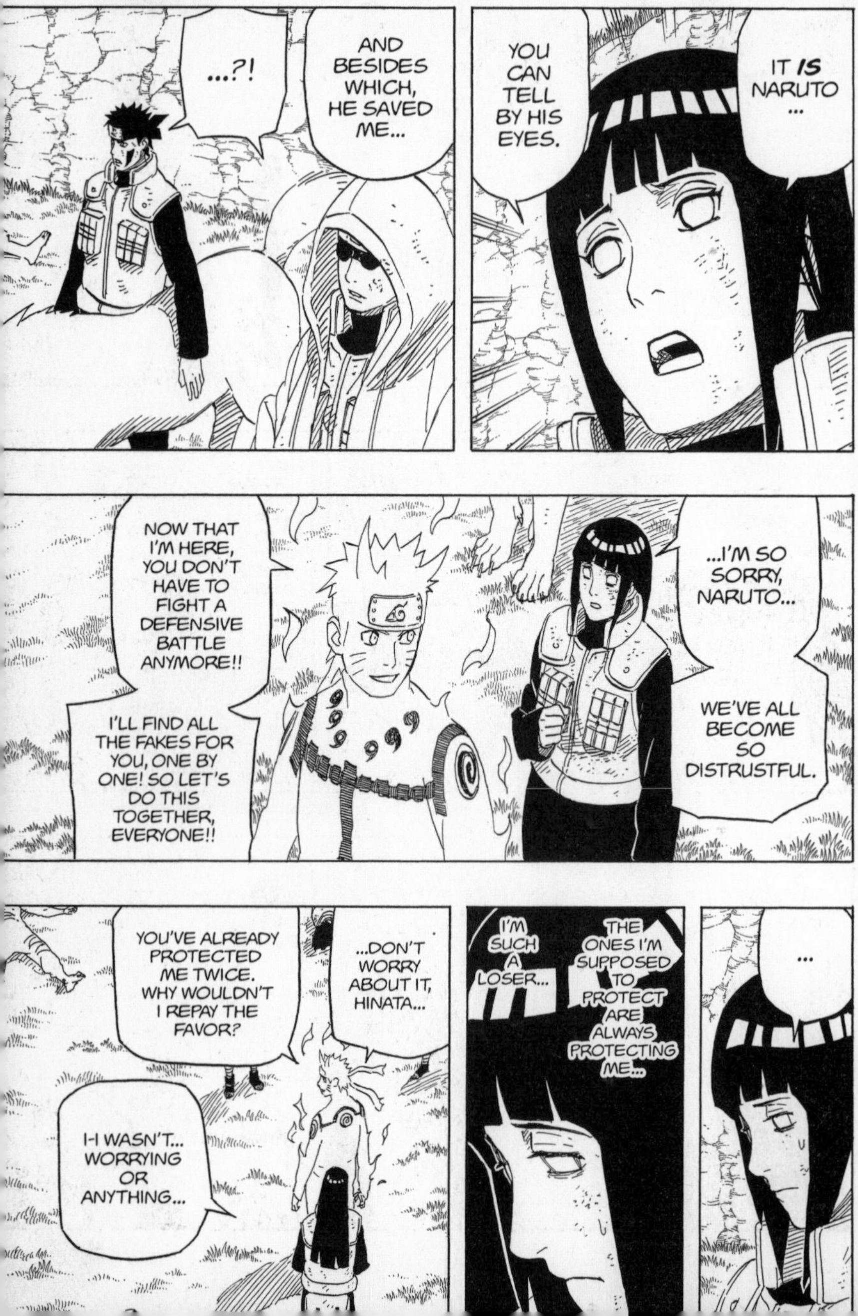
IT *IS* NARUTO ...
YOU CAN TELL BY HIS EYES.
AND BESIDES WHICH, HE SAVED ME...
...?!
...I'M SO SORRY, NARUTO...
WE'VE ALL BECOME SO DISTRUSTFUL.
NOW THAT I'M HERE, YOU DON'T HAVE TO FIGHT A DEFENSIVE BATTLE ANYMORE!!
I'LL FIND ALL THE FAKES FOR YOU, ONE BY ONE! SO LET'S DO THIS TOGETHER, EVERYONE!!
...
THE ONES I'M SUPPOSED TO PROTECT ARE ALWAYS PROTECTING ME...
I'M SUCH A LOSER...
...DON'T WORRY ABOUT IT, HINATA...
YOU'VE ALREADY PROTECTED ME TWICE. WHY WOULDN'T I REPAY THE FAVOR?
I-I WASN'T... WORRYING OR ANYTHING...

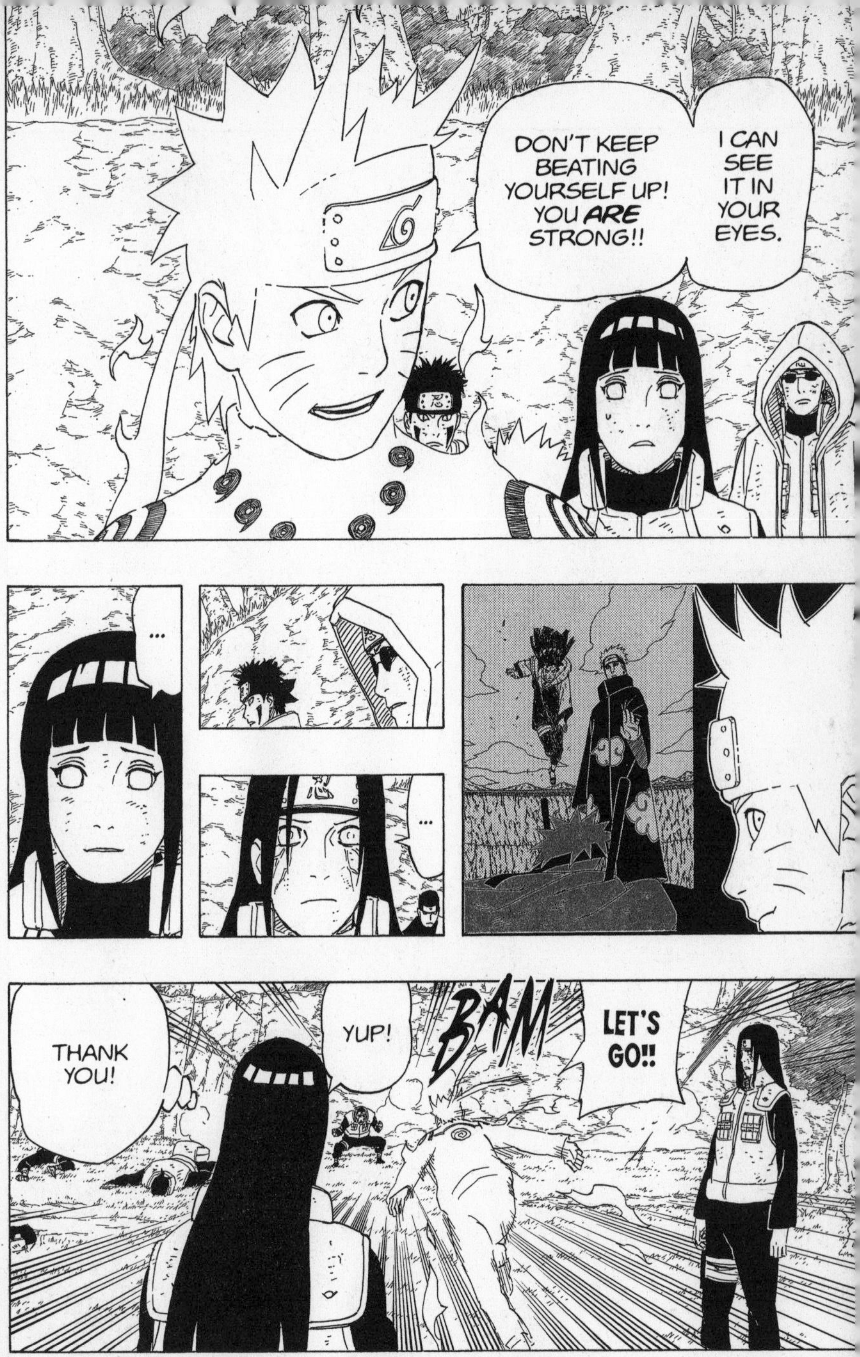
I CAN SEE IT IN YOUR EYES.
DON'T KEEP BEATING YOURSELF UP! YOU **ARE** STRONG!!
...
...
LET'S GO!!
BAM
YUP!
THANK YOU!

READ THIS WAY

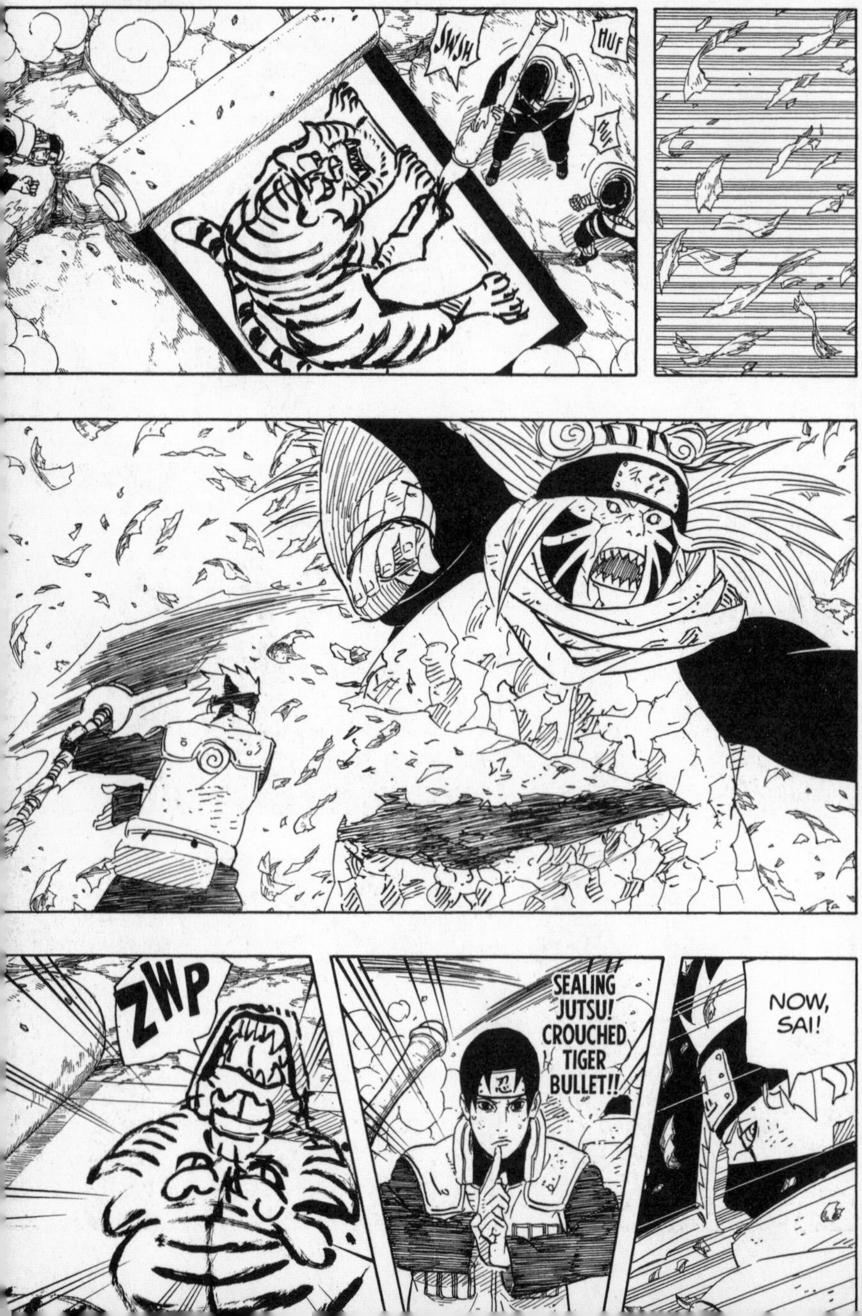
HUF
SWSH
HUF
NOW, SAI!
SEALING JUTSU! CROUCHED TIGER BULLET!!
ZWP

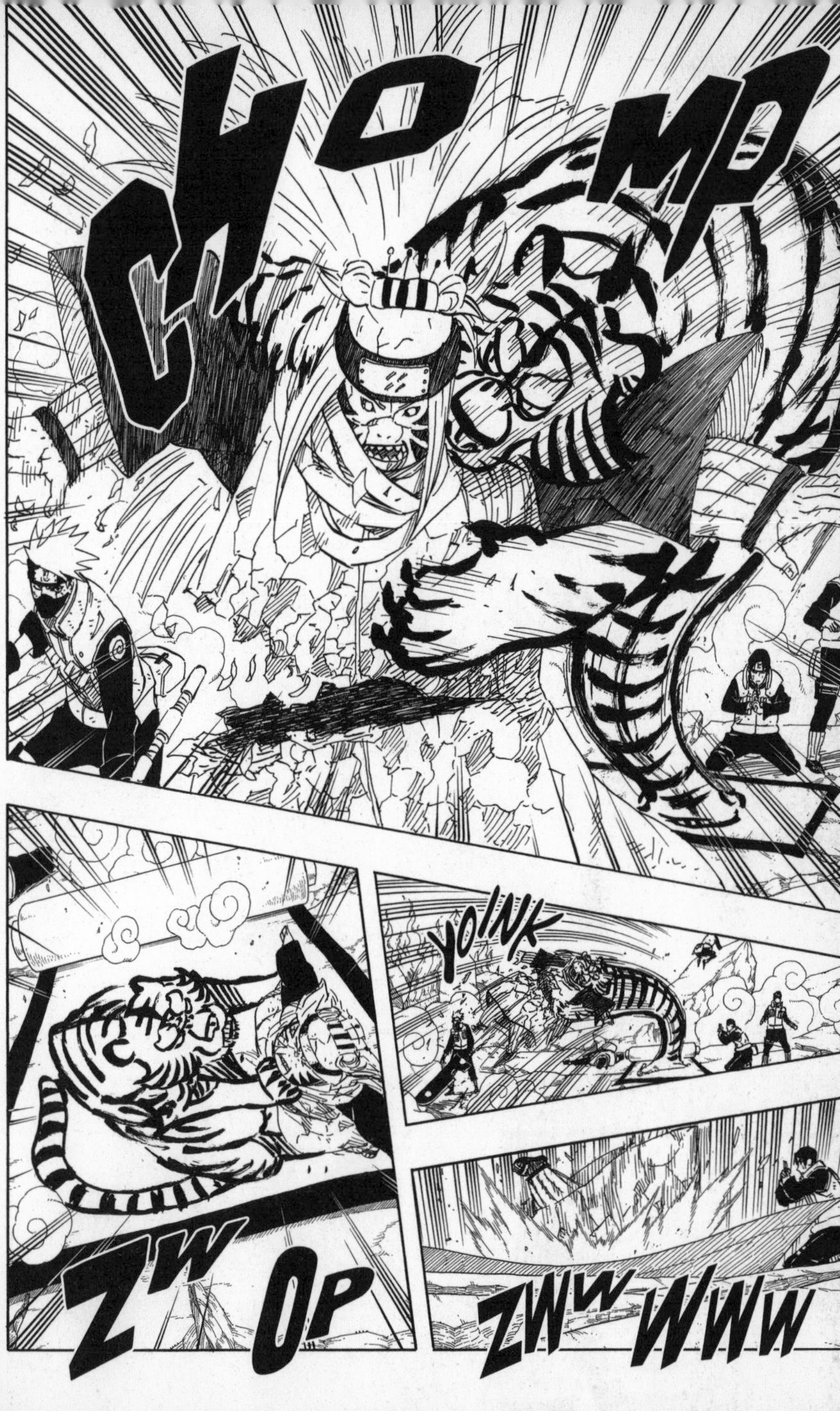
CHOMP
YOINK
ZWWWWW
ZWOP

READ THIS WAY

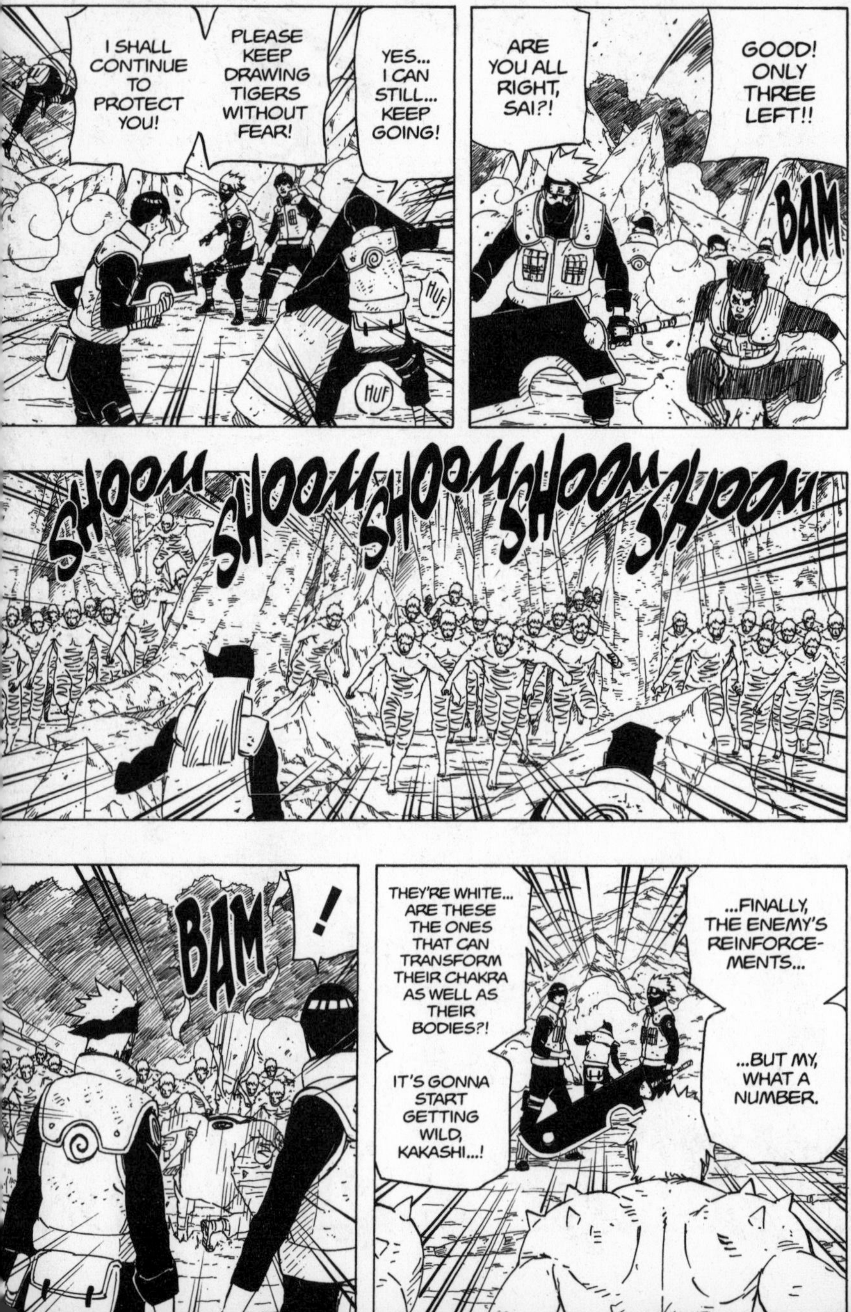
GOOD! ONLY THREE LEFT!!
ARE YOU ALL RIGHT, SAI?!
BAM
YES... I CAN STILL... KEEP GOING!
PLEASE KEEP DRAWING TIGERS WITHOUT FEAR!
I SHALL CONTINUE TO PROTECT YOU!
HUF
HUF
SHOOM SHOOM SHOOM SHOOM SHOOM
...FINALLY, THE ENEMY'S REINFORCE-MENTS...
...BUT MY, WHAT A NUMBER.
THEY'RE WHITE... ARE THESE THE ONES THAT CAN TRANSFORM THEIR CHAKRA AS WELL AS THEIR BODIES?!
IT'S GONNA START GETTING WILD, KAKASHI...!
!
BAM

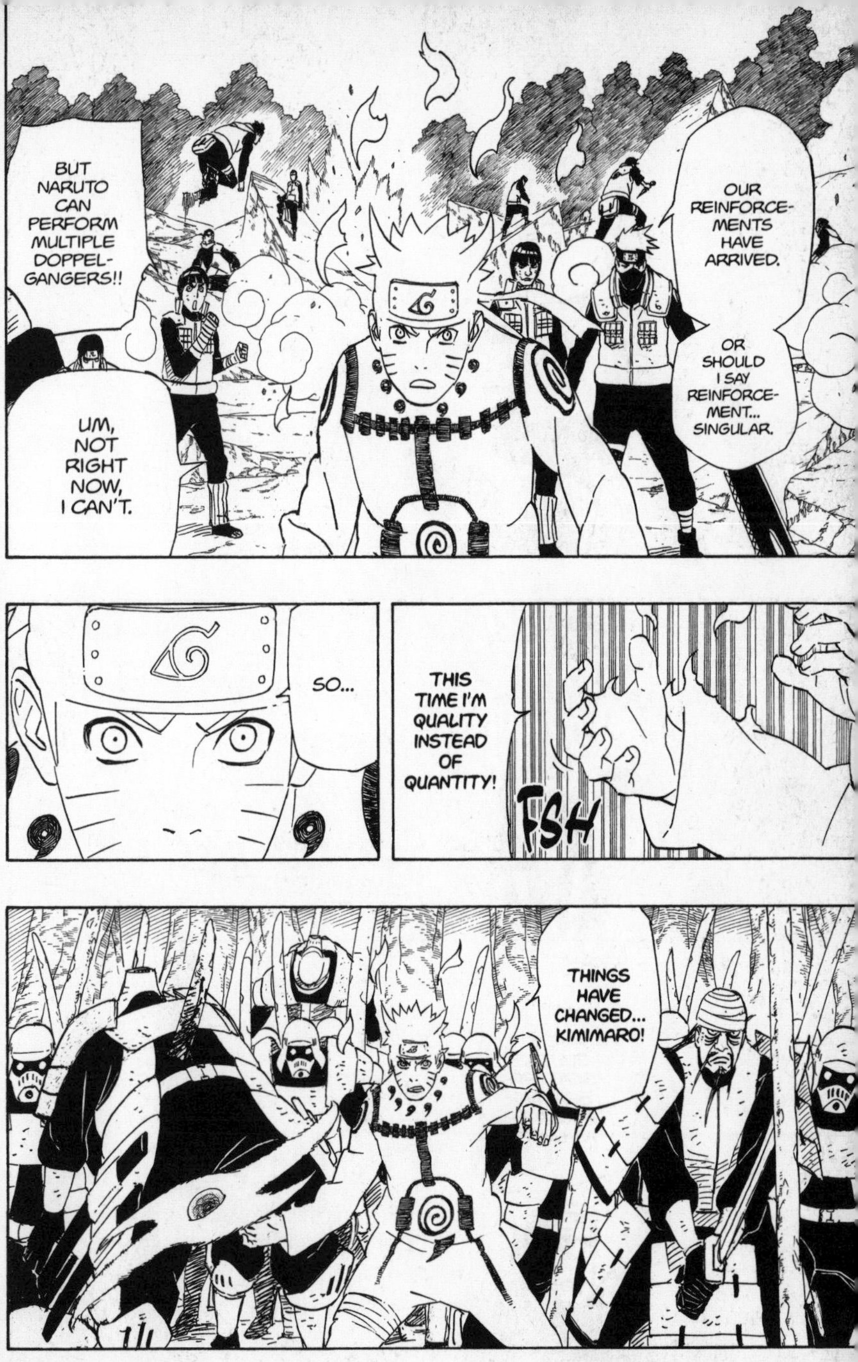
OUR REINFORCEMENTS HAVE ARRIVED.
OR SHOULD I SAY REINFORCEMENT... SINGULAR.
BUT NARUTO CAN PERFORM MULTIPLE DOPPELGANGERS!!
UM, NOT RIGHT NOW, I CAN'T.
THIS TIME I'M QUALITY INSTEAD OF QUANTITY!
FSH
SO...
THINGS HAVE CHANGED... KIMIMARO!

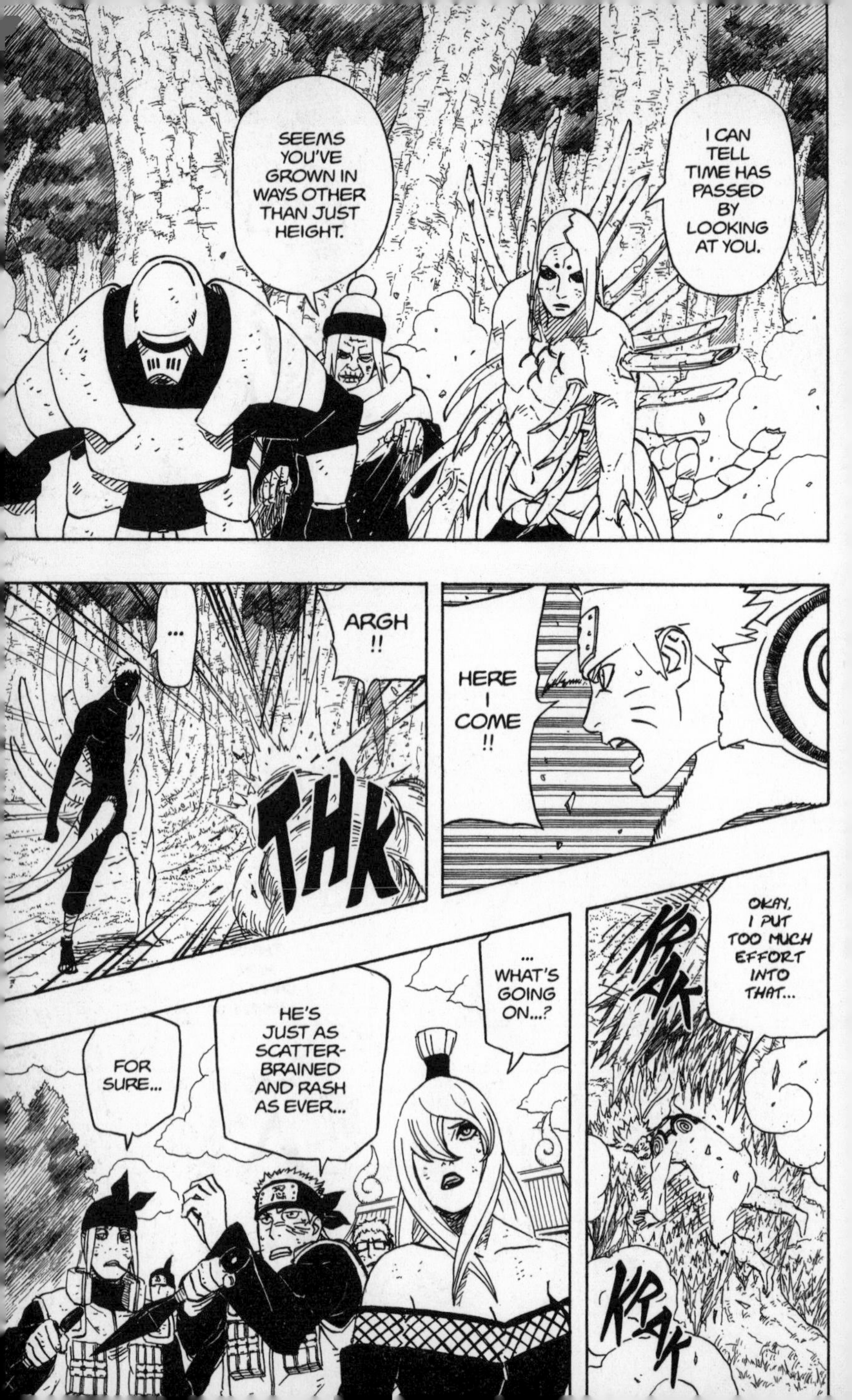
I CAN TELL TIME HAS PASSED BY LOOKING AT YOU.
SEEMS YOU'VE GROWN IN WAYS OTHER THAN JUST HEIGHT.
HERE I COME!!
ARGH!!
...
THK
KRAK
OKAY, I PUT TOO MUCH EFFORT INTO THAT...
KRAK
... WHAT'S GOING ON...?
HE'S JUST AS SCATTER-BRAINED AND RASH AS EVER...
FOR SURE...

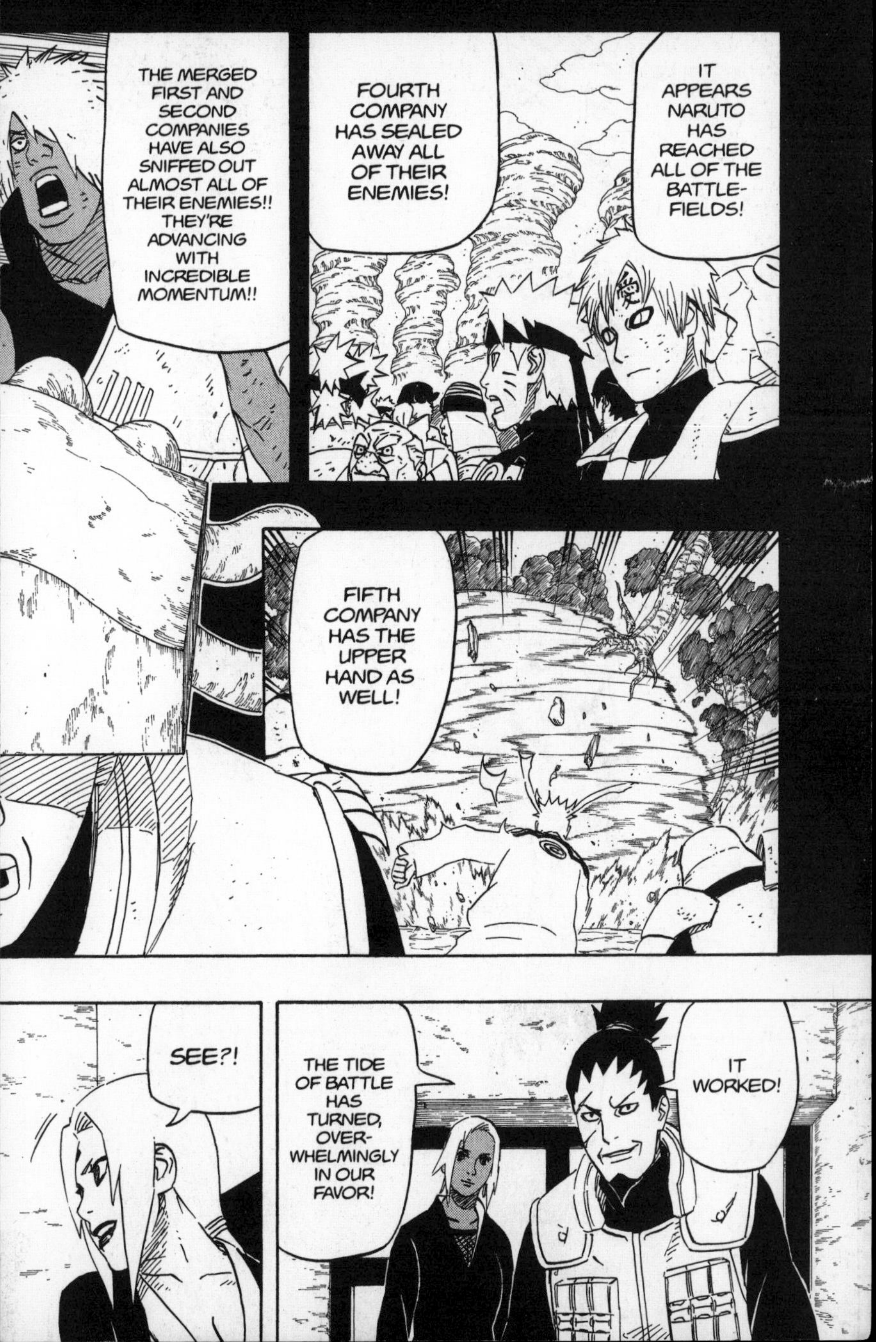
IT APPEARS NARUTO HAS REACHED ALL OF THE BATTLE-FIELDS!
FOURTH COMPANY HAS SEALED AWAY ALL OF THEIR ENEMIES!
THE MERGED FIRST AND SECOND COMPANIES HAVE ALSO SNIFFED OUT ALMOST ALL OF THEIR ENEMIES!! THEY'RE ADVANCING WITH INCREDIBLE MOMENTUM!!
FIFTH COMPANY HAS THE UPPER HAND AS WELL!
IT WORKED!
THE TIDE OF BATTLE HAS TURNED, OVER-WHELMINGLY IN OUR FAVOR!
SEE?!

READ THIS WAY

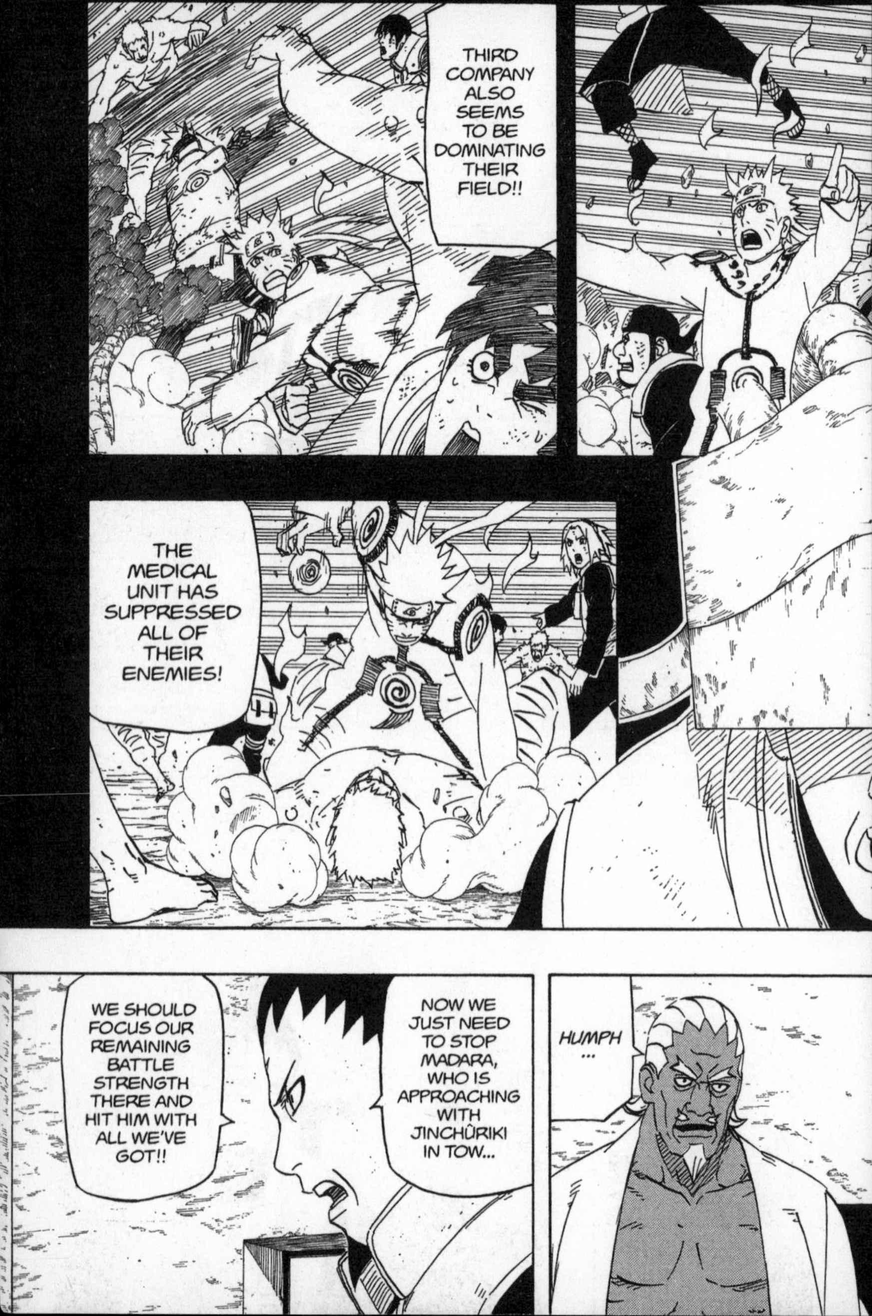
THIRD COMPANY ALSO SEEMS TO BE DOMINATING THEIR FIELD!!
THE MEDICAL UNIT HAS SUPPRESSED ALL OF THEIR ENEMIES!
HUMPH...
NOW WE JUST NEED TO STOP MADARA, WHO IS APPROACHING WITH JINCHŪRIKI IN TOW...
WE SHOULD FOCUS OUR REMAINING BATTLE STRENGTH THERE AND HIT HIM WITH ALL WE'VE GOT!!

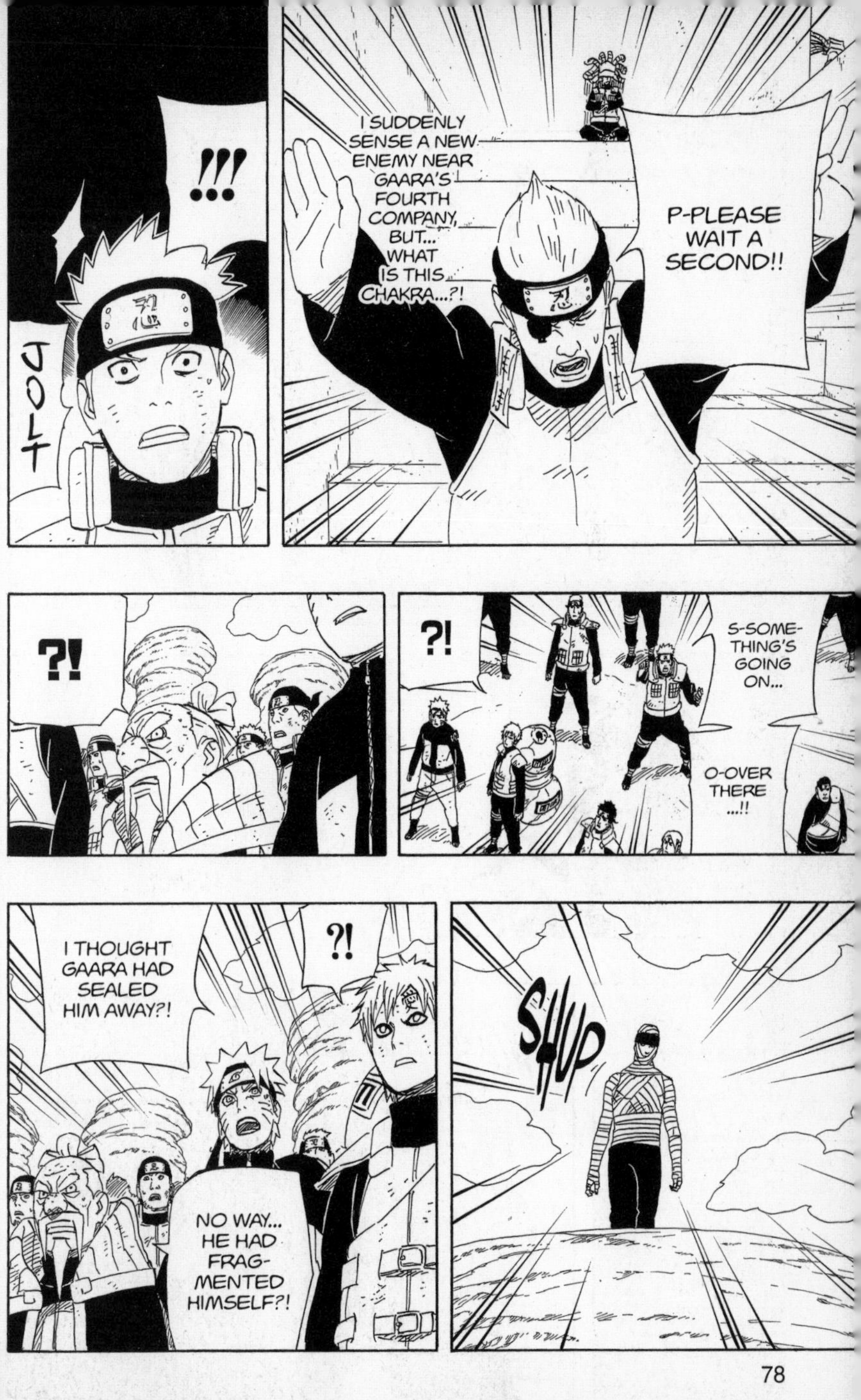
P-PLEASE WAIT A SECOND!!
I SUDDENLY SENSE A NEW ENEMY NEAR GAARA'S FOURTH COMPANY, BUT... WHAT IS THIS CHAKRA...?!
!!!...
JOLT
S-SOMETHING'S GOING ON...
O-OVER THERE ...!!
?!
?!
SHUP
?!
I THOUGHT GAARA HAD SEALED HIM AWAY?!
NO WAY... HE HAD FRAGMENTED HIMSELF?!

READ THIS WAY

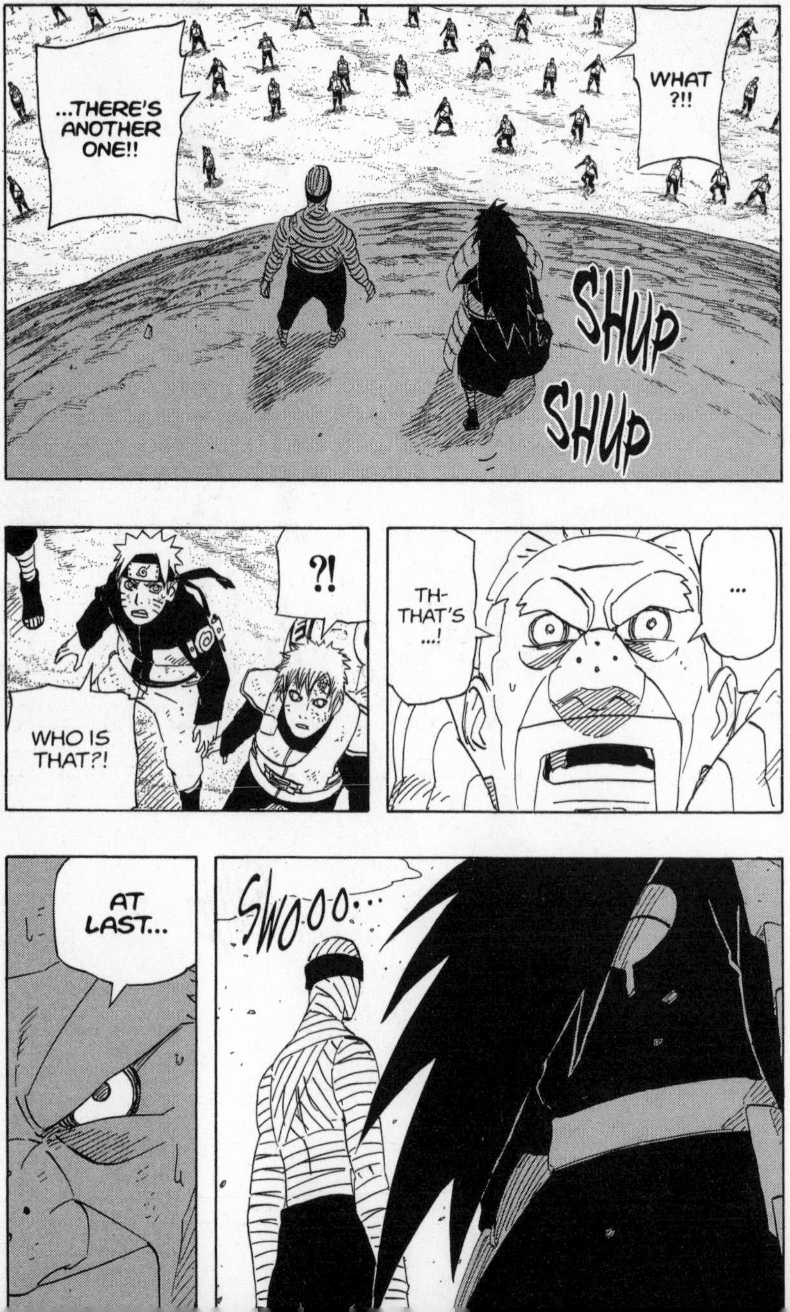
WHAT ?!!
...THERE'S ANOTHER ONE!!
SHUP
SHUP
...
TH- THAT'S ...!
?!
WHO IS THAT?!
SWOOO...
AT LAST...

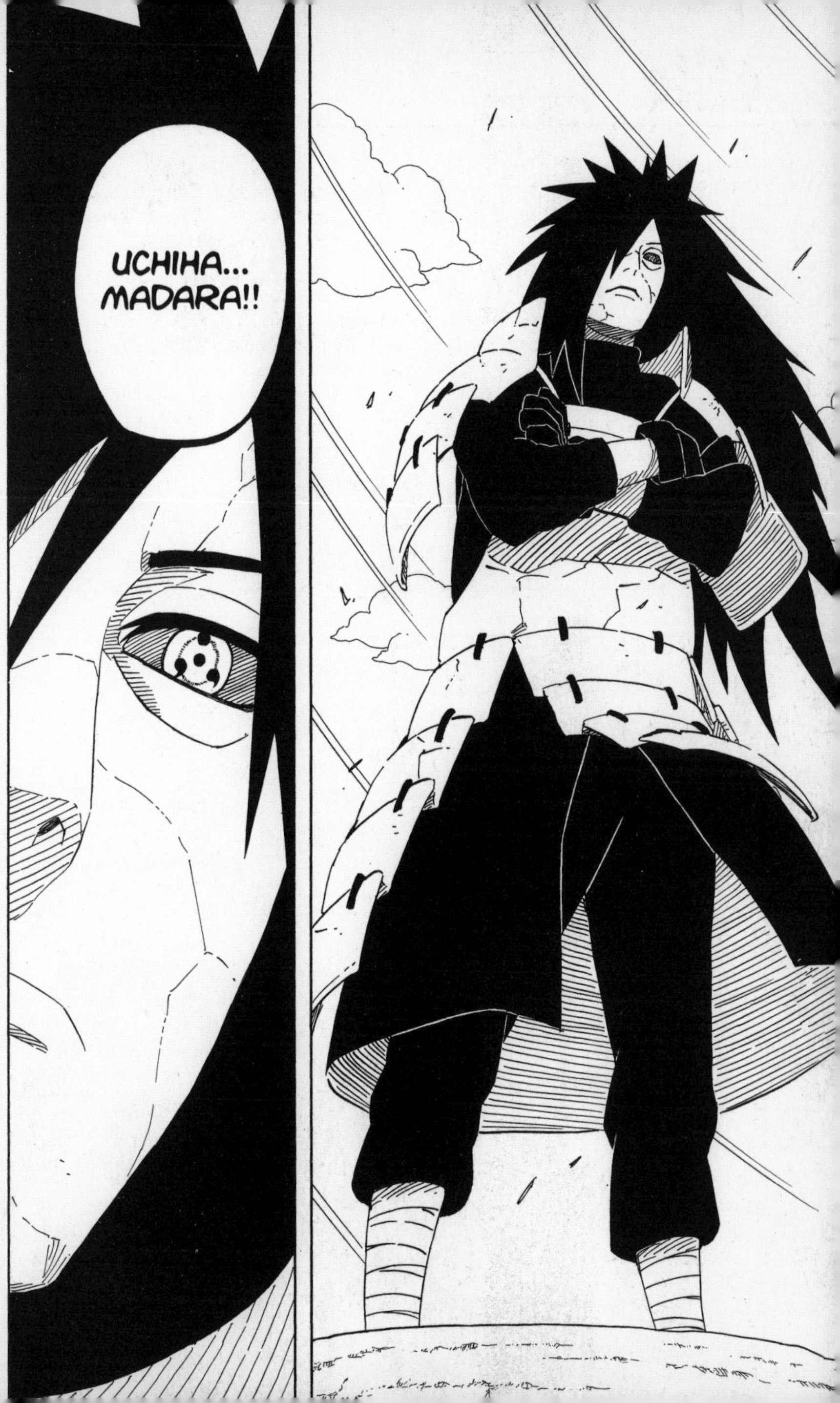
UCHIHA... MADARA!!

READ THIS WAY

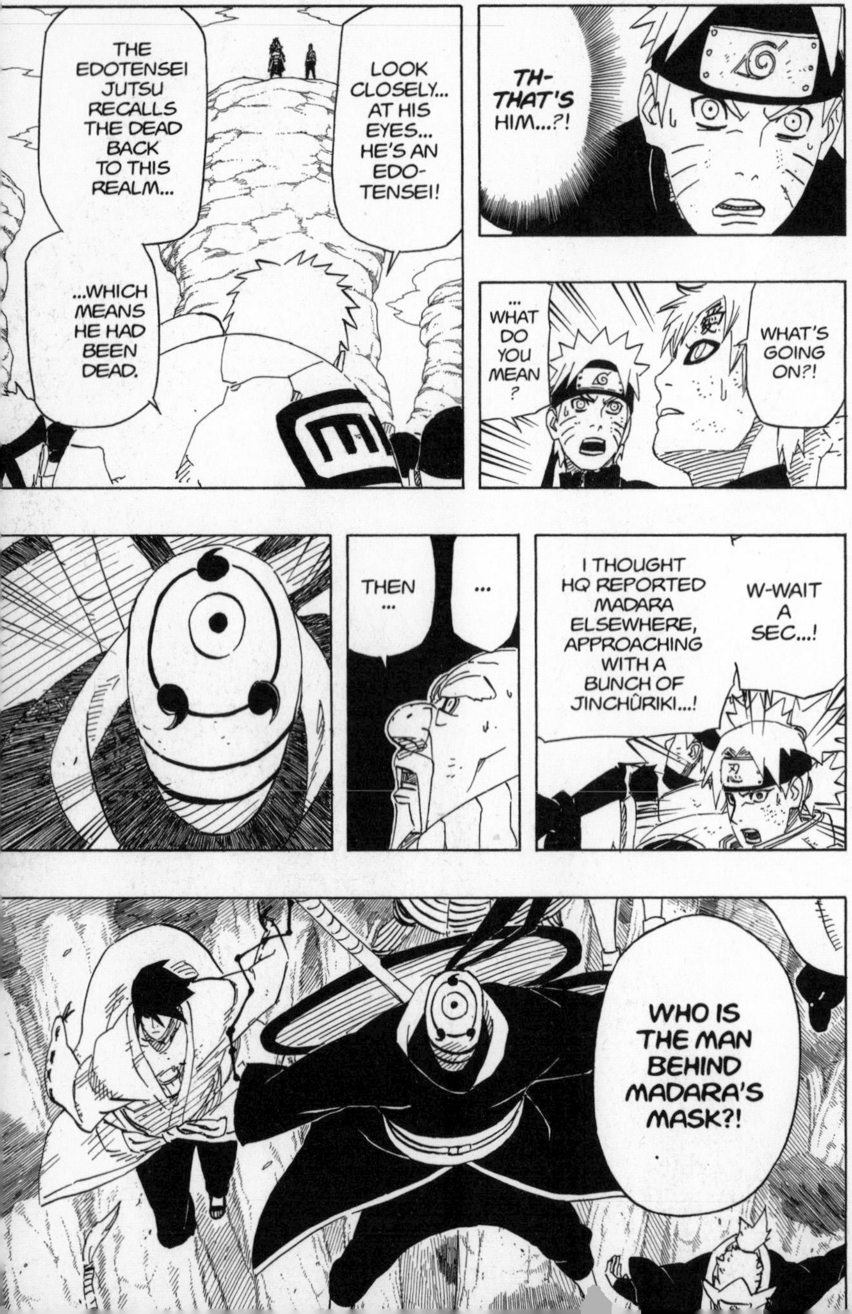
TH-THAT'S HIM...?!
WHAT'S GOING ON?!
...WHAT DO YOU MEAN?
LOOK CLOSELY... AT HIS EYES... HE'S AN EDO-TENSEI!
THE EDOTENSEI JUTSU RECALLS THE DEAD BACK TO THIS REALM...
...WHICH MEANS HE HAD BEEN DEAD.
W-WAIT A SEC...!
I THOUGHT HQ REPORTED MADARA ELSEWHERE, APPROACHING WITH A BUNCH OF JINCHÛRIKI...!
...
THEN ...
WHO IS THE MAN BEHIND MADARA'S MASK?!

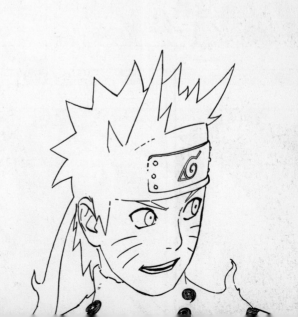

Number 560: Uchiha Madara

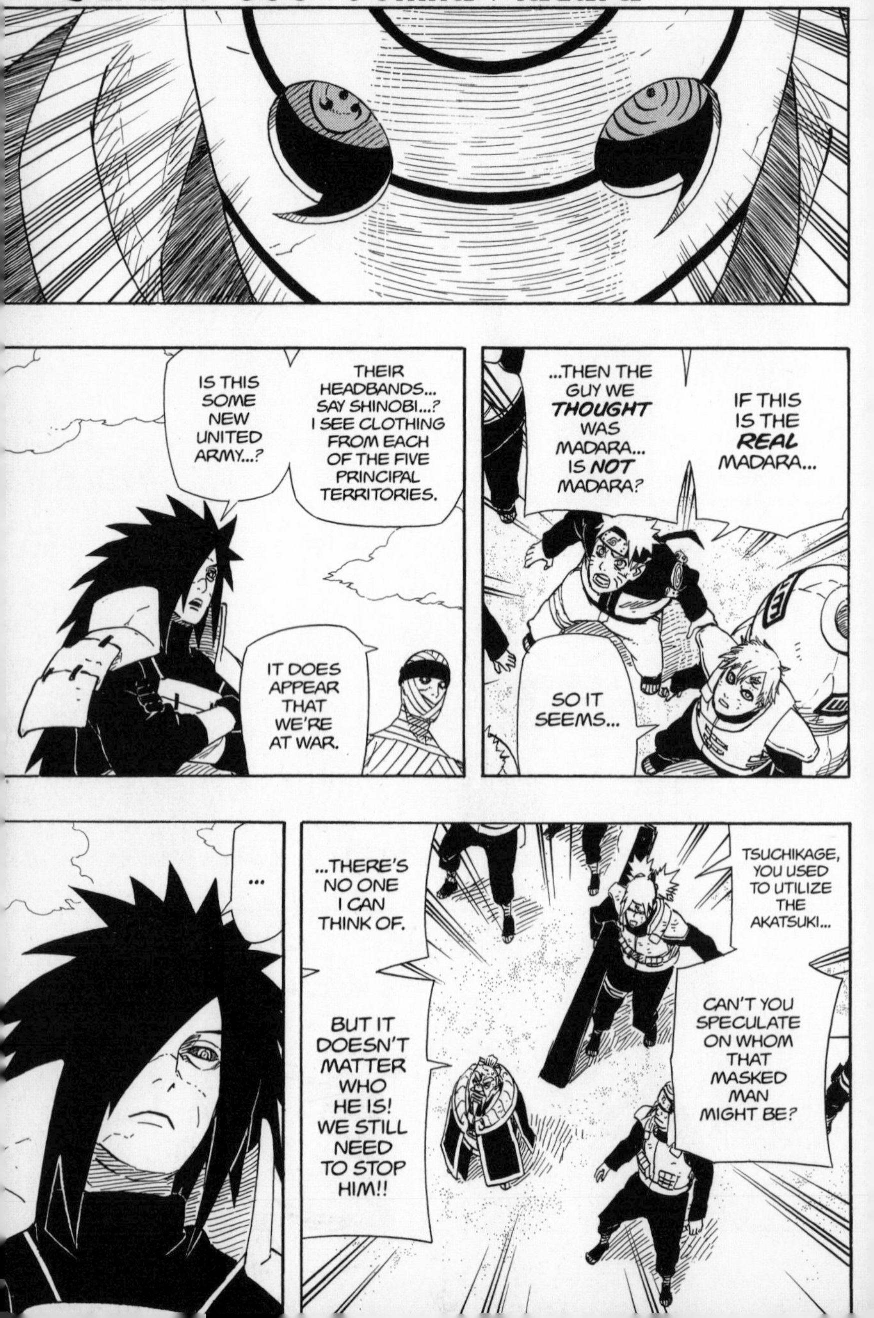
IF THIS IS THE REAL MADARA...
...THEN THE GUY WE THOUGHT WAS MADARA... IS NOT MADARA?
SO IT SEEMS...
THEIR HEADBANDS... SAY SHINOBI...? I SEE CLOTHING FROM EACH OF THE FIVE PRINCIPAL TERRITORIES.
IS THIS SOME NEW UNITED ARMY...?
IT DOES APPEAR THAT WE'RE AT WAR.
TSUCHIKAGE, YOU USED TO UTILIZE THE AKATSUKI...
CAN'T YOU SPECULATE ON WHOM THAT MASKED MAN MIGHT BE?
...THERE'S NO ONE I CAN THINK OF.
BUT IT DOESN'T MATTER WHO HE IS! WE STILL NEED TO STOP HIM!!
...

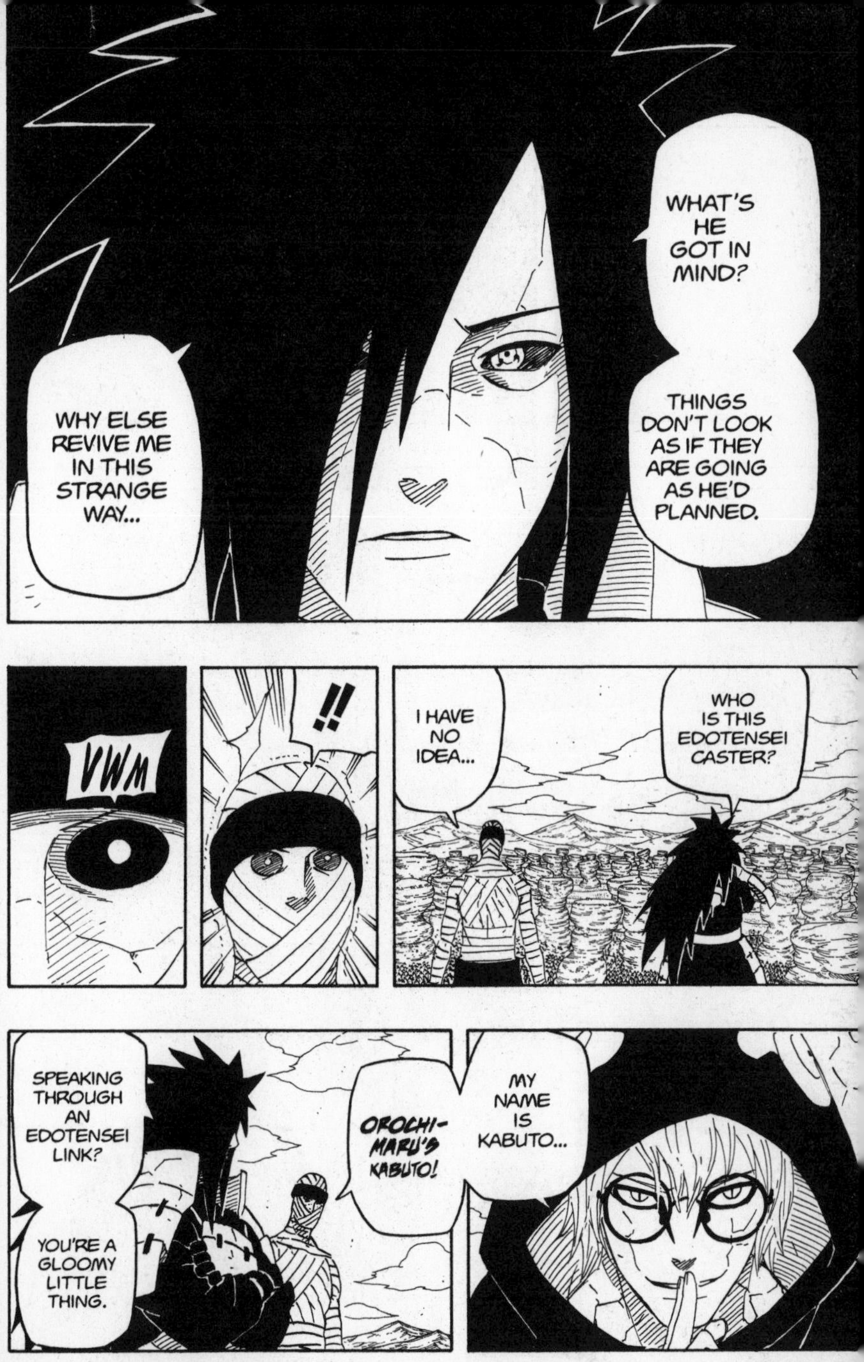
WHAT'S HE GOT IN MIND?
THINGS DON'T LOOK AS IF THEY ARE GOING AS HE'D PLANNED.
WHY ELSE REVIVE ME IN THIS STRANGE WAY...
WHO IS THIS EDOTENSEI CASTER?
I HAVE NO IDEA...
!!
VWM
MY NAME IS KABUTO...
OROCHIMARU'S KABUTO!
SPEAKING THROUGH AN EDOTENSEI LINK?
YOU'RE A GLOOMY LITTLE THING.

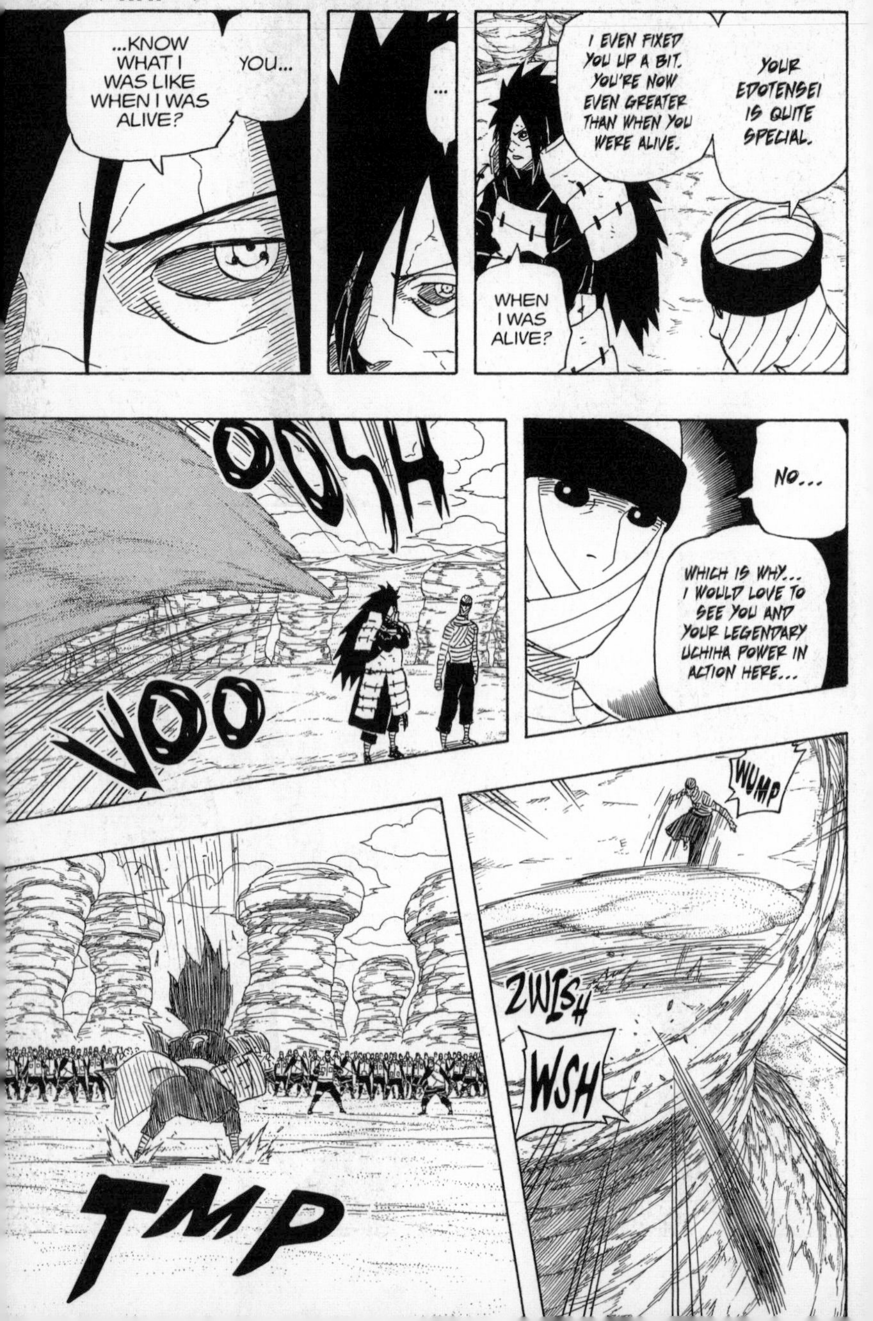
READ THIS WAY
YOUR EDOTENSEI IS QUITE SPECIAL.
I EVEN FIXED YOU UP A BIT. YOU'RE NOW EVEN GREATER THAN WHEN YOU WERE ALIVE.
WHEN I WAS ALIVE?
...
YOU...
...KNOW WHAT I WAS LIKE WHEN I WAS ALIVE?
NO...
WHICH IS WHY... I WOULD LOVE TO SEE YOU AND YOUR LEGENDARY UCHIHA POWER IN ACTION HERE...
VOOOOOSH
WUMP
ZWISH
WSH
TMP

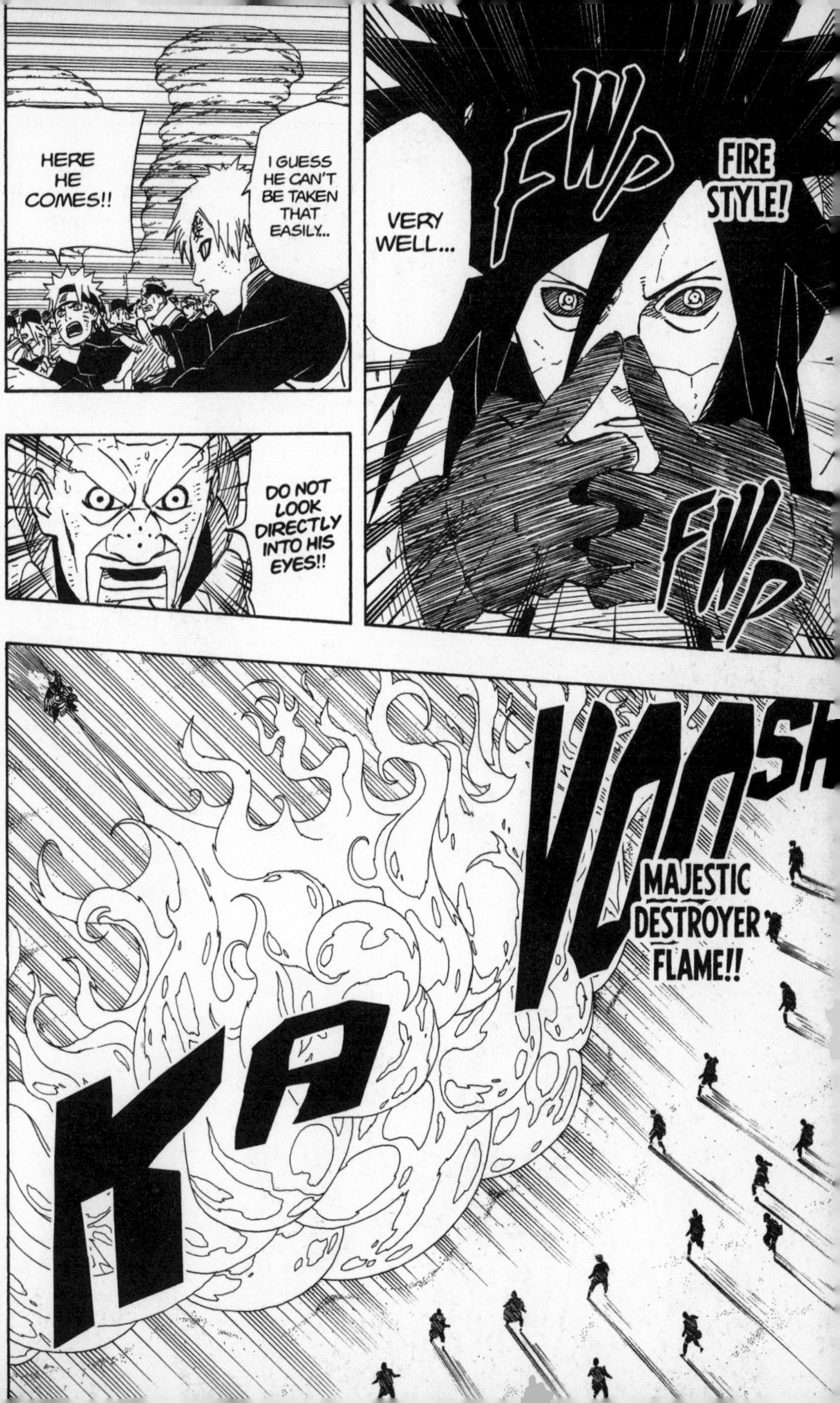

FIRE STYLE!
FWP
VERY WELL...
FWP
I GUESS HE CAN'T BE TAKEN THAT EASILY...
HERE HE COMES!!
DO NOT LOOK DIRECTLY INTO HIS EYES!!
VOOSH
MAJESTIC DESTROYER FLAME!!
KA

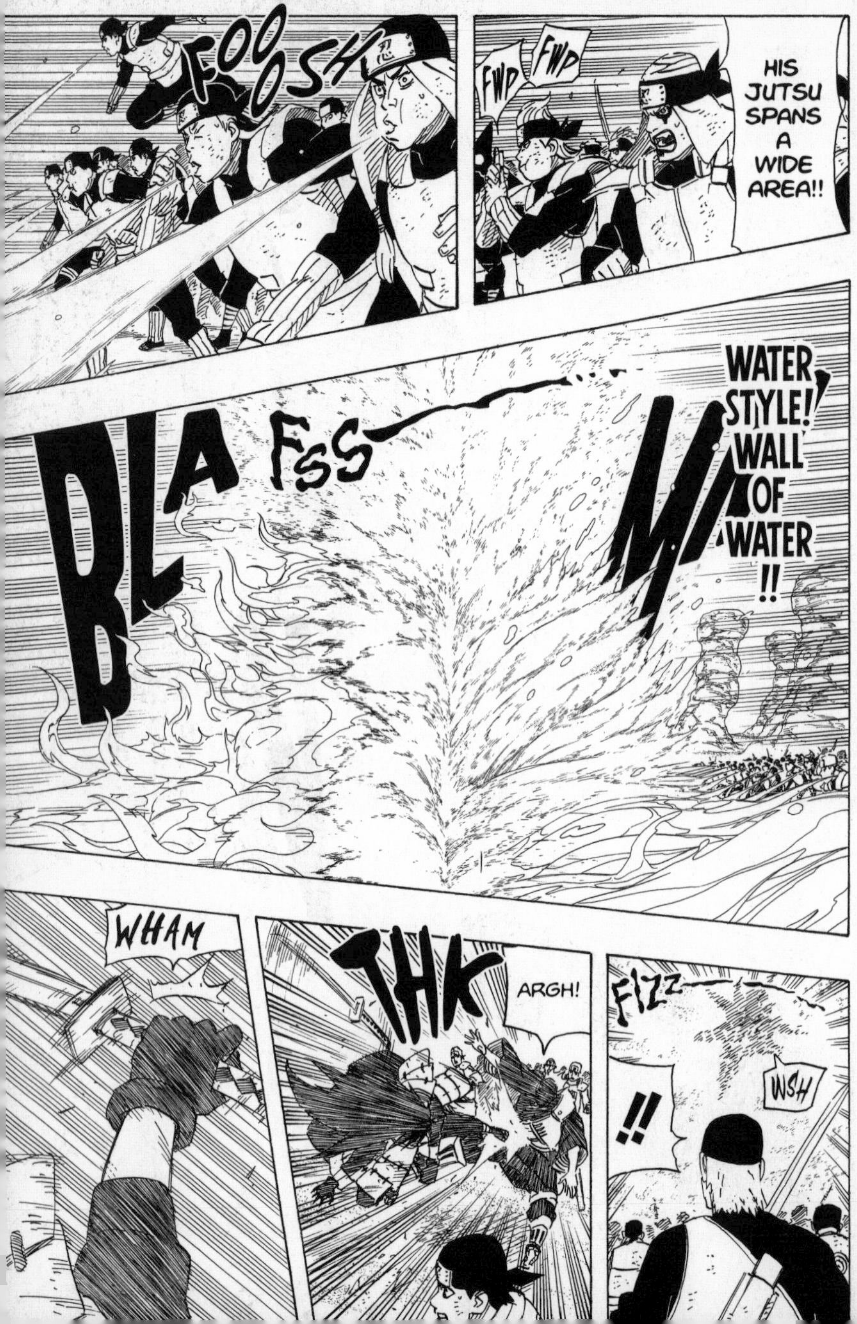
HIS JUTSU SPANS A WIDE AREA!!
FWP
FWP
FWP
FOOOSH
WATER STYLE! WALL OF WATER!!
BLAM
FSS
FIZZ
WSH
!!
THK
ARGH!
WHAM

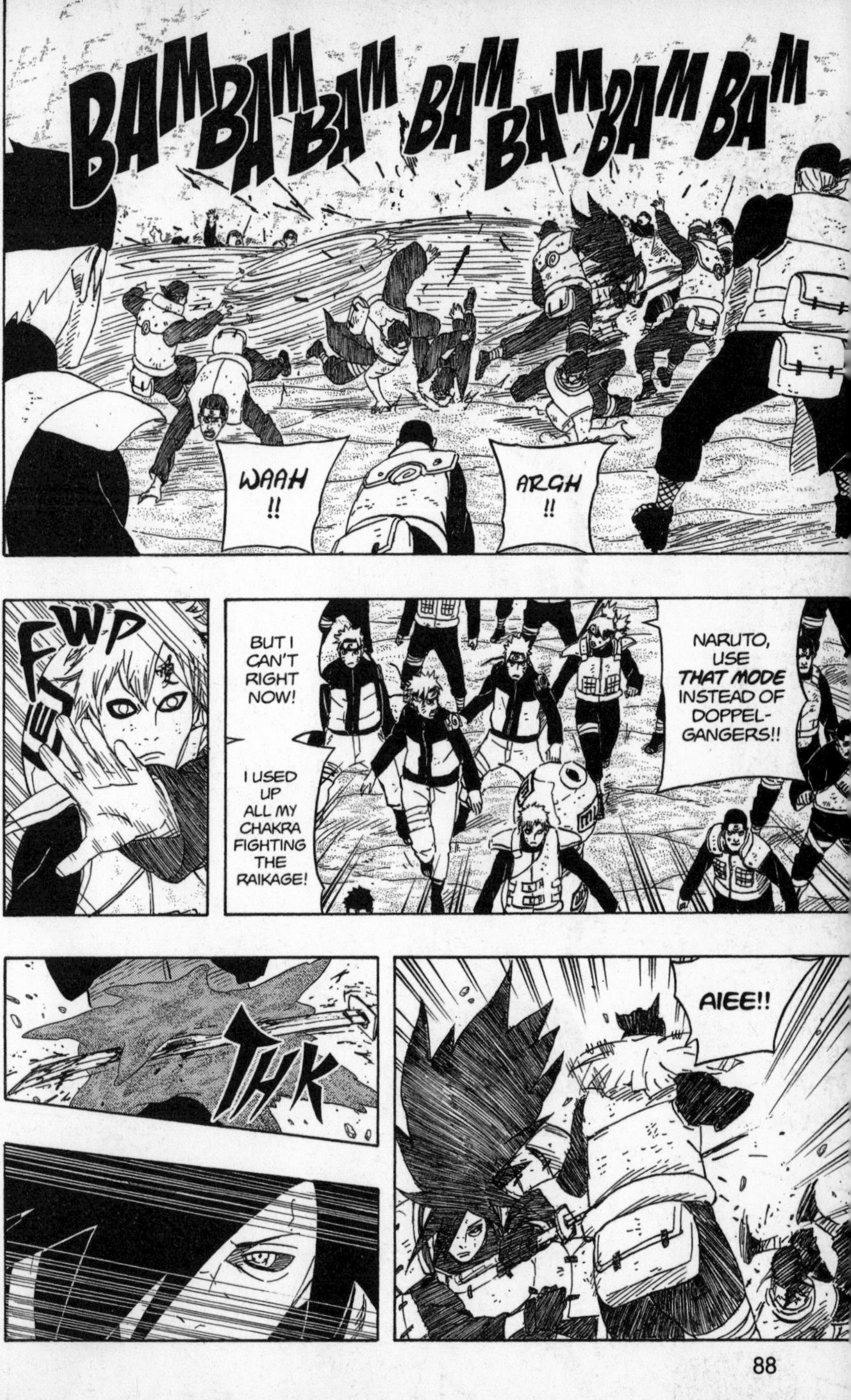
BAM BAM BAM BAM BAM BAM BAM
ARGH!!
WAAH!!
NARUTO, USE *THAT MODE* INSTEAD OF DOPPELGANGERS!!
BUT I CAN'T RIGHT NOW!
I USED UP ALL MY CHAKRA FIGHTING THE RAIKAGE!
FWP
AIEE!!
THK

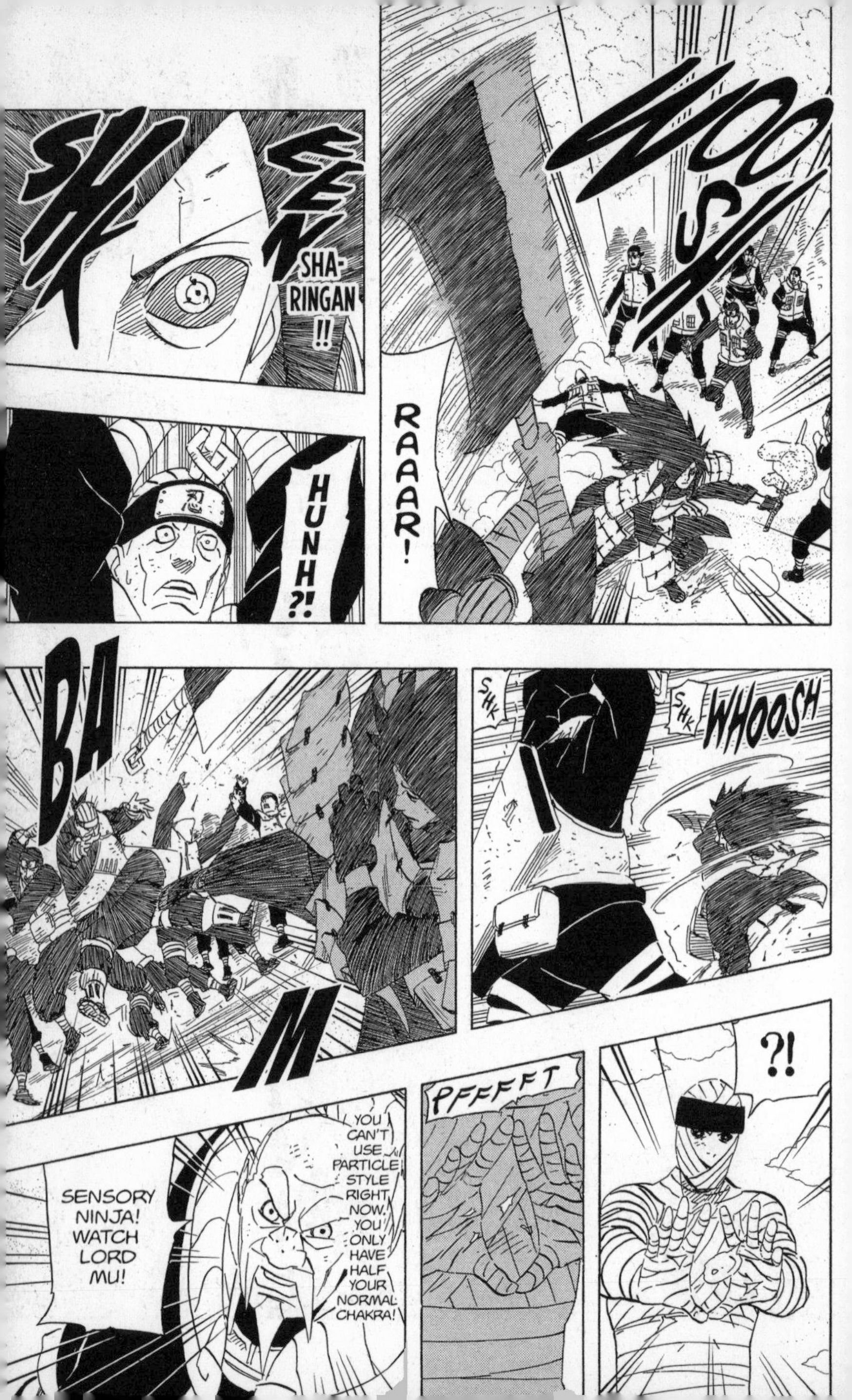

WHOOSH
RAAAAR!
SHKEEN
SHA-RINGAN!!
HUNH?!
SHK
SHK
WHOOSH
BAM
?!
PFFFFT
YOU CAN'T USE PARTICLE STYLE RIGHT NOW! YOU ONLY HAVE HALF YOUR NORMAL CHAKRA!
SENSORY NINJA! WATCH LORD MU!

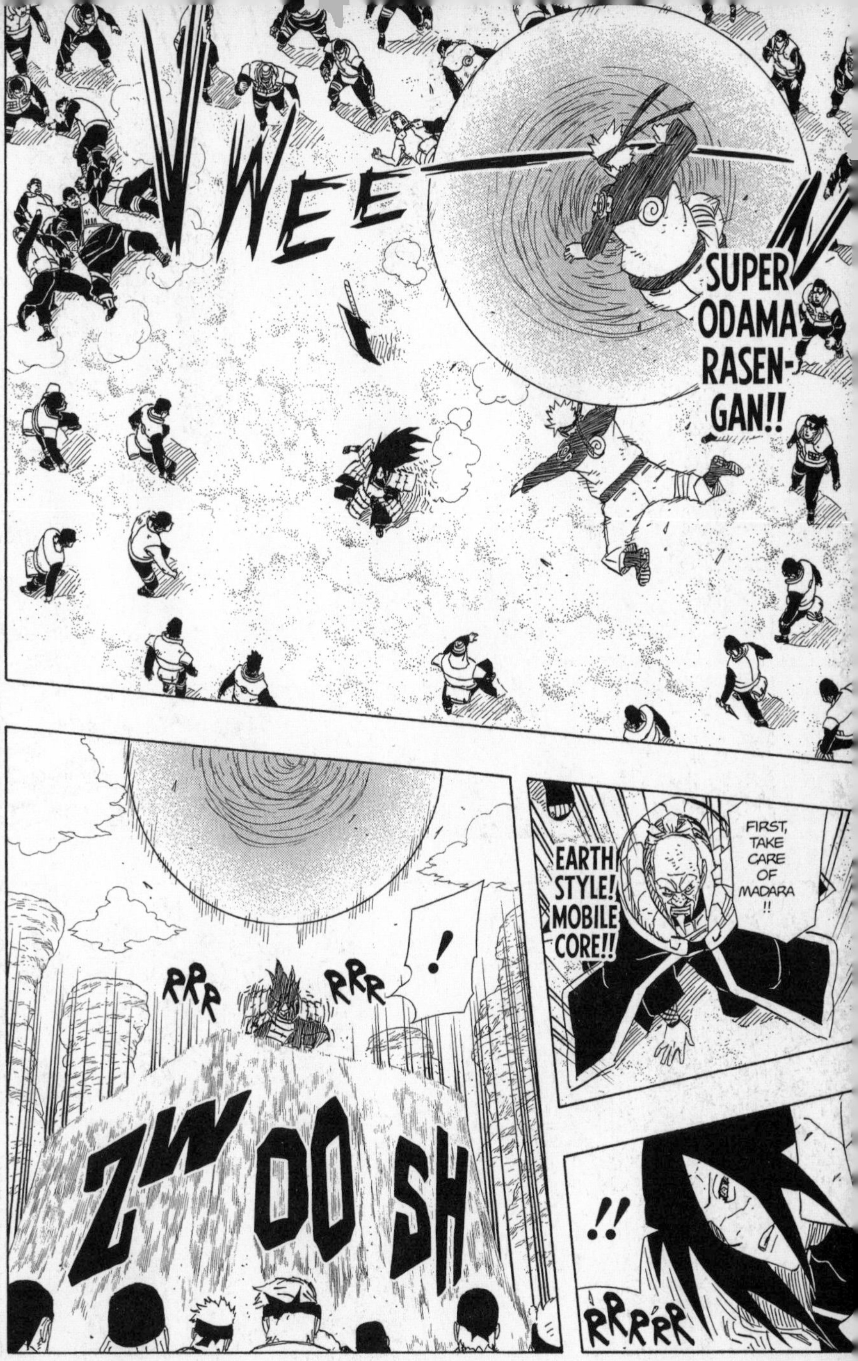
WWEEN
SUPER ODAMA RASEN-GAN!!
FIRST, TAKE CARE OF MADARA!!
EARTH STYLE! MOBILE CORE!!
!!
RRRRR
!
RRR
RRR
ZWOOSH

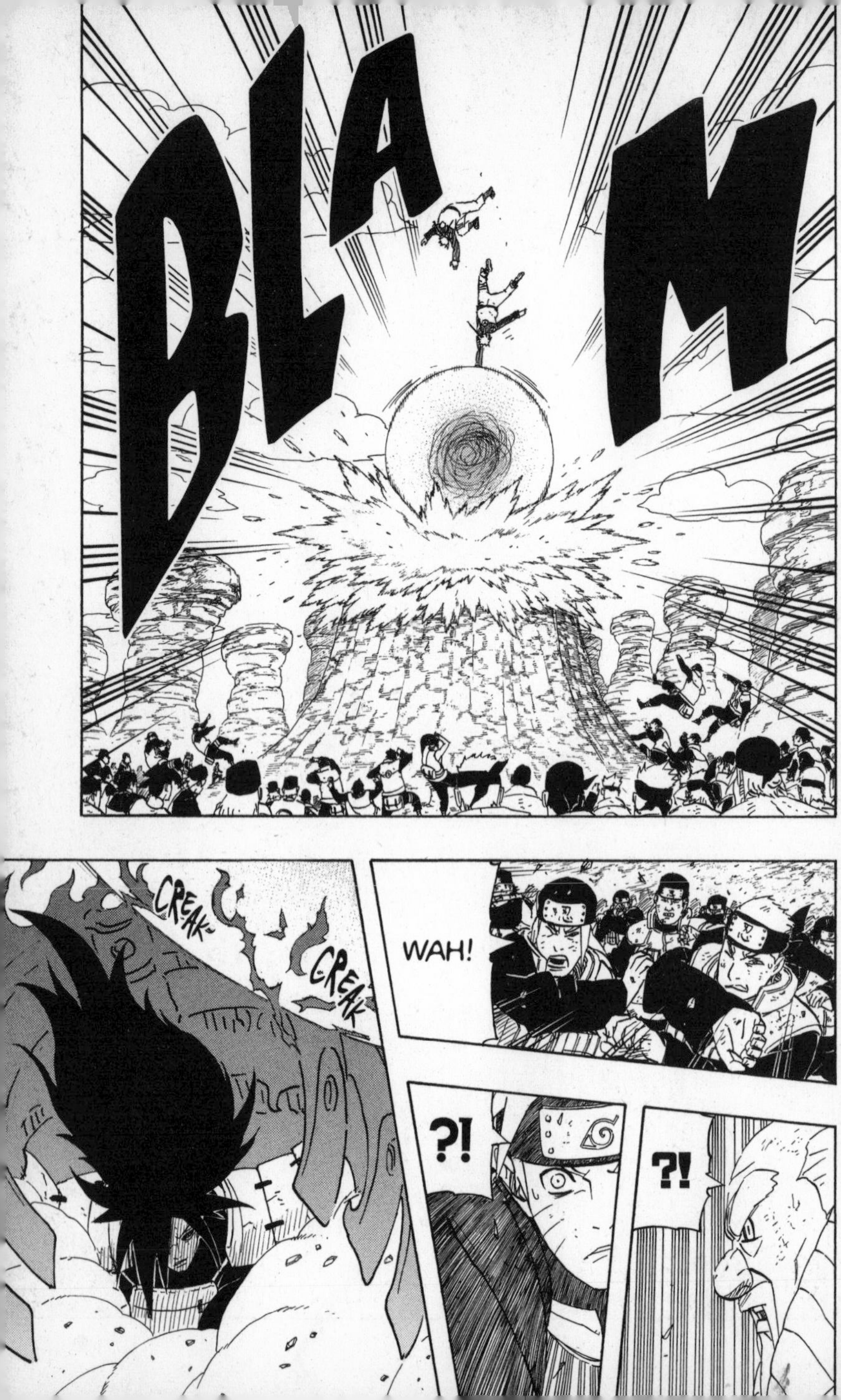
BLAM
WAH!
?!
?!
CREAK
CREAK

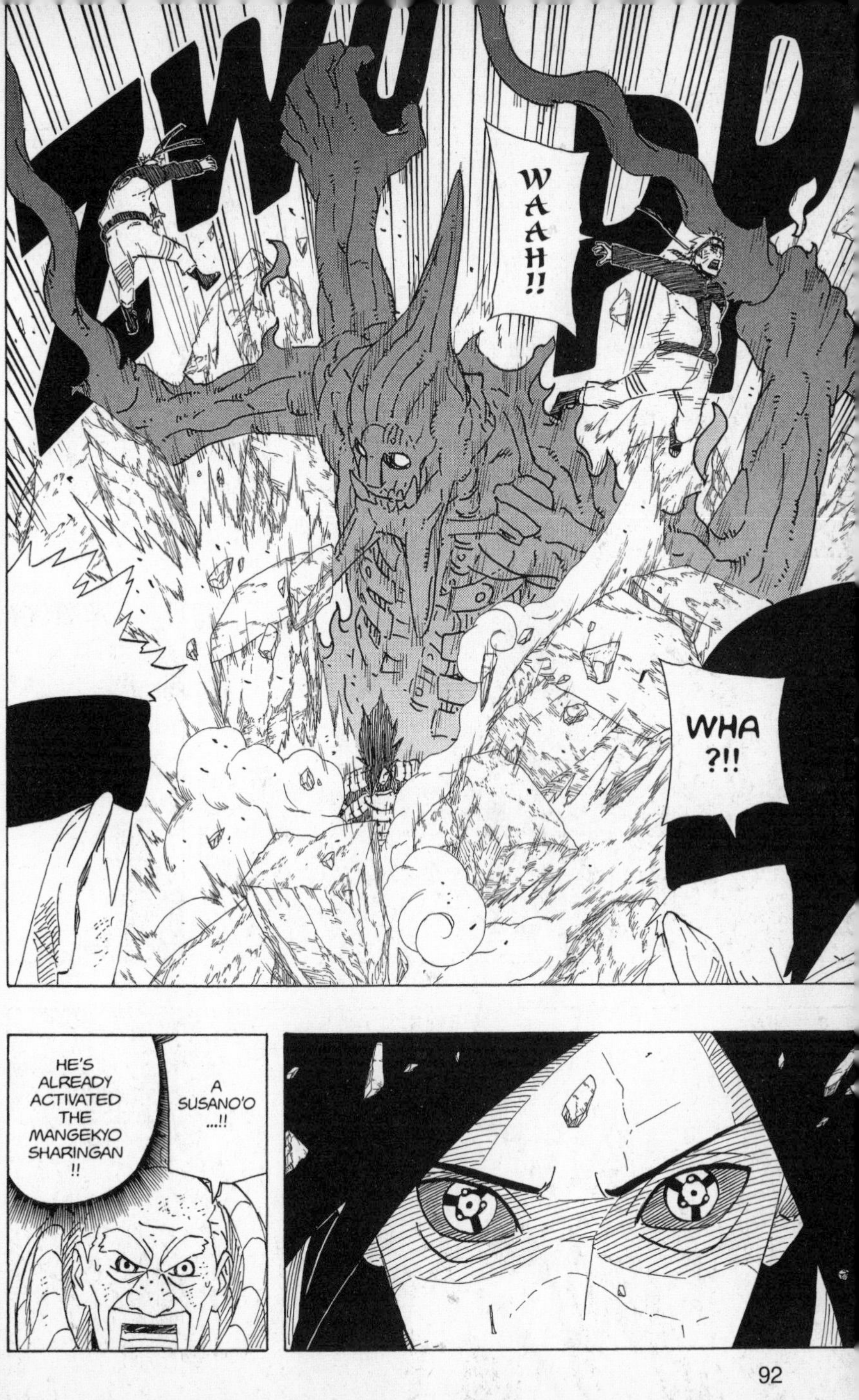
WAAH!!
WHA ?!!
A SUSANO'O ...!!
HE'S ALREADY ACTIVATED THE MANGEKYO SHARINGAN !!

READ THIS WAY

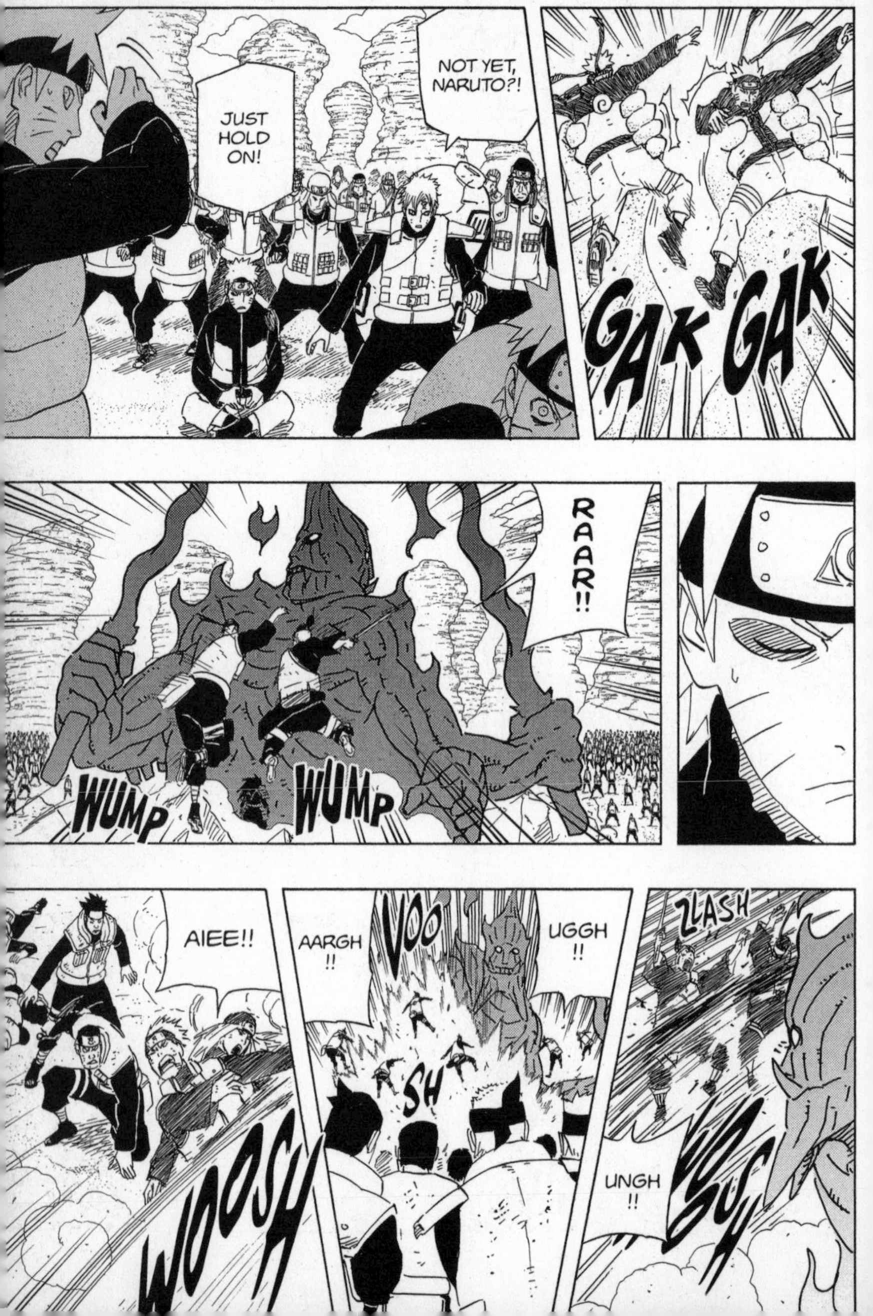
GAK GAK
NOT YET, NARUTO?!
JUST HOLD ON!
RAAAR!!
WUMP
WUMP
ZLASH
UNGH !!
UGGH !!
VOO
AARGH !!
SH
AIEE!!
WOOSH

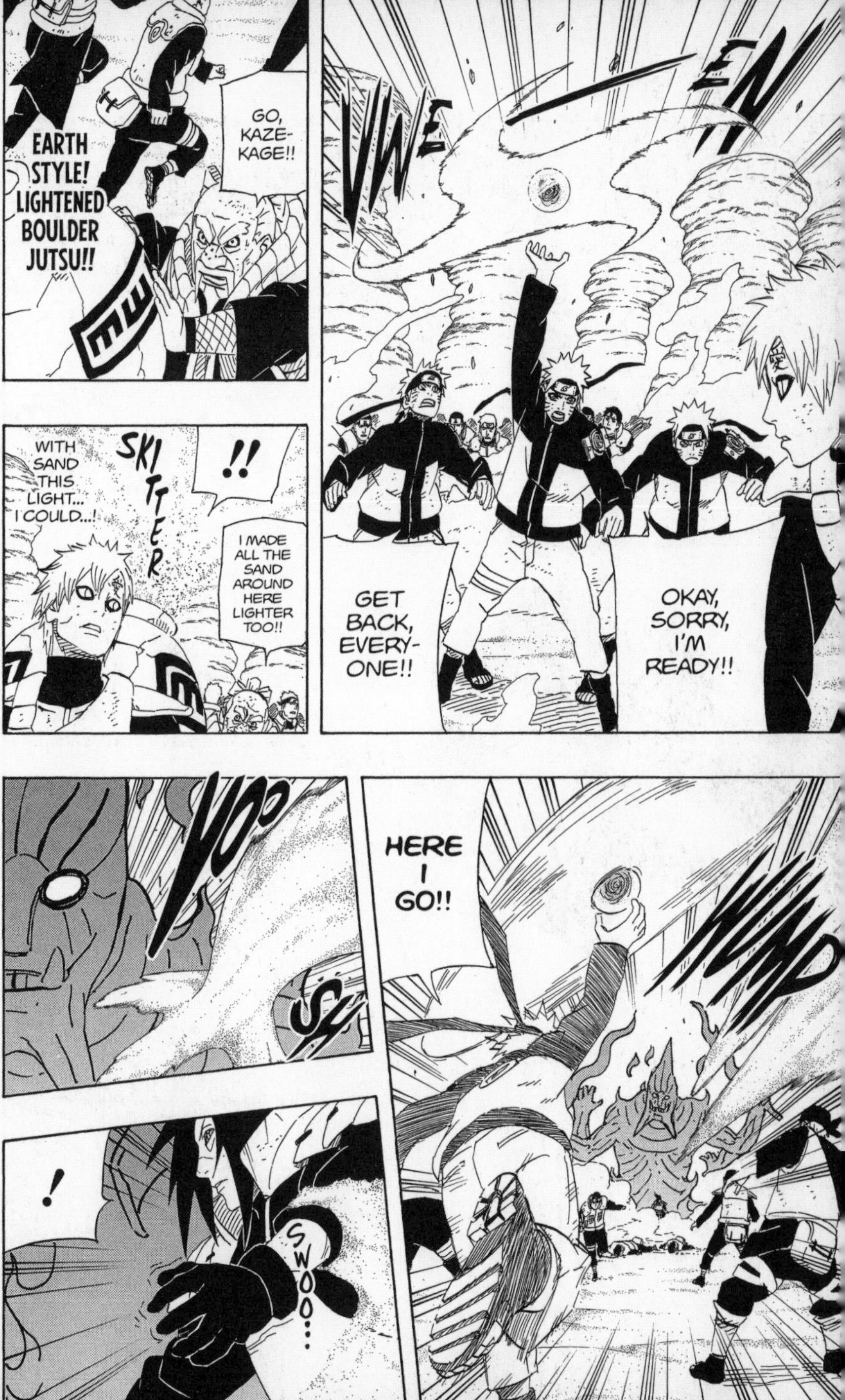
VWEEN
OKAY, SORRY, I'M READY!!
GET BACK, EVERY-ONE!!
GO, KAZE-KAGE!!
EARTH STYLE! LIGHTENED BOULDER JUTSU!!
!!
SKITTER
WITH SAND THIS LIGHT... I COULD...!
I MADE ALL THE SAND AROUND HERE LIGHTER TOO!!
HERE I GO!!
SH
!
SWOOO...

READ THIS WAY

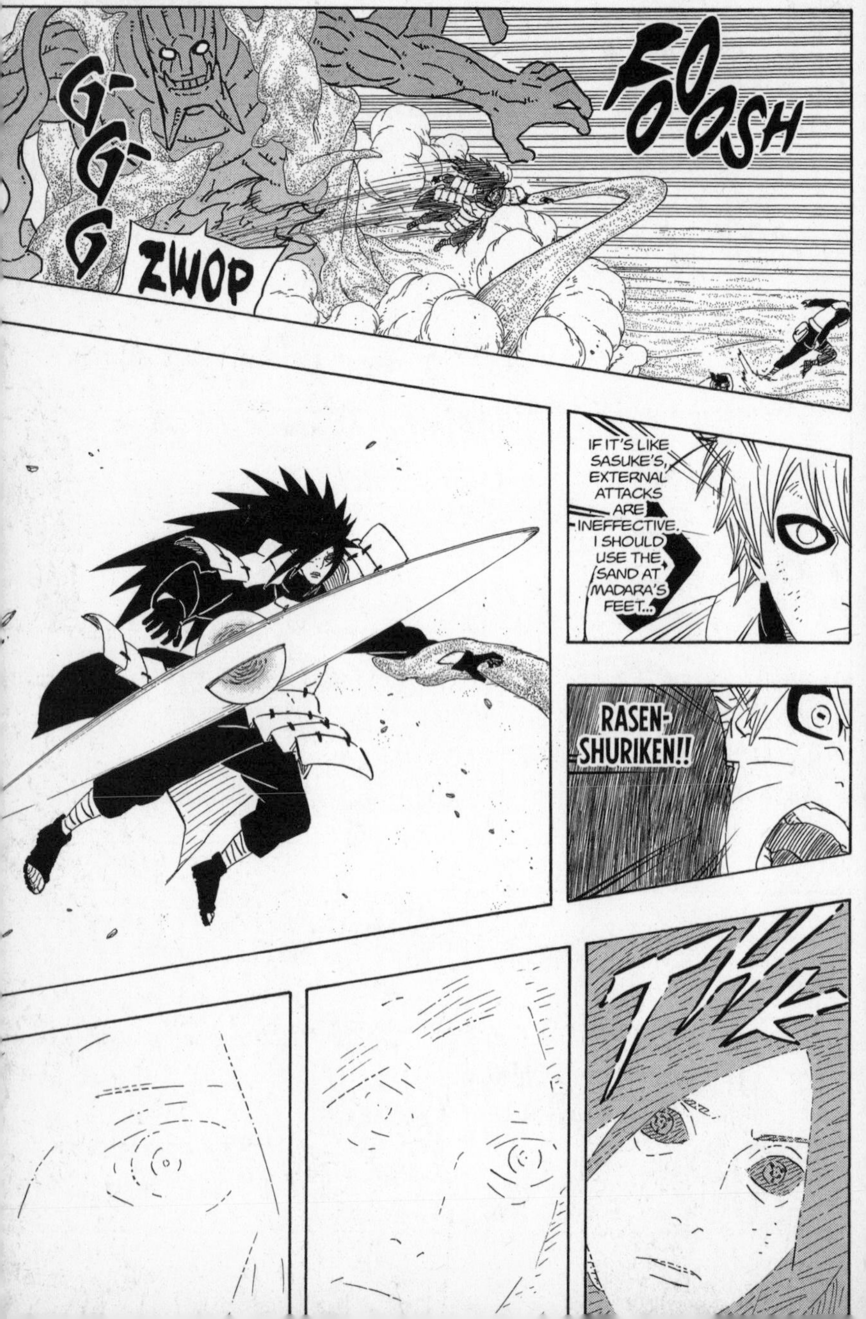
FOOOOSH
G-G-G
ZWOP
IF IT'S LIKE SASUKE'S, EXTERNAL ATTACKS ARE INEFFECTIVE. I SHOULD USE THE SAND AT MADARA'S FEET...
RASEN-SHURIKEN!!
THK

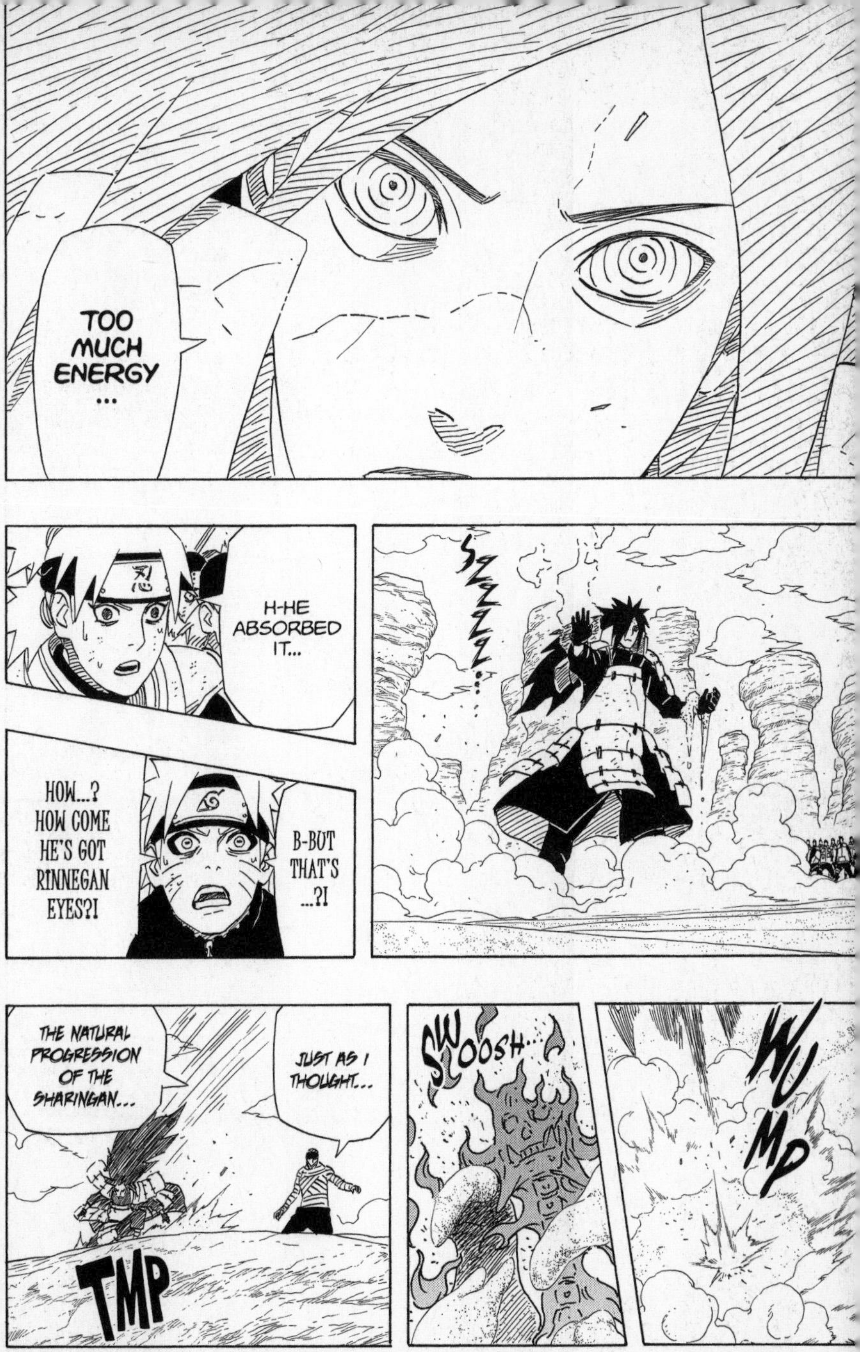
TOO MUCH ENERGY ...
SZZZZZ...
H-HE ABSORBED IT...
B-BUT THAT'S ...?!
HOW...? HOW COME HE'S GOT RINNEGAN EYES?!
WUMP
SWOOSH...
JUST AS I THOUGHT...
THE NATURAL PROGRESSION OF THE SHARINGAN...
TMP

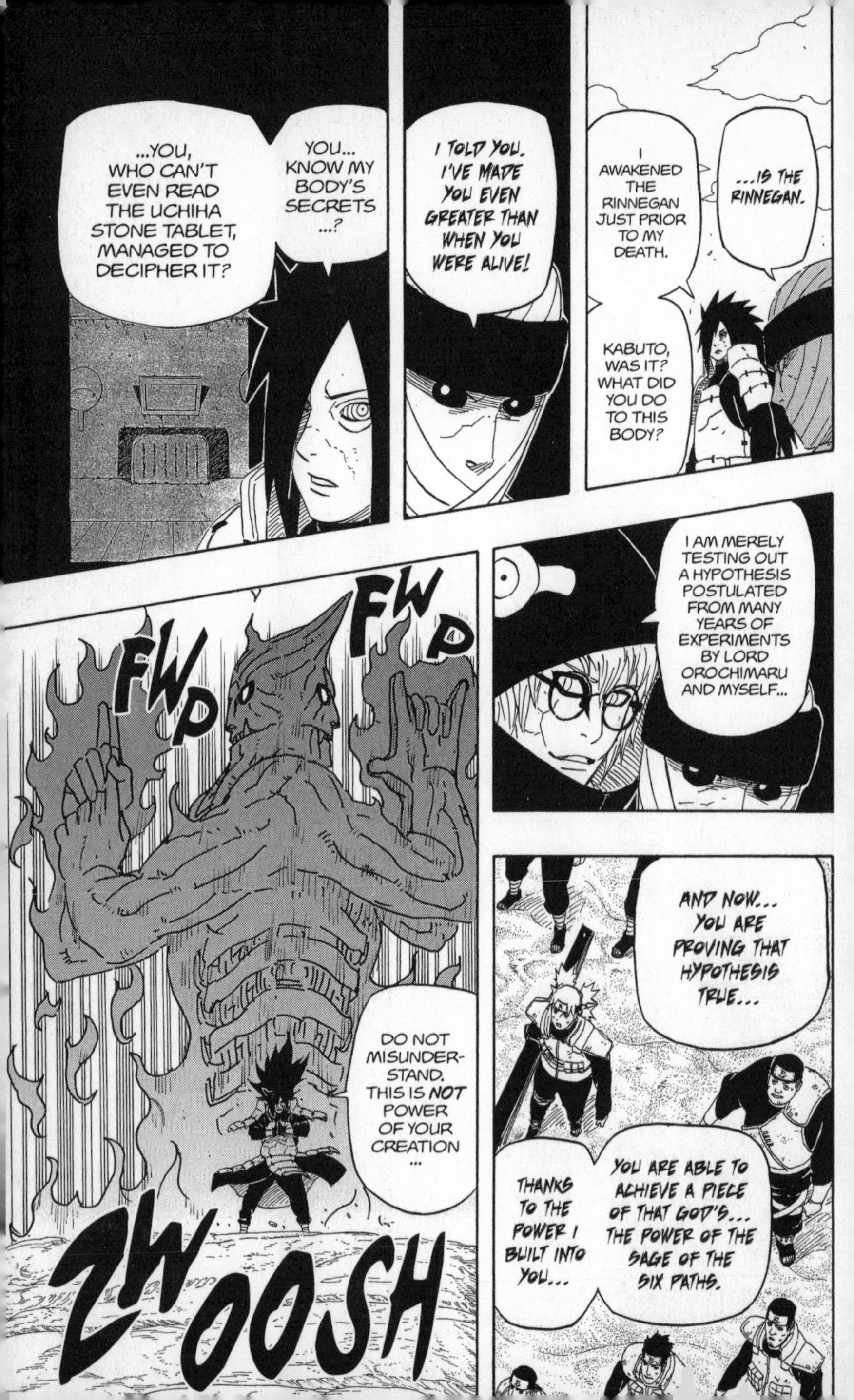
...IS THE RINNEGAN.
I AWAKENED THE RINNEGAN JUST PRIOR TO MY DEATH.
KABUTO, WAS IT? WHAT DID YOU DO TO THIS BODY?
I TOLD YOU. I'VE MADE YOU EVEN GREATER THAN WHEN YOU WERE ALIVE!
YOU... KNOW MY BODY'S SECRETS ...?
...YOU, WHO CAN'T EVEN READ THE UCHIHA STONE TABLET, MANAGED TO DECIPHER IT?
I AM MERELY TESTING OUT A HYPOTHESIS POSTULATED FROM MANY YEARS OF EXPERIMENTS BY LORD OROCHIMARU AND MYSELF...
AND NOW... YOU ARE PROVING THAT HYPOTHESIS TRUE...
YOU ARE ABLE TO ACHIEVE A PIECE OF THAT GOD'S... THE POWER OF THE SAGE OF THE SIX PATHS.
THANKS TO THE POWER I BUILT INTO YOU...
FWP
FWP
DO NOT MISUNDERSTAND. THIS IS NOT POWER OF YOUR CREATION ...
ZWOOSH

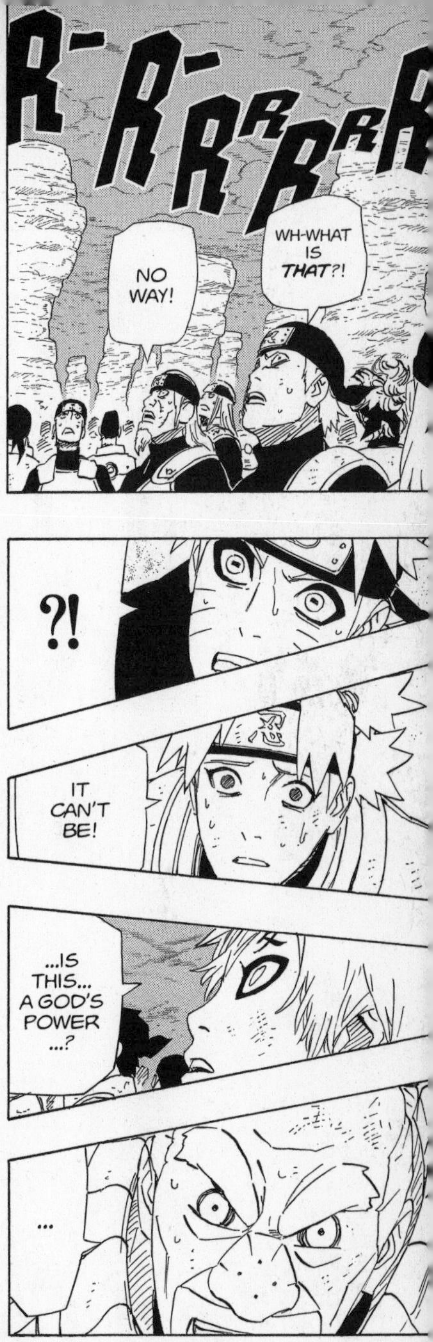
R-R-RRRRRR
NO WAY!
WH-WHAT IS THAT?!
?!
IT CAN'T BE!
...IS THIS... A GOD'S POWER ...?
...

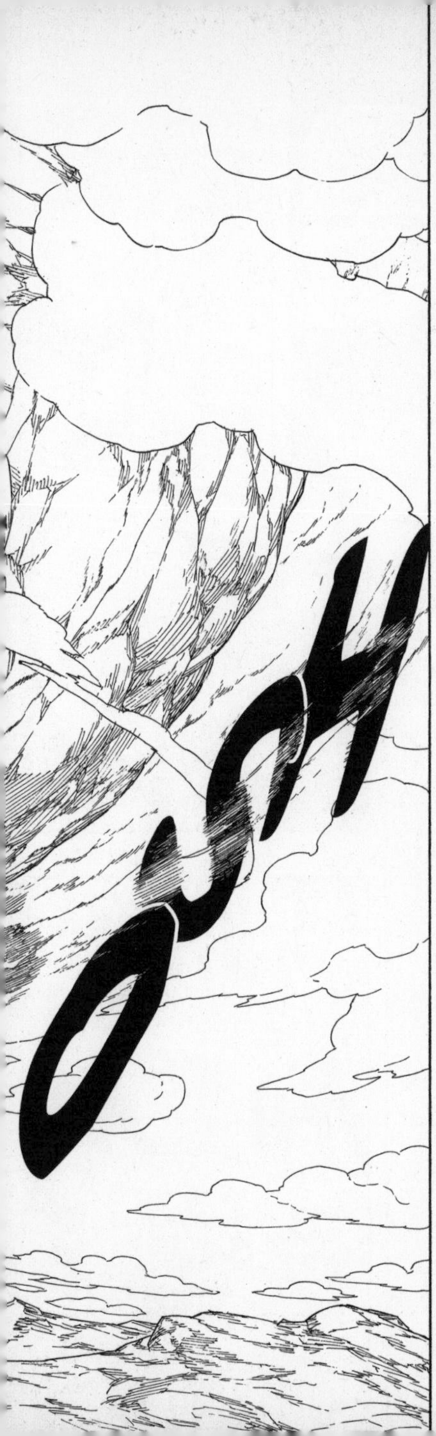
OSH

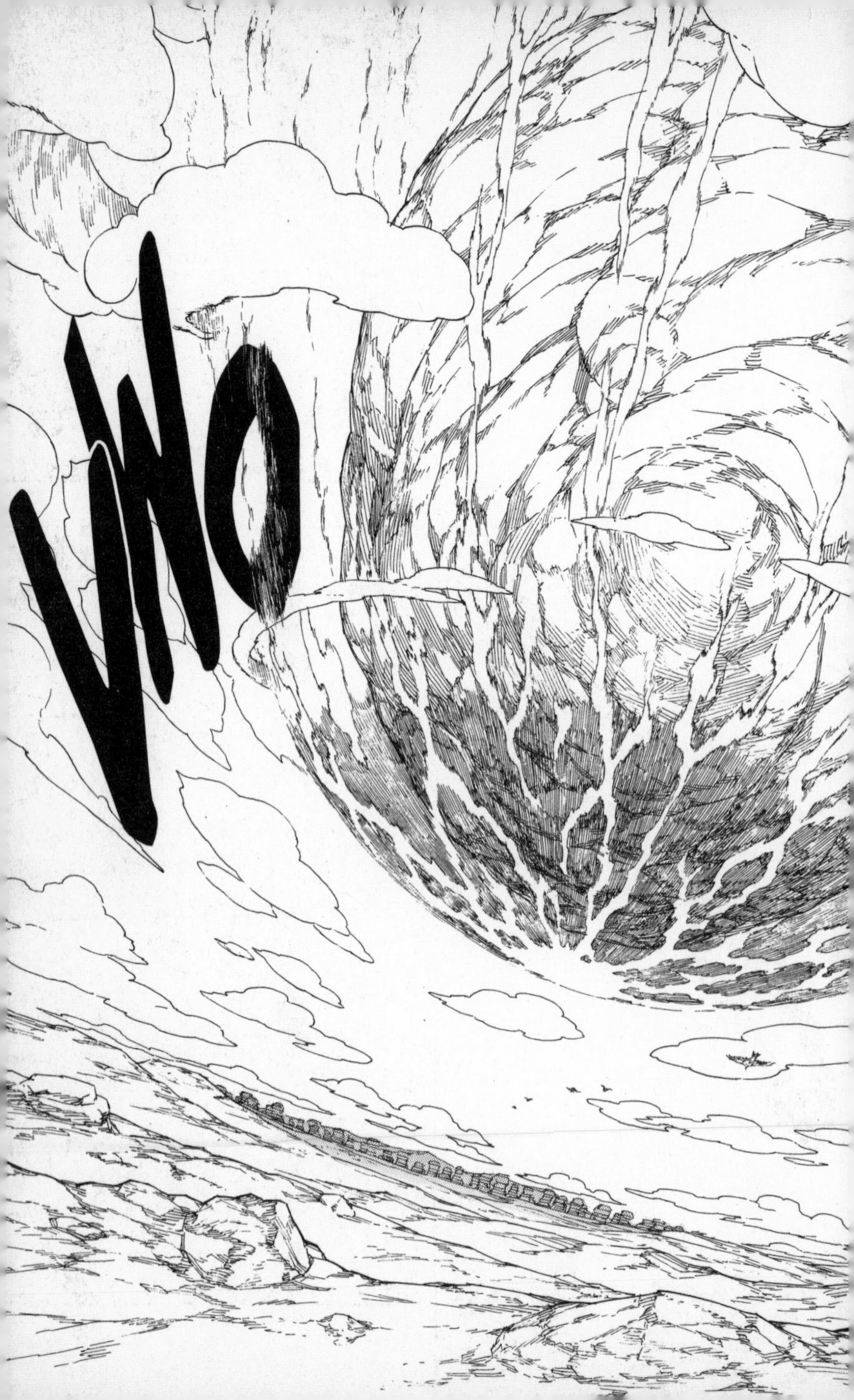
WO

NARUTO

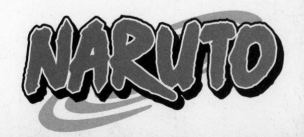

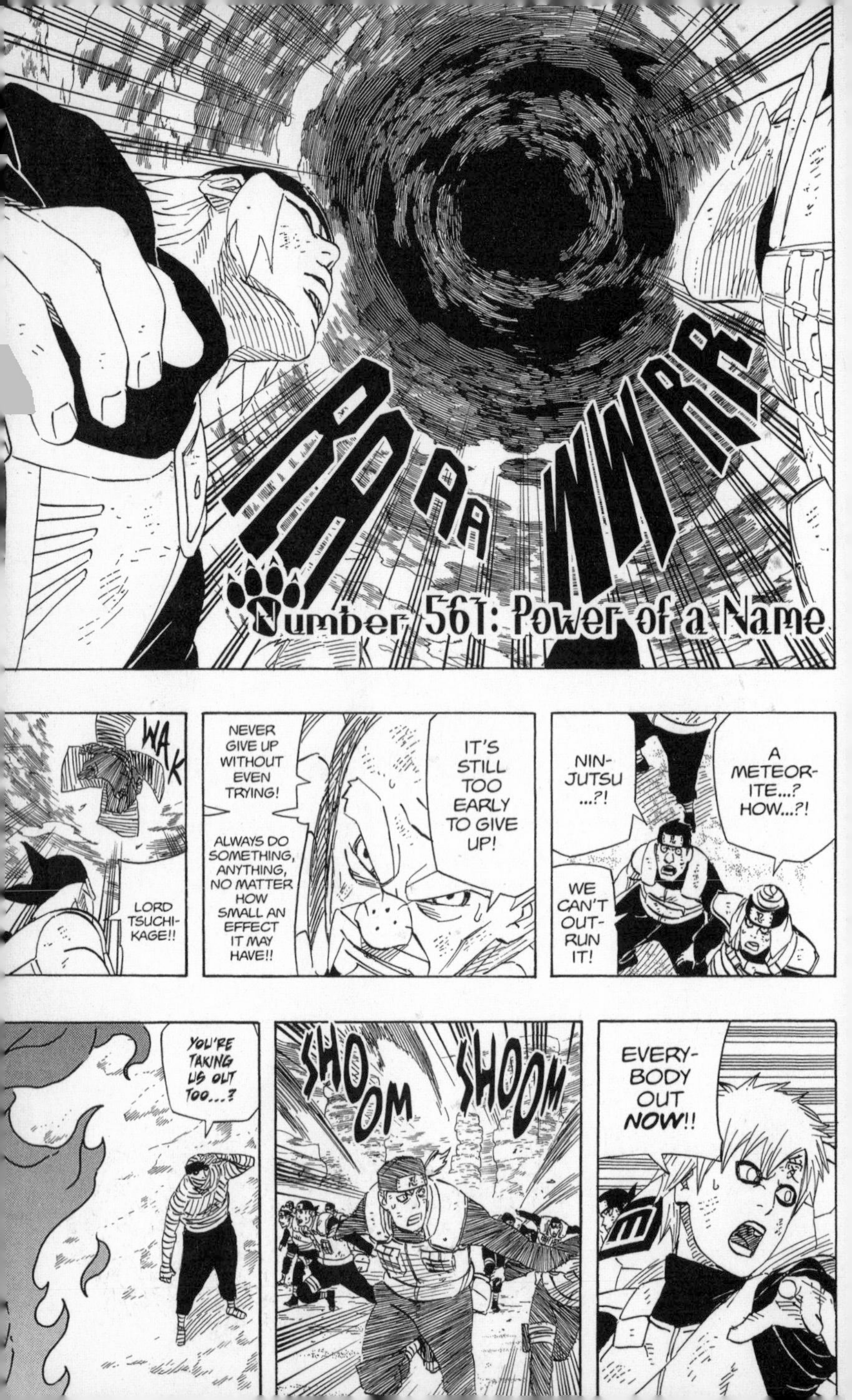
Number 561: Power of a Name
A METEORITE...? HOW...?!
NINJUTSU ...?!
WE CAN'T OUTRUN IT!
IT'S STILL TOO EARLY TO GIVE UP!
NEVER GIVE UP WITHOUT EVEN TRYING!
ALWAYS DO SOMETHING, ANYTHING, NO MATTER HOW SMALL AN EFFECT IT MAY HAVE!!
WAK
LORD TSUCHIKAGE!!
EVERYBODY OUT NOW!!
SHOOM SHOOM
YOU'RE TAKING US OUT TOO...?

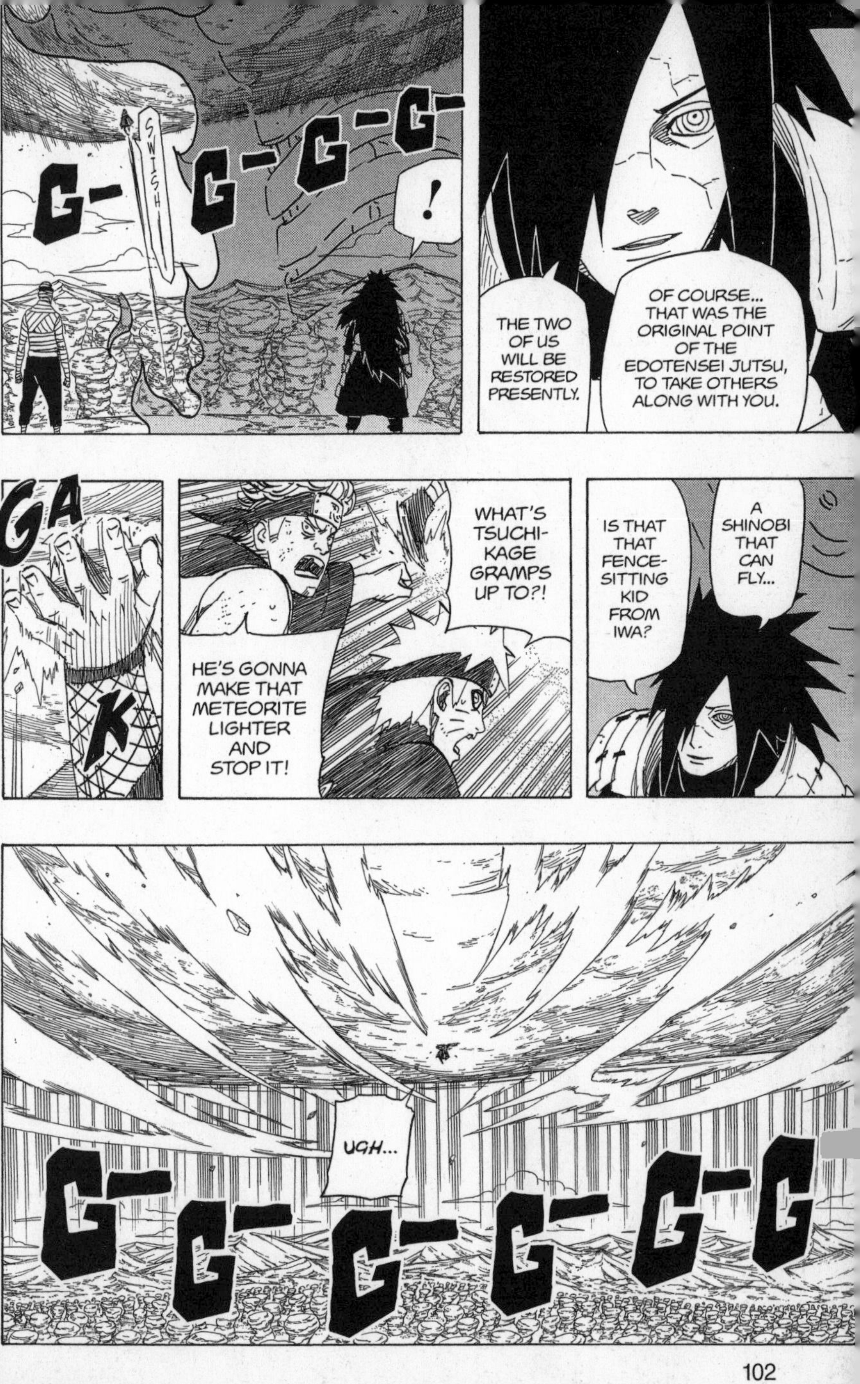
OF COURSE... THAT WAS THE ORIGINAL POINT OF THE EDOTENSEI JUTSU, TO TAKE OTHERS ALONG WITH YOU.
THE TWO OF US WILL BE RESTORED PRESENTLY.
G-G-G-G-G-
SWISH
!
A SHINOBI THAT CAN FLY...
IS THAT THAT FENCE-SITTING KID FROM IWA?
WHAT'S TSUCHI-KAGE GRAMPS UP TO?!
HE'S GONNA MAKE THAT METEORITE LIGHTER AND STOP IT!
GAK
UGH...
G-G-G-G-G-G

READ THIS WAY

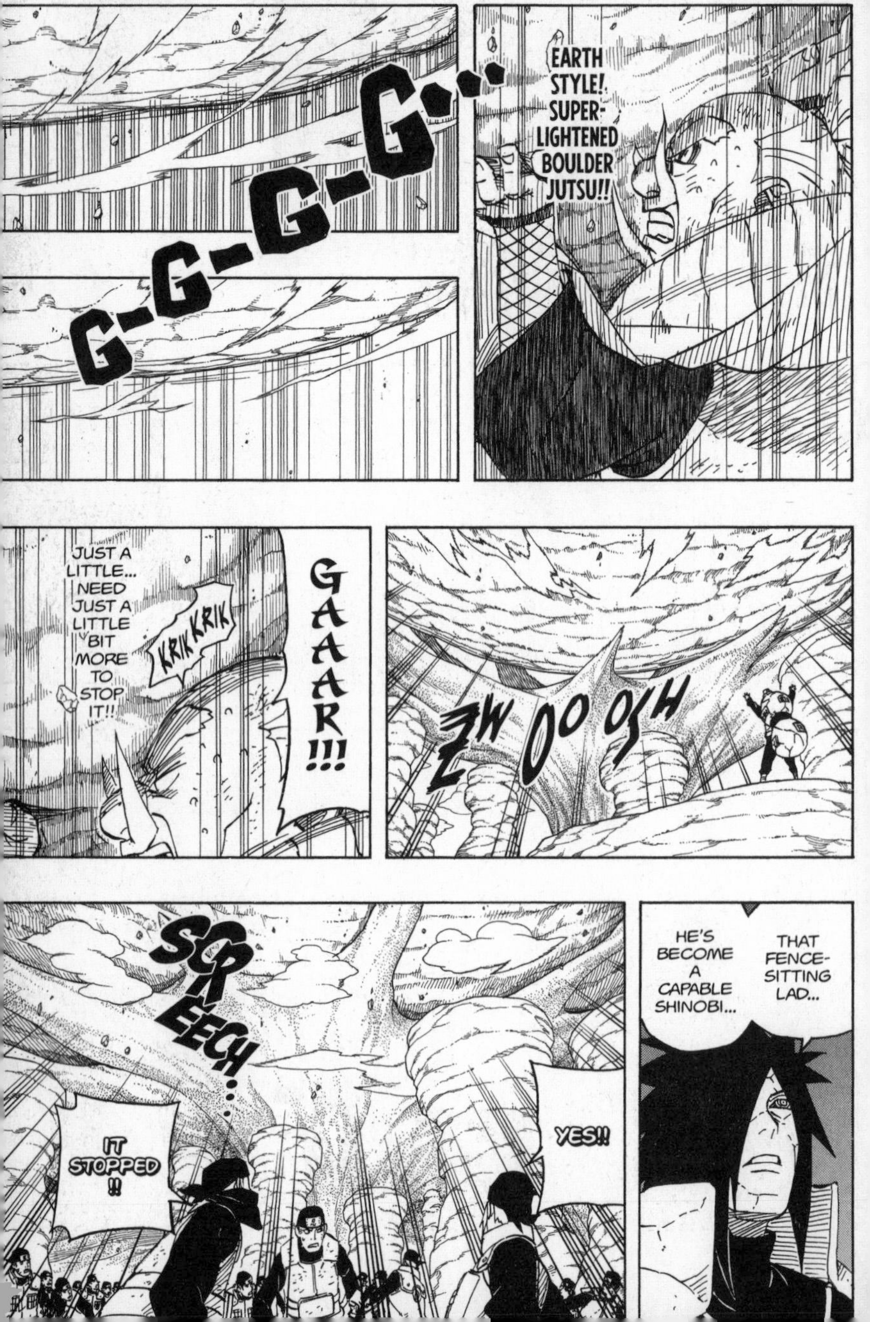
EARTH STYLE! SUPER-LIGHTENED BOULDER JUTSU!!
G-G-G-G
ZWOOOSH
GAAAAR!!!
KRIK KRIK
JUST A LITTLE... NEED JUST A LITTLE BIT MORE TO STOP IT!!
THAT FENCE-SITTING LAD...
HE'S BECOME A CAPABLE SHINOBI...
SCREEECH...
YES!!
IT STOPPED!!

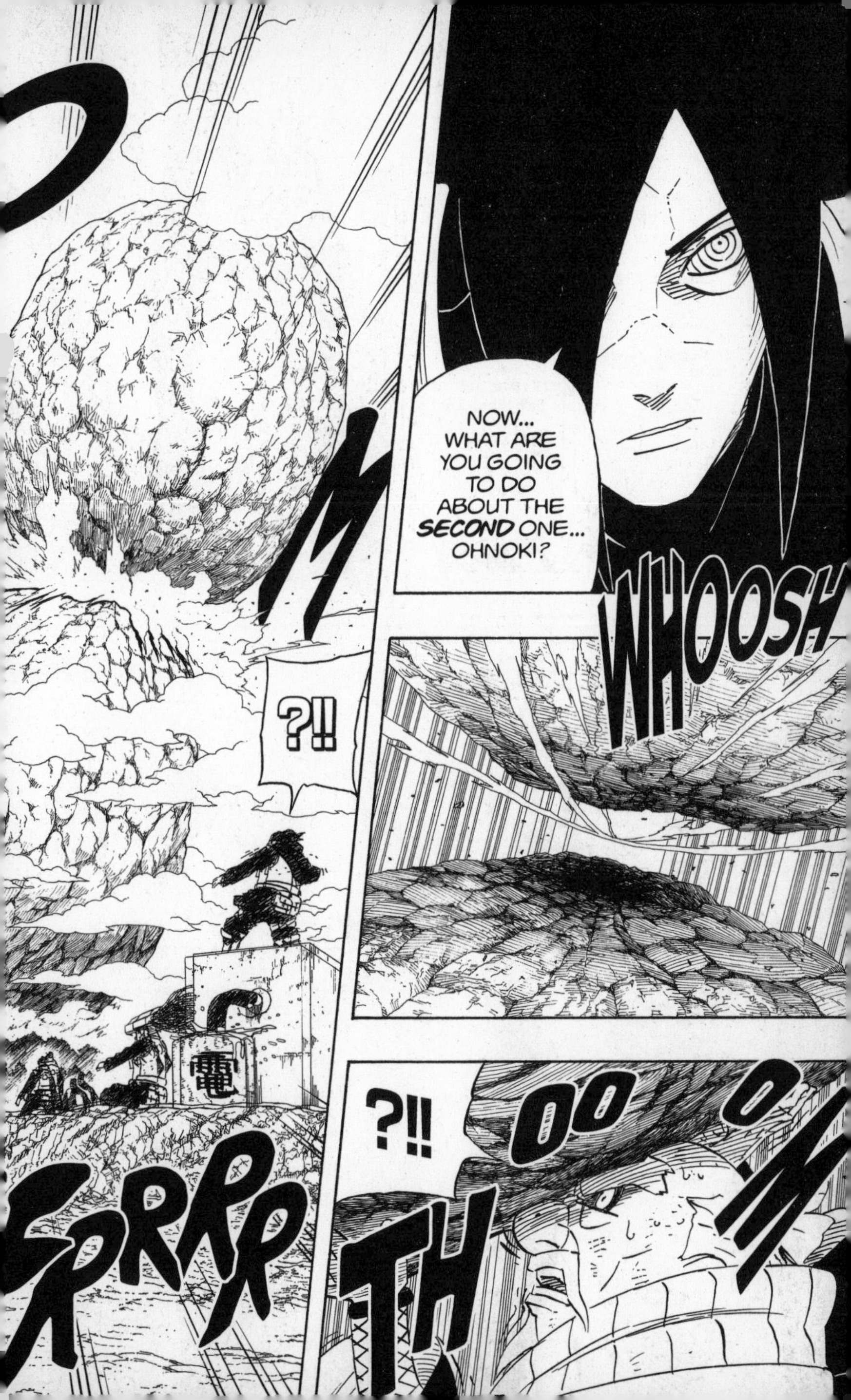
NOW... WHAT ARE YOU GOING TO DO ABOUT THE **SECOND** ONE... OHNOKI?
WHOOSH
?!!
OOOM
TH
?!!
SPRRR

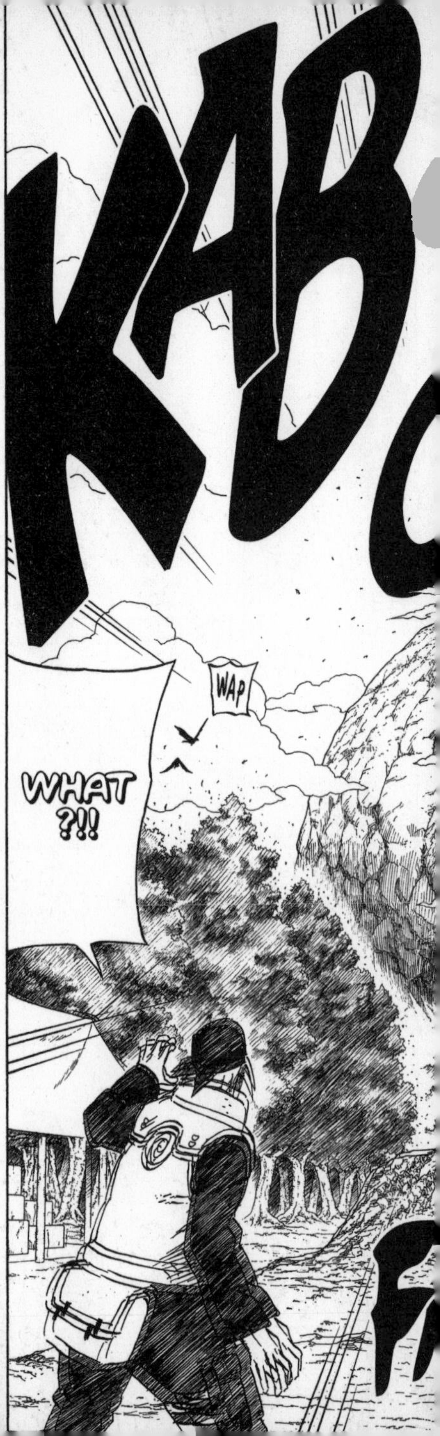
KAB
WAP
WHAT ?!!

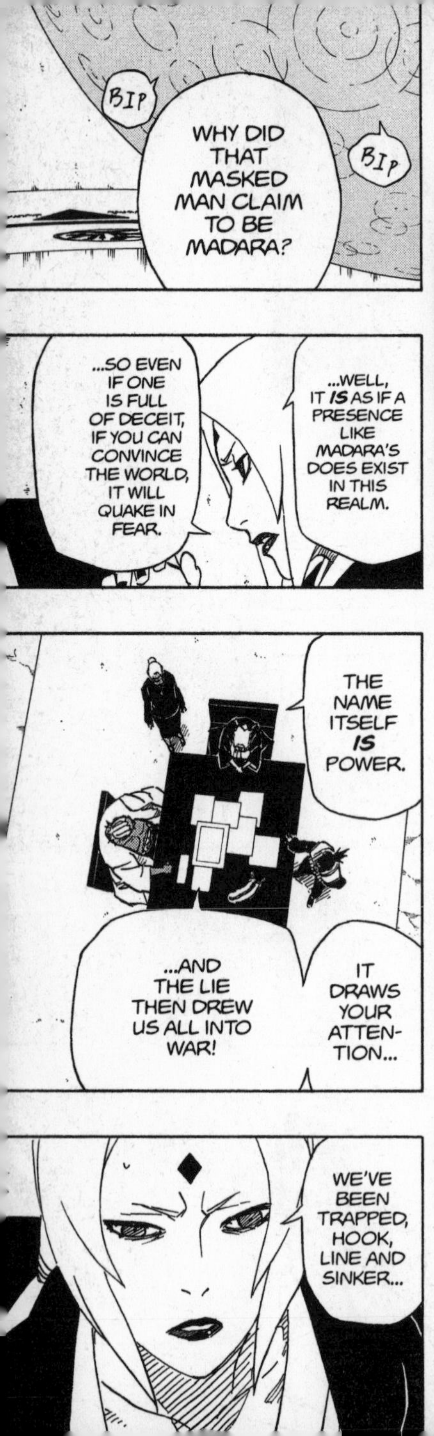
BIP
WHY DID THAT MASKED MAN CLAIM TO BE MADARA?
BIP
...WELL, IT *IS* AS IF A PRESENCE LIKE MADARA'S DOES EXIST IN THIS REALM.
...SO EVEN IF ONE IS FULL OF DECEIT, IF YOU CAN CONVINCE THE WORLD, IT WILL QUAKE IN FEAR.
THE NAME ITSELF *IS* POWER.
IT DRAWS YOUR ATTENTION...
...AND THE LIE THEN DREW US ALL INTO WAR!
WE'VE BEEN TRAPPED, HOOK, LINE AND SINKER...

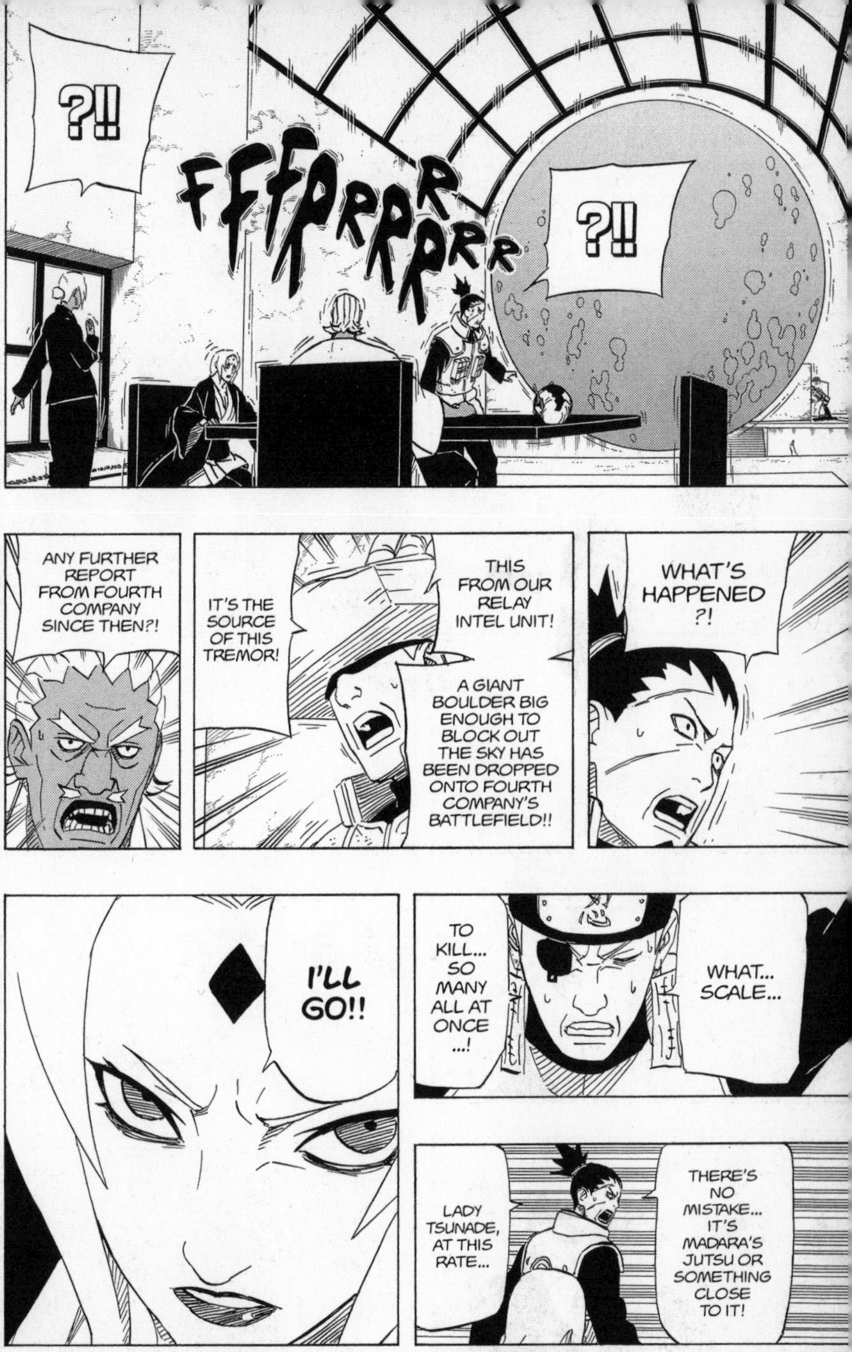
?!!
FFFRRRRRRR
?!!
WHAT'S HAPPENED?!
THIS FROM OUR RELAY INTEL UNIT!
A GIANT BOULDER BIG ENOUGH TO BLOCK OUT THE SKY HAS BEEN DROPPED ONTO FOURTH COMPANY'S BATTLEFIELD!!
IT'S THE SOURCE OF THIS TREMOR!
ANY FURTHER REPORT FROM FOURTH COMPANY SINCE THEN?!
WHAT... SCALE...
TO KILL... SO MANY ALL AT ONCE...!
THERE'S NO MISTAKE... IT'S MADARA'S JUTSU OR SOMETHING CLOSE TO IT!
LADY TSUNADE, AT THIS RATE...
I'LL GO!!

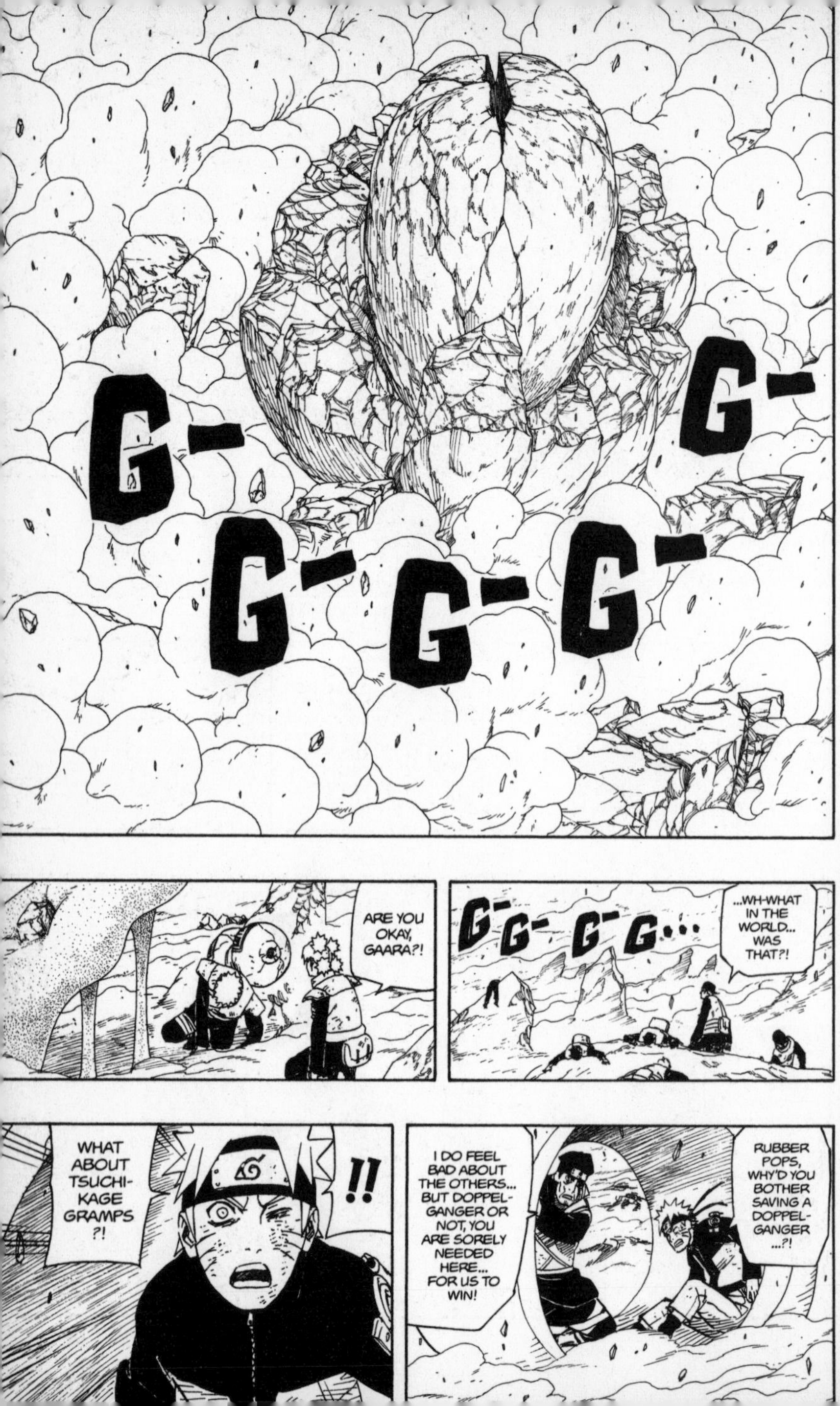
G- G- G- G- G- G-
G-G-G-G...
...WH-WHAT IN THE WORLD... WAS THAT?!
ARE YOU OKAY, GAARA?!
RUBBER POPS, WHY'D YOU BOTHER SAVING A DOPPELGANGER ...?!
I DO FEEL BAD ABOUT THE OTHERS... BUT DOPPELGANGER OR NOT, YOU ARE SORELY NEEDED HERE... FOR US TO WIN!
WHAT ABOUT TSUCHIKAGE GRAMPS ?!
!!

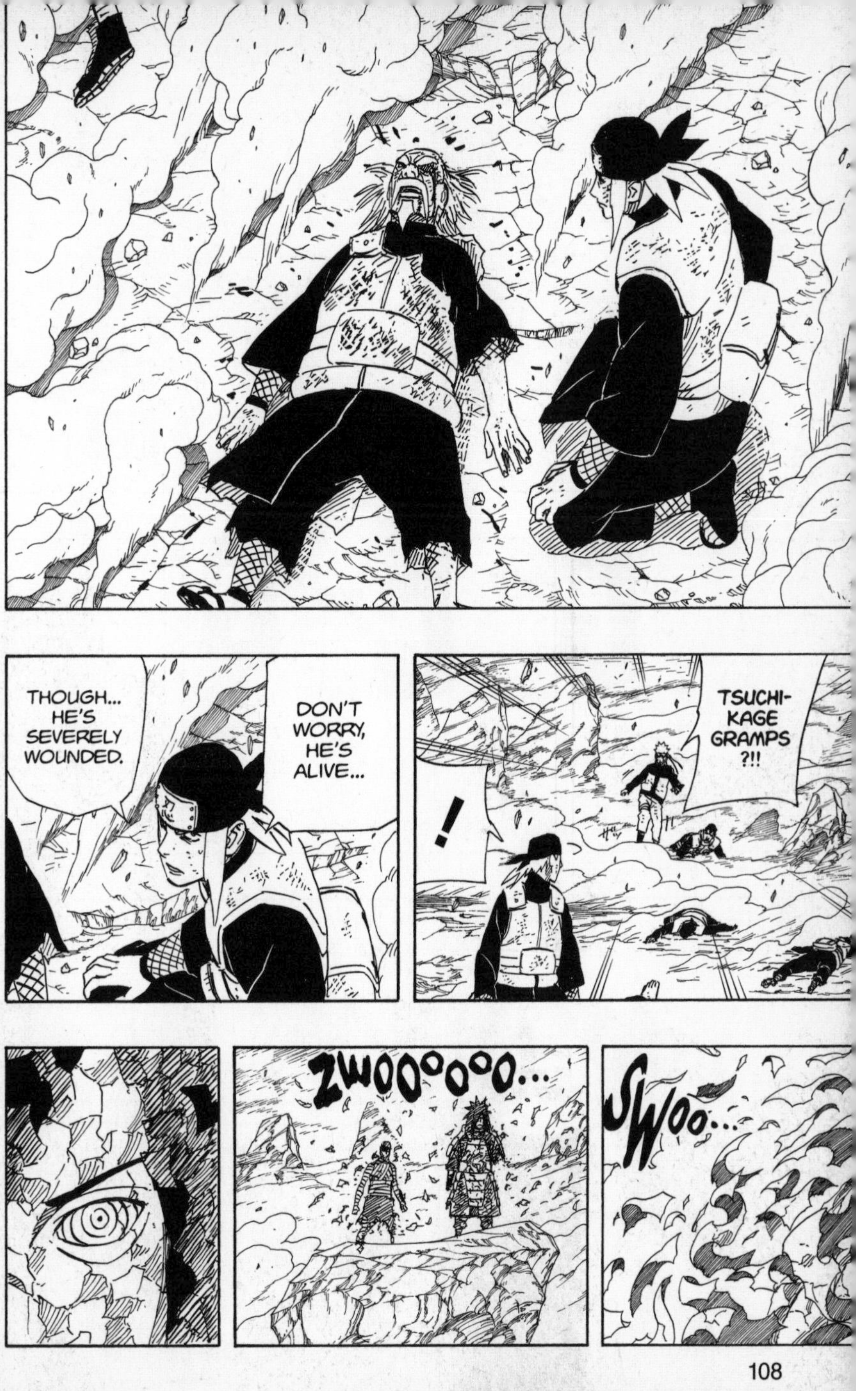
TSUCHI-KAGE GRAMPS ?!!
!
DON'T WORRY, HE'S ALIVE...
THOUGH... HE'S SEVERELY WOUNDED.
SWOO...
ZWOOOOOO...

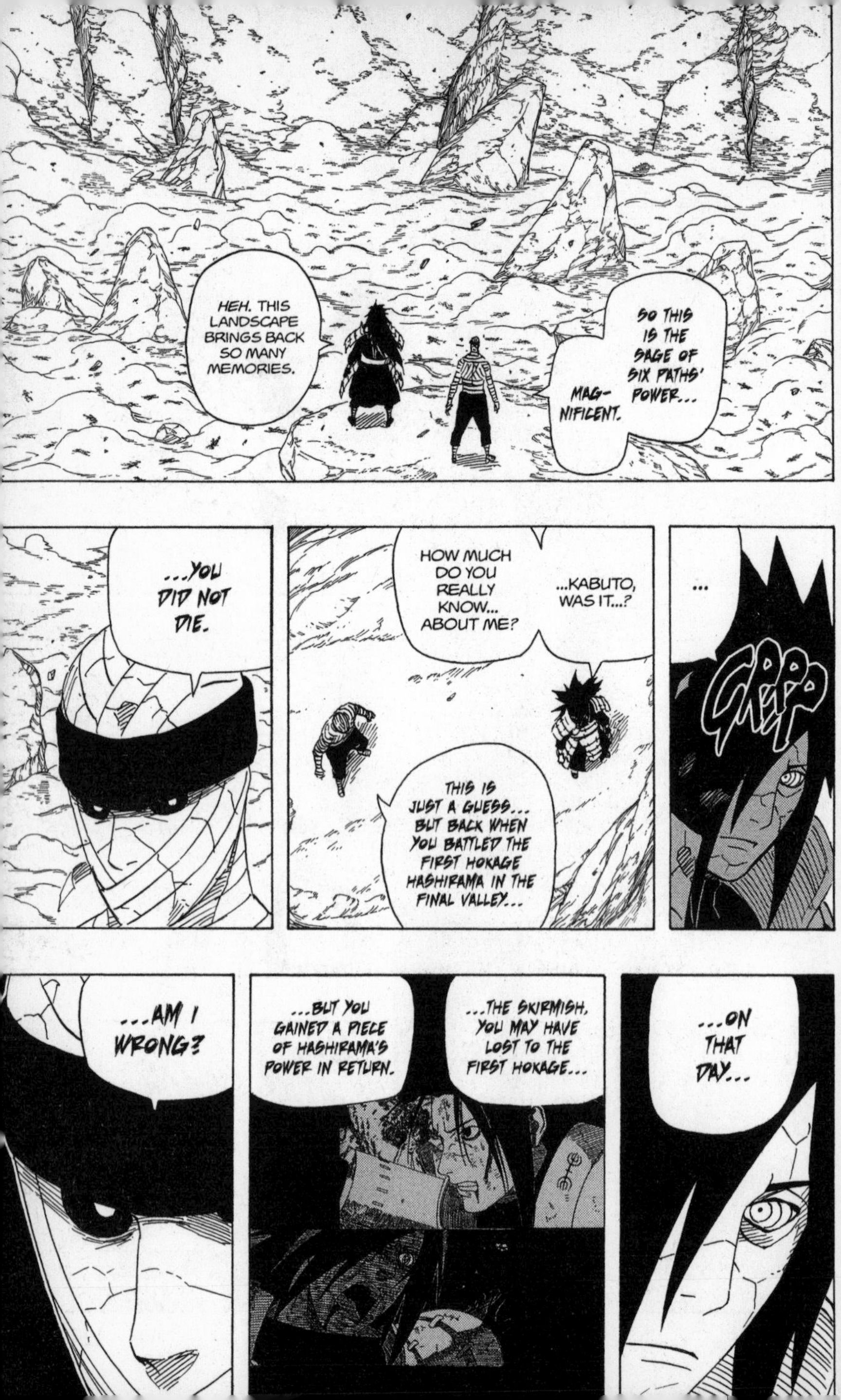
SO THIS IS THE SAGE OF SIX PATHS' POWER...
MAG-NIFICENT.
HEH. THIS LANDSCAPE BRINGS BACK SO MANY MEMORIES.
...
...KABUTO, WAS IT...?
HOW MUCH DO YOU REALLY KNOW... ABOUT ME?
THIS IS JUST A GUESS... BUT BACK WHEN YOU BATTLED THE FIRST HOKAGE HASHIRAMA IN THE FINAL VALLEY...
...YOU DID NOT DIE.
...ON THAT DAY...
...THE SKIRMISH, YOU MAY HAVE LOST TO THE FIRST HOKAGE...
...BUT YOU GAINED A PIECE OF HASHIRAMA'S POWER IN RETURN.
...AM I WRONG?

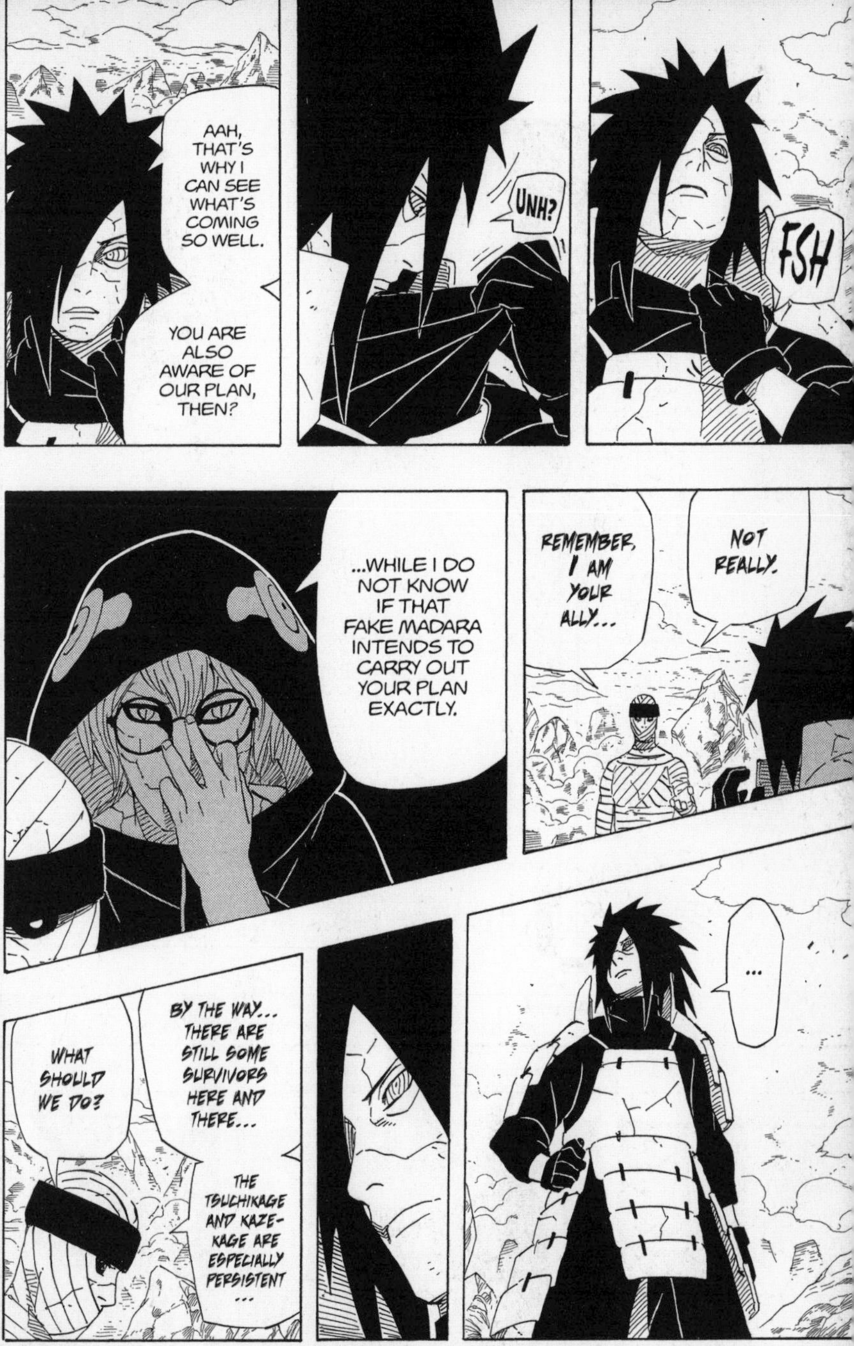
FSH
UNH?
AAH, THAT'S WHY I CAN SEE WHAT'S COMING SO WELL.
YOU ARE ALSO AWARE OF OUR PLAN, THEN?
NOT REALLY.
REMEMBER, I AM YOUR ALLY...
...WHILE I DO NOT KNOW IF THAT FAKE MADARA INTENDS TO CARRY OUT YOUR PLAN EXACTLY.
...
BY THE WAY... THERE ARE STILL SOME SURVIVORS HERE AND THERE...
WHAT SHOULD WE DO?
THE TSUCHIKAGE AND KAZE-KAGE ARE ESPECIALLY PERSISTENT...

READ THIS WAY

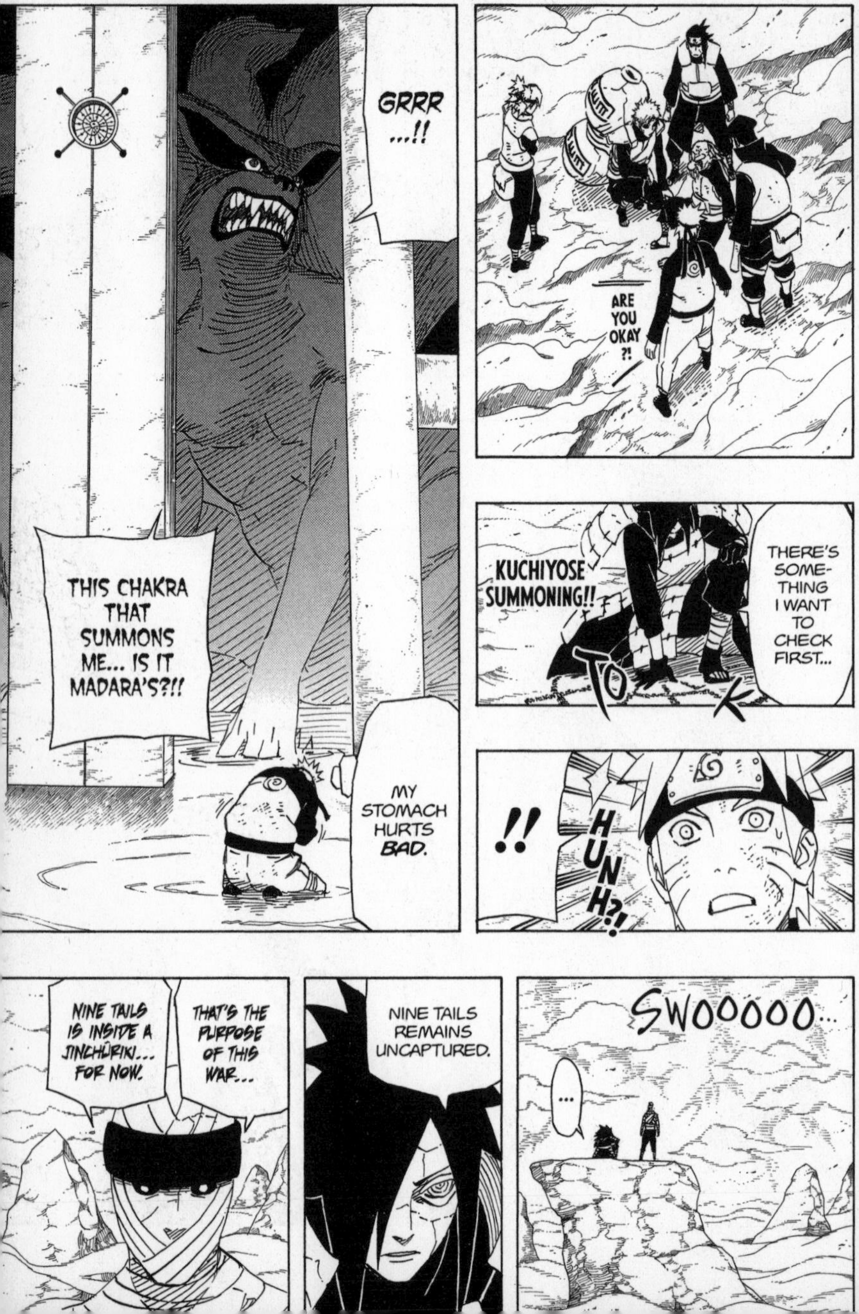
ARE YOU OKAY ?!
THERE'S SOMETHING I WANT TO CHECK FIRST...
KUCHIYOSE SUMMONING!!
TOK
HUNH?!
!!
GRRR ...!!
THIS CHAKRA THAT SUMMONS ME... IS IT MADARA'S?!!
MY STOMACH HURTS BAD.
SWOOOOO...
...
NINE TAILS REMAINS UNCAPTURED.
THAT'S THE PURPOSE OF THIS WAR...
NINE TAILS IS INSIDE A JINCHŪRIKI... FOR NOW.

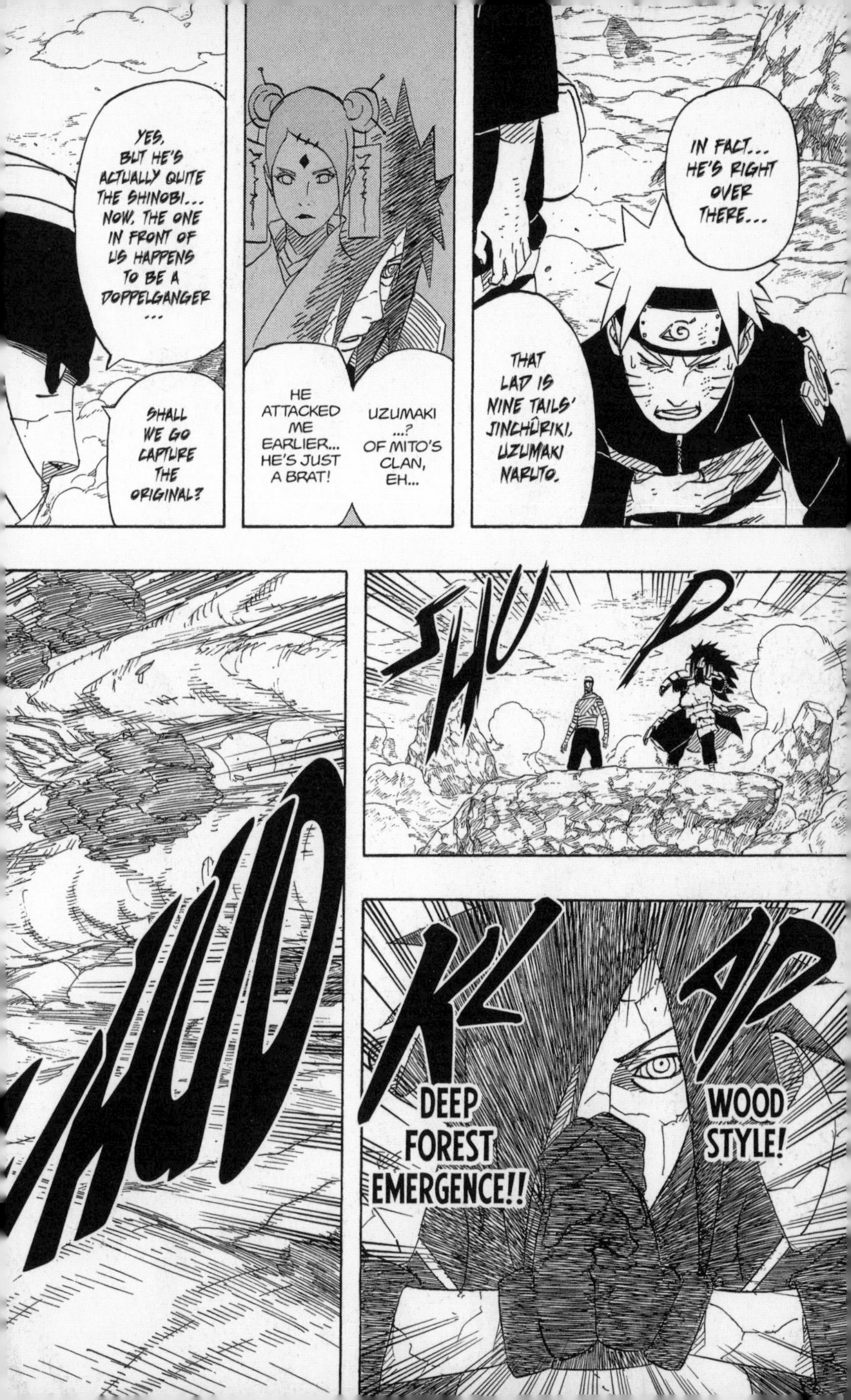
IN FACT... HE'S RIGHT OVER THERE...
THAT LAD IS NINE TAILS' JINCHÛRIKI, UZUMAKI NARUTO.
UZUMAKI ...? OF MITO'S CLAN, EH...
HE ATTACKED ME EARLIER... HE'S JUST A BRAT!
YES, BUT HE'S ACTUALLY QUITE THE SHINOBI... NOW, THE ONE IN FRONT OF US HAPPENS TO BE A DOPPELGANGER...
SHALL WE GO CAPTURE THE ORIGINAL?
SHUP
KLAP
WOOD STYLE!
DEEP FOREST EMERGENCE!!
WHUD

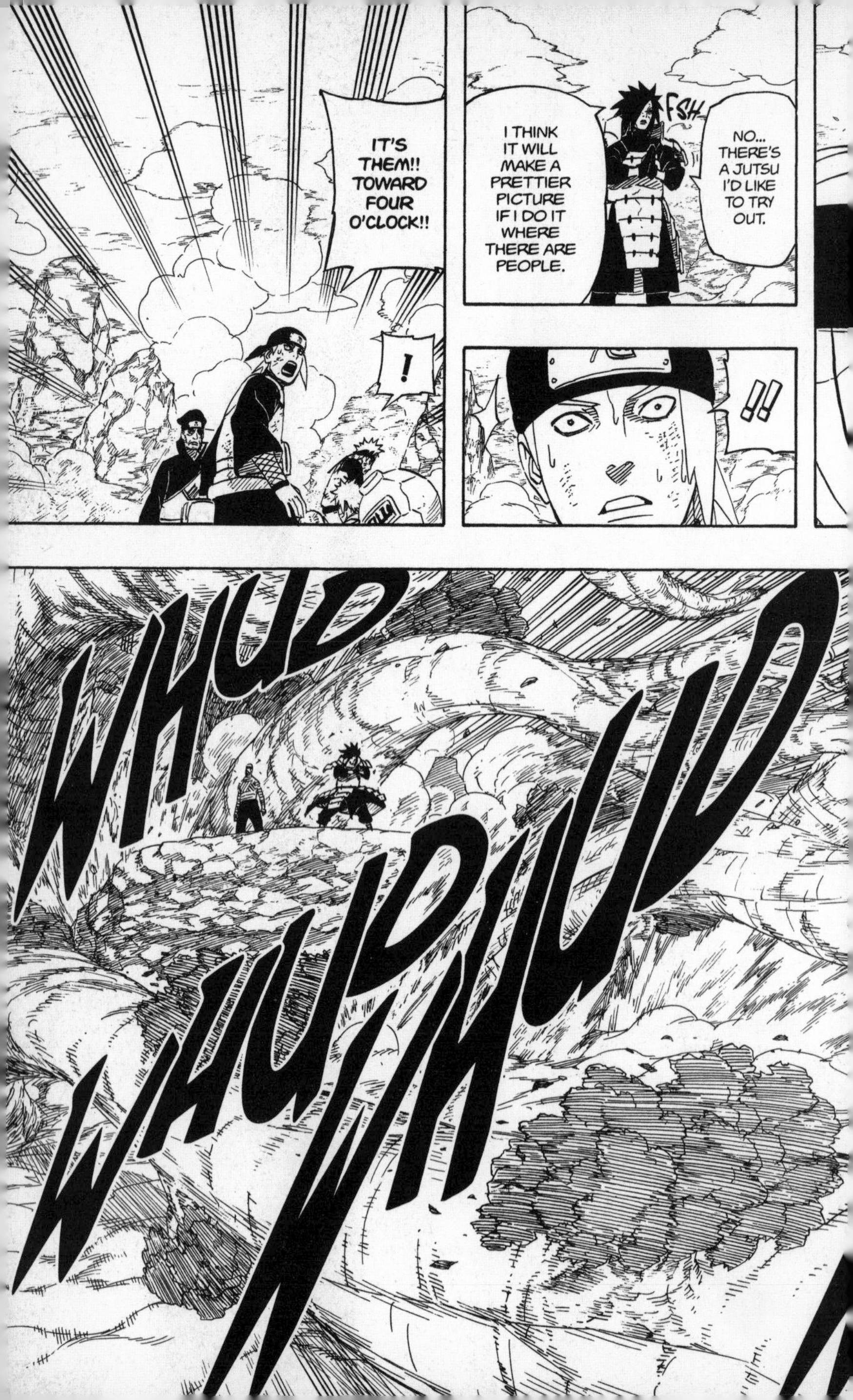
NO... THERE'S A JUTSU I'D LIKE TO TRY OUT.
FSH
I THINK IT WILL MAKE A PRETTIER PICTURE IF I DO IT WHERE THERE ARE PEOPLE.
!!
IT'S THEM!! TOWARD FOUR O'CLOCK!!
!
WHUD
WHUDUD

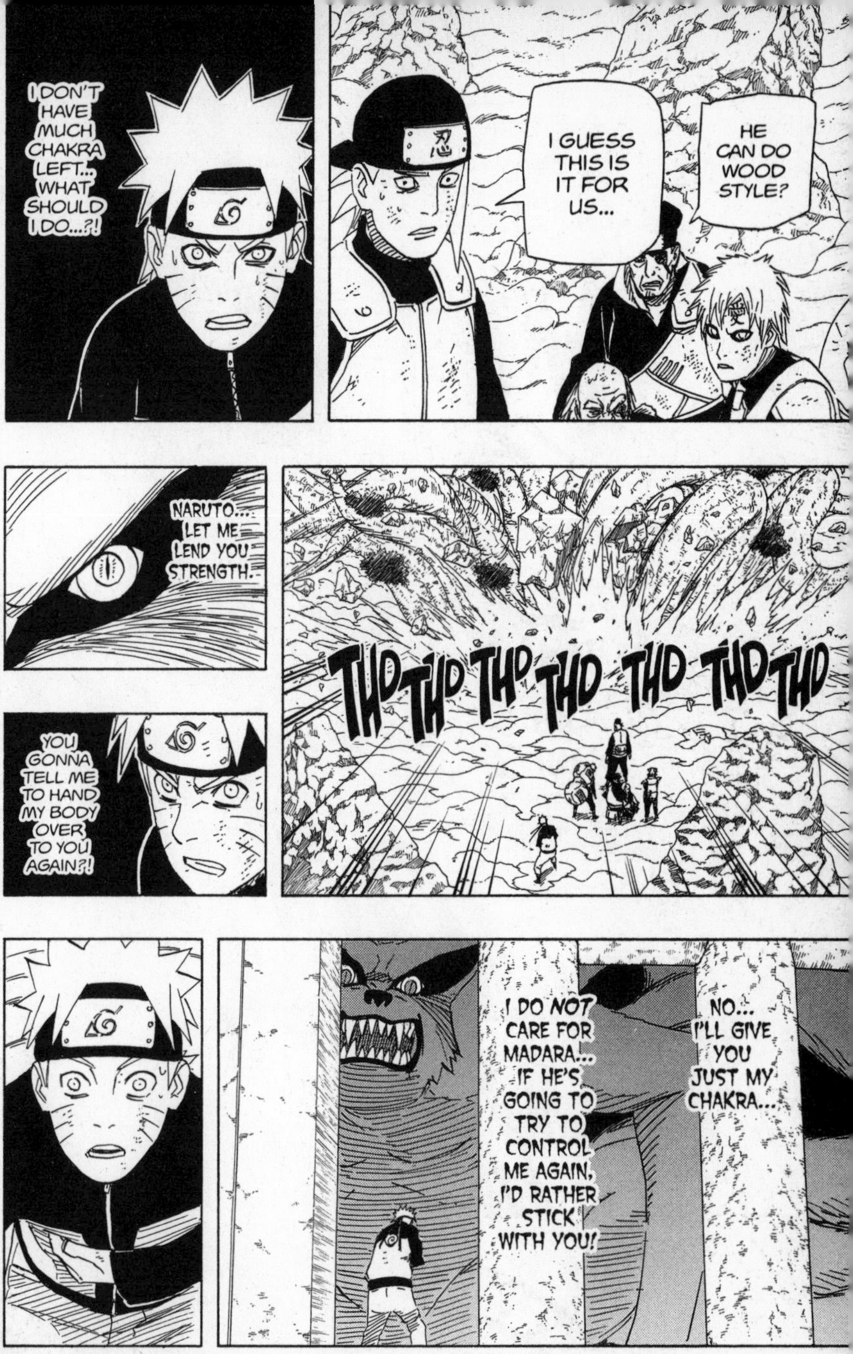
HE CAN DO WOOD STYLE?
I GUESS THIS IS IT FOR US...
I DON'T HAVE MUCH CHAKRA LEFT... WHAT SHOULD I DO...?!
THD THD THD THD THD THD THD
NARUTO... LET ME LEND YOU STRENGTH.
YOU GONNA TELL ME TO HAND MY BODY OVER TO YOU AGAIN?!
NO... I'LL GIVE YOU JUST MY CHAKRA...
I DO NOT CARE FOR MADARA... IF HE'S GOING TO TRY TO CONTROL ME AGAIN, I'D RATHER STICK WITH YOU!

READ THIS WAY

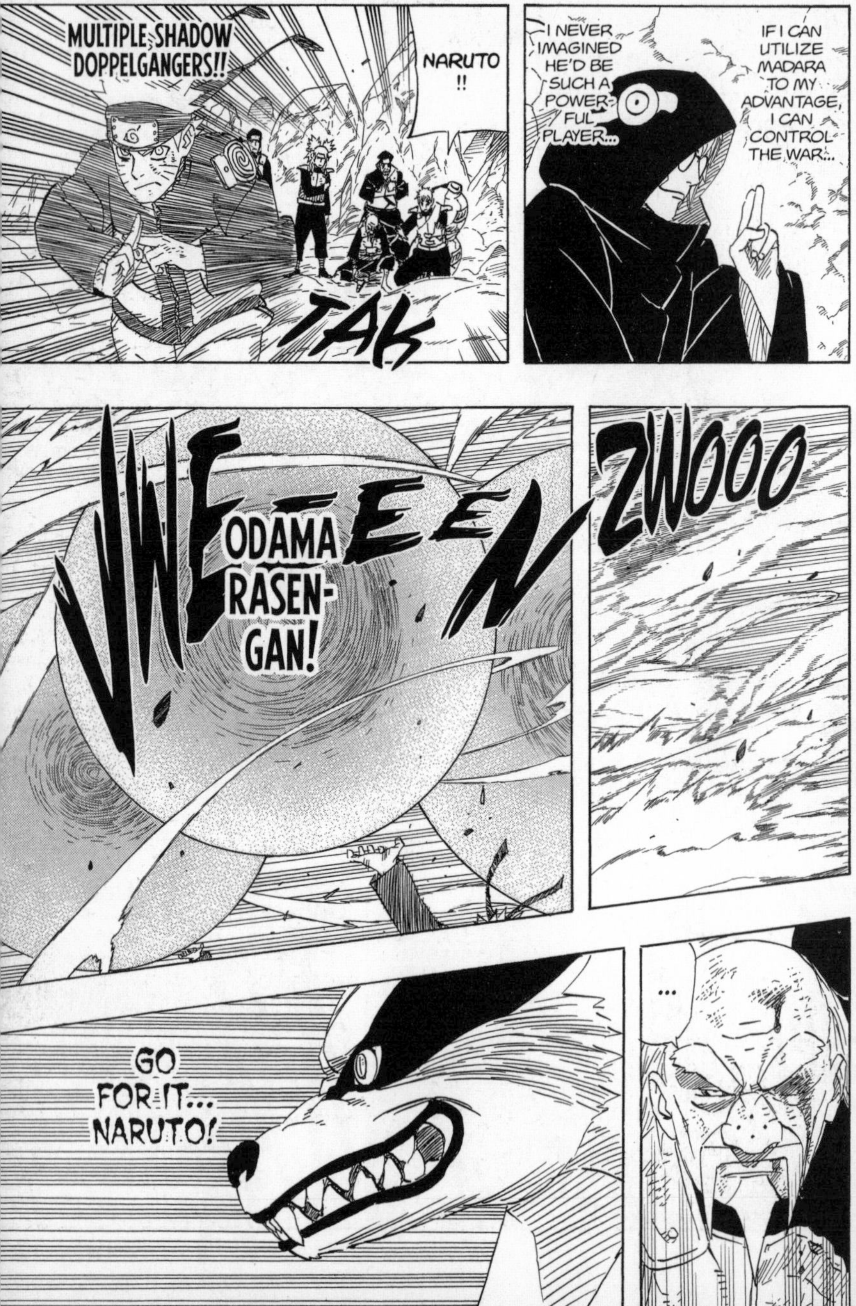
IF I CAN UTILIZE MADARA TO MY ADVANTAGE, I CAN CONTROL THE WAR...
I NEVER IMAGINED HE'D BE SUCH A POWERFUL PLAYER...
NARUTO !!
MULTIPLE SHADOW DOPPELGANGERS!!
TAK
ZWOOO
VWEEEEN
ODAMA RASEN-GAN!
...
GO FOR IT... NARUTO!

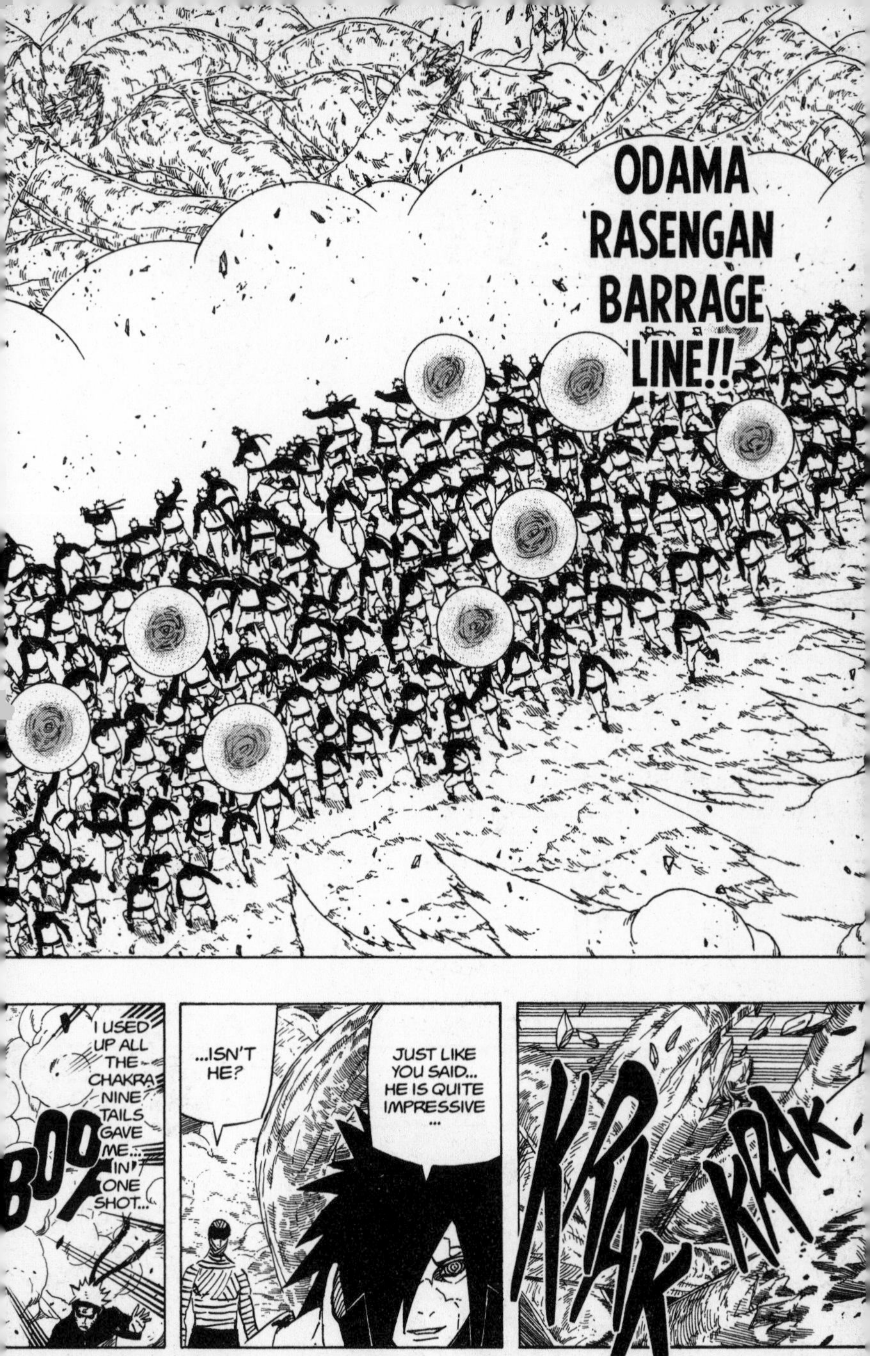
ODAMA RASENGAN BARRAGE LINE!!
KRAK
KRAK
JUST LIKE YOU SAID... HE IS QUITE IMPRESSIVE ...
...ISN'T HE?
I USED UP ALL THE CHAKRA NINE TAILS GAVE ME... IN ONE SHOT...
BOOF

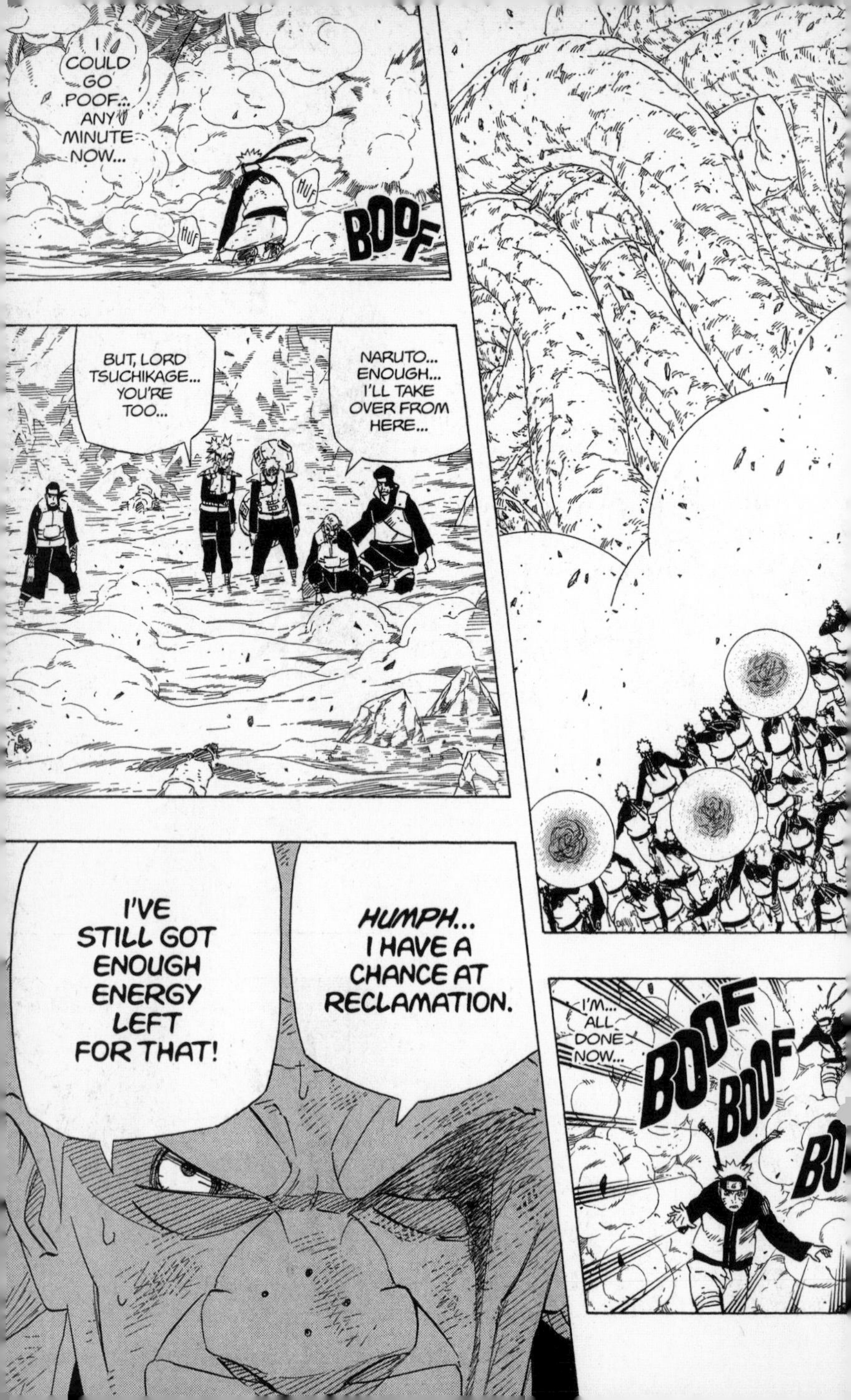
I'M... ALL DONE NOW...
BOOF
BOOF
BO
I COULD GO POOF... ANY MINUTE NOW...
HUF
HUF
BOOF
NARUTO... ENOUGH... I'LL TAKE OVER FROM HERE...
BUT, LORD TSUCHIKAGE... YOU'RE TOO...
HUMPH... I HAVE A CHANCE AT RECLAMATION.
I'VE STILL GOT ENOUGH ENERGY LEFT FOR THAT!

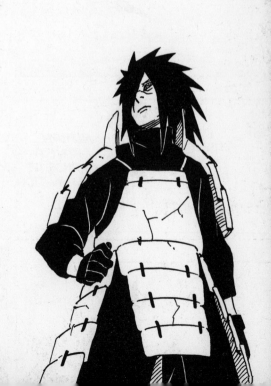

Number 562: Reclamation

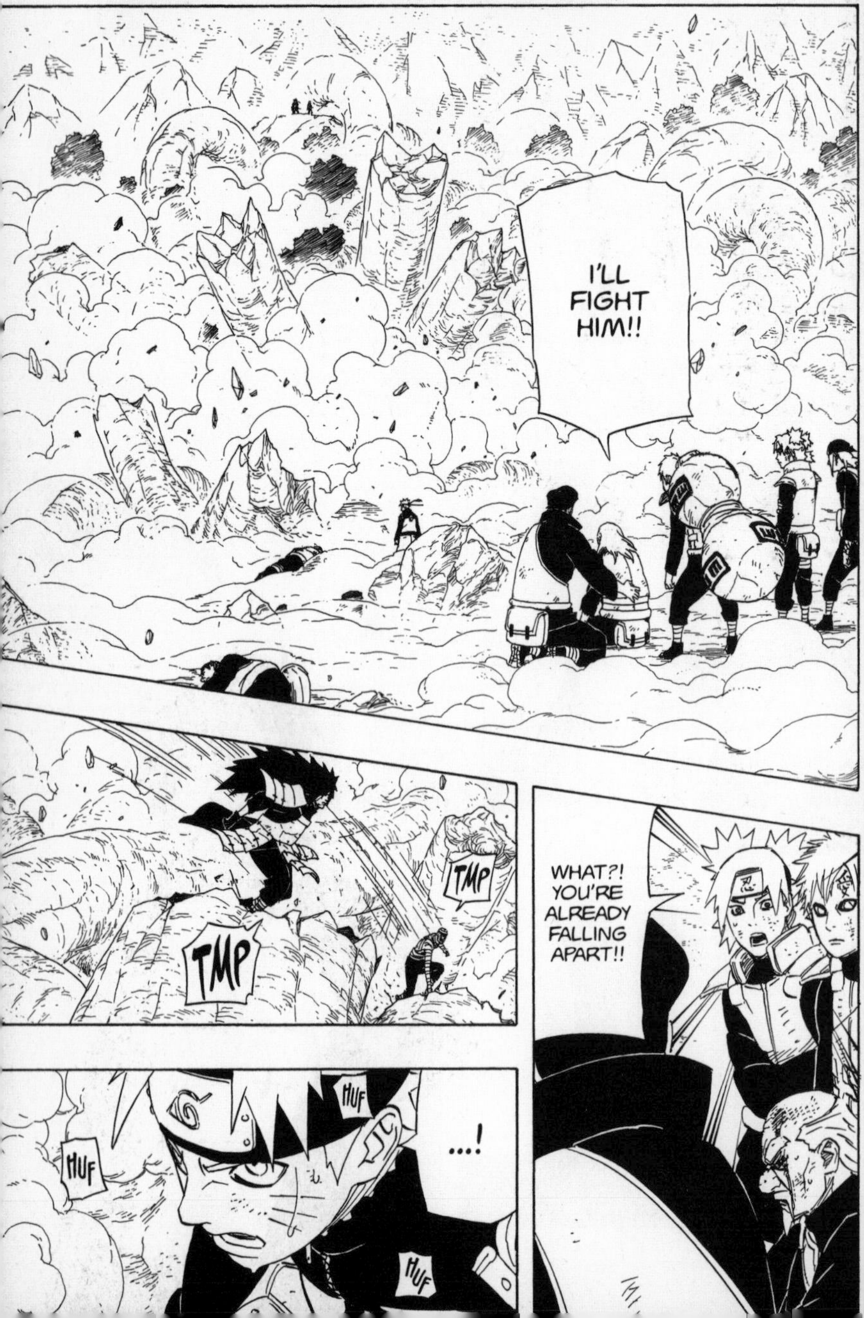
I'LL FIGHT HIM!!
WHAT?! YOU'RE ALREADY FALLING APART!!
TMP
TMP
HUF
HUF
...!
HUF

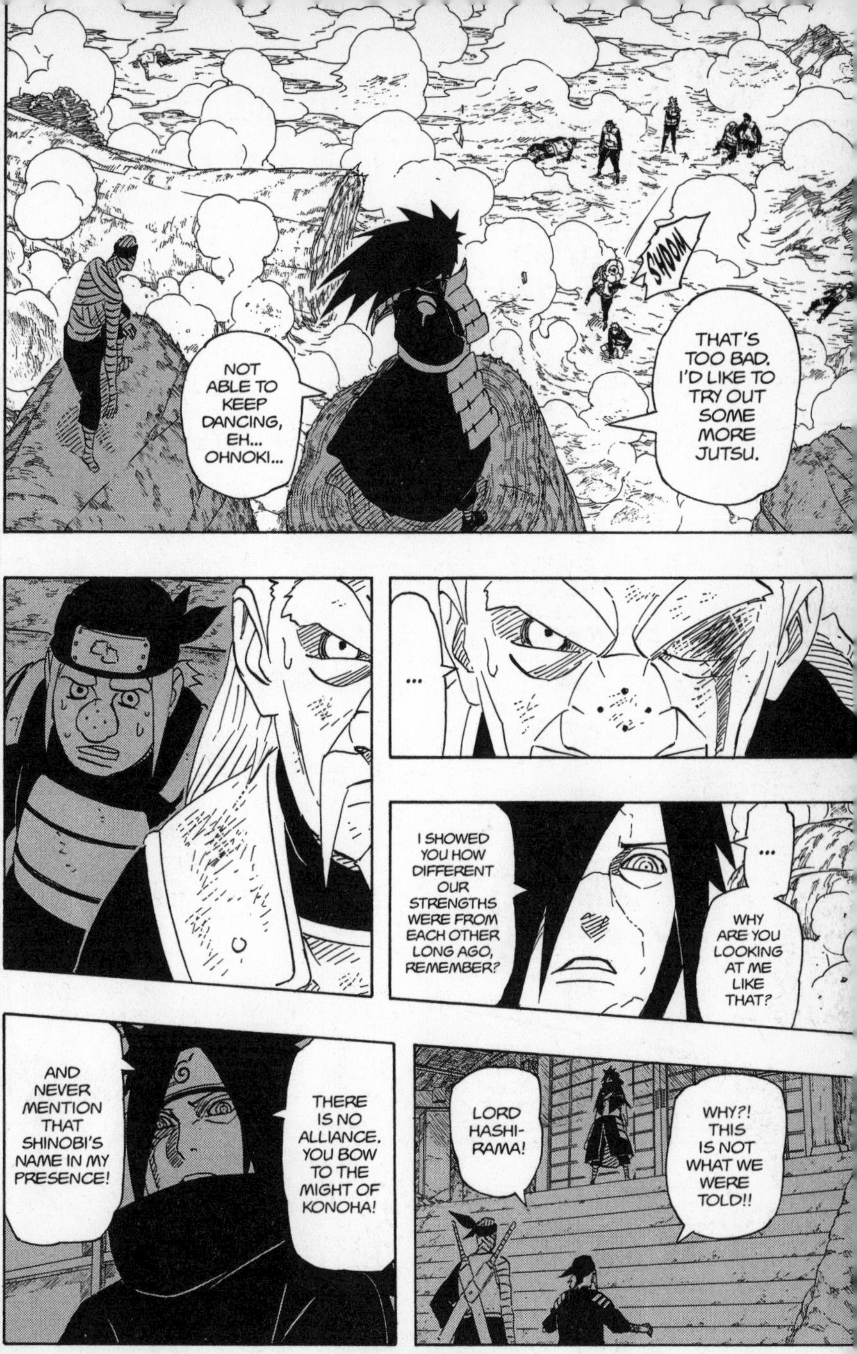
SHOOM
THAT'S TOO BAD. I'D LIKE TO TRY OUT SOME MORE JUTSU.
NOT ABLE TO KEEP DANCING, EH... OHNOKI...
...
...
WHY ARE YOU LOOKING AT ME LIKE THAT?
I SHOWED YOU HOW DIFFERENT OUR STRENGTHS WERE FROM EACH OTHER LONG AGO, REMEMBER?
WHY?! THIS IS NOT WHAT WE WERE TOLD!!
LORD HASHI-RAMA!
THERE IS NO ALLIANCE. YOU BOW TO THE MIGHT OF KONOHA!
AND NEVER MENTION THAT SHINOBI'S NAME IN MY PRESENCE!

READ THIS WAY

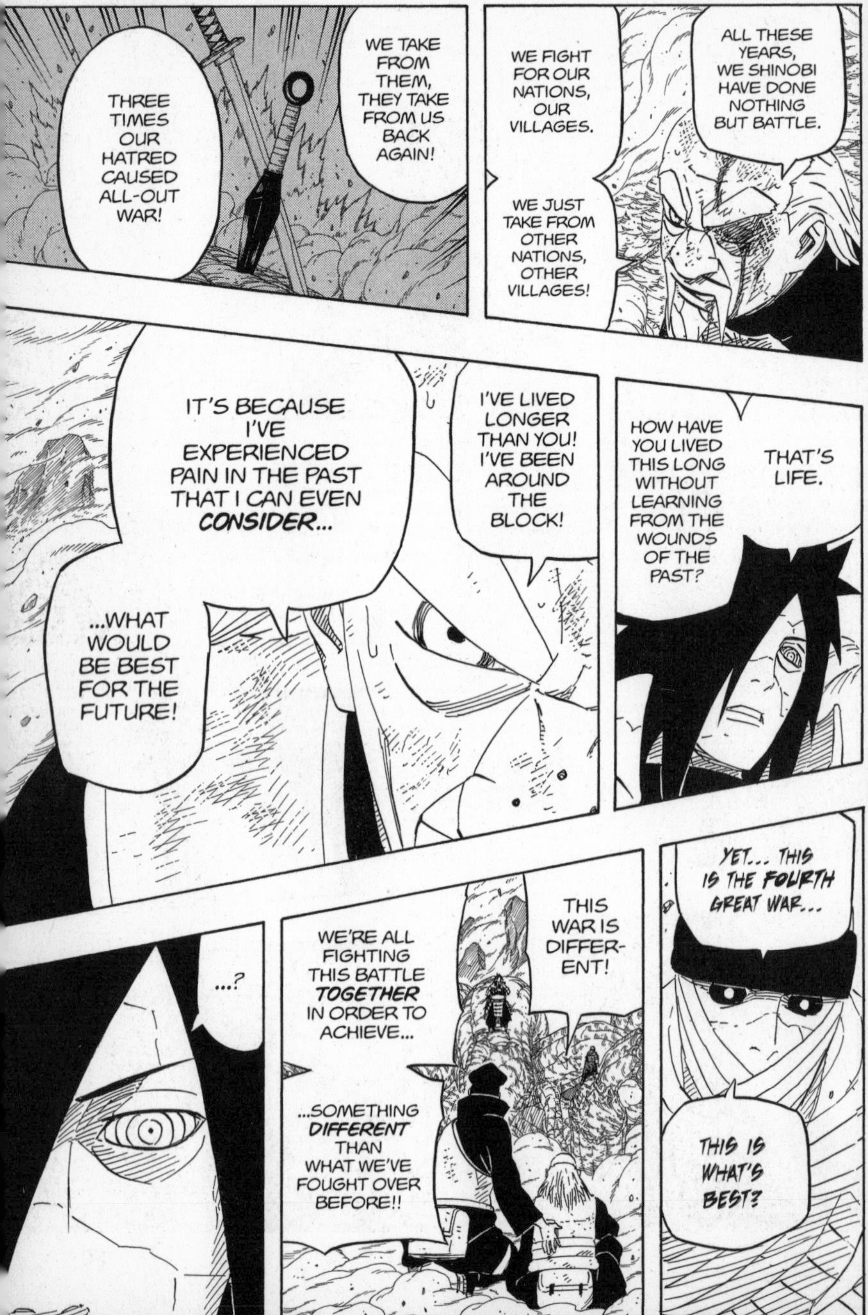
ALL THESE YEARS, WE SHINOBI HAVE DONE NOTHING BUT BATTLE.
WE FIGHT FOR OUR NATIONS, OUR VILLAGES.
WE JUST TAKE FROM OTHER NATIONS, OTHER VILLAGES!
WE TAKE FROM THEM, THEY TAKE FROM US BACK AGAIN!
THREE TIMES OUR HATRED CAUSED ALL-OUT WAR!
THAT'S LIFE.
HOW HAVE YOU LIVED THIS LONG WITHOUT LEARNING FROM THE WOUNDS OF THE PAST?
I'VE LIVED LONGER THAN YOU! I'VE BEEN AROUND THE BLOCK!
IT'S BECAUSE I'VE EXPERIENCED PAIN IN THE PAST THAT I CAN EVEN ***CONSIDER...***
...WHAT WOULD BE BEST FOR THE FUTURE!
YET... THIS IS THE ***FOURTH*** GREAT WAR...
THIS IS WHAT'S BEST?
THIS WAR IS DIFFERENT!
WE'RE ALL FIGHTING THIS BATTLE ***TOGETHER*** IN ORDER TO ACHIEVE...
...SOMETHING ***DIFFERENT*** THAN WHAT WE'VE FOUGHT OVER BEFORE!!
...?

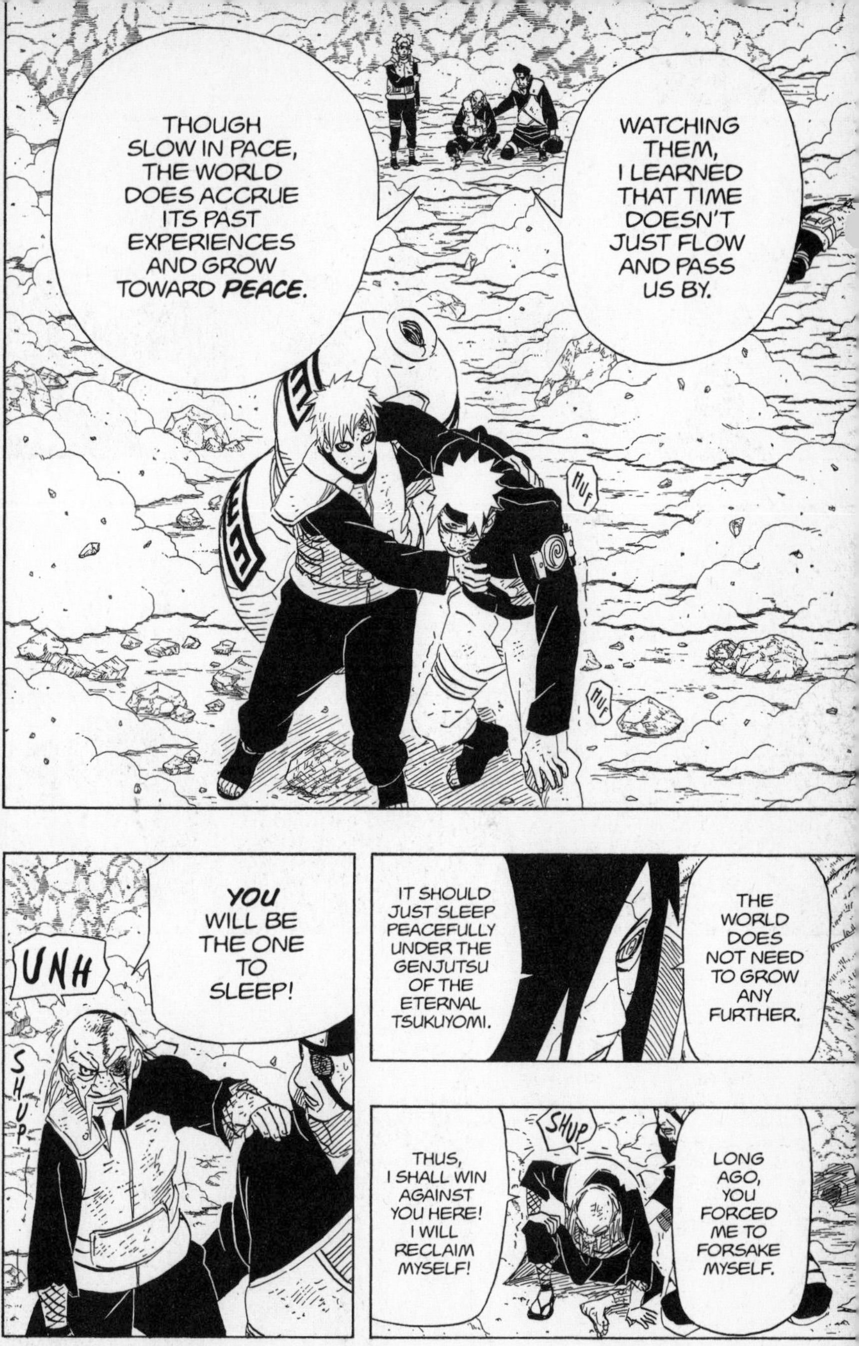
WATCHING THEM, I LEARNED THAT TIME DOESN'T JUST FLOW AND PASS US BY.
THOUGH SLOW IN PACE, THE WORLD DOES ACCRUE ITS PAST EXPERIENCES AND GROW TOWARD PEACE.
HUF
HUF
THE WORLD DOES NOT NEED TO GROW ANY FURTHER.
IT SHOULD JUST SLEEP PEACEFULLY UNDER THE GENJUTSU OF THE ETERNAL TSUKUYOMI.
LONG AGO, YOU FORCED ME TO FORSAKE MYSELF.
SHUP
THUS, I SHALL WIN AGAINST YOU HERE! I WILL RECLAIM MYSELF!
YOU WILL BE THE ONE TO SLEEP!
UNH
SHUP

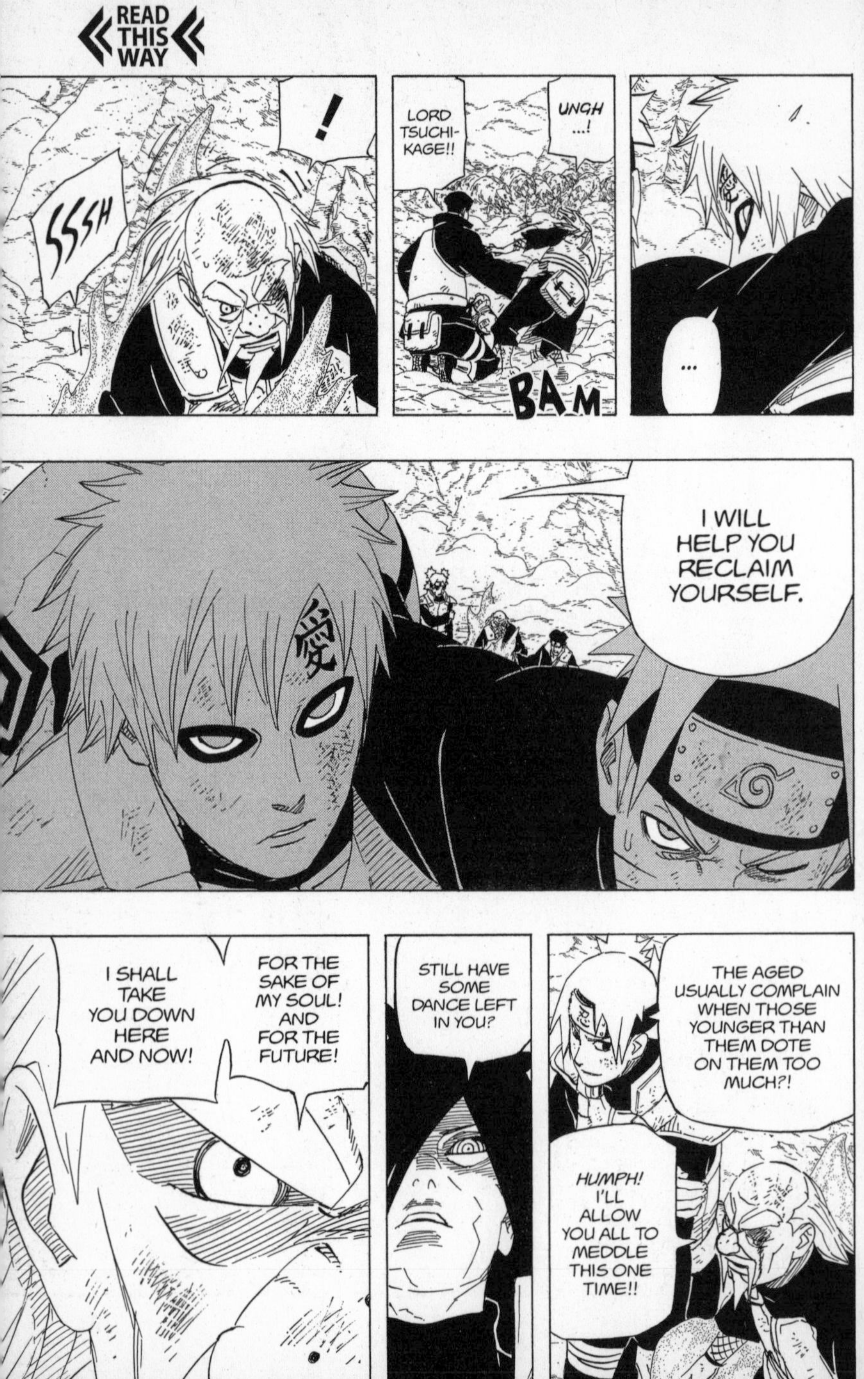
READ THIS WAY
...
UNGH ...!
LORD TSUCHIKAGE!!
BAM
!
SSSH
I WILL HELP YOU RECLAIM YOURSELF.
THE AGED USUALLY COMPLAIN WHEN THOSE YOUNGER THAN THEM DOTE ON THEM TOO MUCH?!
HUMPH! I'LL ALLOW YOU ALL TO MEDDLE THIS ONE TIME!!
STILL HAVE SOME DANCE LEFT IN YOU?
FOR THE SAKE OF MY SOUL! AND FOR THE FUTURE!
I SHALL TAKE YOU DOWN HERE AND NOW!

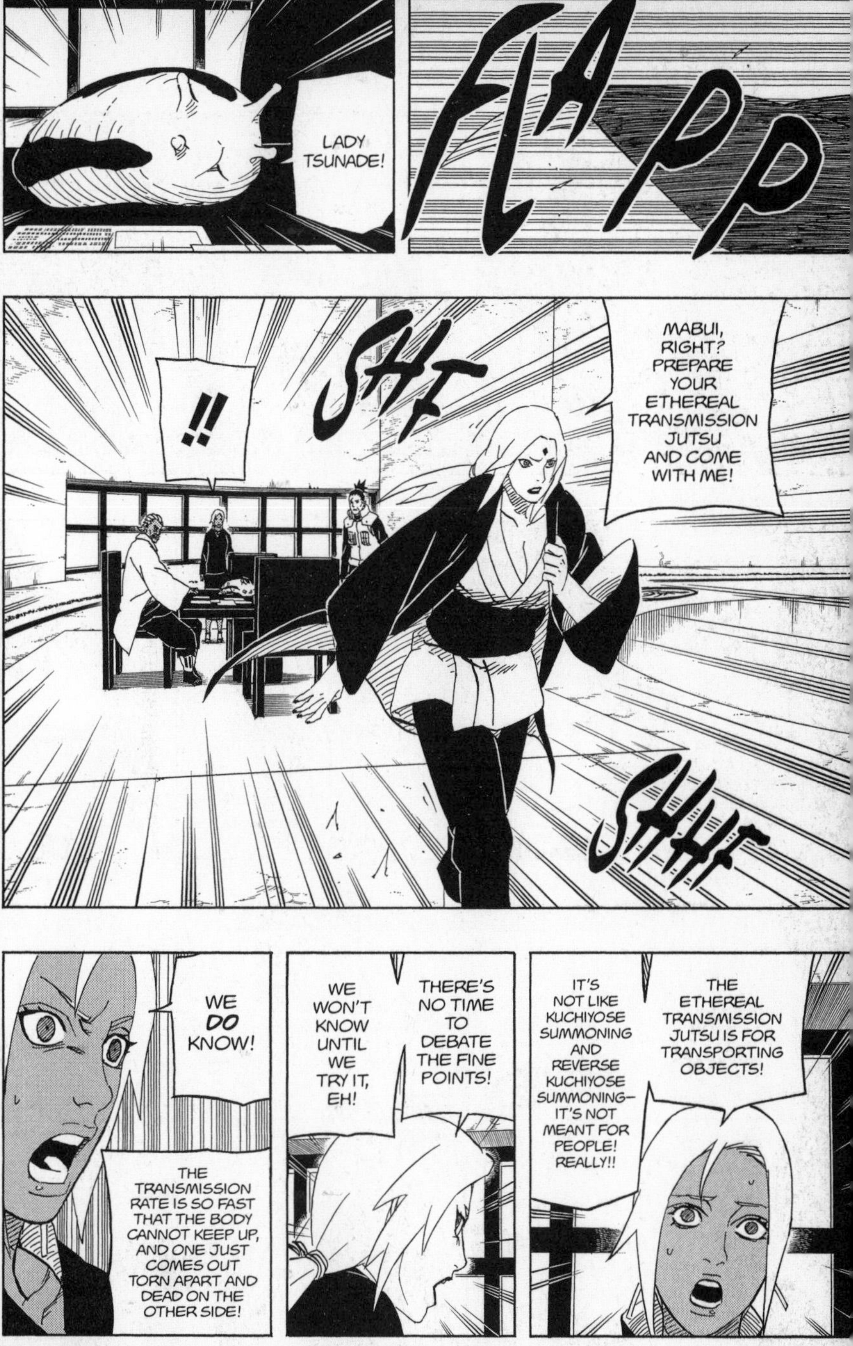
FLAPP
LADY TSUNADE!
MABUI, RIGHT? PREPARE YOUR ETHEREAL TRANSMISSION JUTSU AND COME WITH ME!
SHF
!!
SHHF
THE ETHEREAL TRANSMISSION JUTSU IS FOR TRANSPORTING OBJECTS!
IT'S NOT LIKE KUCHIYOSE SUMMONING AND REVERSE KUCHIYOSE SUMMONING— IT'S NOT MEANT FOR PEOPLE! REALLY!!
THERE'S NO TIME TO DEBATE THE FINE POINTS!
WE WON'T KNOW UNTIL WE TRY IT, EH!
WE **DO** KNOW!
THE TRANSMISSION RATE IS SO FAST THAT THE BODY CANNOT KEEP UP, AND ONE JUST COMES OUT TORN APART AND DEAD ON THE OTHER SIDE!

READ THIS WAY

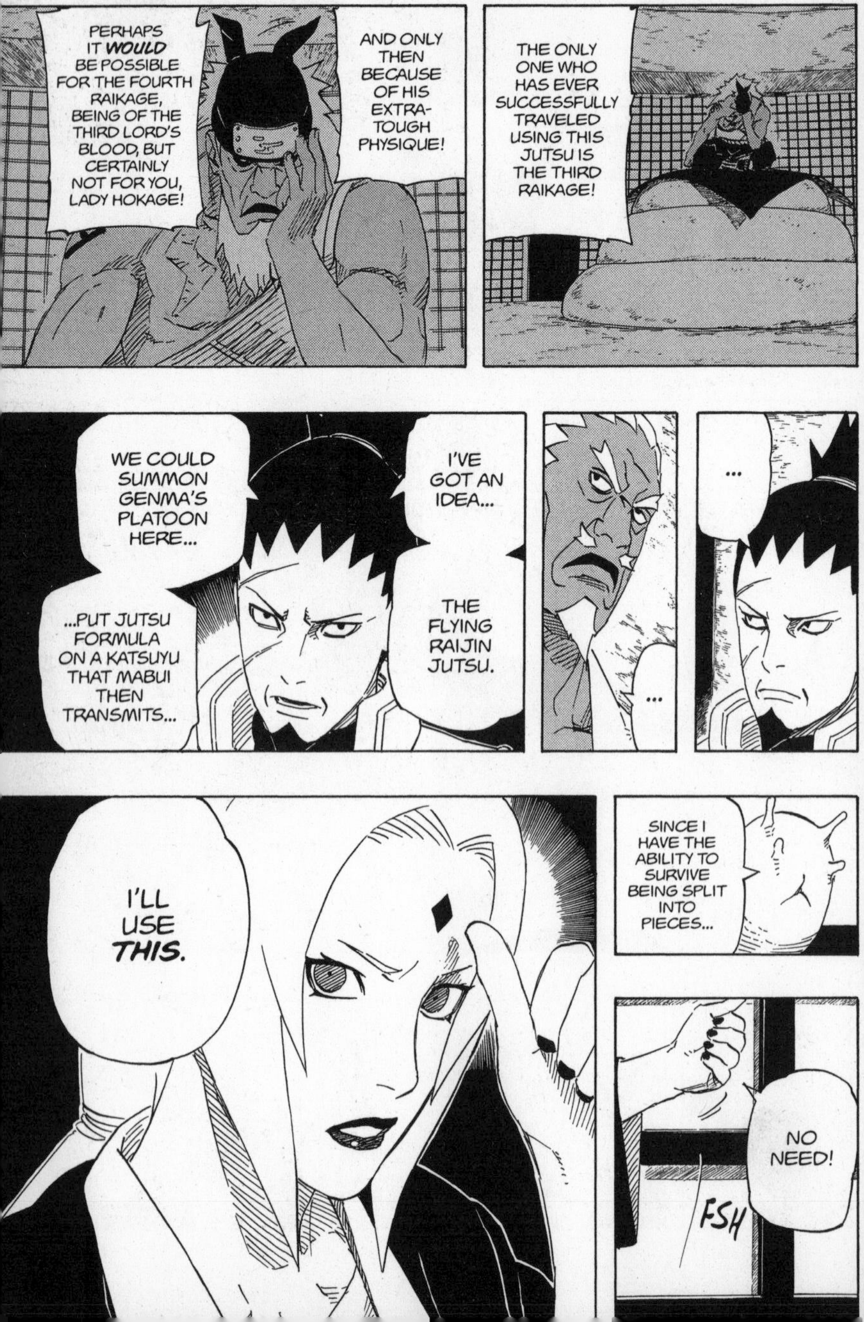
THE ONLY ONE WHO HAS EVER SUCCESSFULLY TRAVELED USING THIS JUTSU IS THE THIRD RAIKAGE!
AND ONLY THEN BECAUSE OF HIS EXTRA-TOUGH PHYSIQUE!
PERHAPS IT *WOULD* BE POSSIBLE FOR THE FOURTH RAIKAGE, BEING OF THE THIRD LORD'S BLOOD, BUT CERTAINLY NOT FOR YOU, LADY HOKAGE!
...
...
I'VE GOT AN IDEA...
WE COULD SUMMON GENMA'S PLATOON HERE...
THE FLYING RAIJIN JUTSU.
...PUT JUTSU FORMULA ON A KATSUYU THAT MABUI THEN TRANSMITS...
SINCE I HAVE THE ABILITY TO SURVIVE BEING SPLIT INTO PIECES...
NO NEED!
FSH
I'LL USE *THIS*.

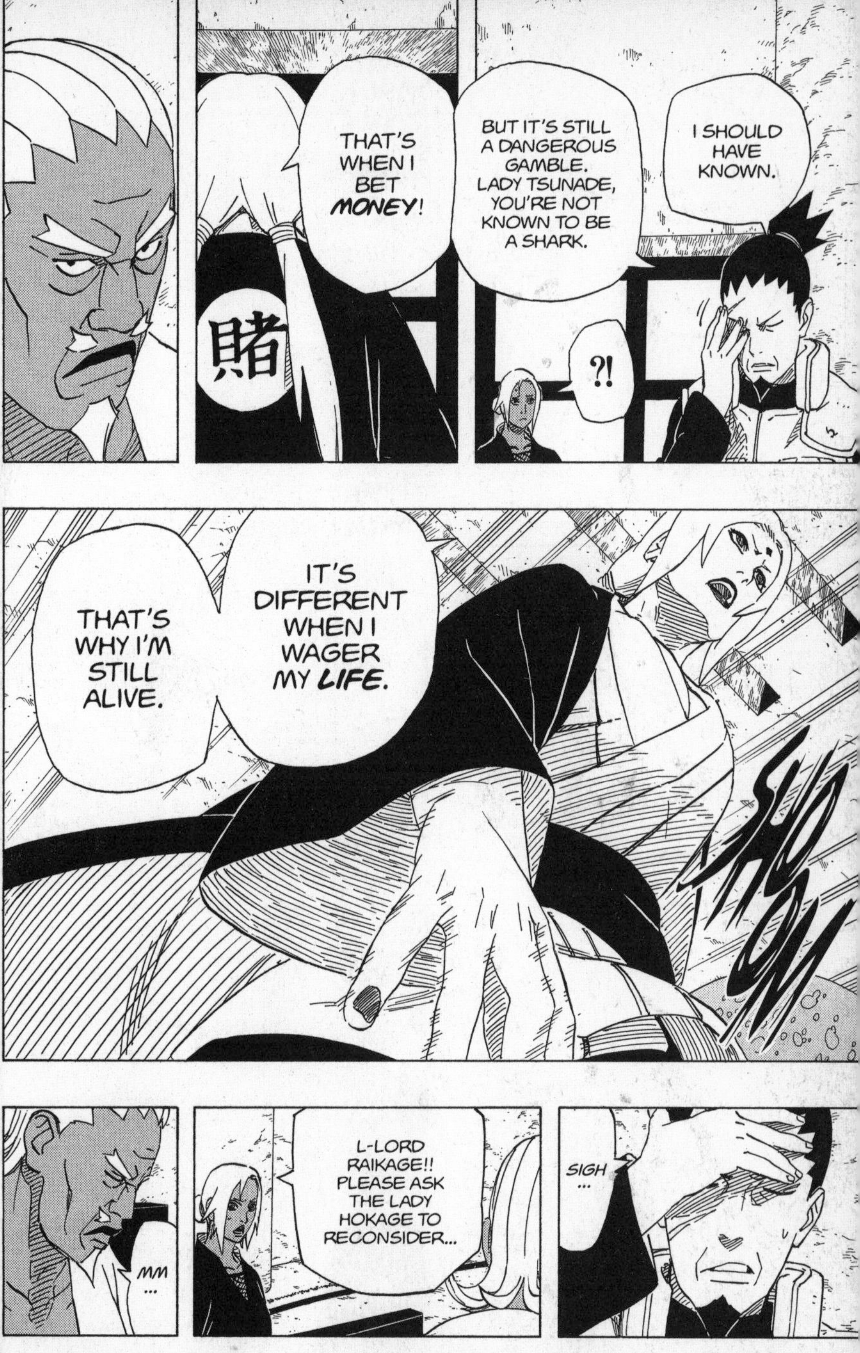
I SHOULD HAVE KNOWN.
BUT IT'S STILL A DANGEROUS GAMBLE. LADY TSUNADE, YOU'RE NOT KNOWN TO BE A SHARK.
?!
THAT'S WHEN I BET MONEY!
賭
IT'S DIFFERENT WHEN I WAGER MY LIFE.
THAT'S WHY I'M STILL ALIVE.
SIGH...
L-LORD RAIKAGE!! PLEASE ASK THE LADY HOKAGE TO RECONSIDER...
MM...

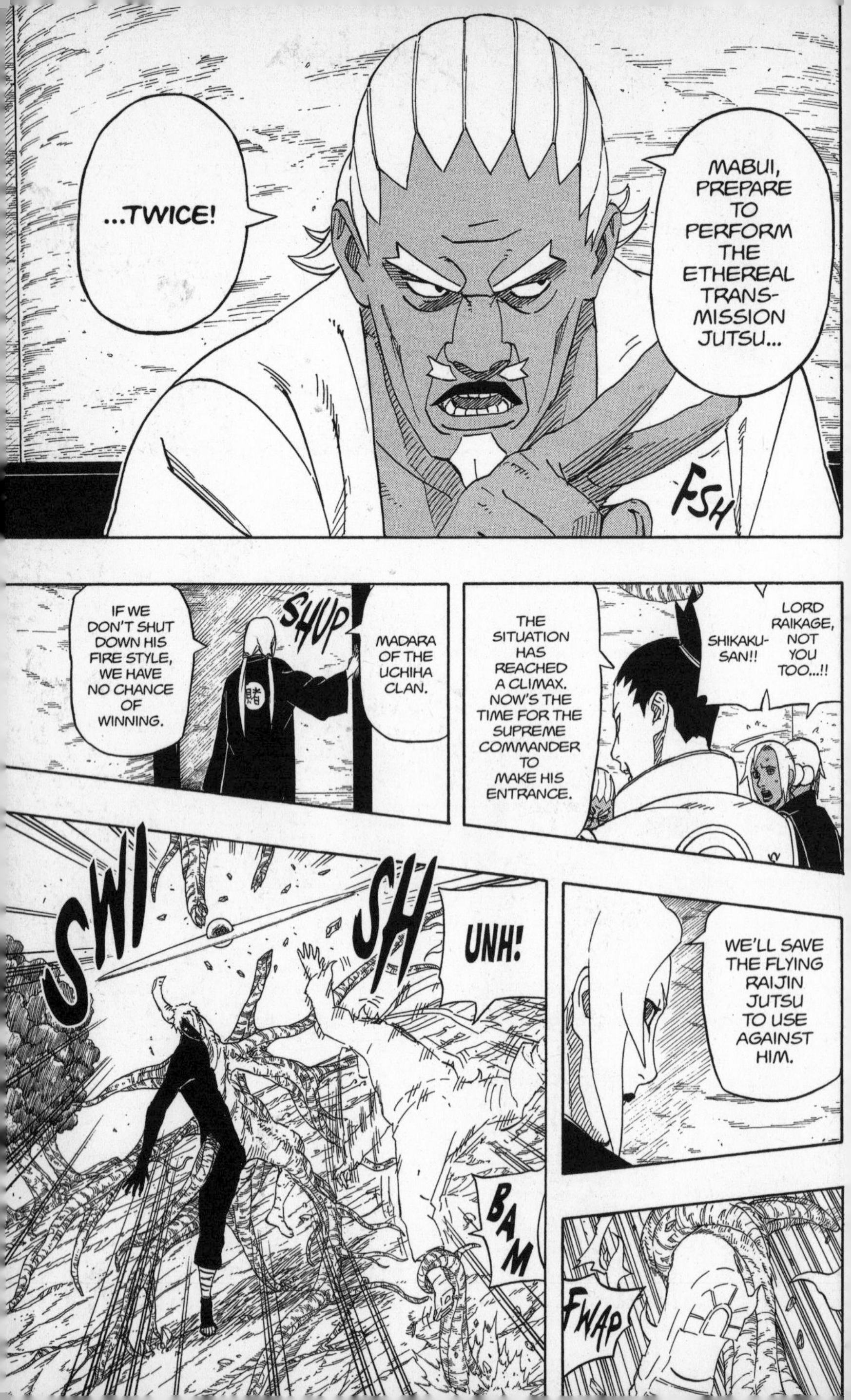

MABUI, PREPARE TO PERFORM THE ETHEREAL TRANSMISSION JUTSU...
...TWICE!
FSH
LORD RAIKAGE, NOT YOU TOO...!!
SHIKAKU-SAN!!
THE SITUATION HAS REACHED A CLIMAX. NOW'S THE TIME FOR THE SUPREME COMMANDER TO MAKE HIS ENTRANCE.
MADARA OF THE UCHIHA CLAN.
SHUP
IF WE DON'T SHUT DOWN HIS FIRE STYLE, WE HAVE NO CHANCE OF WINNING.
WE'LL SAVE THE FLYING RAIJIN JUTSU TO USE AGAINST HIM.
FWAP
UNH!
SH
SWI
BAM

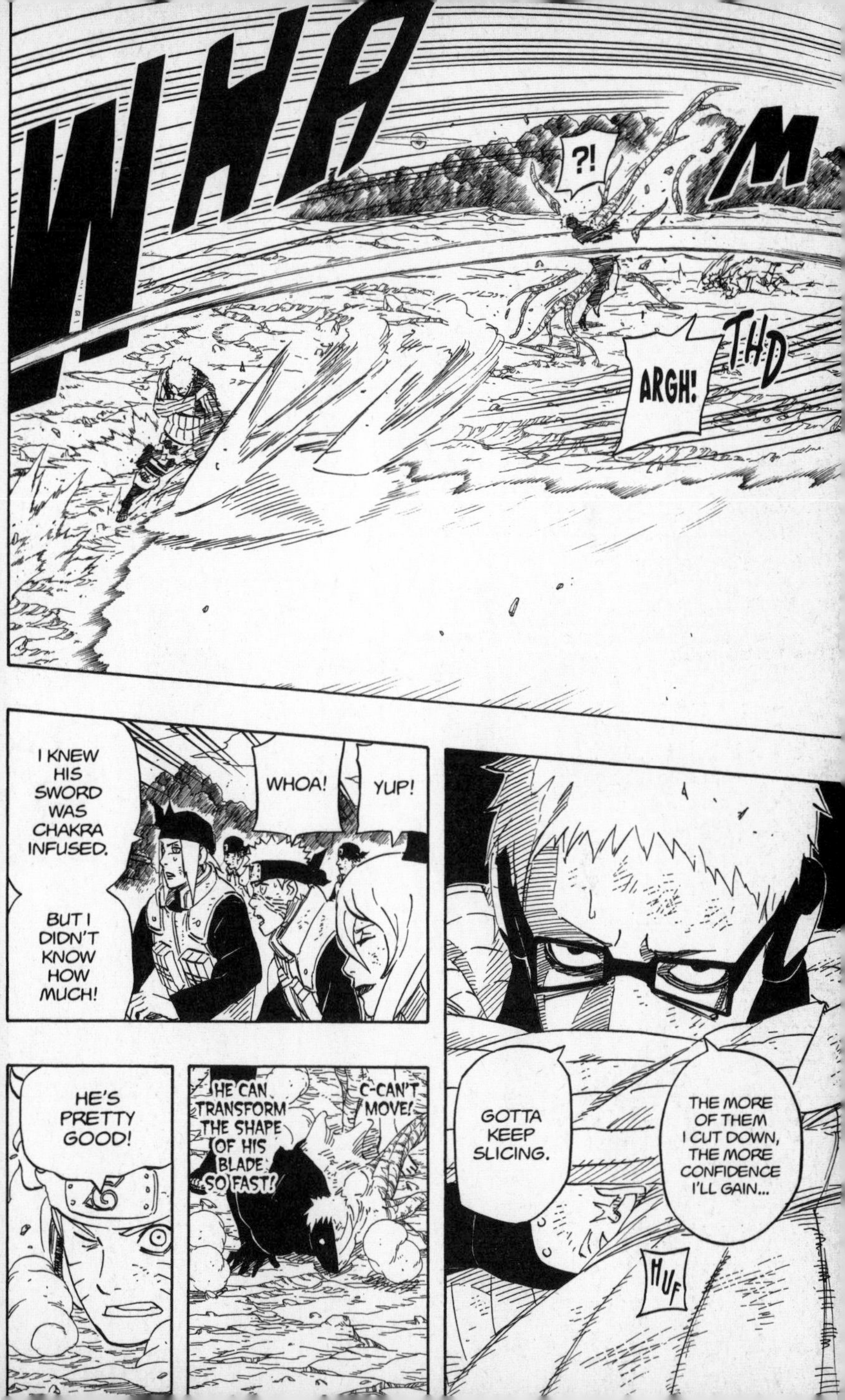
?!
M
ARGH!
THD
WHAB
THE MORE OF THEM I CUT DOWN, THE MORE CONFIDENCE I'LL GAIN...
GOTTA KEEP SLICING.
HUF
YUP!
WHOA!
I KNEW HIS SWORD WAS CHAKRA INFUSED.
BUT I DIDN'T KNOW HOW MUCH!
C-CAN'T MOVE!
HE CAN TRANSFORM THE SHAPE OF HIS BLADE SO FAST!
HE'S PRETTY GOOD!

READ THIS WAY

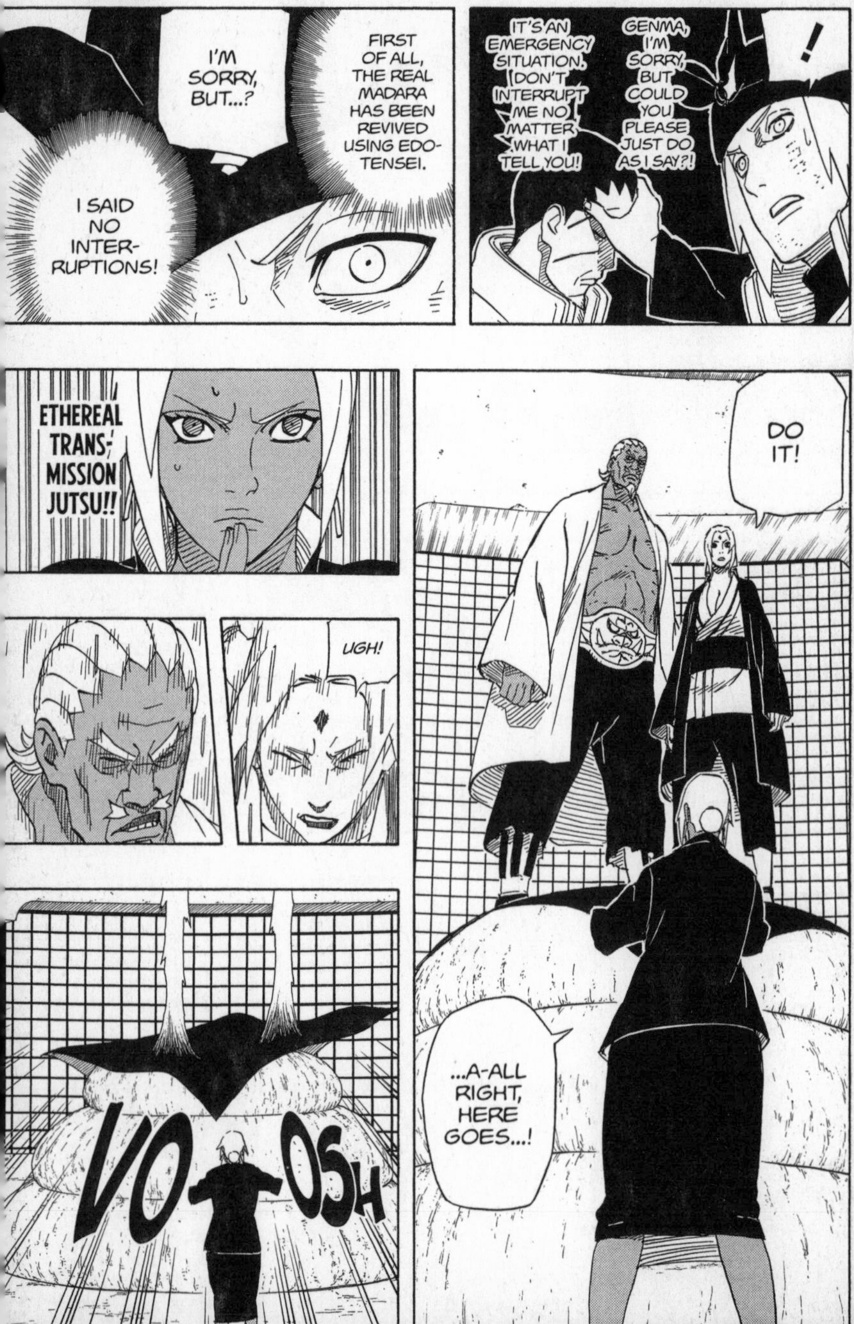
!
GENMA, I'M SORRY, BUT COULD YOU PLEASE JUST DO AS I SAY?!
IT'S AN EMERGENCY SITUATION. DON'T INTERRUPT ME NO MATTER WHAT I TELL YOU!
FIRST OF ALL, THE REAL MADARA HAS BEEN REVIVED USING EDO-TENSEI.
I'M SORRY, BUT...?
I SAID NO INTER-RUPTIONS!
DO IT!
...A-ALL RIGHT, HERE GOES...!
ETHEREAL TRANS-MISSION JUTSU!!
UGH!
VOOSH

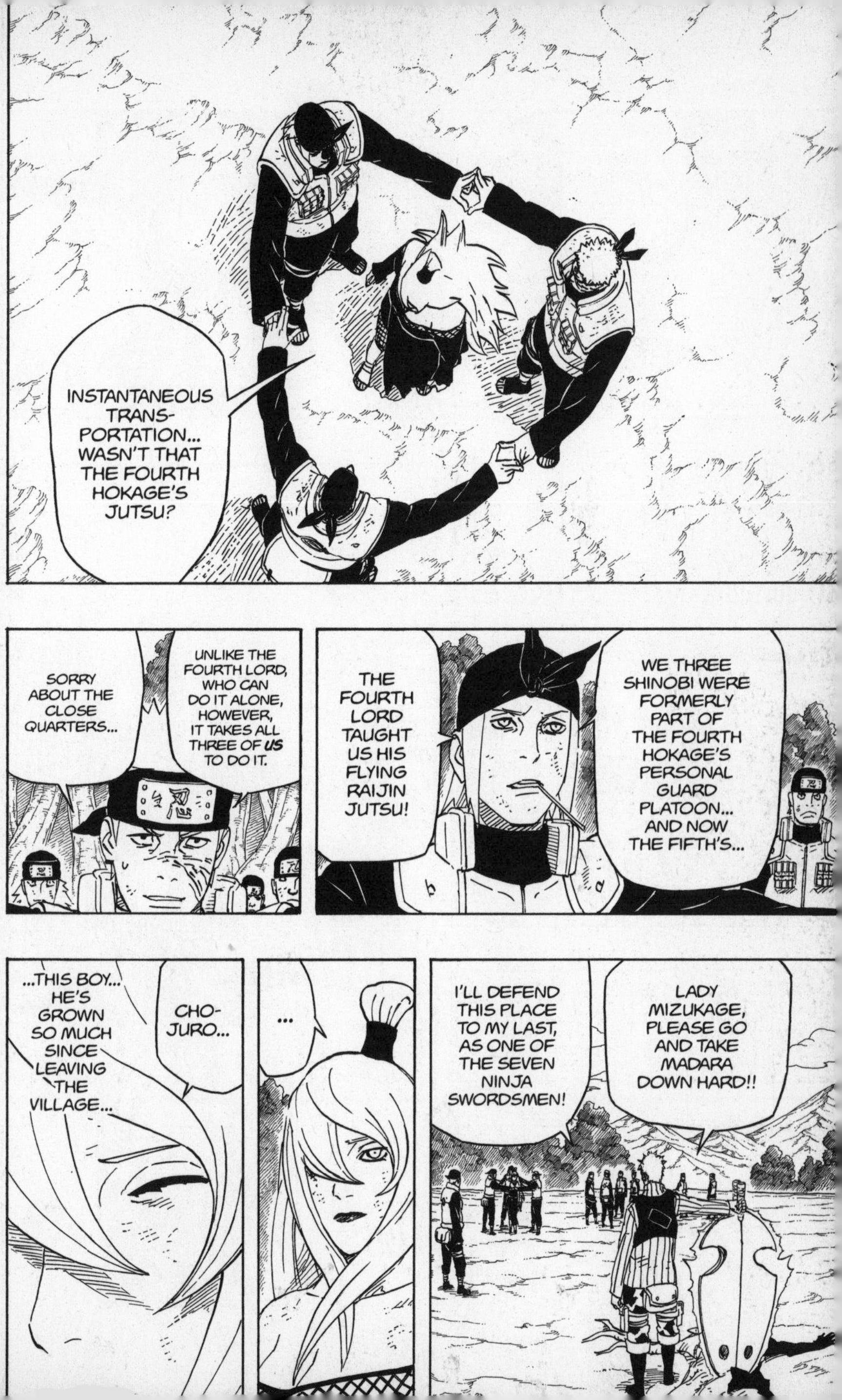
INSTANTANEOUS TRANS-PORTATION... WASN'T THAT THE FOURTH HOKAGE'S JUTSU?
WE THREE SHINOBI WERE FORMERLY PART OF THE FOURTH HOKAGE'S PERSONAL GUARD PLATOON... AND NOW THE FIFTH'S...
THE FOURTH LORD TAUGHT US HIS FLYING RAIJIN JUTSU!
UNLIKE THE FOURTH LORD, WHO CAN DO IT ALONE, HOWEVER, IT TAKES ALL THREE OF *US* TO DO IT.
SORRY ABOUT THE CLOSE QUARTERS...
LADY MIZUKAGE, PLEASE GO AND TAKE MADARA DOWN HARD!!
I'LL DEFEND THIS PLACE TO MY LAST, AS ONE OF THE SEVEN NINJA SWORDSMEN!
...
CHO-JURO...
...THIS BOY... HE'S GROWN SO MUCH SINCE LEAVING THE VILLAGE...

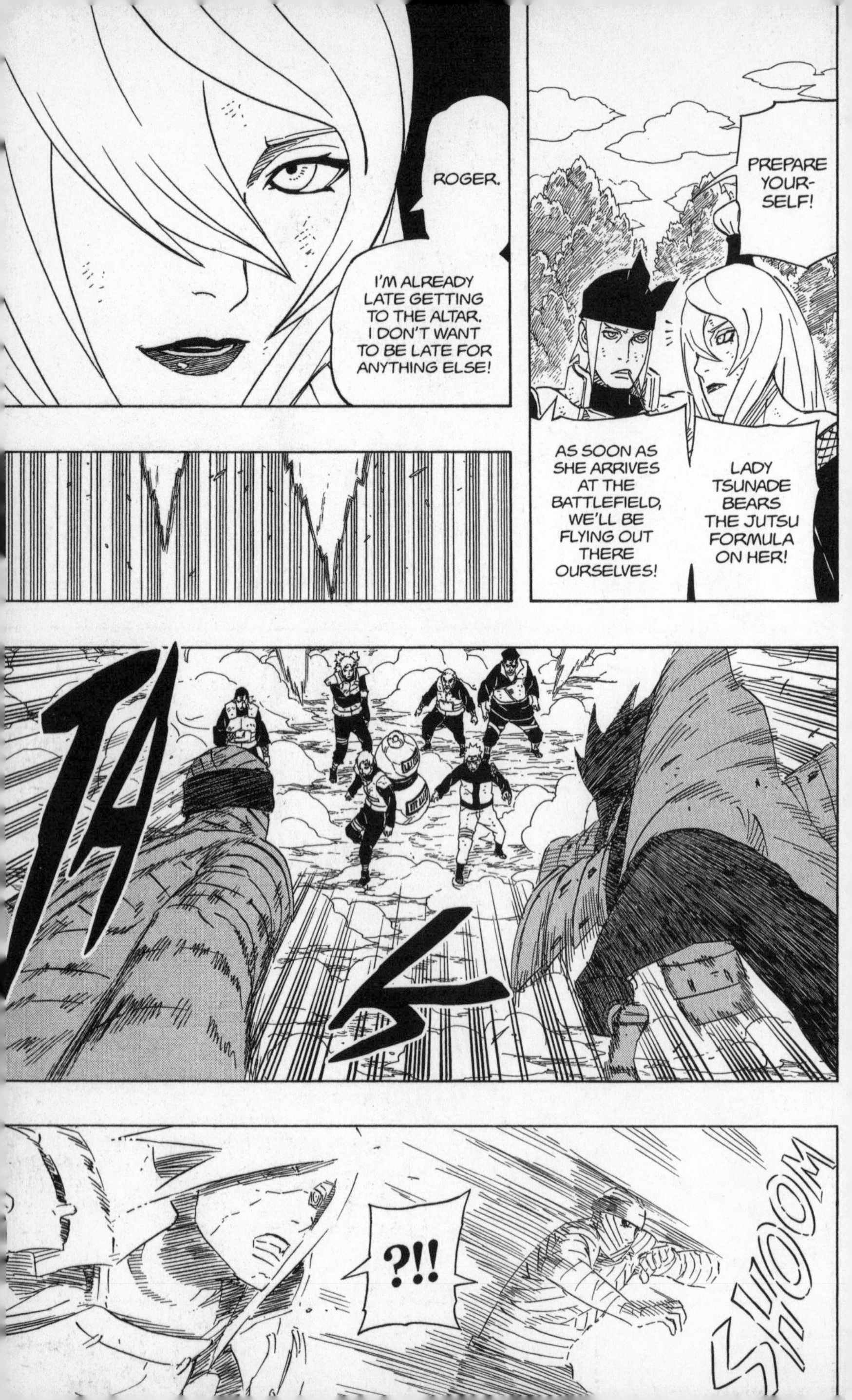
PREPARE YOURSELF!
LADY TSUNADE BEARS THE JUTSU FORMULA ON HER!
AS SOON AS SHE ARRIVES AT THE BATTLEFIELD, WE'LL BE FLYING OUT THERE OURSELVES!
ROGER.
I'M ALREADY LATE GETTING TO THE ALTAR. I DON'T WANT TO BE LATE FOR ANYTHING ELSE!
ZA
SHOOM
?!!

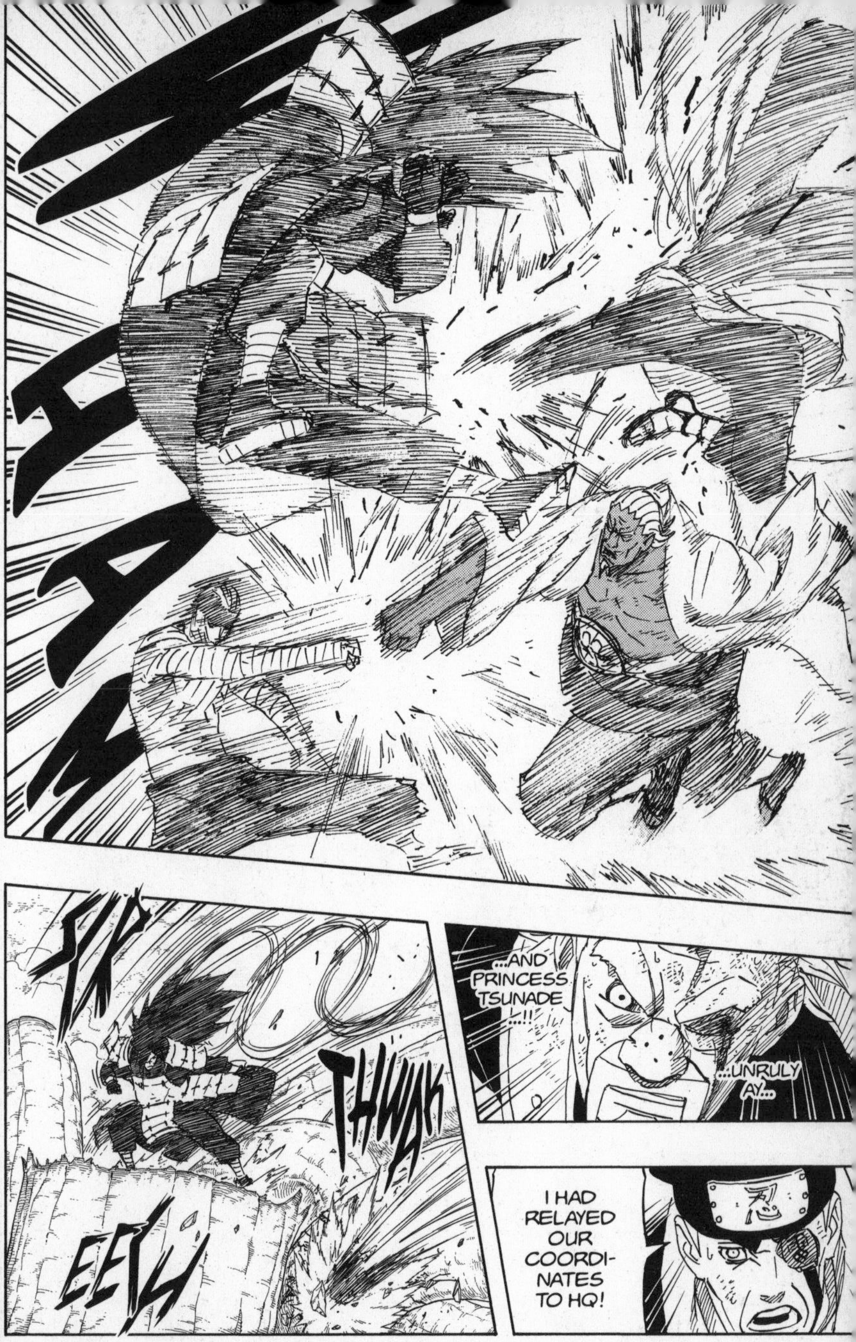
WHAM
...AND PRINCESS TSUNADE...!!
...UNRULY AY...
I HAD RELAYED OUR COORDINATES TO HQ!
THWAK

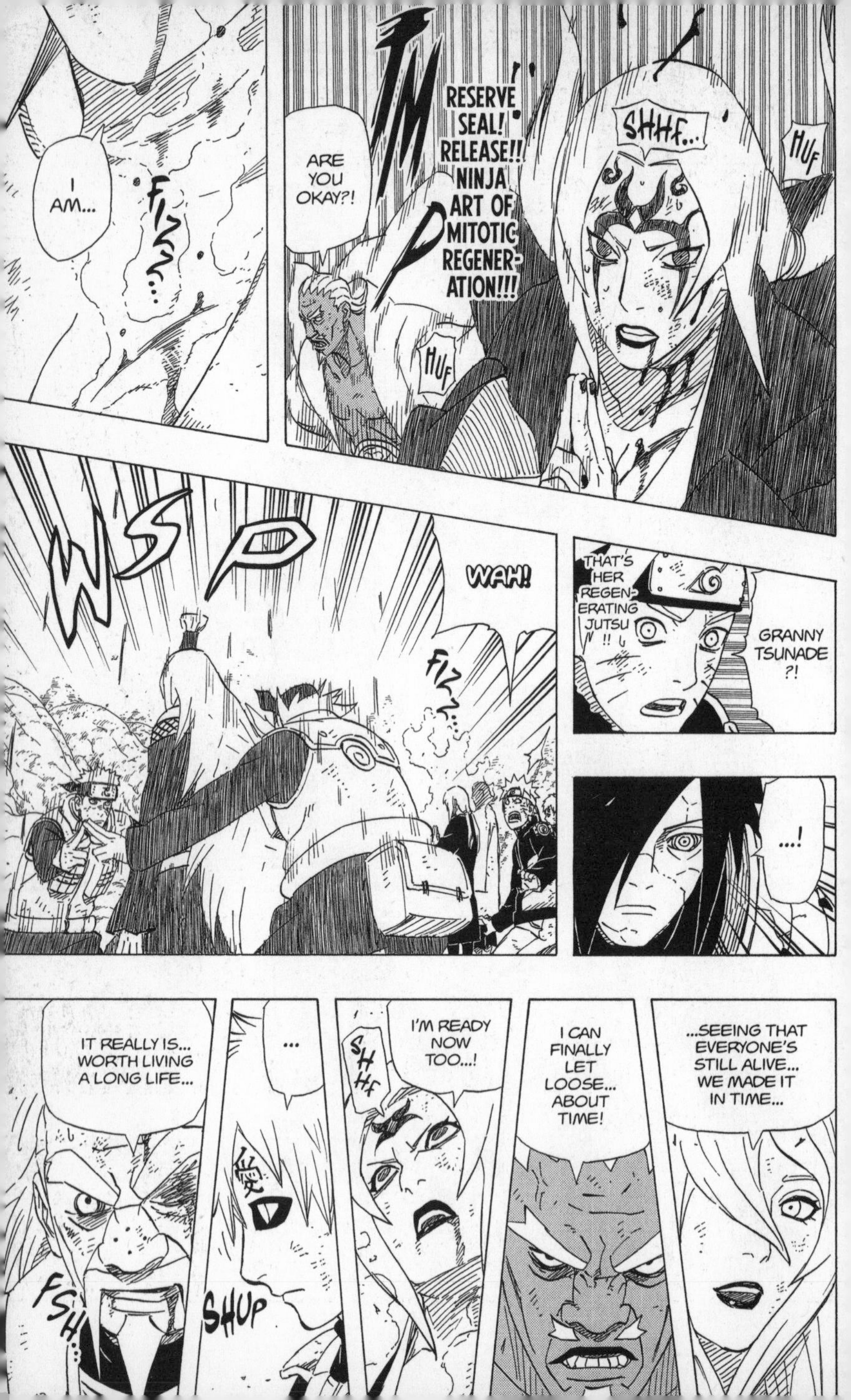
HUF
SHHF...
RESERVE SEAL! RELEASE!! NINJA ART OF MITOTIC REGENERATION!!!
ARE YOU OKAY?!
HUF
I AM...
FIZZZ...
GRANNY TSUNADE?!
THAT'S HER REGENERATING JUTSU!!
...!
WAH!
FIZZZ...
WSP
...SEEING THAT EVERYONE'S STILL ALIVE... WE MADE IT IN TIME...
I CAN FINALLY LET LOOSE... ABOUT TIME!
I'M READY NOW TOO...!
SHHF
...
SHUP
IT REALLY IS... WORTH LIVING A LONG LIFE...
FSH

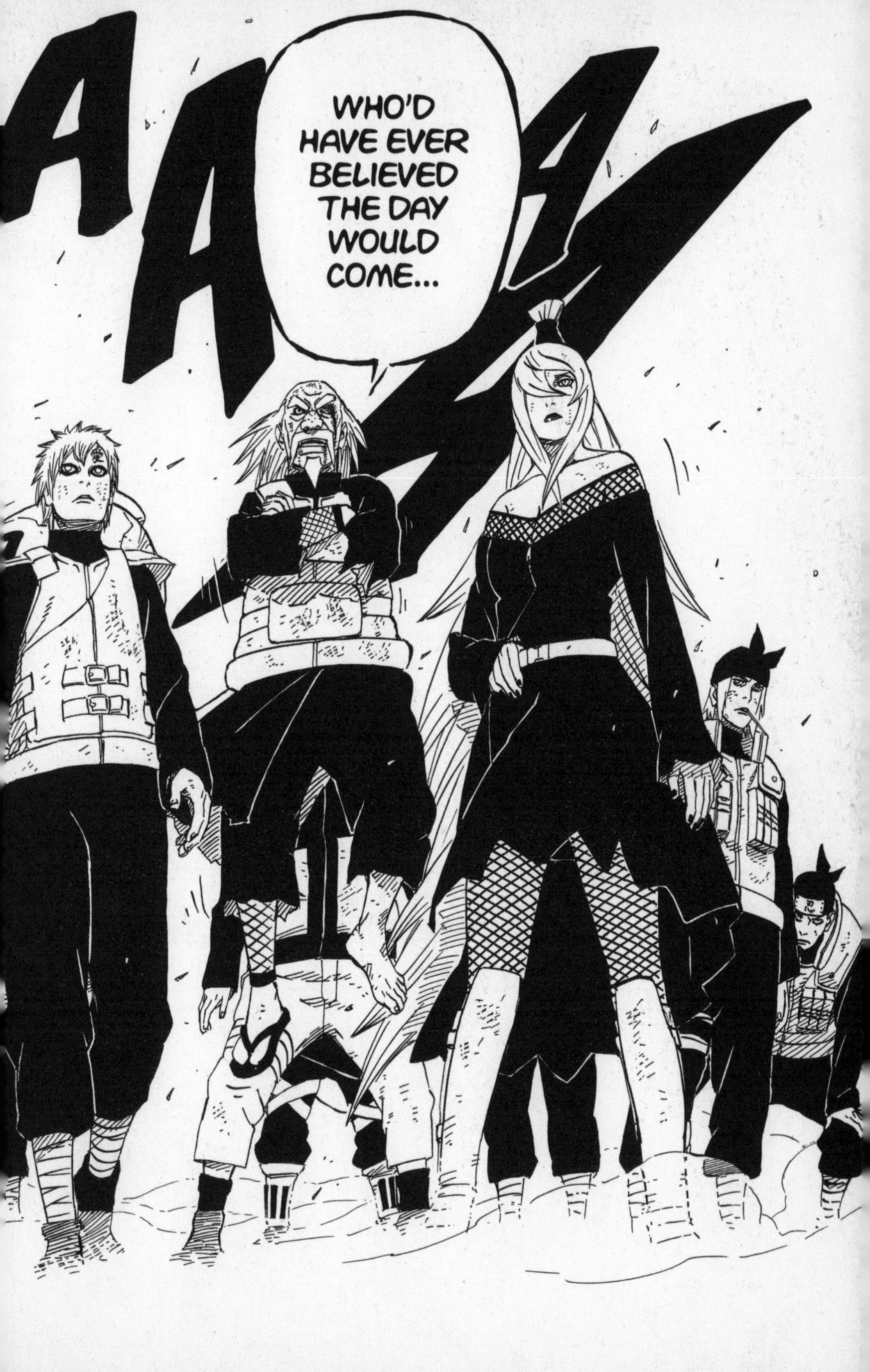
AAAA
WHO'D HAVE EVER BELIEVED THE DAY WOULD COME...

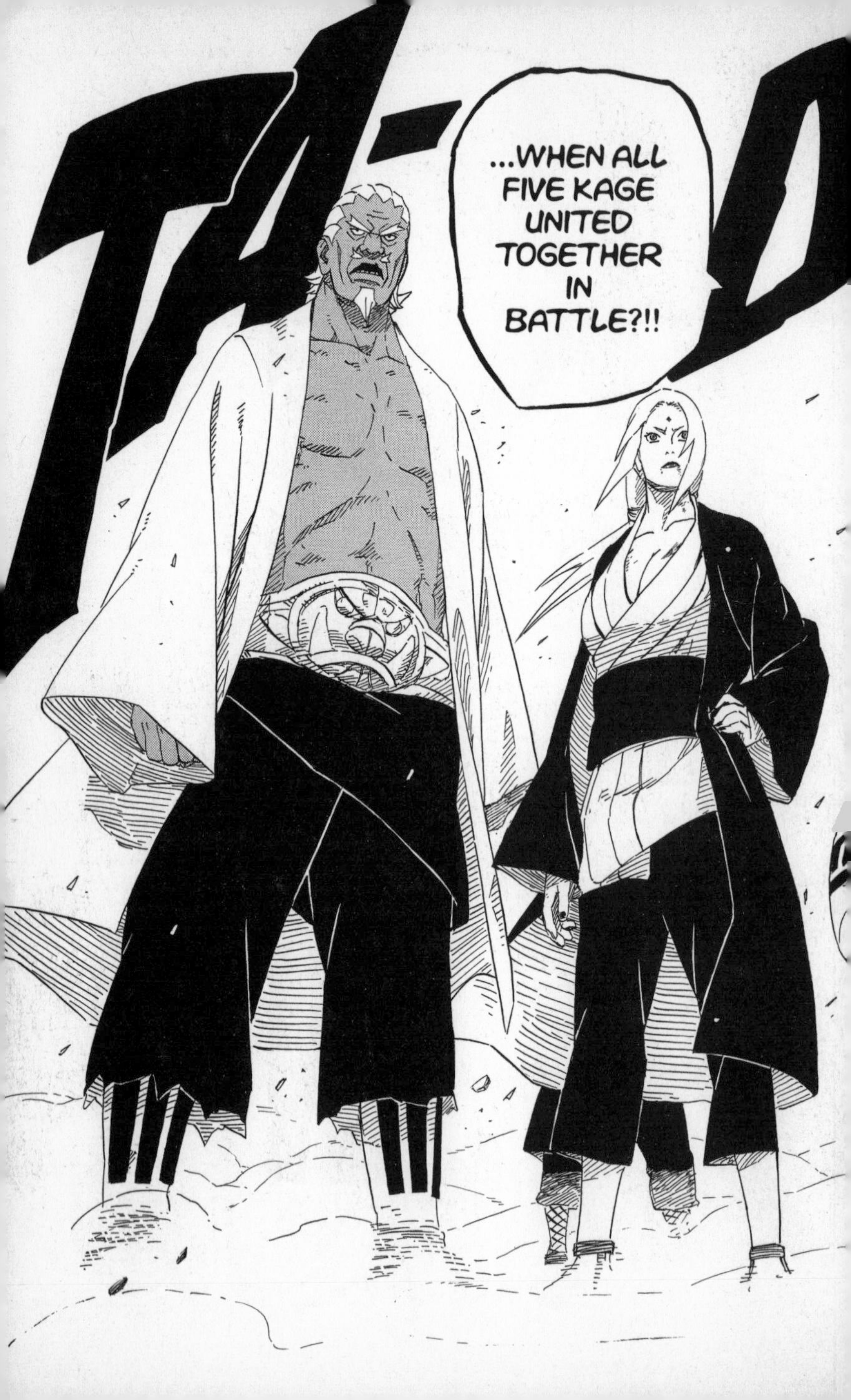
TA-D
...WHEN ALL FIVE KAGE UNITED TOGETHER IN BATTLE?!!

NARUTO

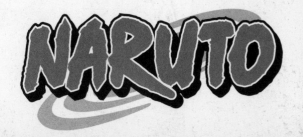

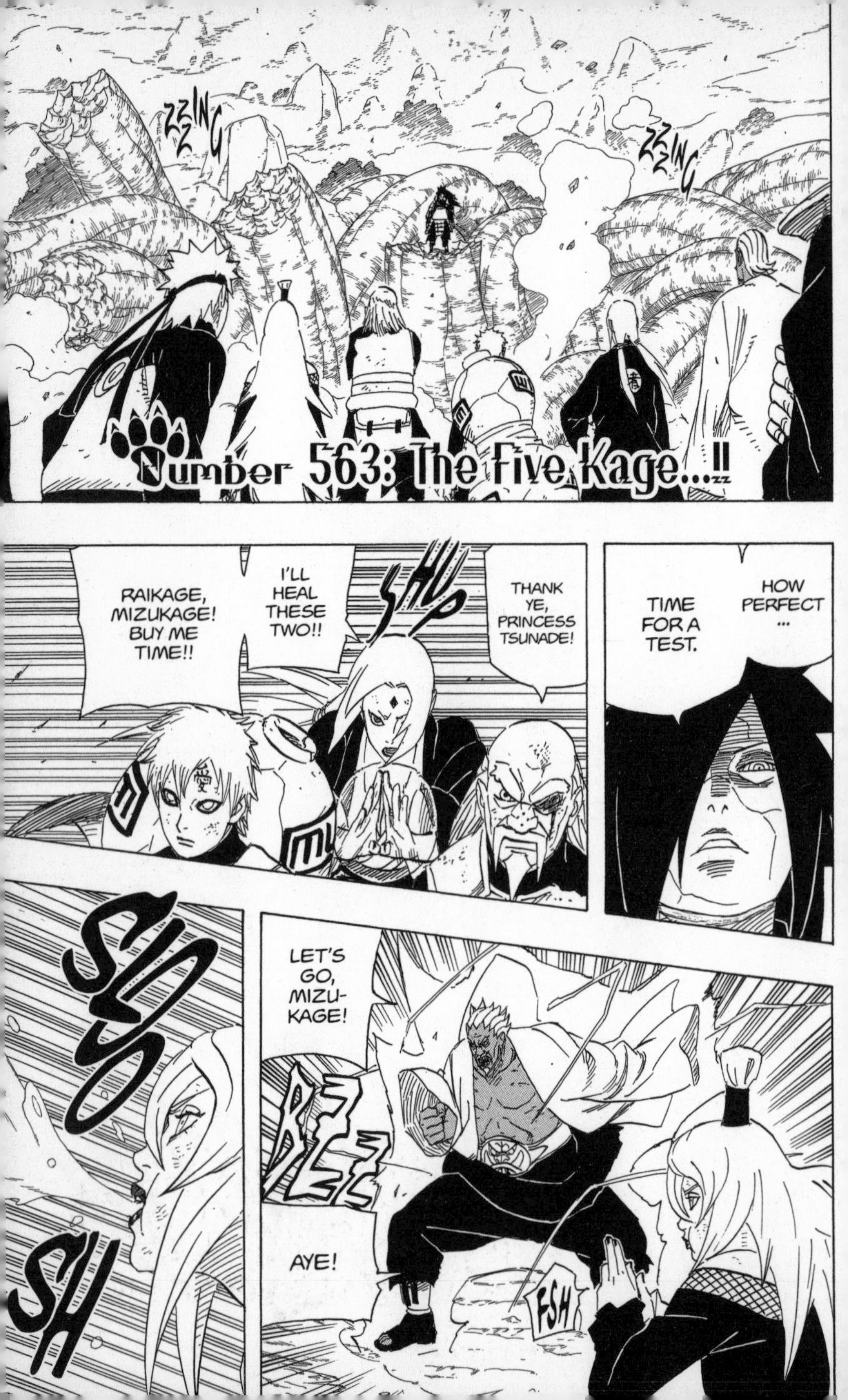
ZZZING
ZZZING
Number 563: The Five Kage...!!
HOW PERFECT ...
TIME FOR A TEST.
THANK YE, PRINCESS TSUNADE!
I'LL HEAL THESE TWO!!
RAIKAGE, MIZUKAGE! BUY ME TIME!!
LET'S GO, MIZUKAGE!
AYE!
FSH
SH

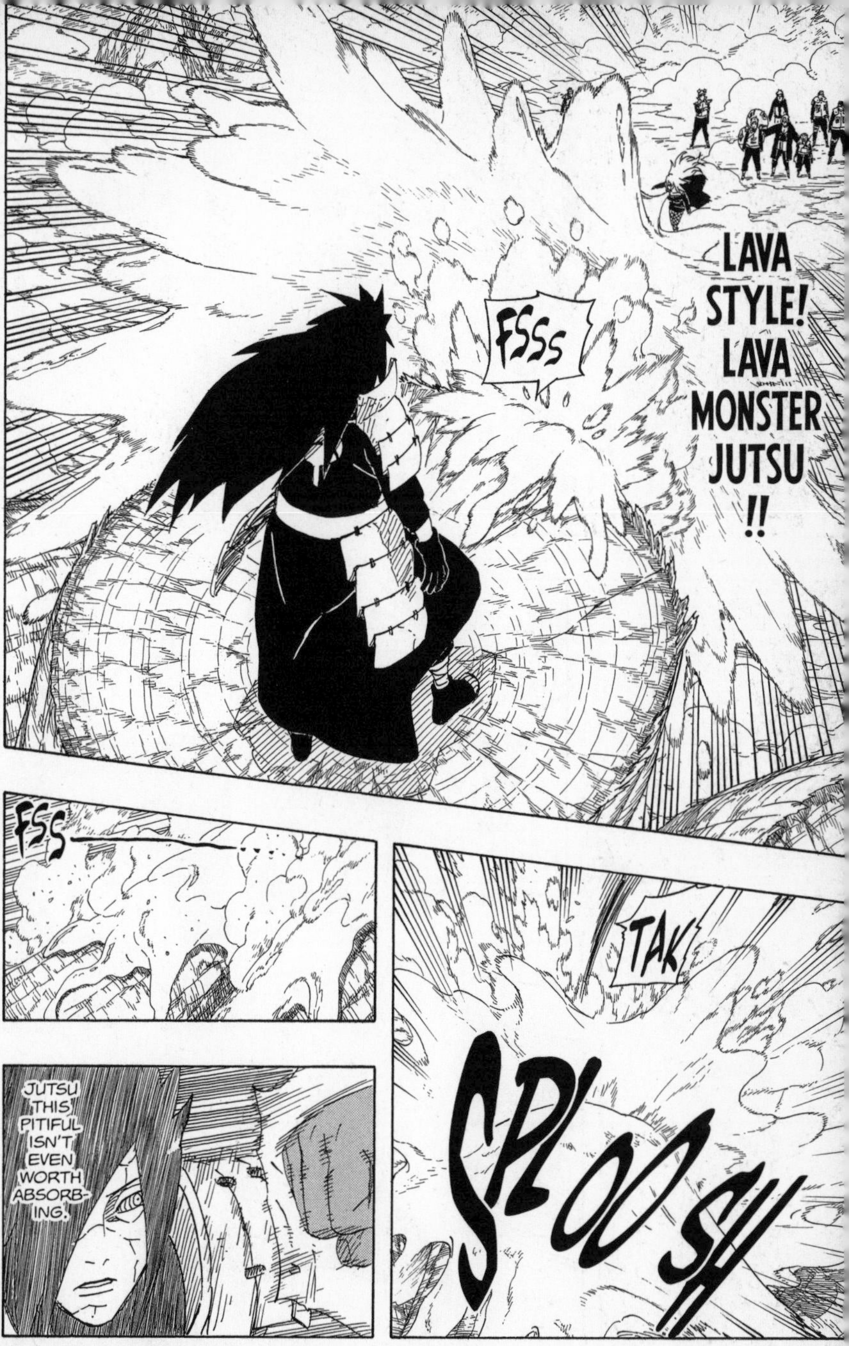
LAVA STYLE! LAVA MONSTER JUTSU!!
FSSS
TAK
SPLOOSH
FSS
JUTSU THIS PITIFUL ISN'T EVEN WORTH ABSORB-ING.

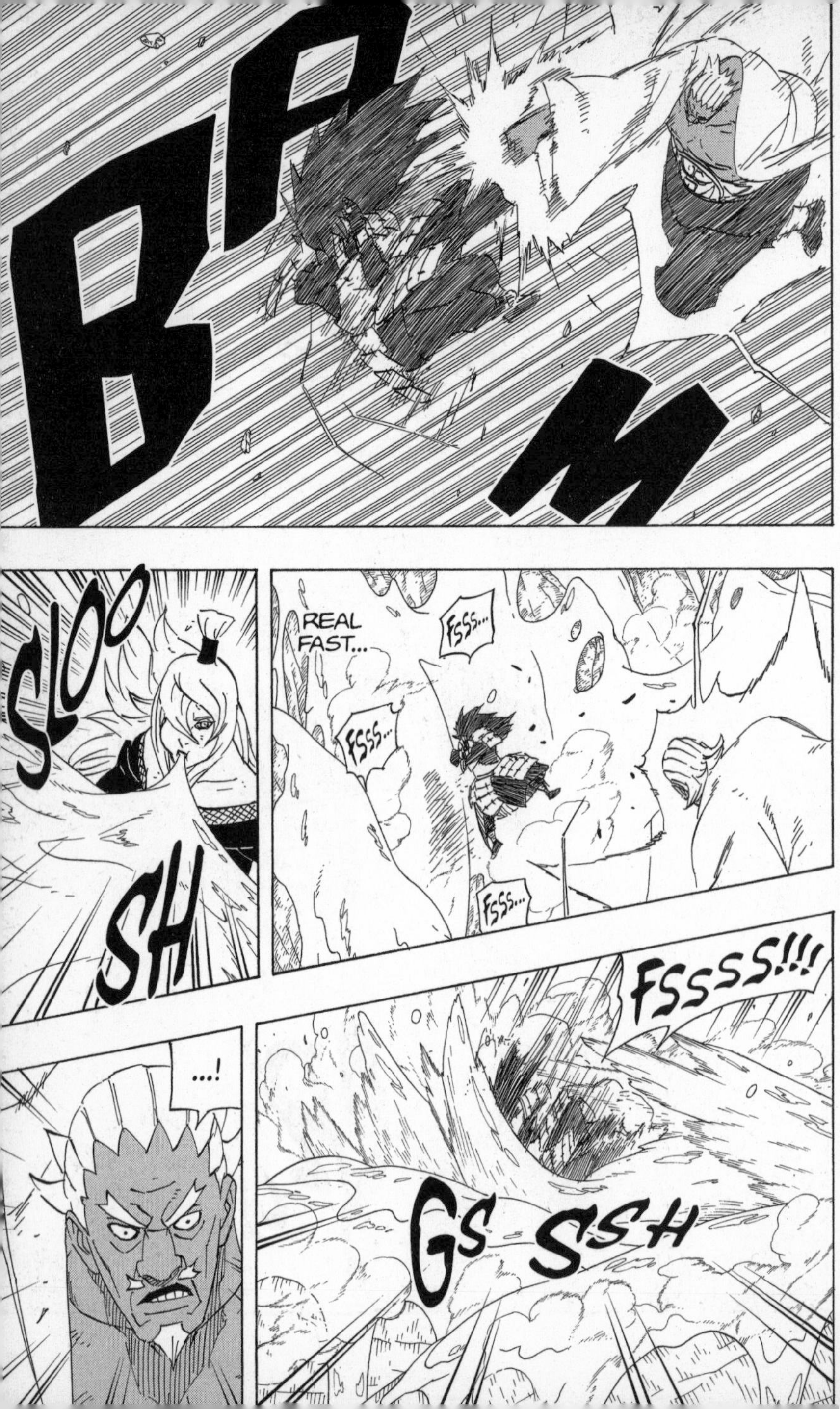
BOOM
FSSS...
REAL FAST...
FSSS...
FSSS...
SLOOSH
FSSSS!!!
GSSSH
...!

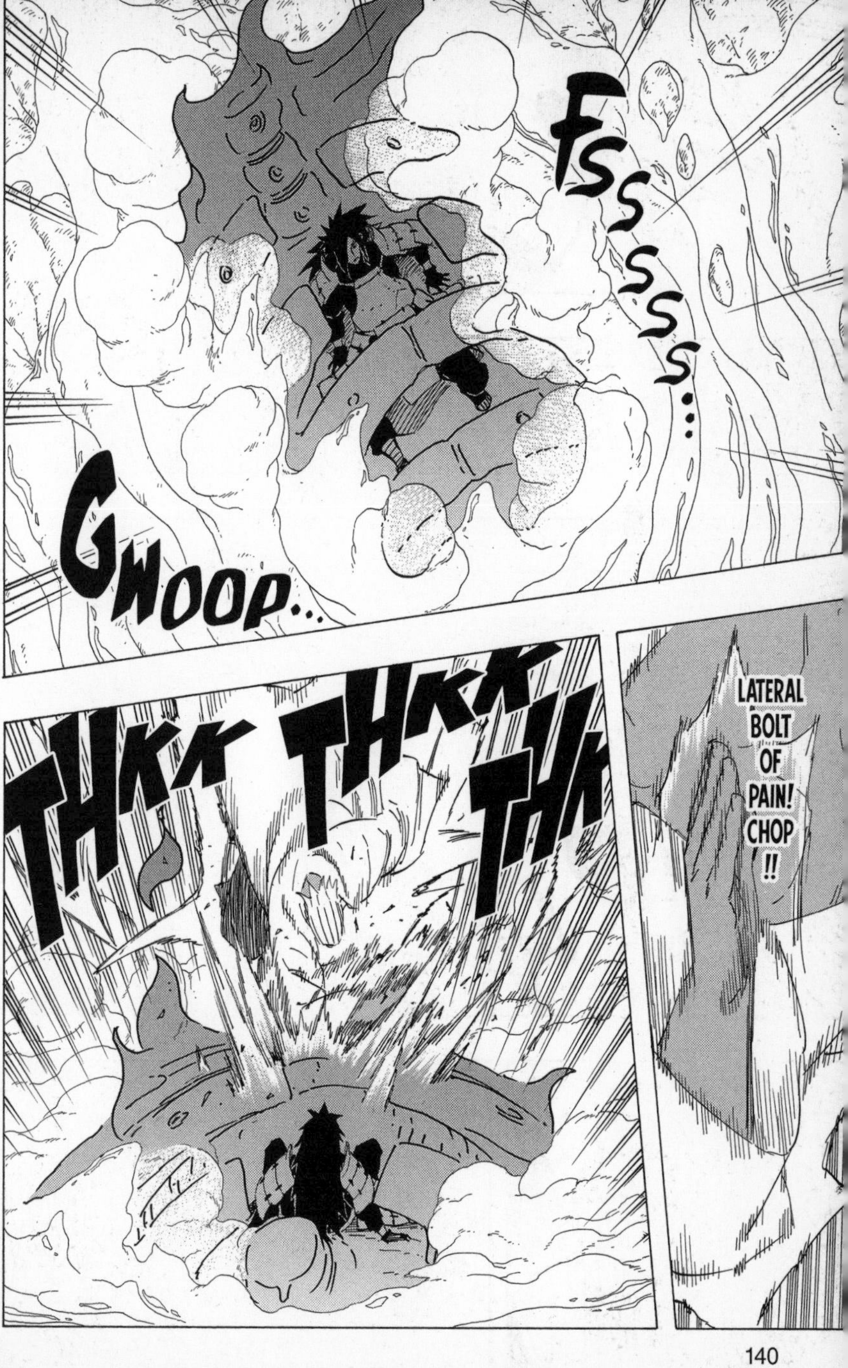
FSSSSSS...
GWOOP...
LATERAL BOLT OF PAIN! CHOP!!
THKK THKK THK

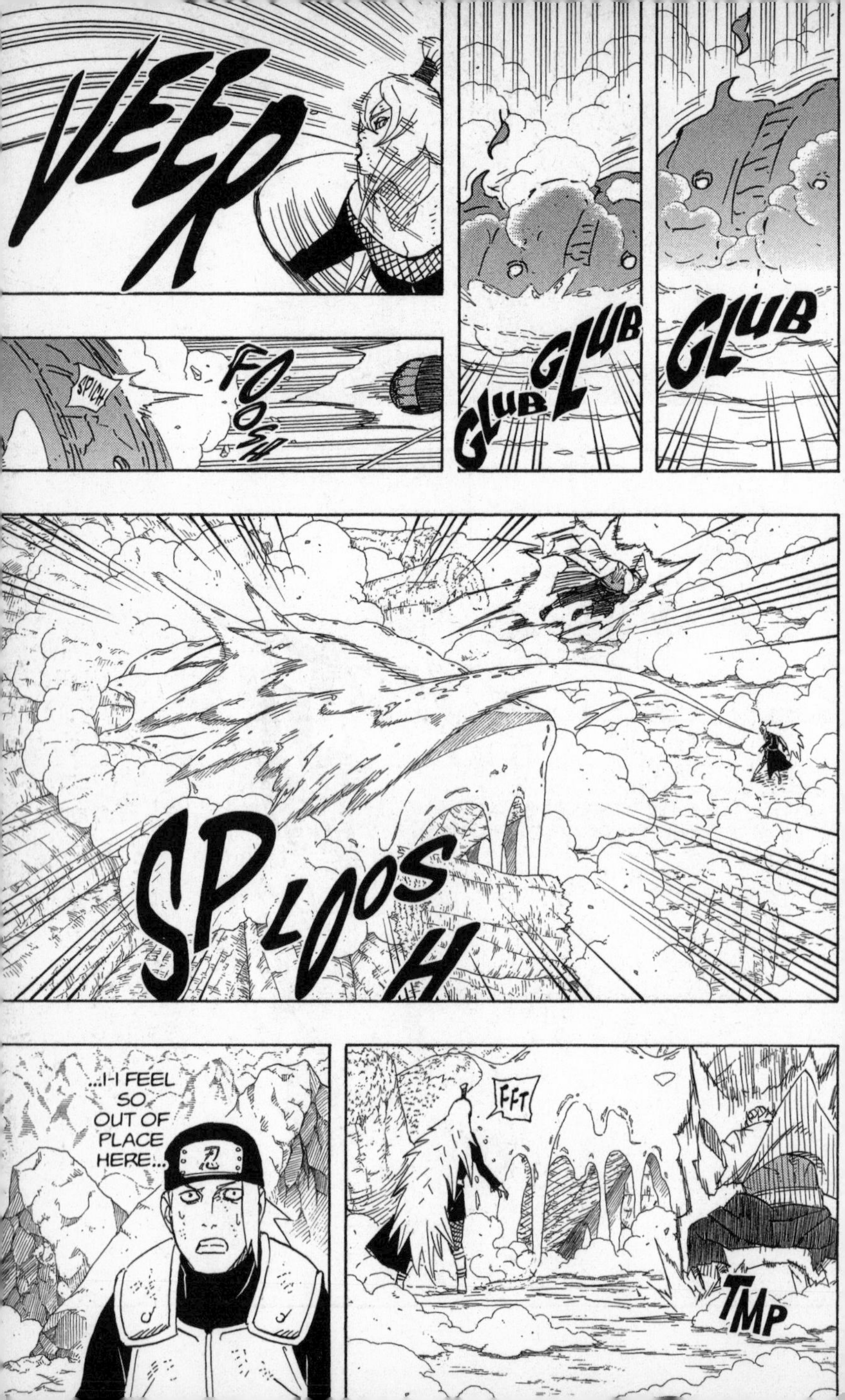
GLUB
GLUB GLUB
VEEP
SPICH
FOOSH
SPLOOSH
FFT
TMP
...I-I FEEL SO OUT OF PLACE HERE...

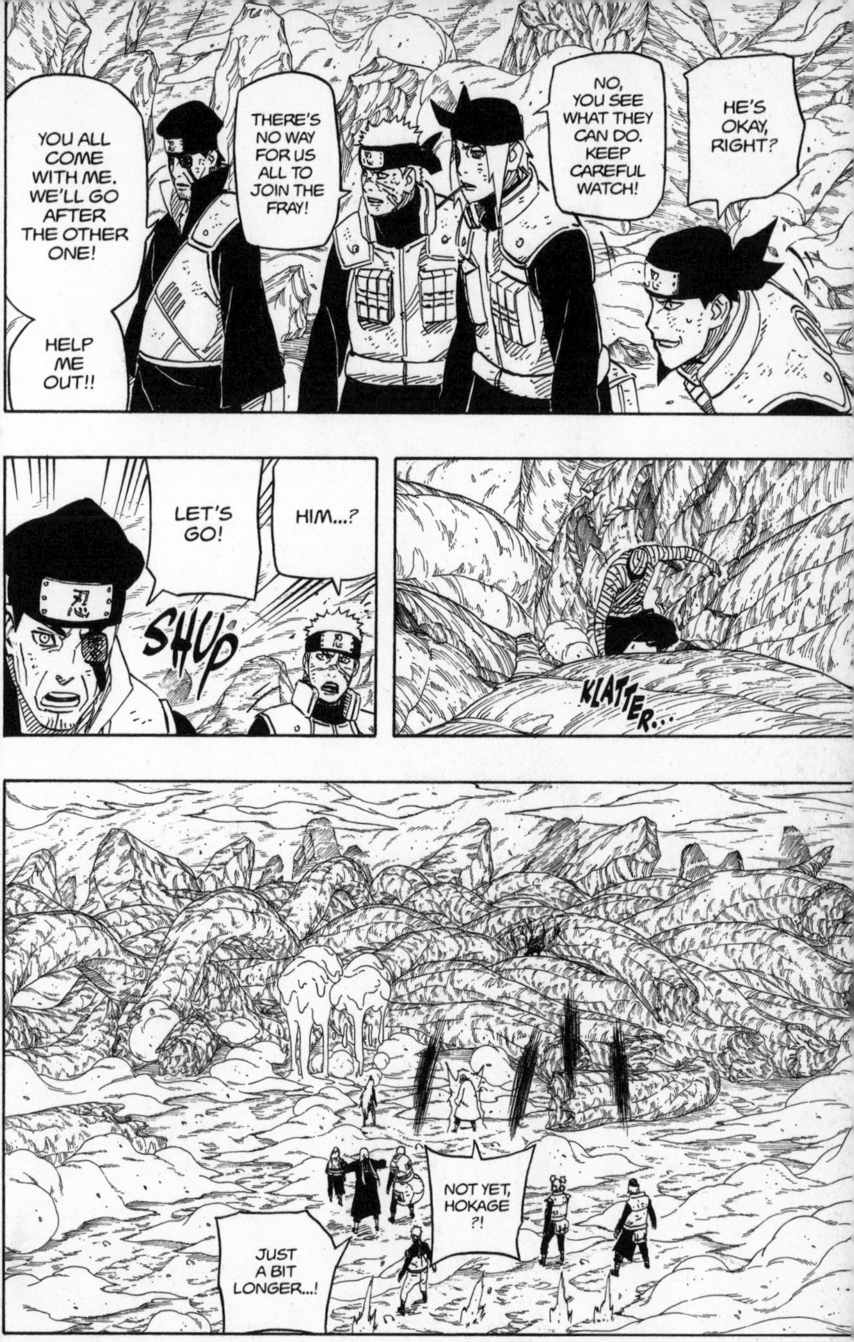
HE'S OKAY, RIGHT?
NO, YOU SEE WHAT THEY CAN DO. KEEP CAREFUL WATCH!
THERE'S NO WAY FOR US ALL TO JOIN THE FRAY!
YOU ALL COME WITH ME. WE'LL GO AFTER THE OTHER ONE!
HELP ME OUT!!
KLATTER...
HIM...?
LET'S GO!
SHUP
NOT YET, HOKAGE ?!
JUST A BIT LONGER...!

READ THIS WAY

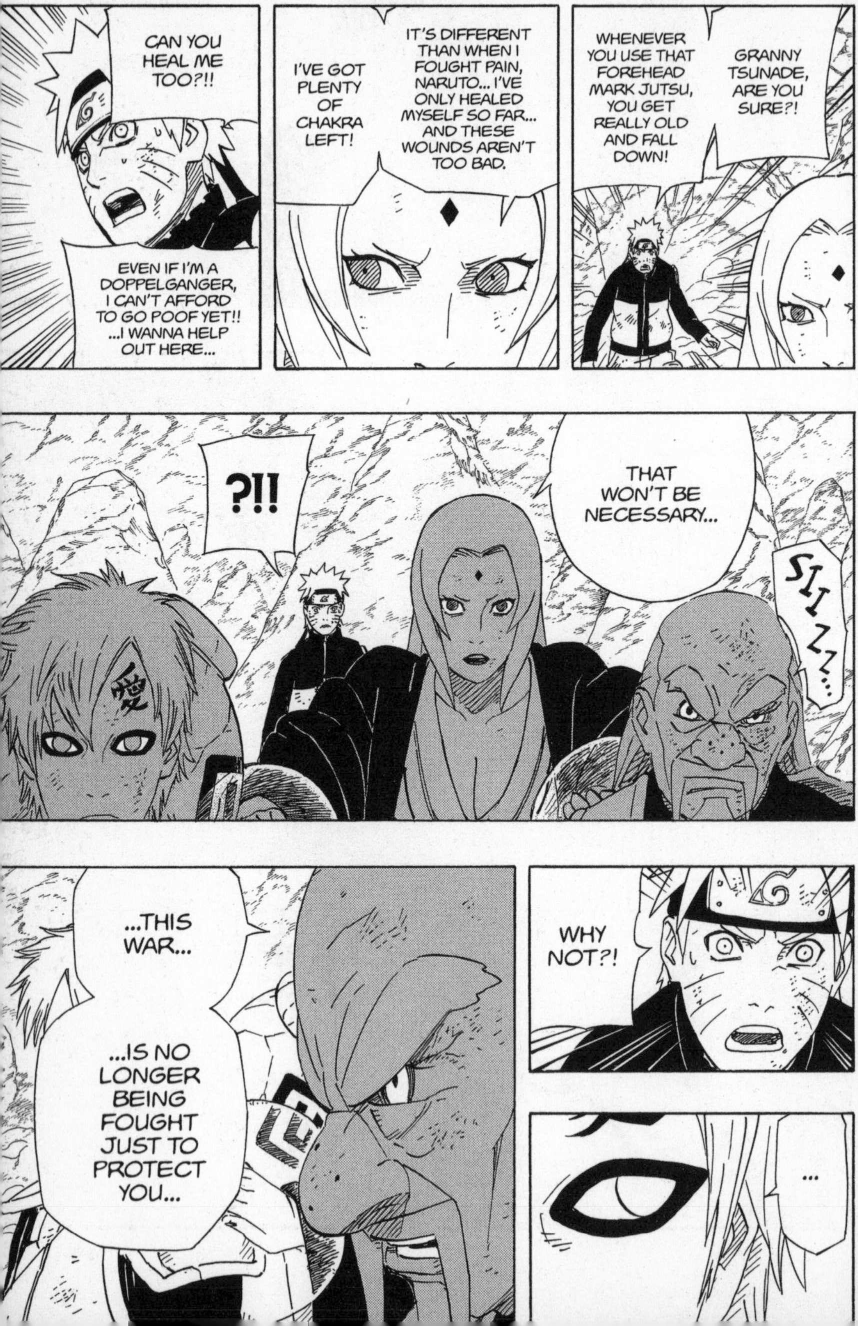
GRANNY TSUNADE, ARE YOU SURE?!
WHENEVER YOU USE THAT FOREHEAD MARK JUTSU, YOU GET REALLY OLD AND FALL DOWN!
IT'S DIFFERENT THAN WHEN I FOUGHT PAIN, NARUTO... I'VE ONLY HEALED MYSELF SO FAR... AND THESE WOUNDS AREN'T TOO BAD.
I'VE GOT PLENTY OF CHAKRA LEFT!
CAN YOU HEAL ME TOO?!!
EVEN IF I'M A DOPPELGANGER, I CAN'T AFFORD TO GO POOF YET!! ...I WANNA HELP OUT HERE...
THAT WON'T BE NECESSARY...
SIIZZZ...
?!!
WHY NOT?!
...
...THIS WAR...
...IS NO LONGER BEING FOUGHT JUST TO PROTECT YOU...

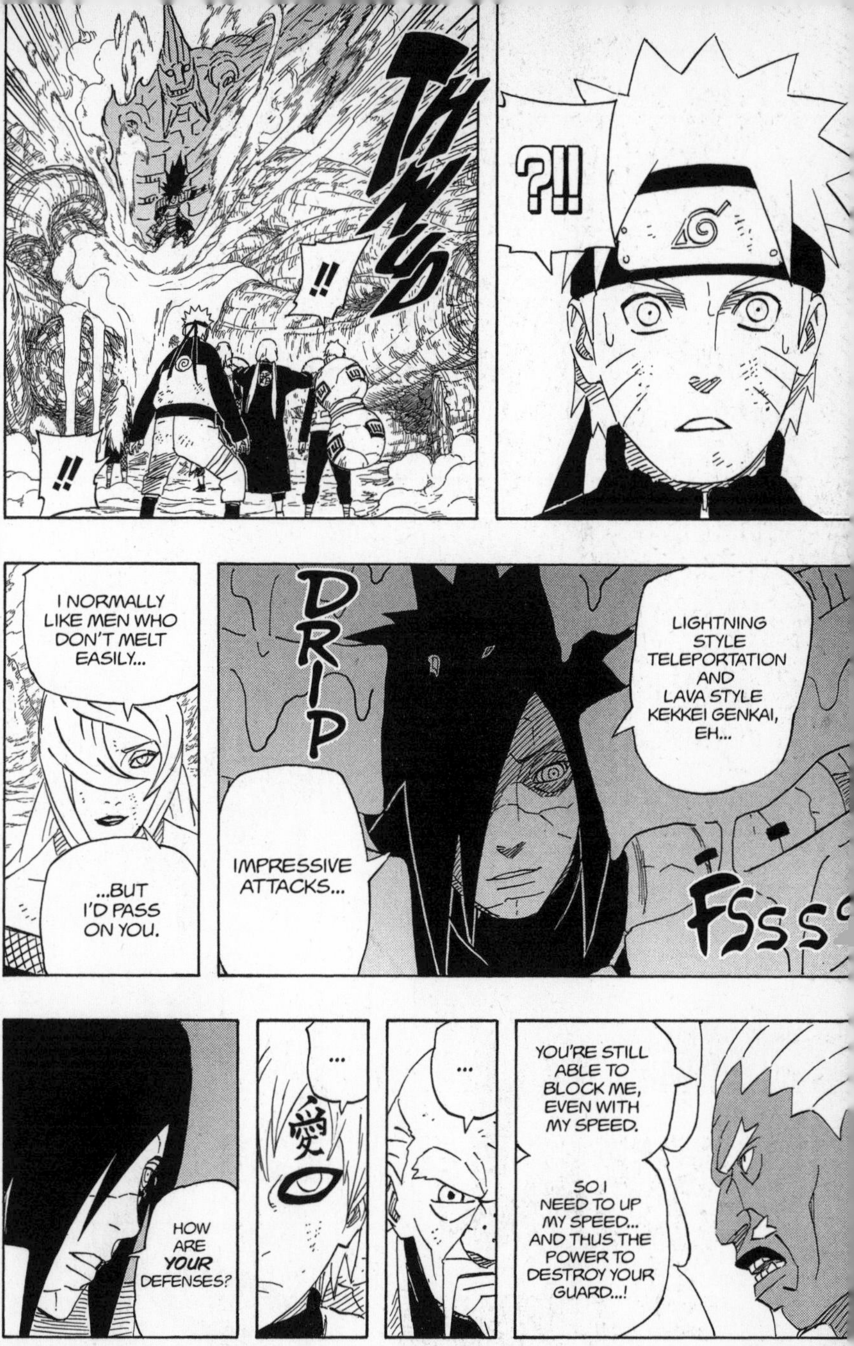
?!!
!!
!!
DRIP
LIGHTNING STYLE TELEPORTATION AND LAVA STYLE KEKKEI GENKAI, EH...
IMPRESSIVE ATTACKS...
FSSS
I NORMALLY LIKE MEN WHO DON'T MELT EASILY...
...BUT I'D PASS ON YOU.
YOU'RE STILL ABLE TO BLOCK ME, EVEN WITH MY SPEED.
SO I NEED TO UP MY SPEED... AND THUS THE POWER TO DESTROY YOUR GUARD...!
...
...
HOW ARE YOUR DEFENSES?

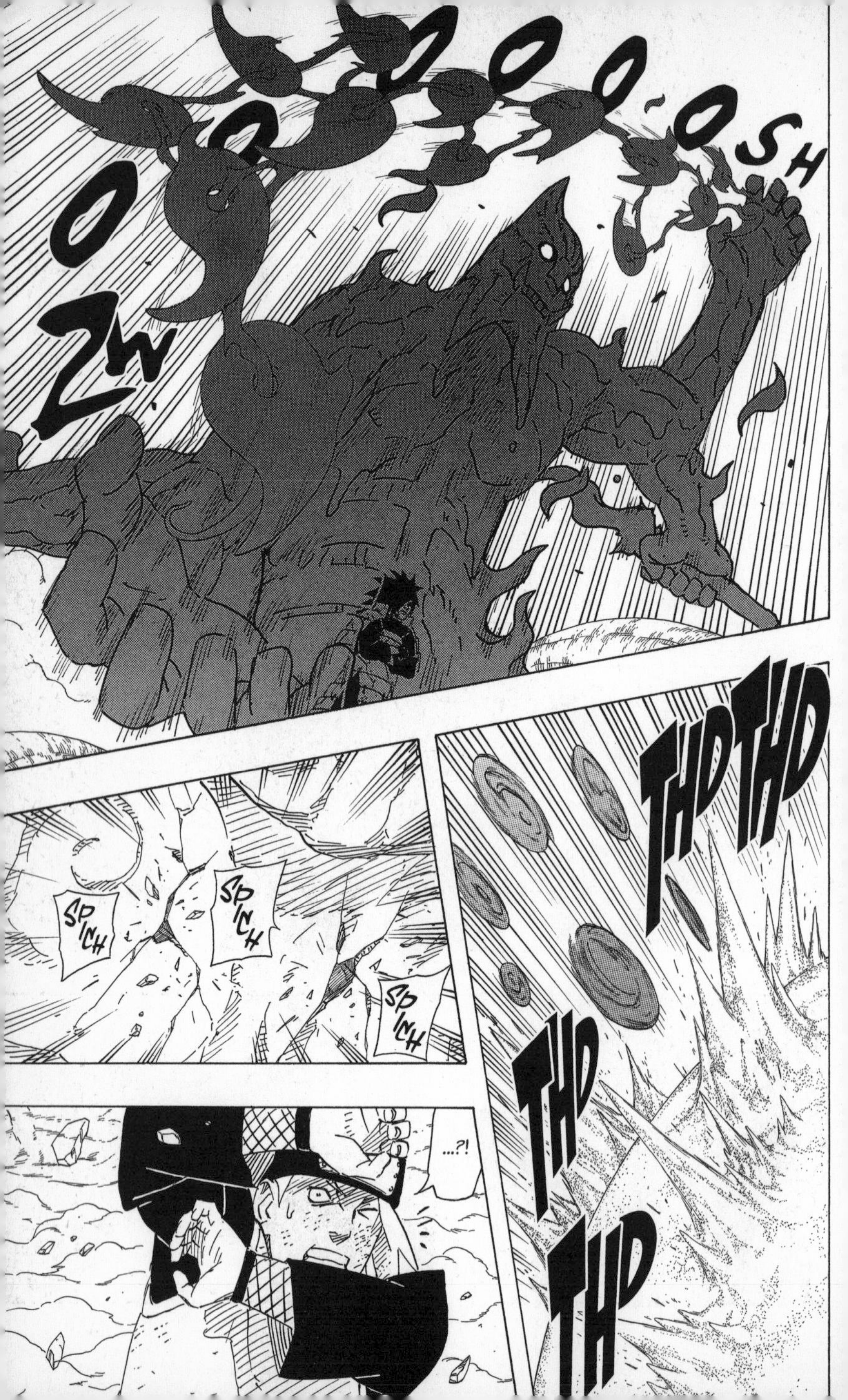
ZWOOOOOOOOSH
THD THD
THD
THD
SPICH
SPICH
SPICH
...?!

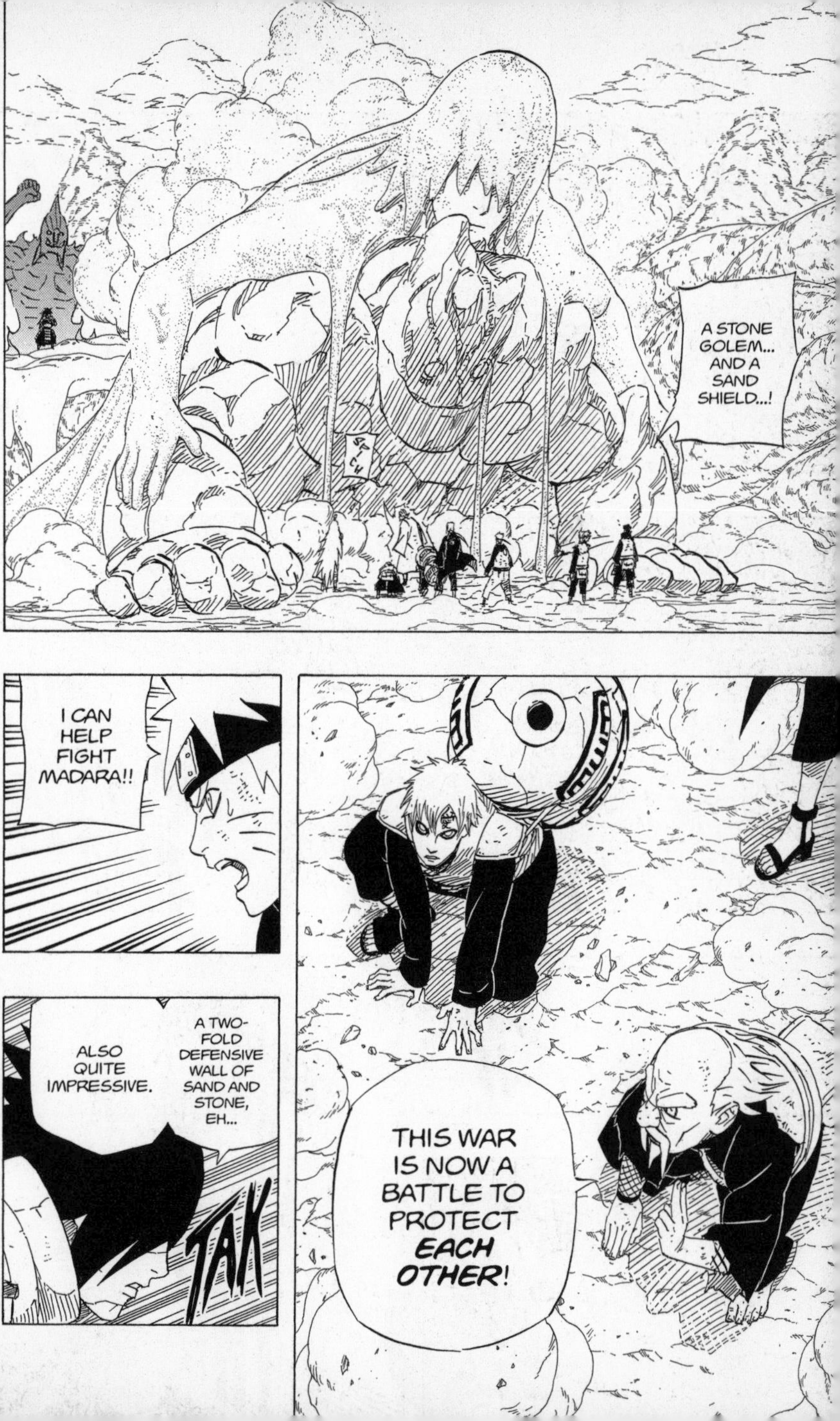
A STONE GOLEM... AND A SAND SHIELD...!
SPICH
THIS WAR IS NOW A BATTLE TO PROTECT EACH OTHER!
I CAN HELP FIGHT MADARA!!
A TWO-FOLD DEFENSIVE WALL OF SAND AND STONE, EH...
ALSO QUITE IMPRESSIVE.
TAK

READ THIS WAY

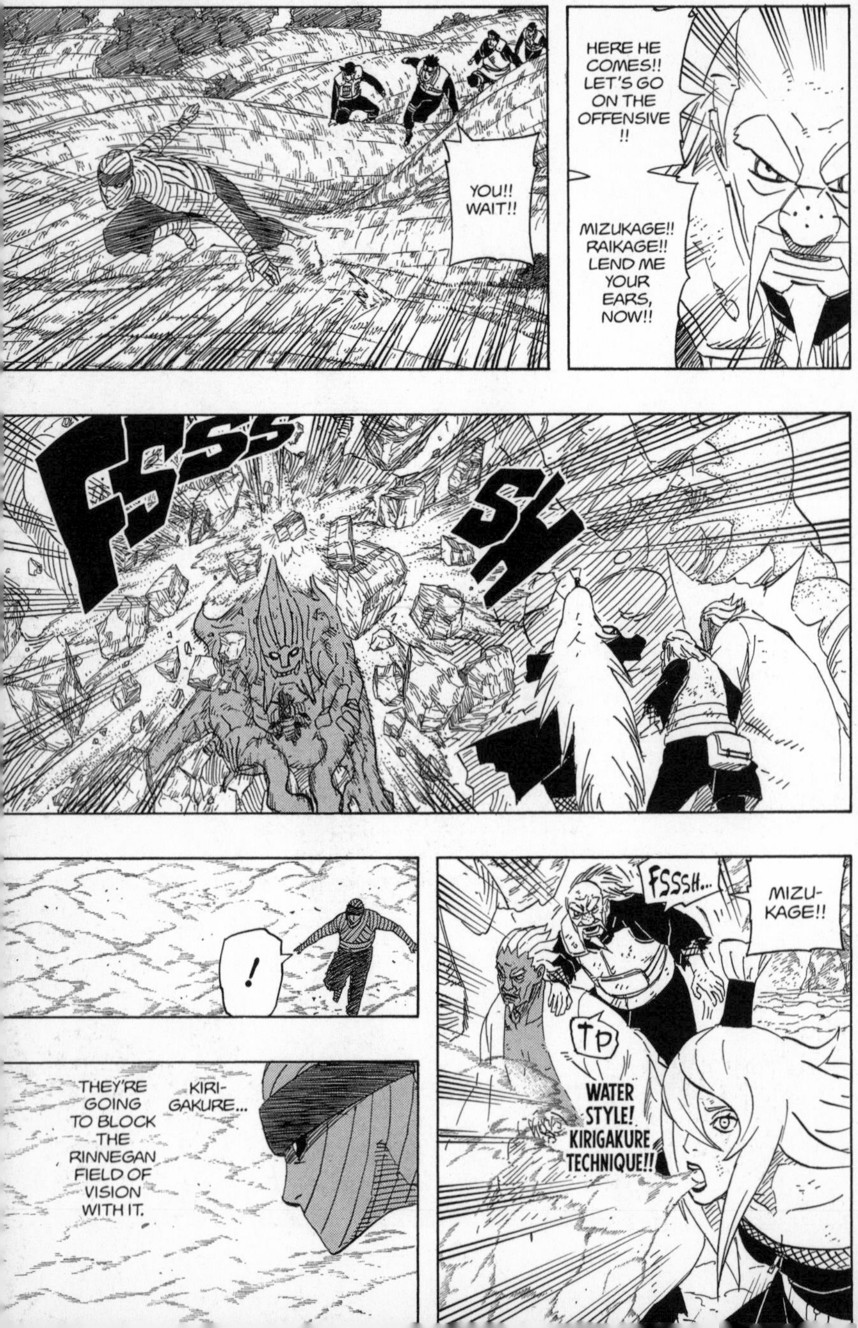
HERE HE COMES!! LET'S GO ON THE OFFENSIVE!!
MIZUKAGE!! RAIKAGE!! LEND ME YOUR EARS, NOW!!
YOU!! WAIT!!
FSSS
SH
FSSSH...
MIZU-KAGE!!
Tp
WATER STYLE! KIRIGAKURE TECHNIQUE!!
!
KIRI-GAKURE...
THEY'RE GOING TO BLOCK THE RINNEGAN FIELD OF VISION WITH IT.

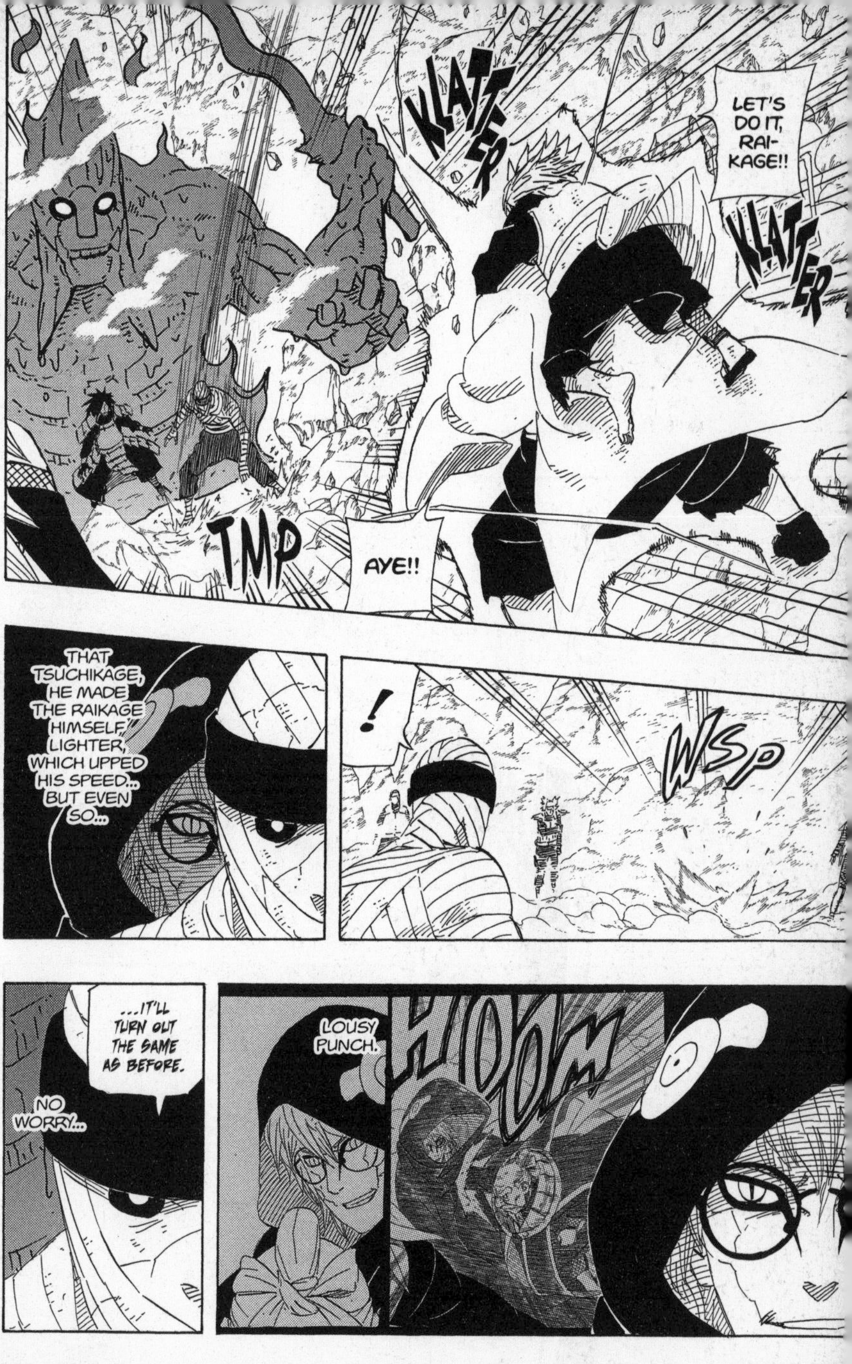
LET'S DO IT, RAI-KAGE!!
KLATTER
KLATTER
AYE!!
TMP
WSP
!
THAT TSUCHIKAGE, HE MADE THE RAIKAGE HIMSELF LIGHTER, WHICH UPPED HIS SPEED... BUT EVEN SO...
HOOM
LOUSY PUNCH.
...IT'LL TURN OUT THE SAME AS BEFORE.
NO WORRY...

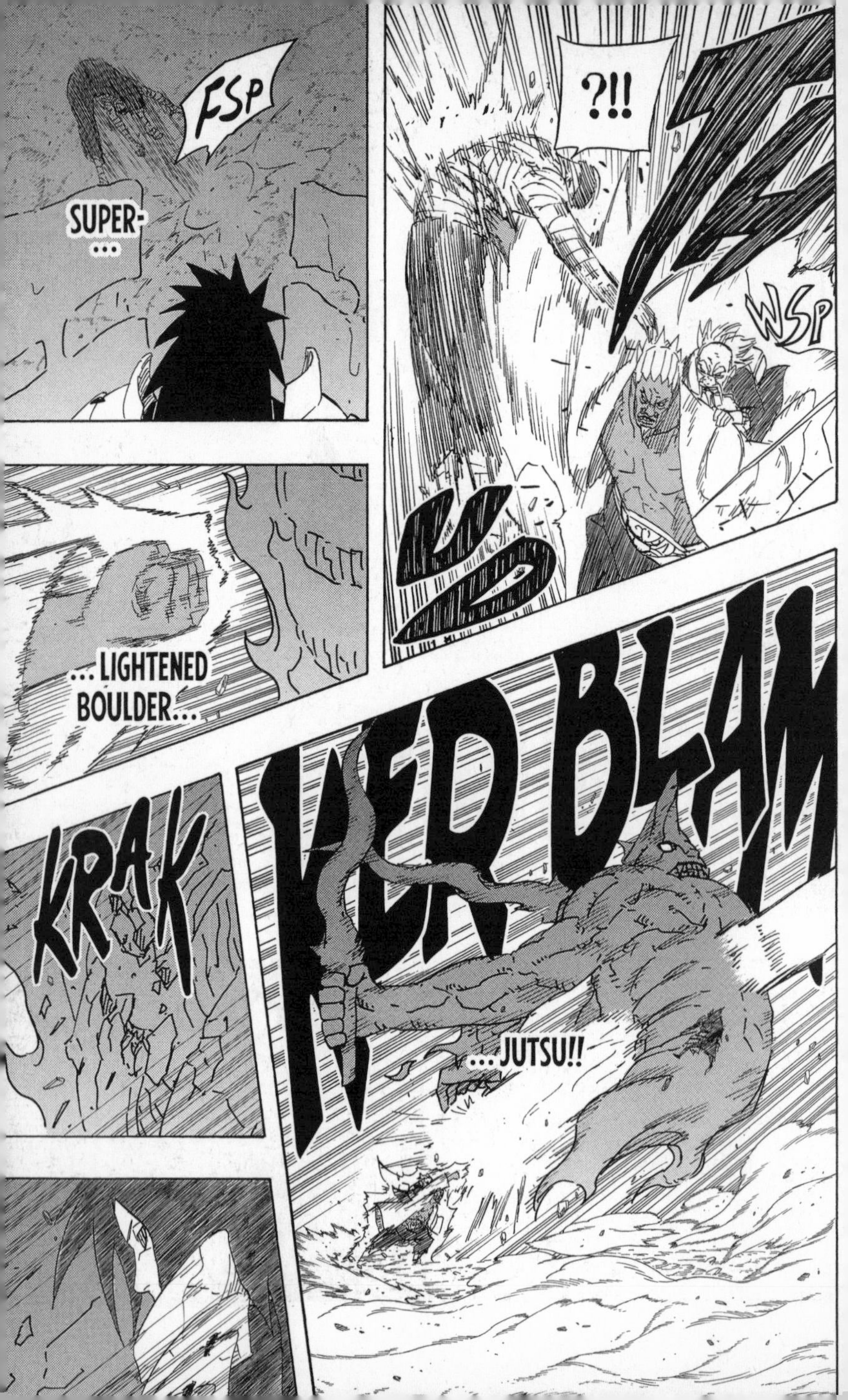
?!!
WSP
FSP
SUPER-
...
... LIGHTENED BOULDER...
...JUTSU!!
KRAK

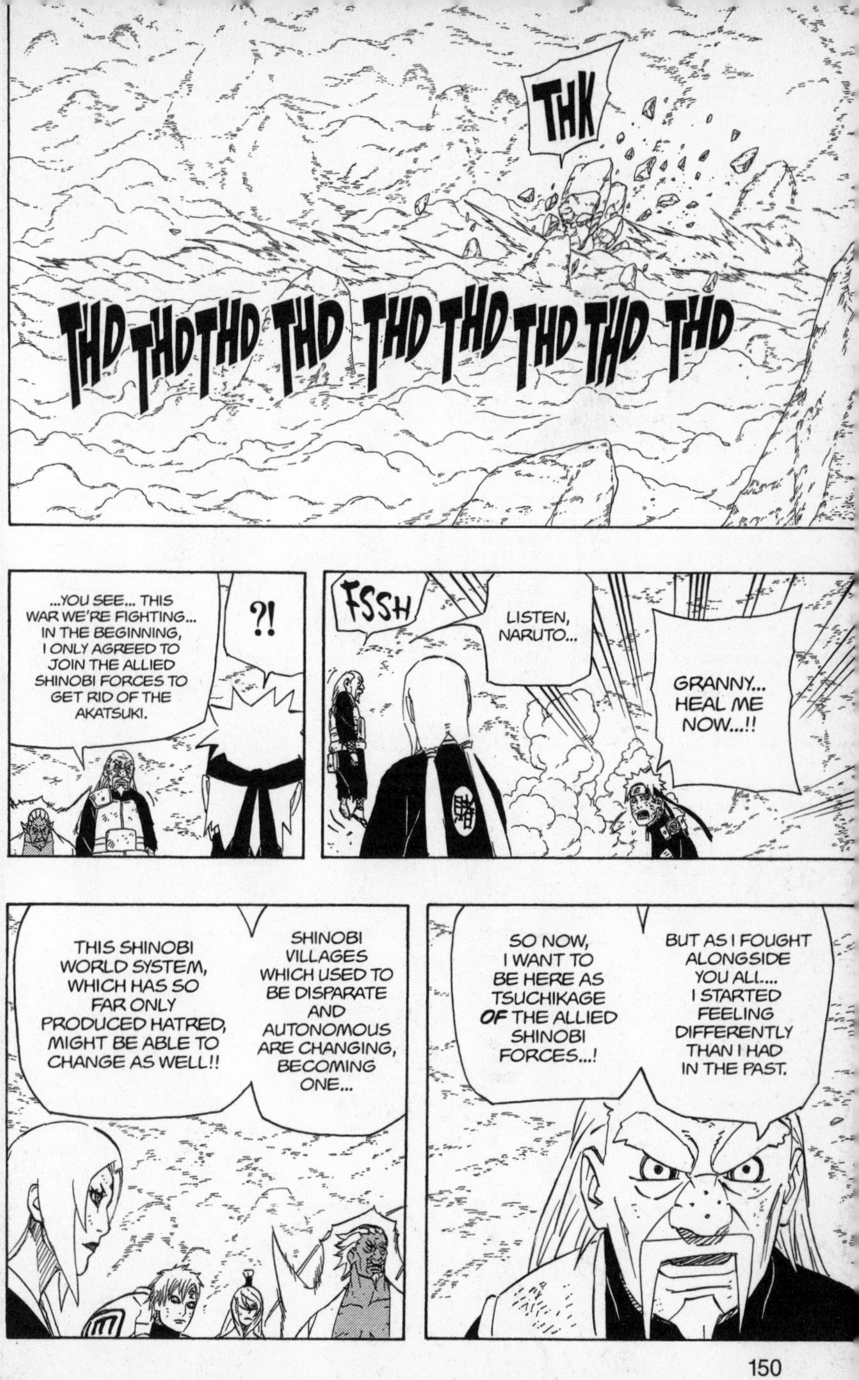
THK
THD THD THD THD THD THD THD THD THD
GRANNY... HEAL ME NOW...!!
LISTEN, NARUTO...
FSSH
?!
...YOU SEE... THIS WAR WE'RE FIGHTING... IN THE BEGINNING, I ONLY AGREED TO JOIN THE ALLIED SHINOBI FORCES TO GET RID OF THE AKATSUKI.
BUT AS I FOUGHT ALONGSIDE YOU ALL.... I STARTED FEELING DIFFERENTLY THAN I HAD IN THE PAST.
SO NOW, I WANT TO BE HERE AS TSUCHIKAGE OF THE ALLIED SHINOBI FORCES...!
SHINOBI VILLAGES WHICH USED TO BE DISPARATE AND AUTONOMOUS ARE CHANGING, BECOMING ONE...
THIS SHINOBI WORLD SYSTEM, WHICH HAS SO FAR ONLY PRODUCED HATRED, MIGHT BE ABLE TO CHANGE AS WELL!!

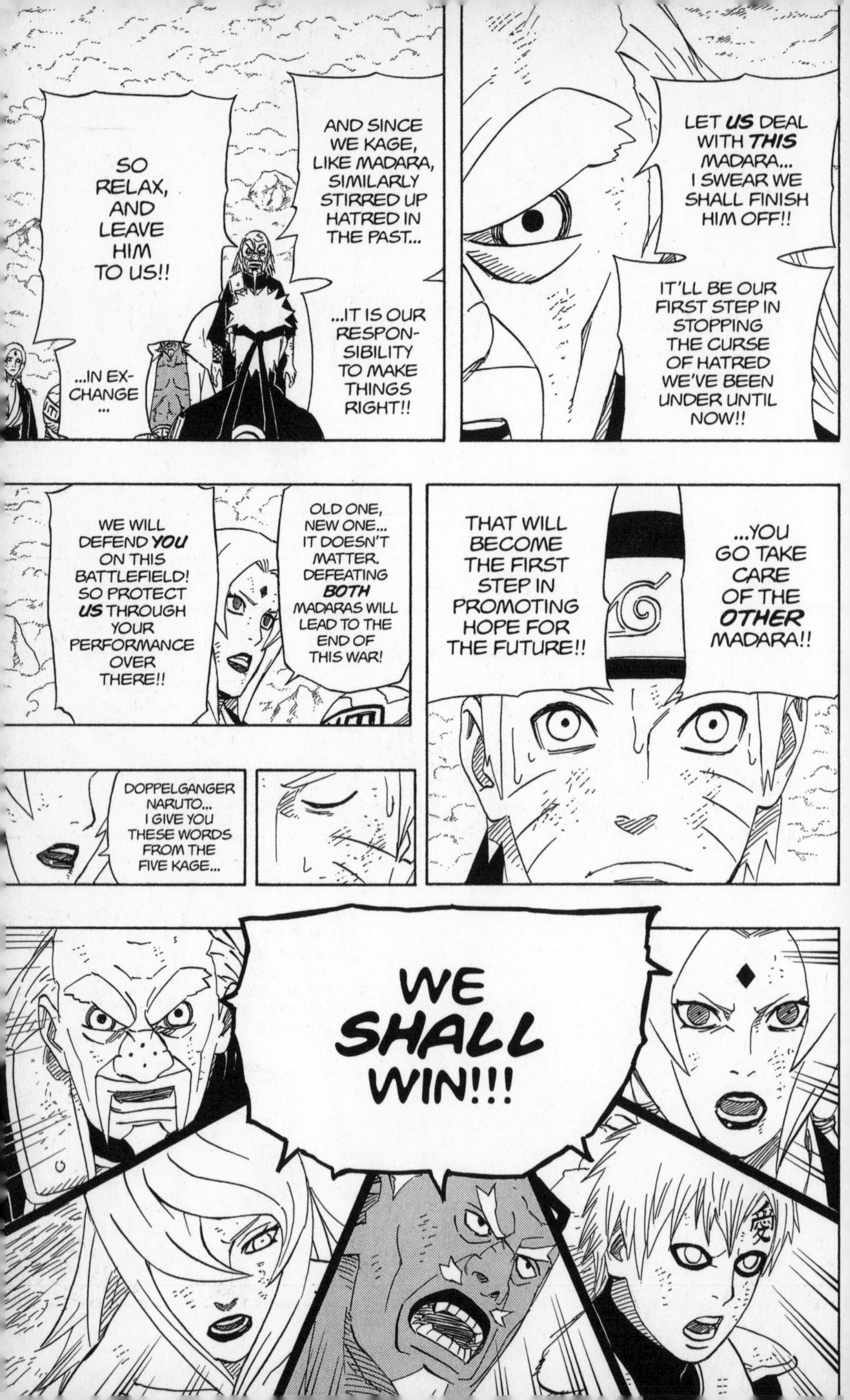
LET US DEAL WITH THIS MADARA... I SWEAR WE SHALL FINISH HIM OFF!!
IT'LL BE OUR FIRST STEP IN STOPPING THE CURSE OF HATRED WE'VE BEEN UNDER UNTIL NOW!!
AND SINCE WE KAGE, LIKE MADARA, SIMILARLY STIRRED UP HATRED IN THE PAST...
...IT IS OUR RESPON-SIBILITY TO MAKE THINGS RIGHT!!
SO RELAX, AND LEAVE HIM TO US!!
...IN EX-CHANGE...
...YOU GO TAKE CARE OF THE OTHER MADARA!!
THAT WILL BECOME THE FIRST STEP IN PROMOTING HOPE FOR THE FUTURE!!
OLD ONE, NEW ONE... IT DOESN'T MATTER. DEFEATING BOTH MADARAS WILL LEAD TO THE END OF THIS WAR!
WE WILL DEFEND YOU ON THIS BATTLEFIELD! SO PROTECT US THROUGH YOUR PERFORMANCE OVER THERE!!
DOPPELGANGER NARUTO... I GIVE YOU THESE WORDS FROM THE FIVE KAGE...
WE SHALL WIN!!!

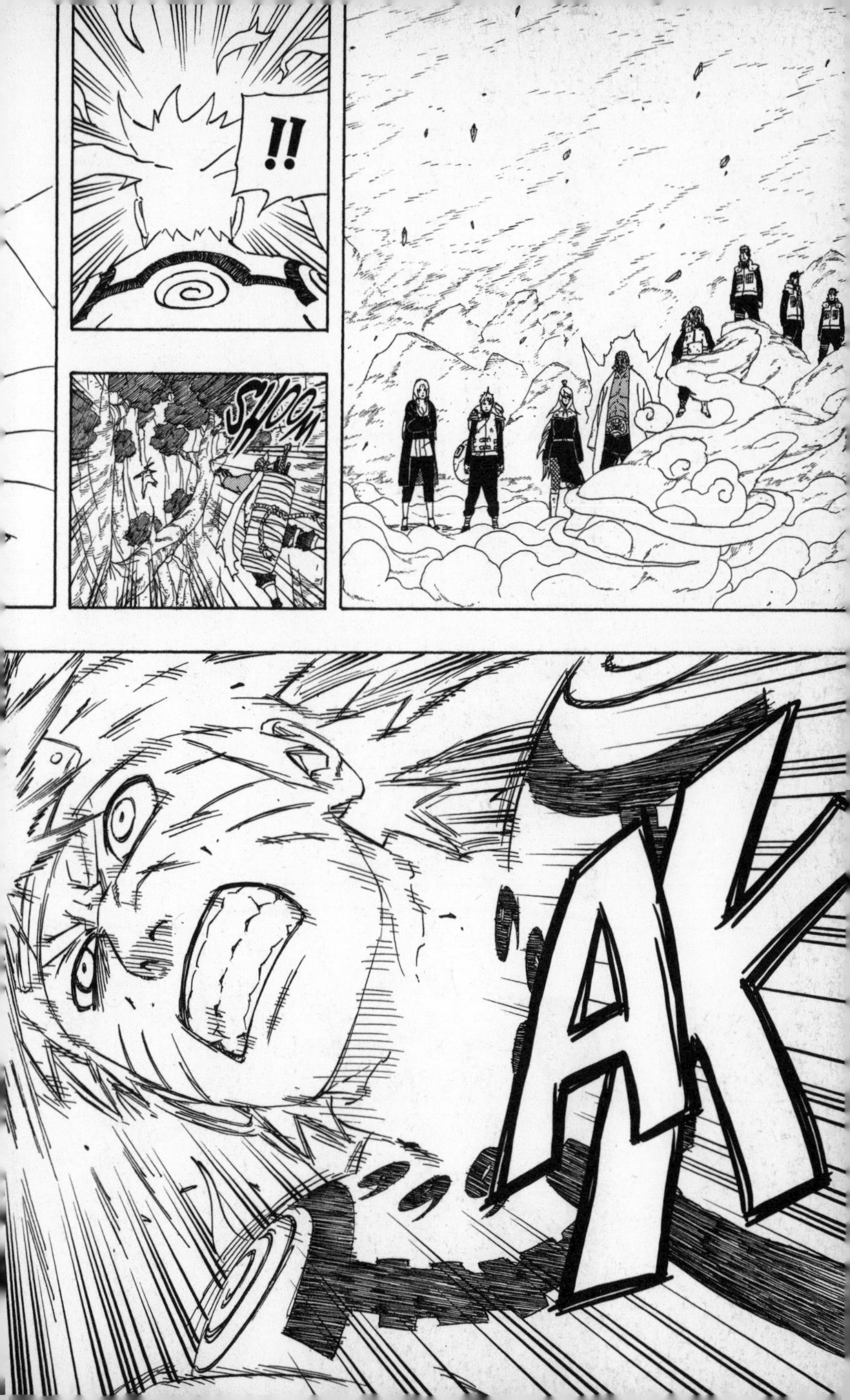
!!
SHOOM
AK

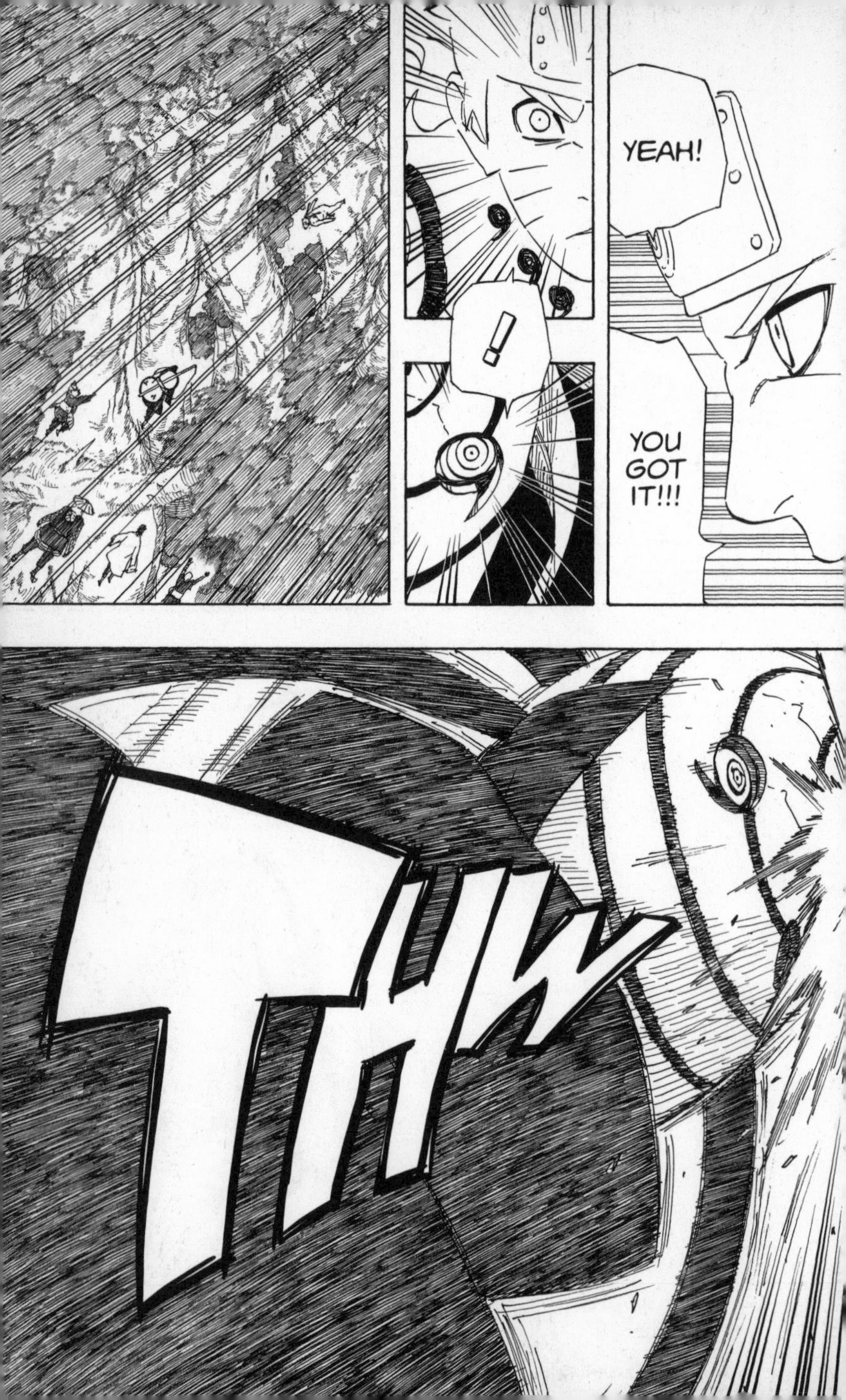
YEAH!
YOU GOT IT!!!
!
THW

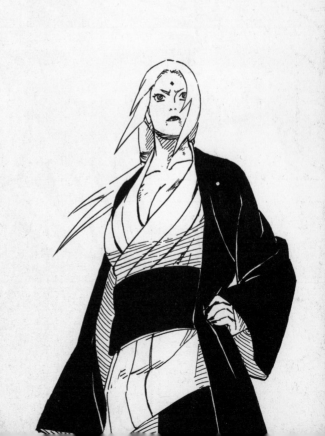

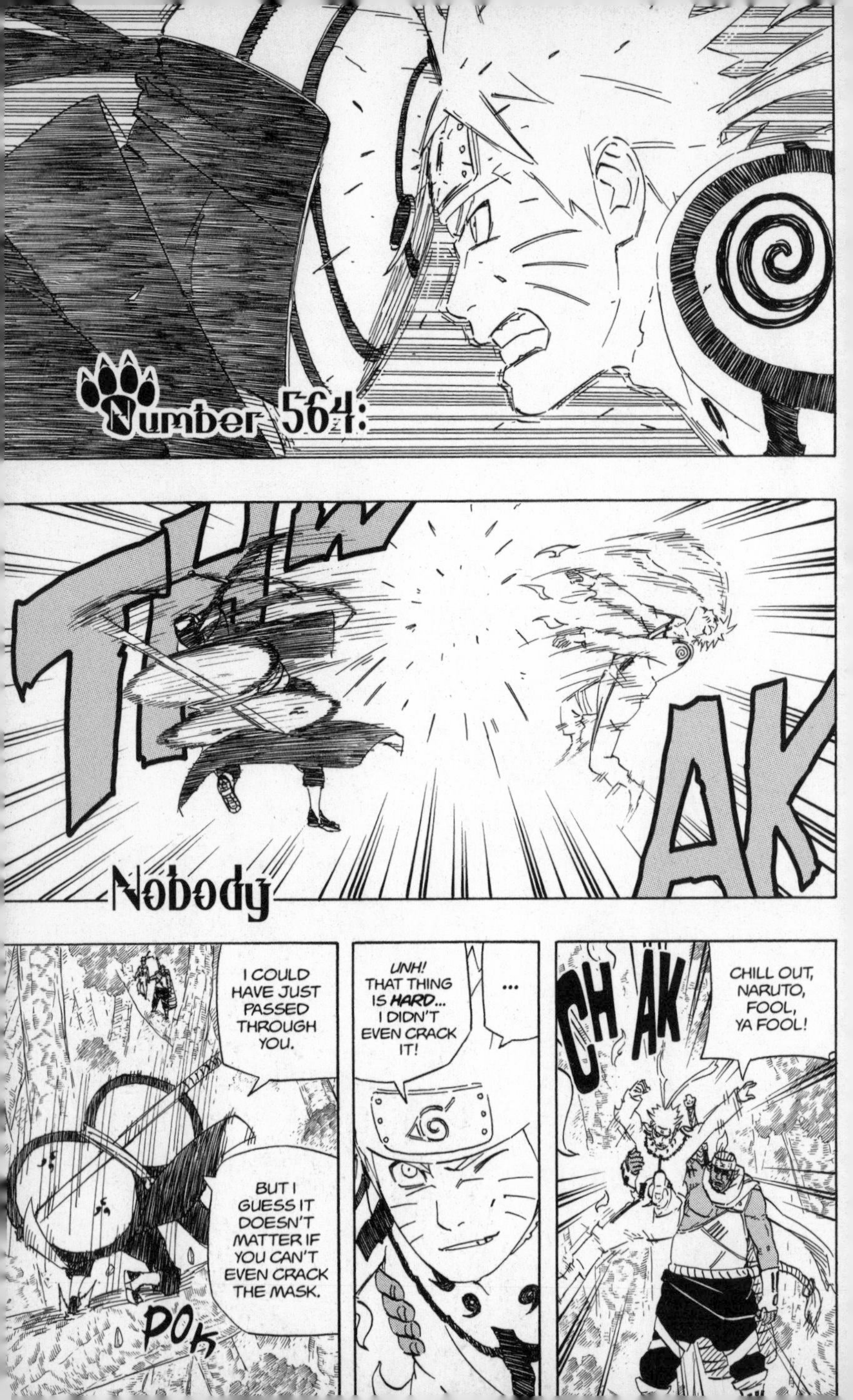
Number 564:
Nobody
AK
TH
CHÄK
CHILL OUT, NARUTO, FOOL, YA FOOL!
...
UNH! THAT THING IS *HARD*... I DIDN'T EVEN CRACK IT!
I COULD HAVE JUST PASSED THROUGH YOU.
BUT I GUESS IT DOESN'T MATTER IF YOU CAN'T EVEN CRACK THE MASK.
POK

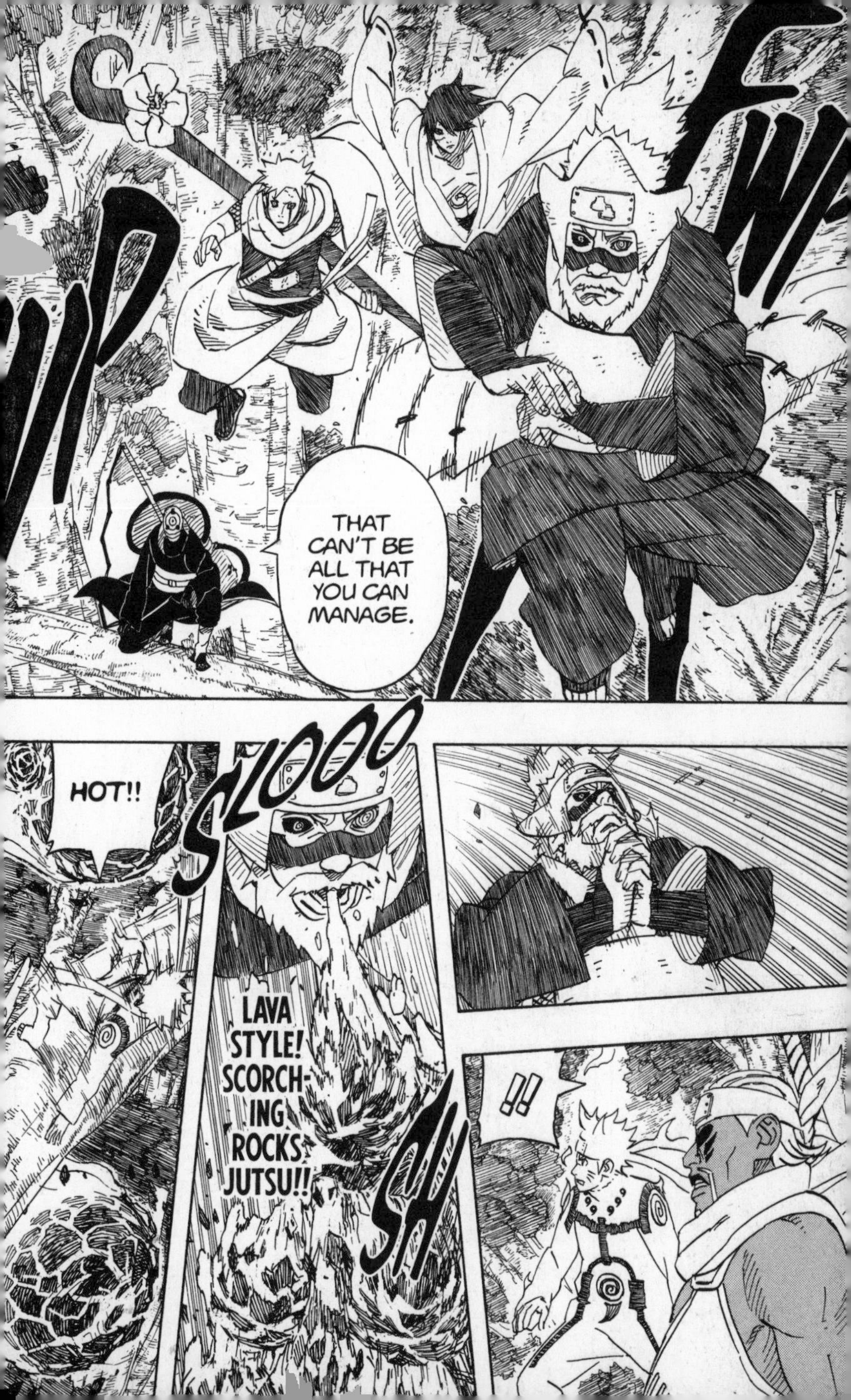
FWIP
THAT CAN'T BE ALL THAT YOU CAN MANAGE.
!!
SCLOOO
LAVA STYLE! SCORCHING ROCKS JUTSU!!
SH
HOT!!

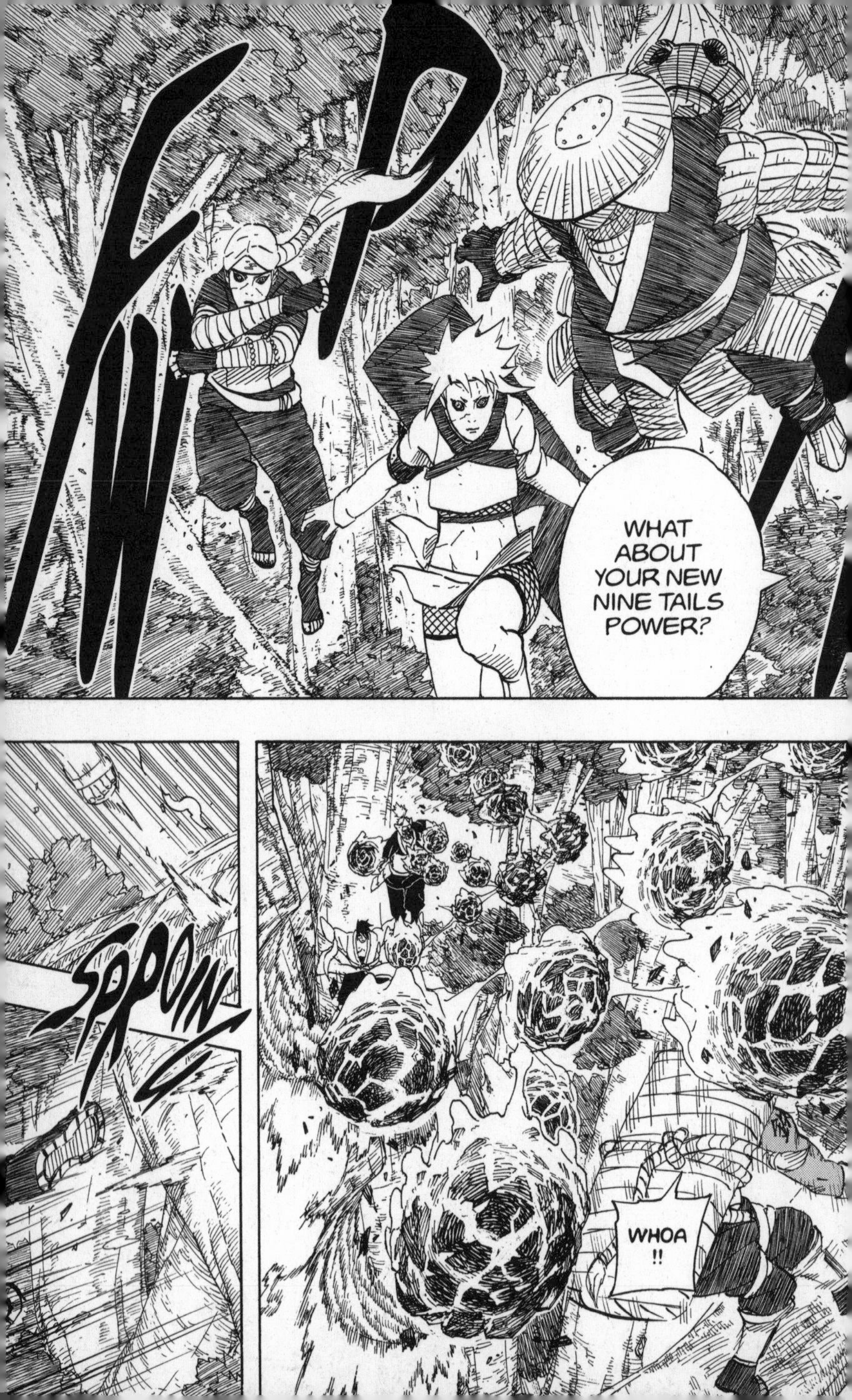
WHAT ABOUT YOUR NEW NINE TAILS POWER?
WHOA !!

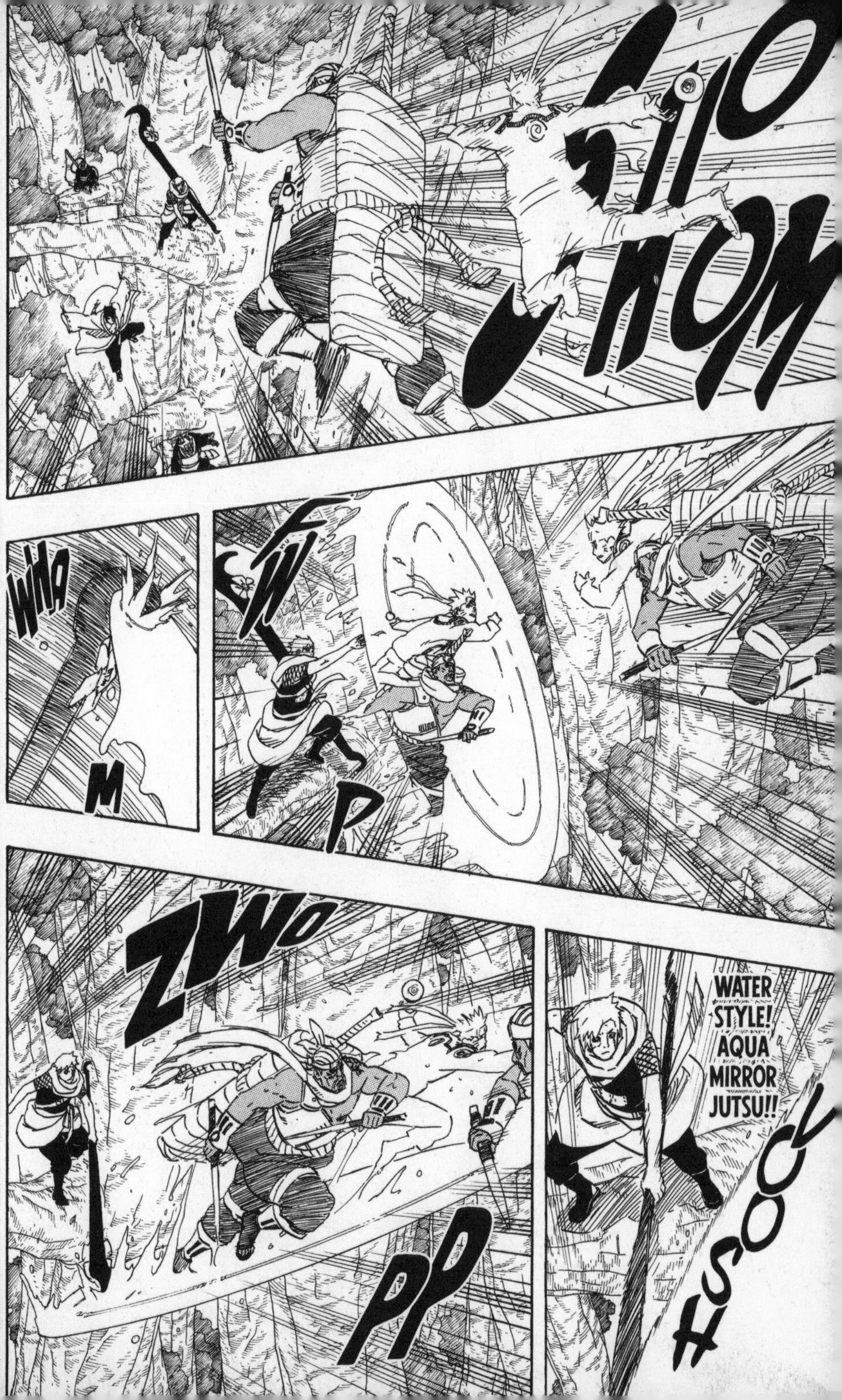
WATER STYLE! AQUA MIRROR JUTSU!!

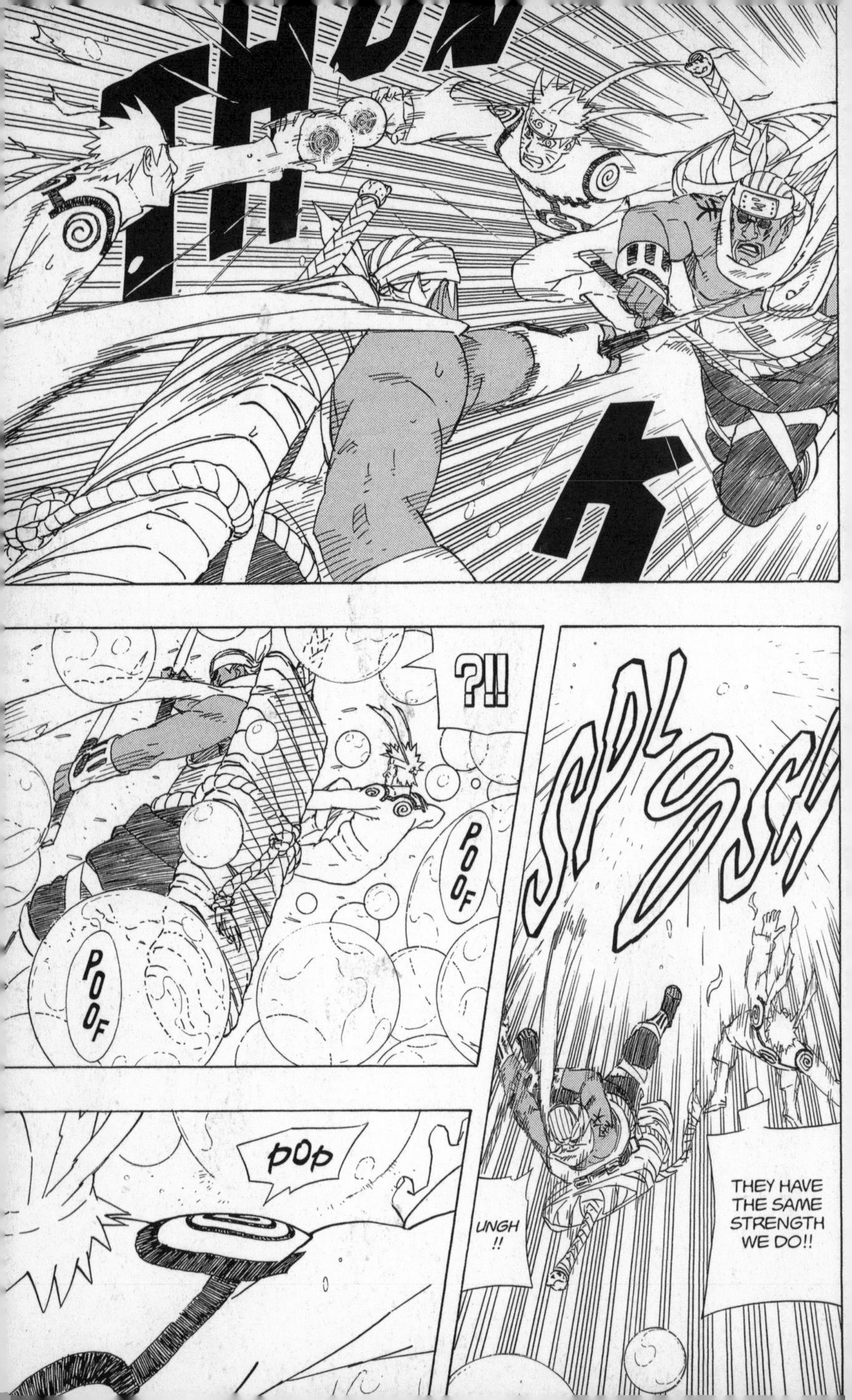
THUNK
SPLOSH
UNGH !!
THEY HAVE THE SAME STRENGTH WE DO!!
?!!
POOF
POOF
POP

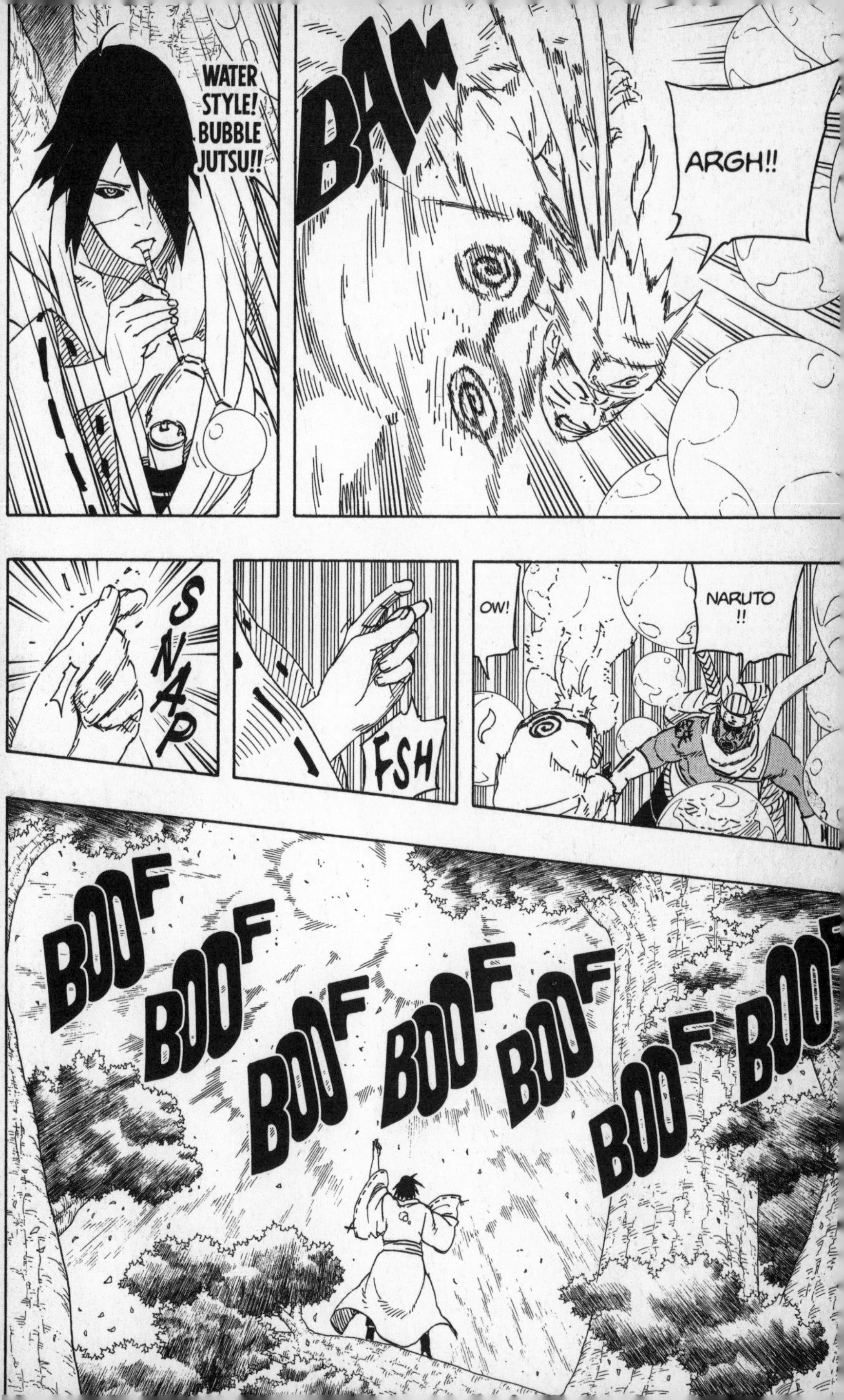
BAM
ARGH!!
WATER STYLE! BUBBLE JUTSU!!
NARUTO !!
OW!
FSH
SNAP
BOOF BOOF BOOF BOOF BOOF BOOF BOO

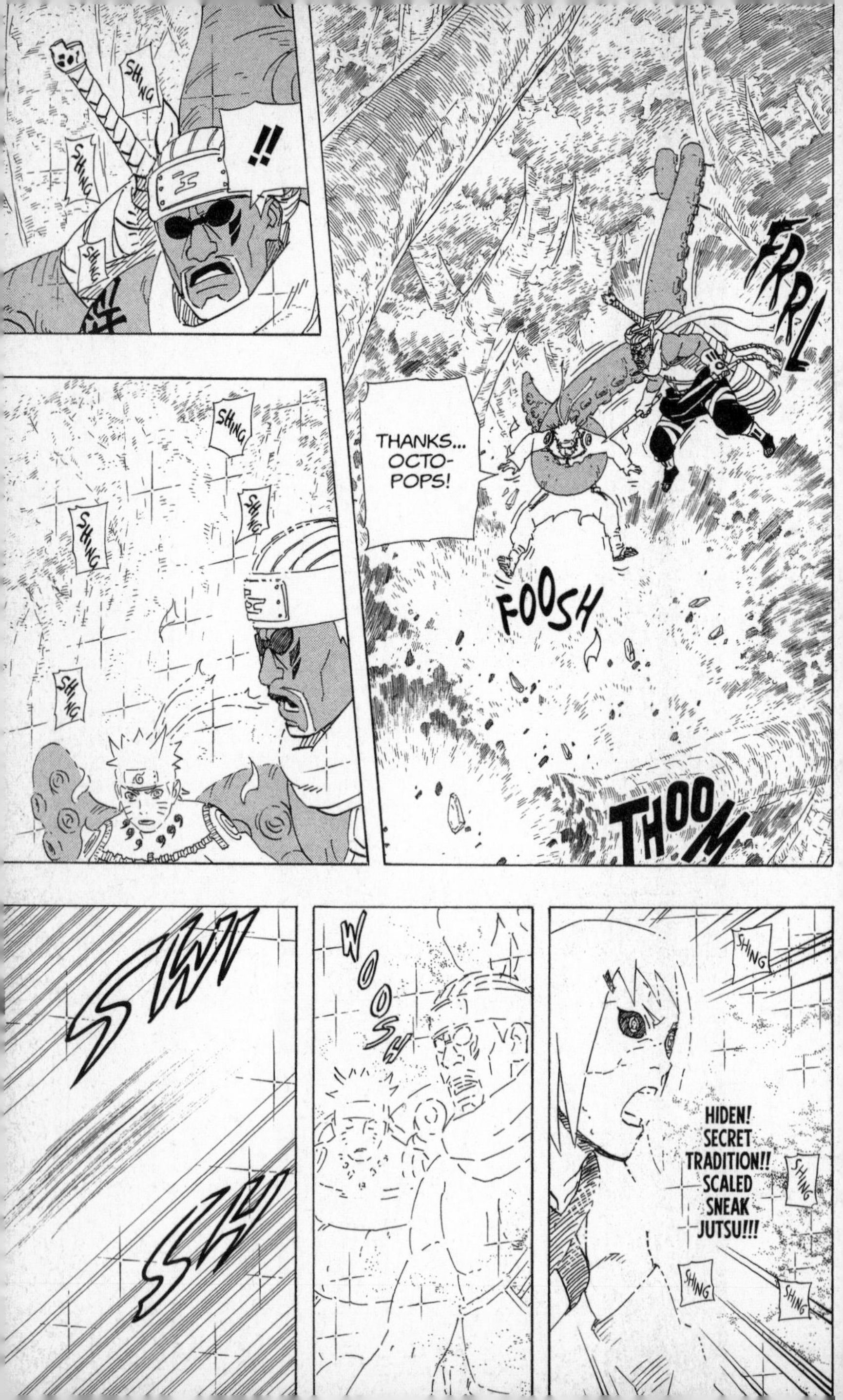
FRRL
THANKS... OCTO-POPS!
FOOSH
THOOM
SHING
SHING
!!
SHING
SHING
SHING
SHING
SHING
SHING
HIDEN! SECRET TRADITION!! SCALED SNEAK JUTSU!!!
SHING
SHING
SHING
WOOOSH
SHH
SHH

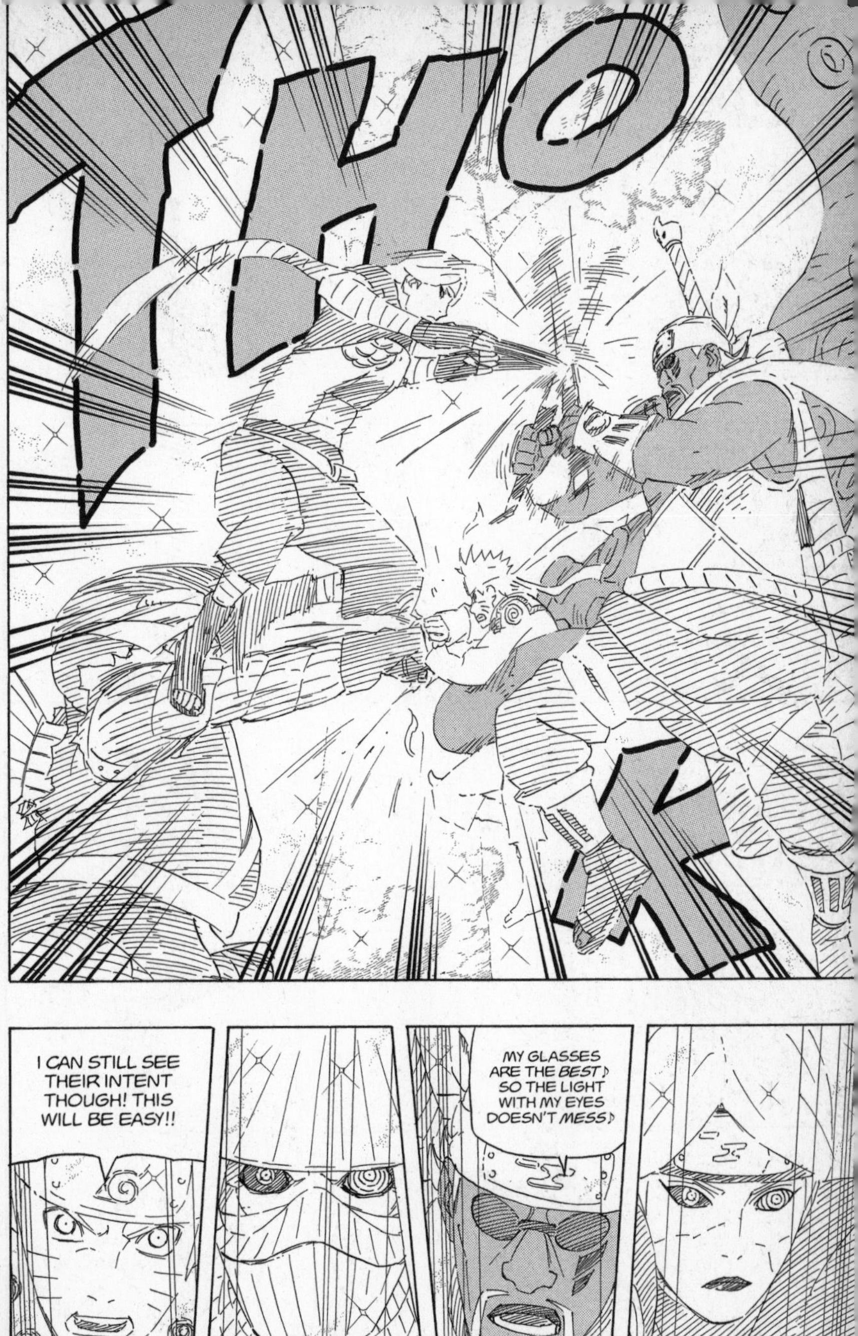
MY GLASSES ARE THE *BEST*♪ SO THE LIGHT WITH MY EYES DOESN'T *MESS*♪
I CAN STILL SEE THEIR INTENT THOUGH! THIS WILL BE EASY!!

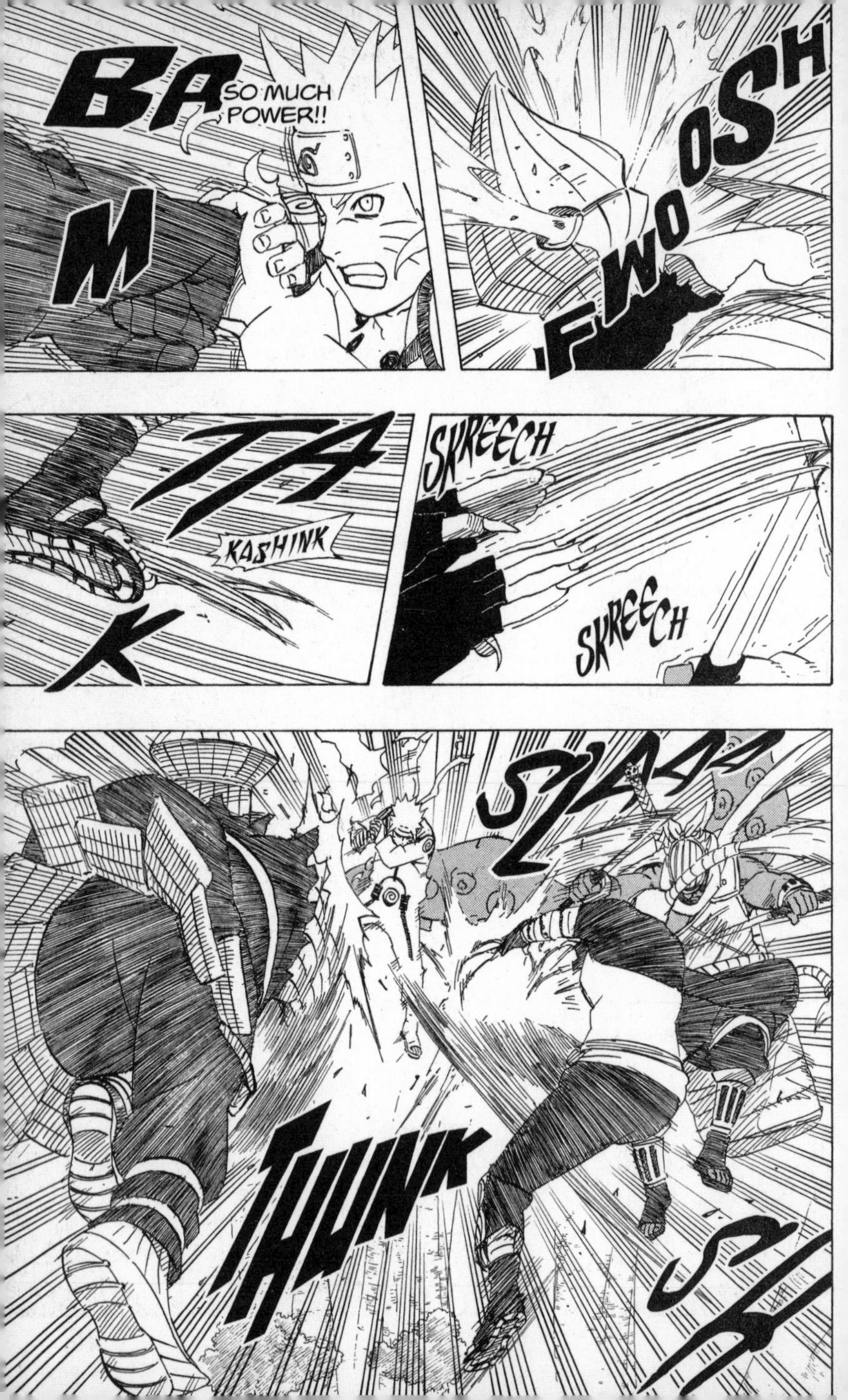
FWOOSH
BAM
SO MUCH POWER!!
SKREECH
SKREECH
TAK
KASHINK
SLAAA
THUNK
SH

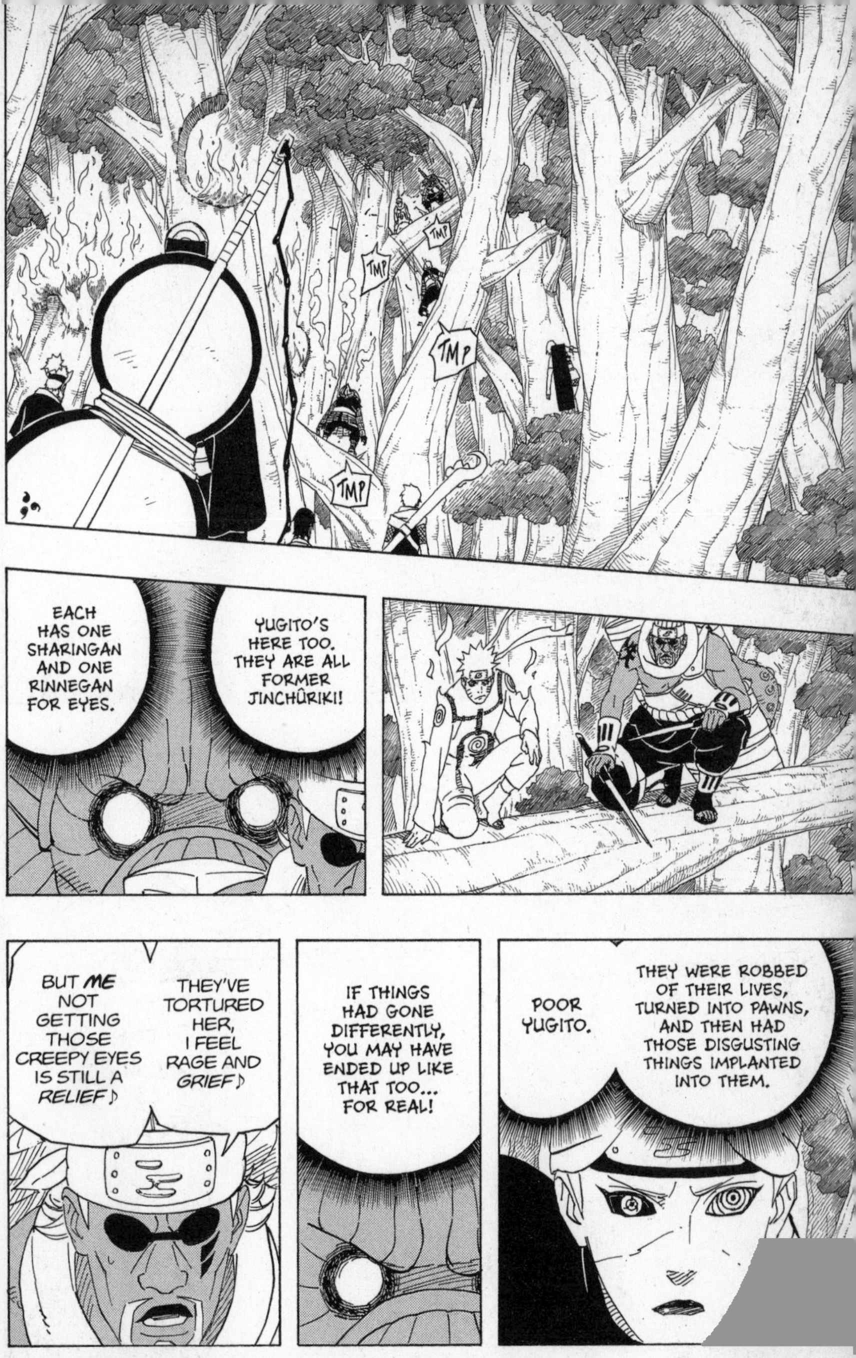
TMP
TMP
TMP
TMP
YUGITO'S HERE TOO. THEY ARE ALL FORMER JINCHÛRIKI!
EACH HAS ONE SHARINGAN AND ONE RINNEGAN FOR EYES.
THEY WERE ROBBED OF THEIR LIVES, TURNED INTO PAWNS, AND THEN HAD THOSE DISGUSTING THINGS IMPLANTED INTO THEM.
POOR YUGITO.
IF THINGS HAD GONE DIFFERENTLY, YOU MAY HAVE ENDED UP LIKE THAT TOO... FOR REAL!
THEY'VE TORTURED HER, I FEEL RAGE AND GRIEF♪
BUT ME NOT GETTING THOSE CREEPY EYES IS STILL A RELIEF♪

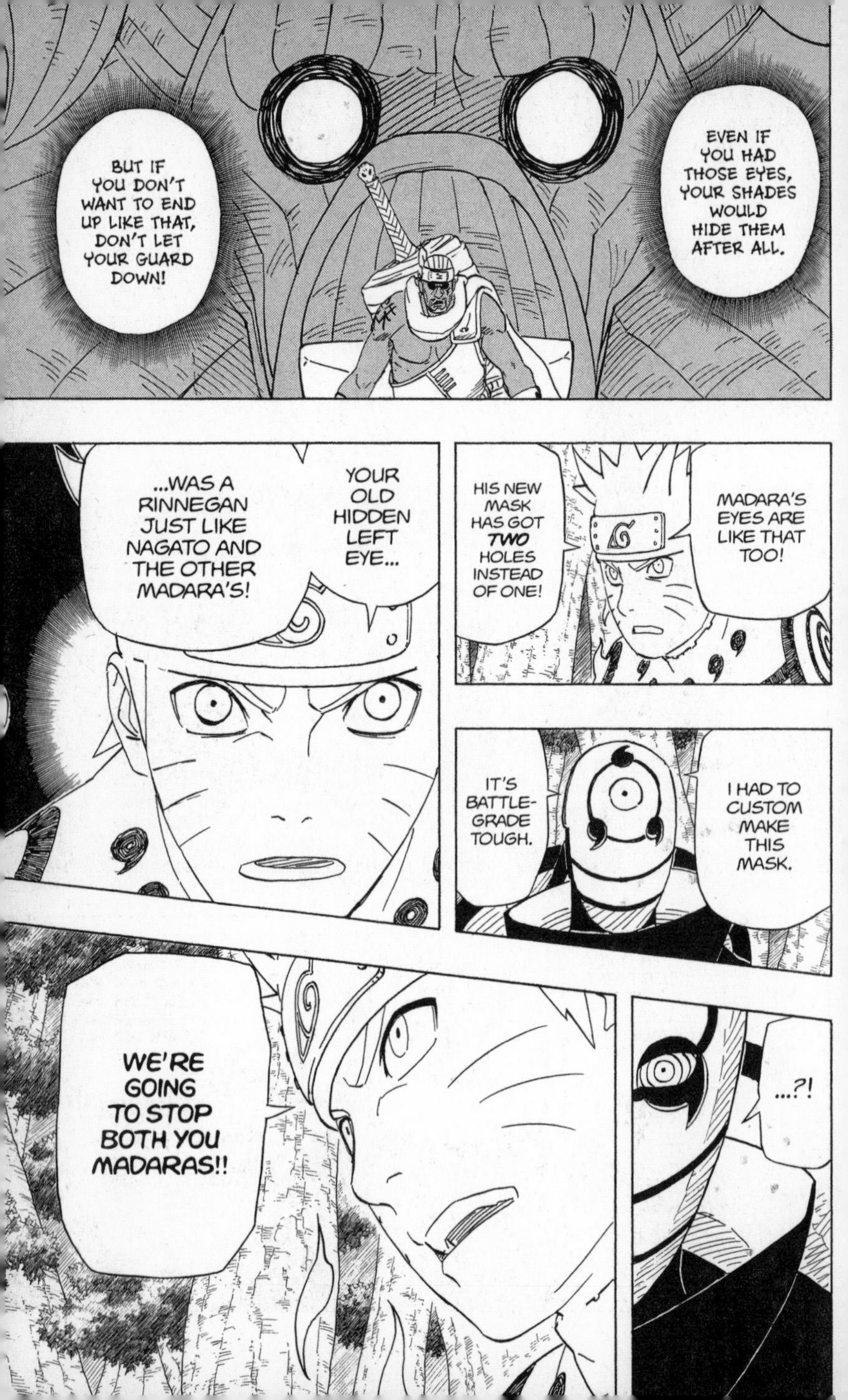
EVEN IF YOU HAD THOSE EYES, YOUR SHADES WOULD HIDE THEM AFTER ALL.
BUT IF YOU DON'T WANT TO END UP LIKE THAT, DON'T LET YOUR GUARD DOWN!
MADARA'S EYES ARE LIKE THAT TOO!
HIS NEW MASK HAS GOT *TWO* HOLES INSTEAD OF ONE!
I HAD TO CUSTOM MAKE THIS MASK.
IT'S BATTLE-GRADE TOUGH.
YOUR OLD HIDDEN LEFT EYE...
...WAS A RINNEGAN JUST LIKE NAGATO AND THE OTHER MADARA'S!
...?!
WE'RE GOING TO STOP BOTH YOU MADARAS!!

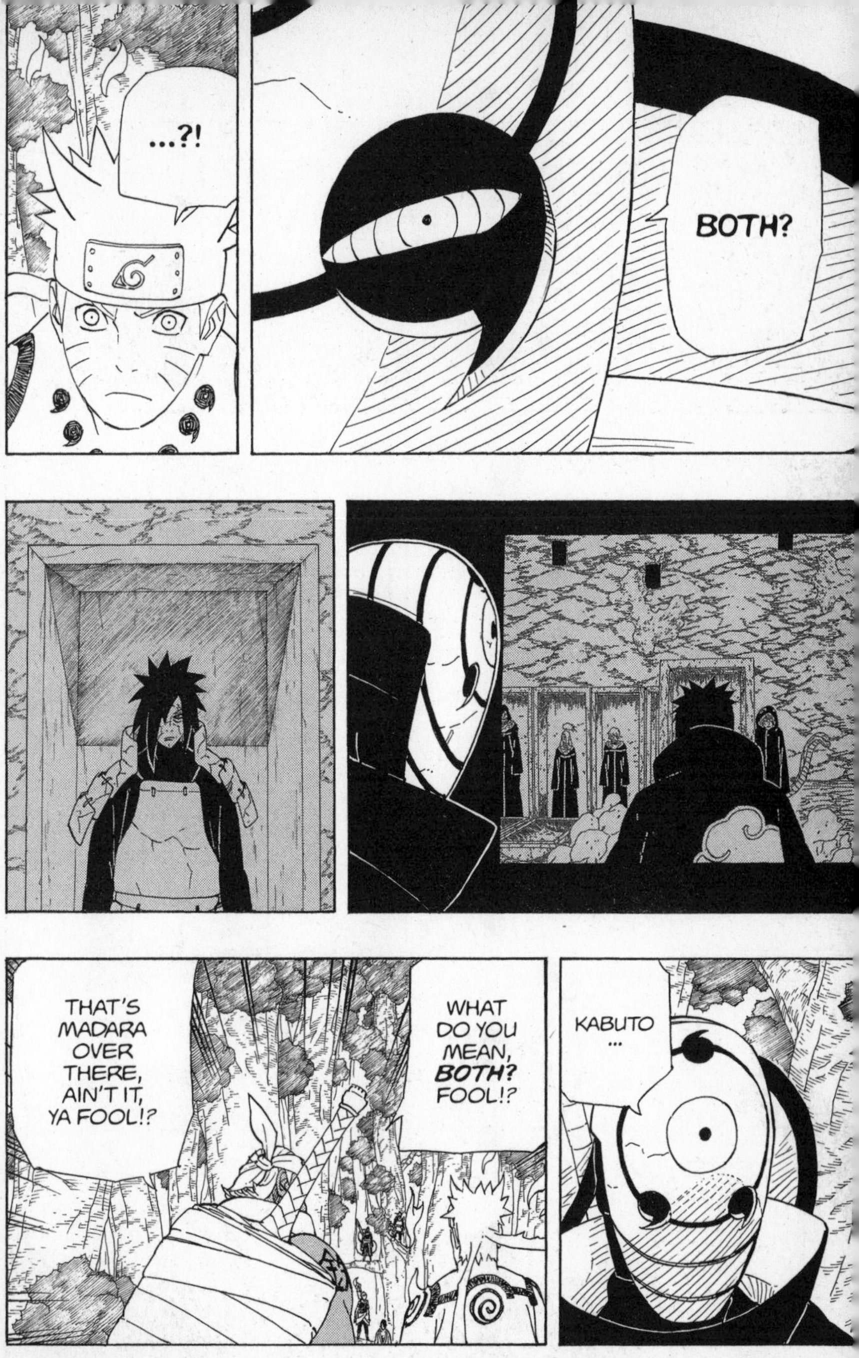
BOTH?
...?!
KABUTO ...
WHAT DO YOU MEAN, **BOTH?** FOOL!?
THAT'S MADARA OVER THERE, AIN'T IT, YA FOOL!?

READ THIS WAY

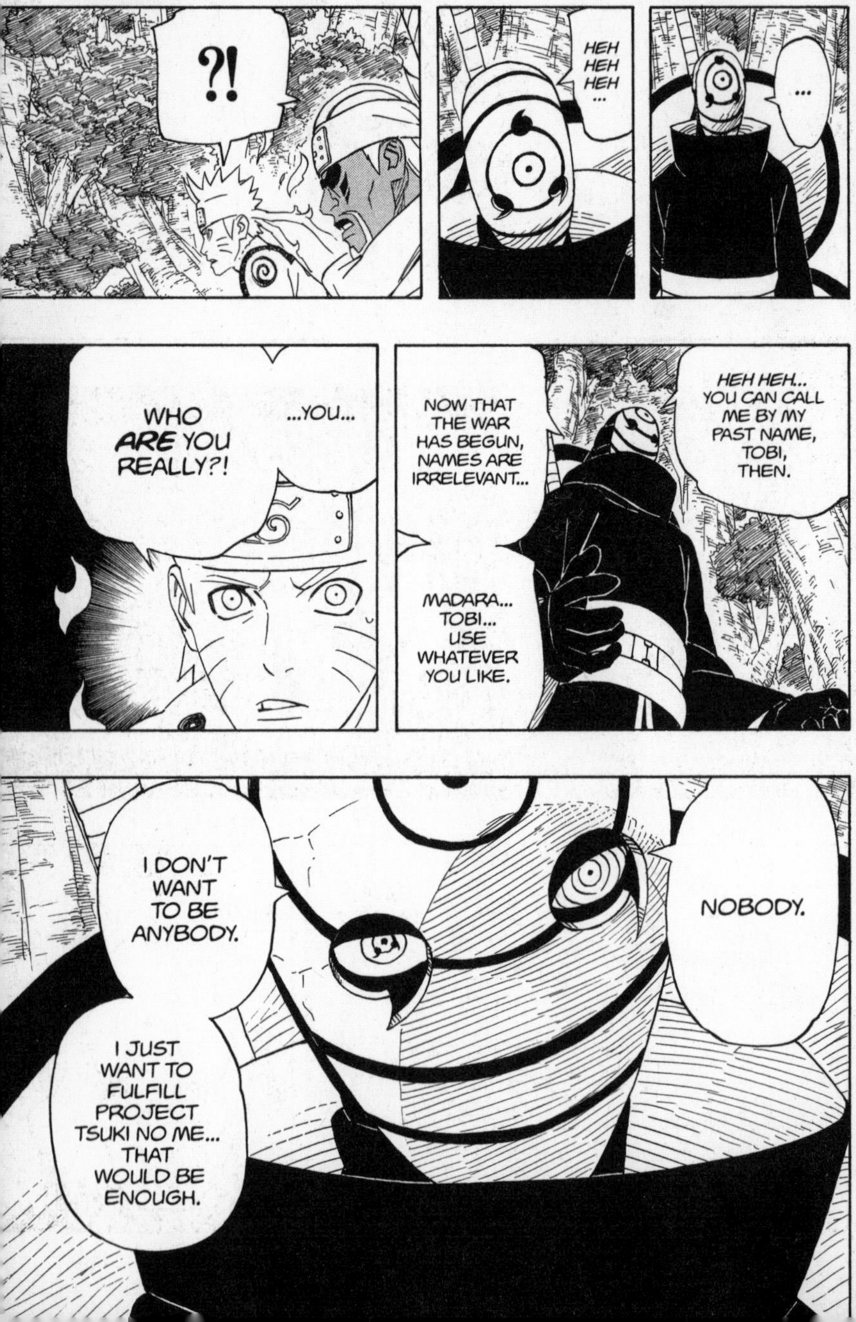
...
HEH HEH HEH ...
?!
HEH HEH... YOU CAN CALL ME BY MY PAST NAME, TOBI, THEN.
NOW THAT THE WAR HAS BEGUN, NAMES ARE IRRELEVANT...
MADARA... TOBI... USE WHATEVER YOU LIKE.
...YOU...
WHO ARE YOU REALLY?!
NOBODY.
I DON'T WANT TO BE ANYBODY.
I JUST WANT TO FULFILL PROJECT TSUKI NO ME... THAT WOULD BE ENOUGH.

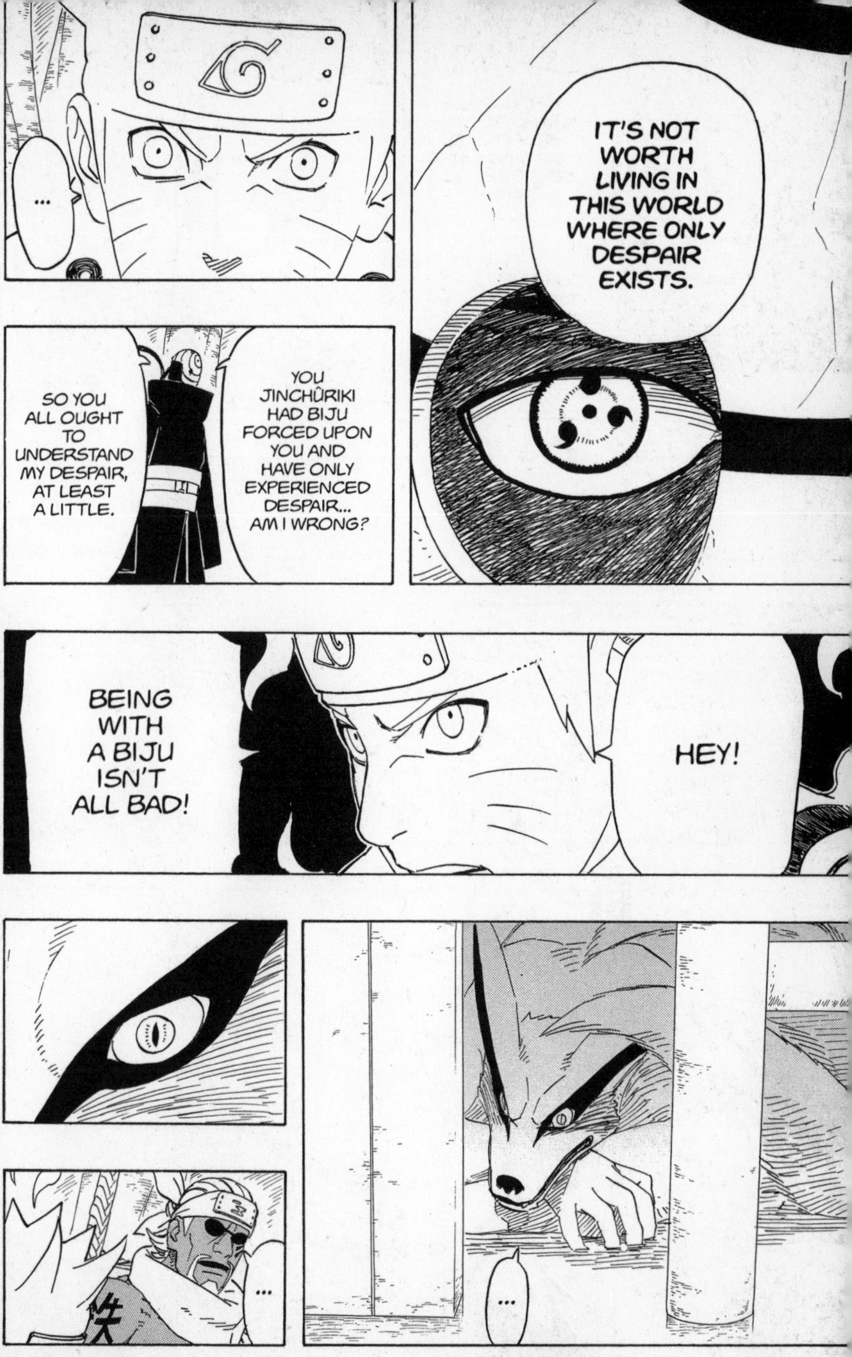
IT'S NOT WORTH LIVING IN THIS WORLD WHERE ONLY DESPAIR EXISTS.
...
YOU JINCHÛRIKI HAD BIJU FORCED UPON YOU AND HAVE ONLY EXPERIENCED DESPAIR... AM I WRONG?
SO YOU ALL OUGHT TO UNDERSTAND MY DESPAIR, AT LEAST A LITTLE.
HEY!
BEING WITH A BIJU ISN'T ALL BAD!
...
...

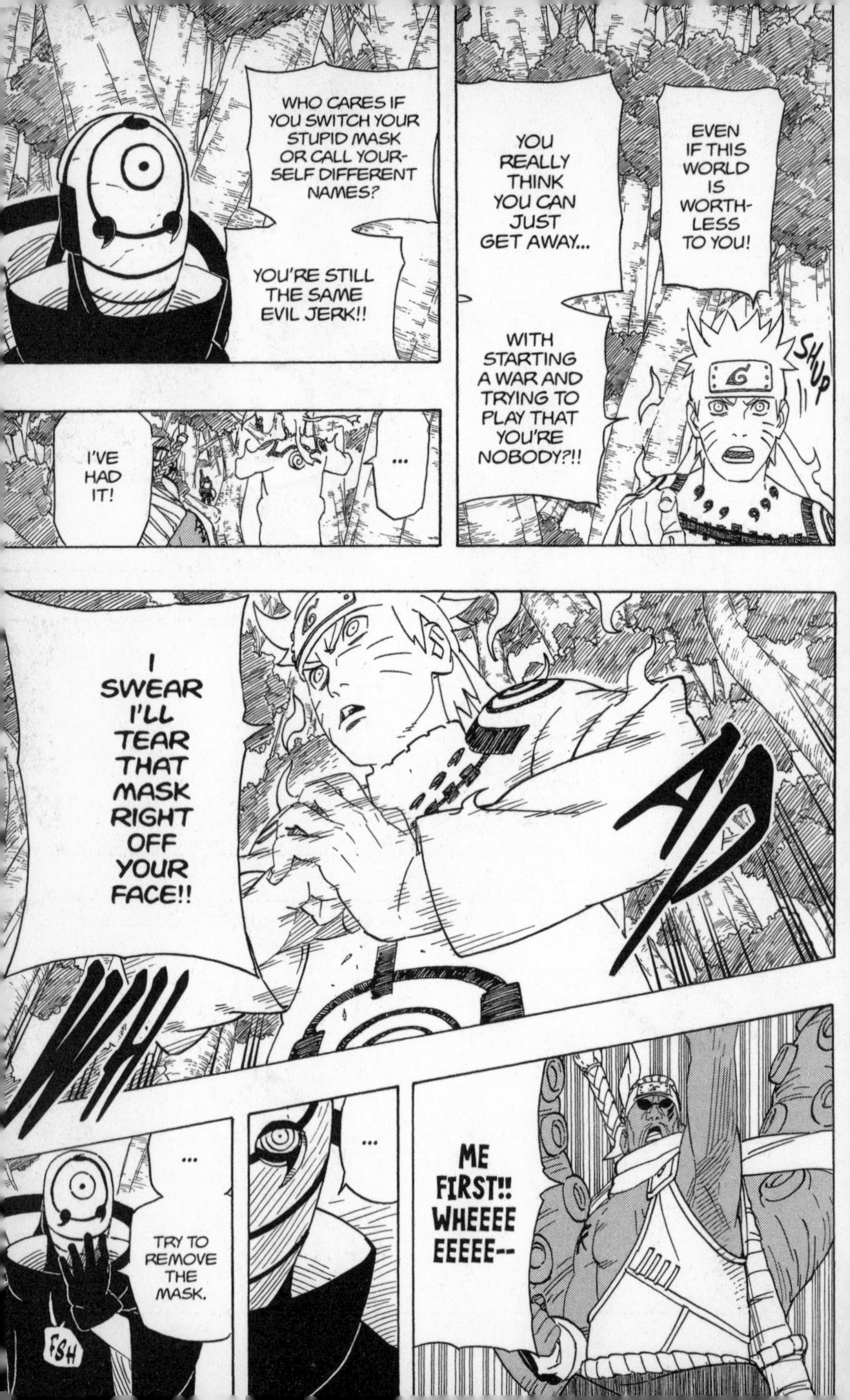
EVEN IF THIS WORLD IS WORTHLESS TO YOU!
YOU REALLY THINK YOU CAN JUST GET AWAY...
WITH STARTING A WAR AND TRYING TO PLAY THAT YOU'RE NOBODY?!!
SHUP
WHO CARES IF YOU SWITCH YOUR STUPID MASK OR CALL YOURSELF DIFFERENT NAMES?
YOU'RE STILL THE SAME EVIL JERK!!
...
I'VE HAD IT!
I SWEAR I'LL TEAR THAT MASK RIGHT OFF YOUR FACE!!
ME FIRST!! WHEEEE EEEEE--
...
...
TRY TO REMOVE THE MASK.
FSH

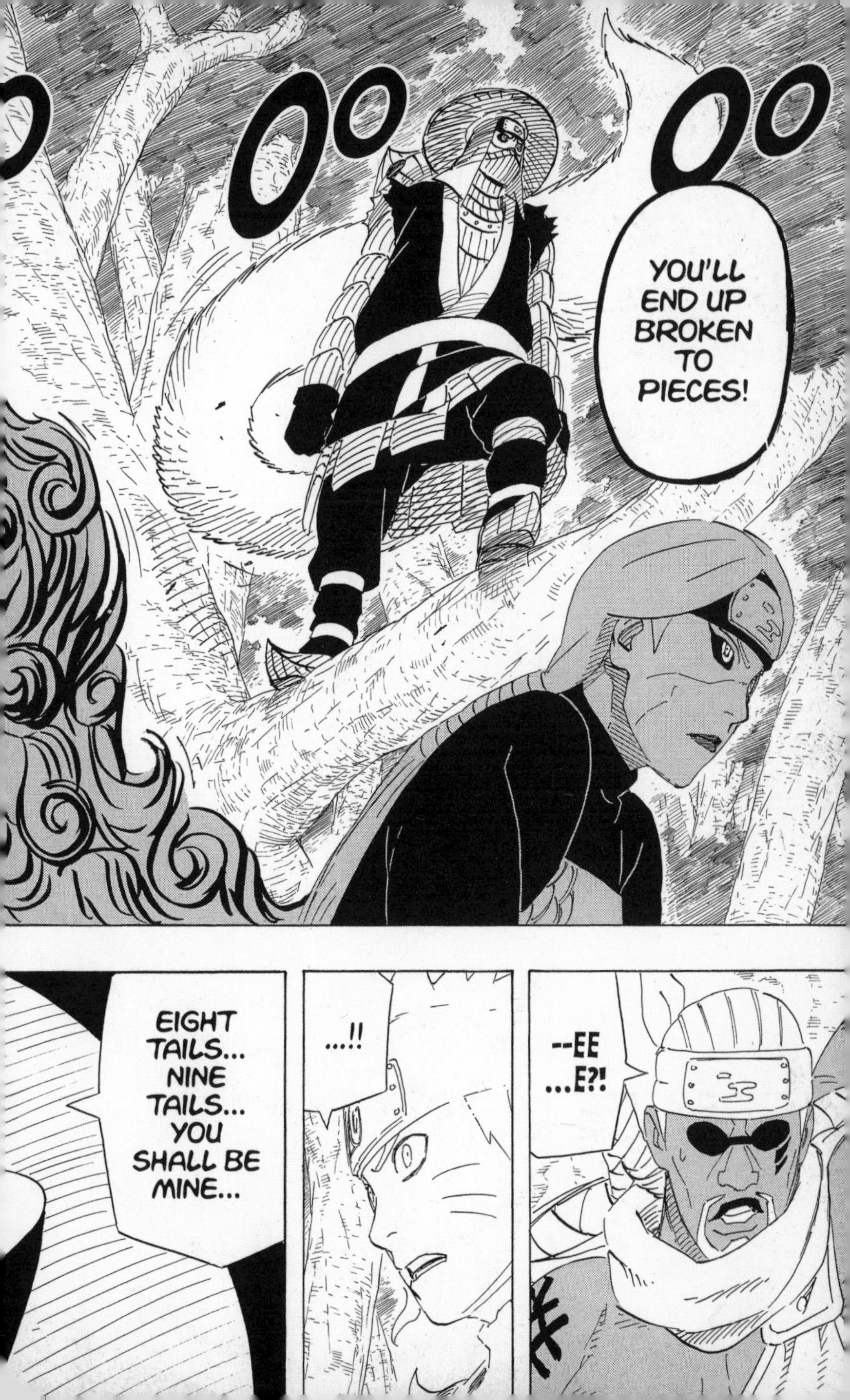
OOO
YOU'LL END UP BROKEN TO PIECES!
--EE ...E?!
...!!
EIGHT TAILS... NINE TAILS... YOU SHALL BE MINE...

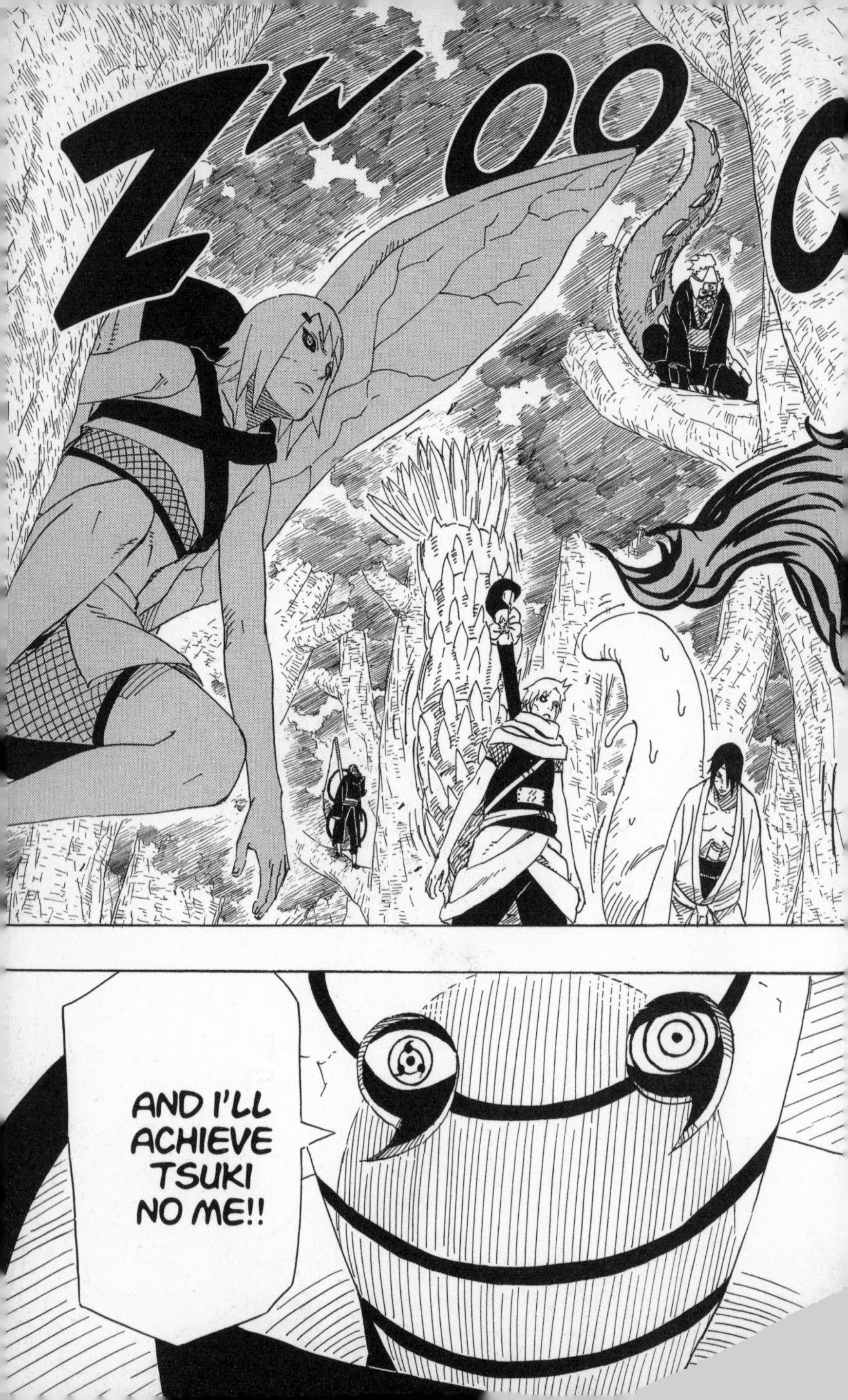
ZWOOO
AND I'LL ACHIEVE TSUKI NO ME!!

NARUTO

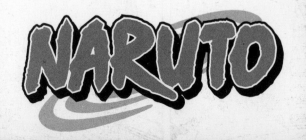

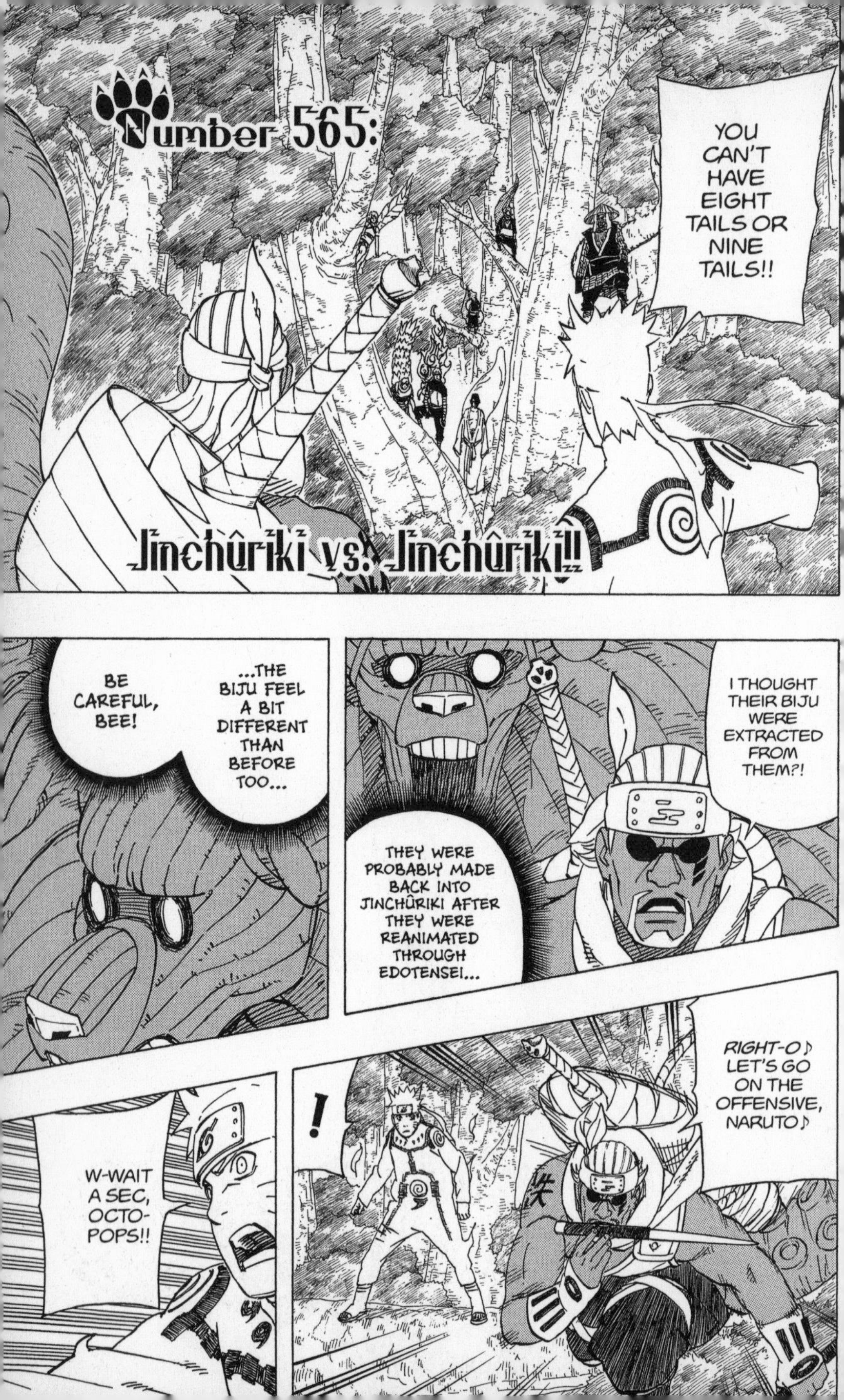
Number 565:
Jinchûriki vs. Jinchûriki!!
YOU CAN'T HAVE EIGHT TAILS OR NINE TAILS!!
I THOUGHT THEIR BIJU WERE EXTRACTED FROM THEM?!
THEY WERE PROBABLY MADE BACK INTO JINCHÛRIKI AFTER THEY WERE REANIMATED THROUGH EDOTENSEI...
BE CAREFUL, BEE!
...THE BIJU FEEL A BIT DIFFERENT THAN BEFORE TOO...
RIGHT-O♪ LET'S GO ON THE OFFENSIVE, NARUTO♪
!
W-WAIT A SEC, OCTO-POPS!!

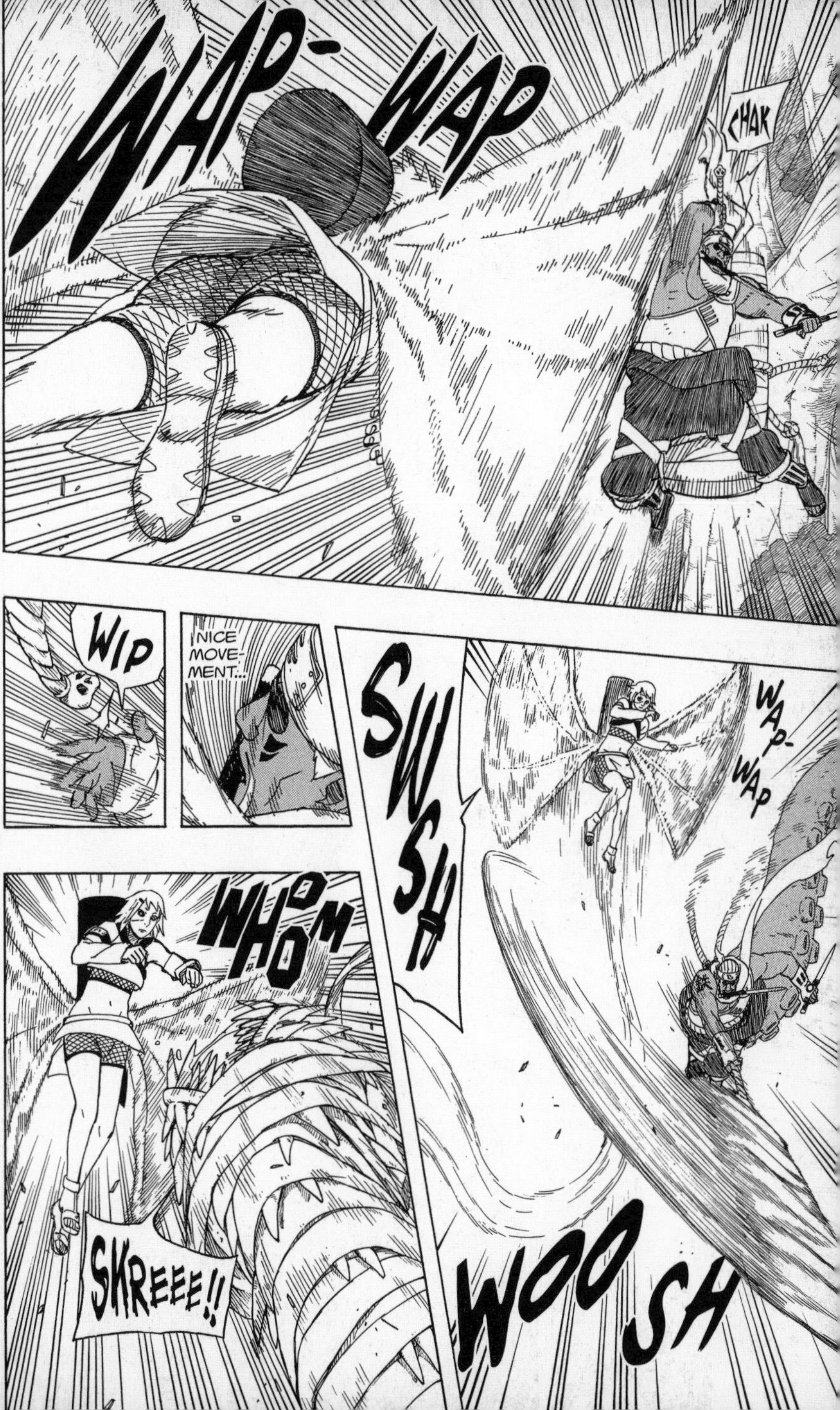
WAP-WAP
CHAK
SWSH
WAP-WAP
WOOSH
NICE MOVEMENT...
WIP
WHOOM
SKREEE!!

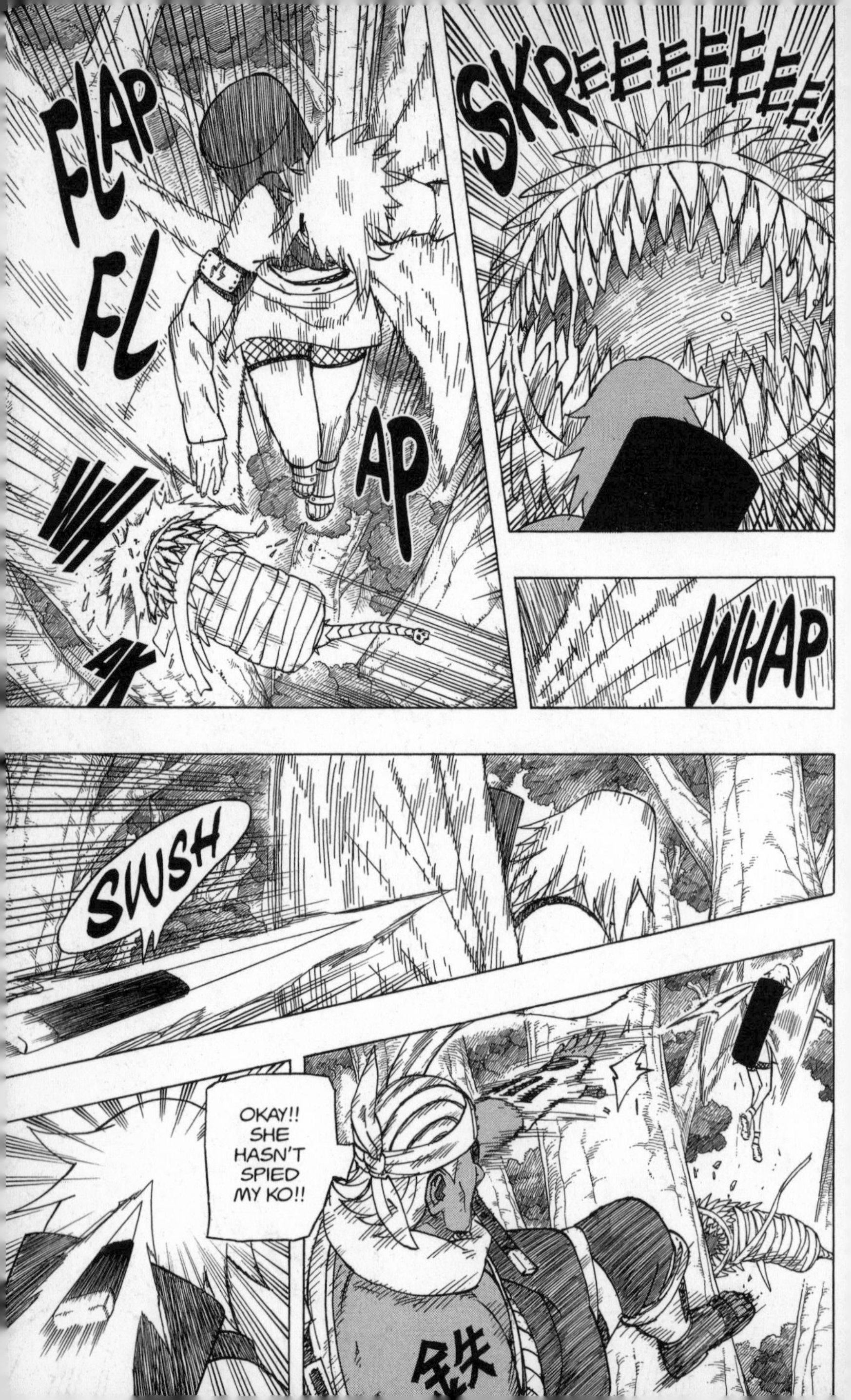
SKREEEEEEEEEE!!
WHAP
FLAP
FL
AP
WH
AK
SWUSH
OKAY!! SHE HASN'T SPIED MY KO!!

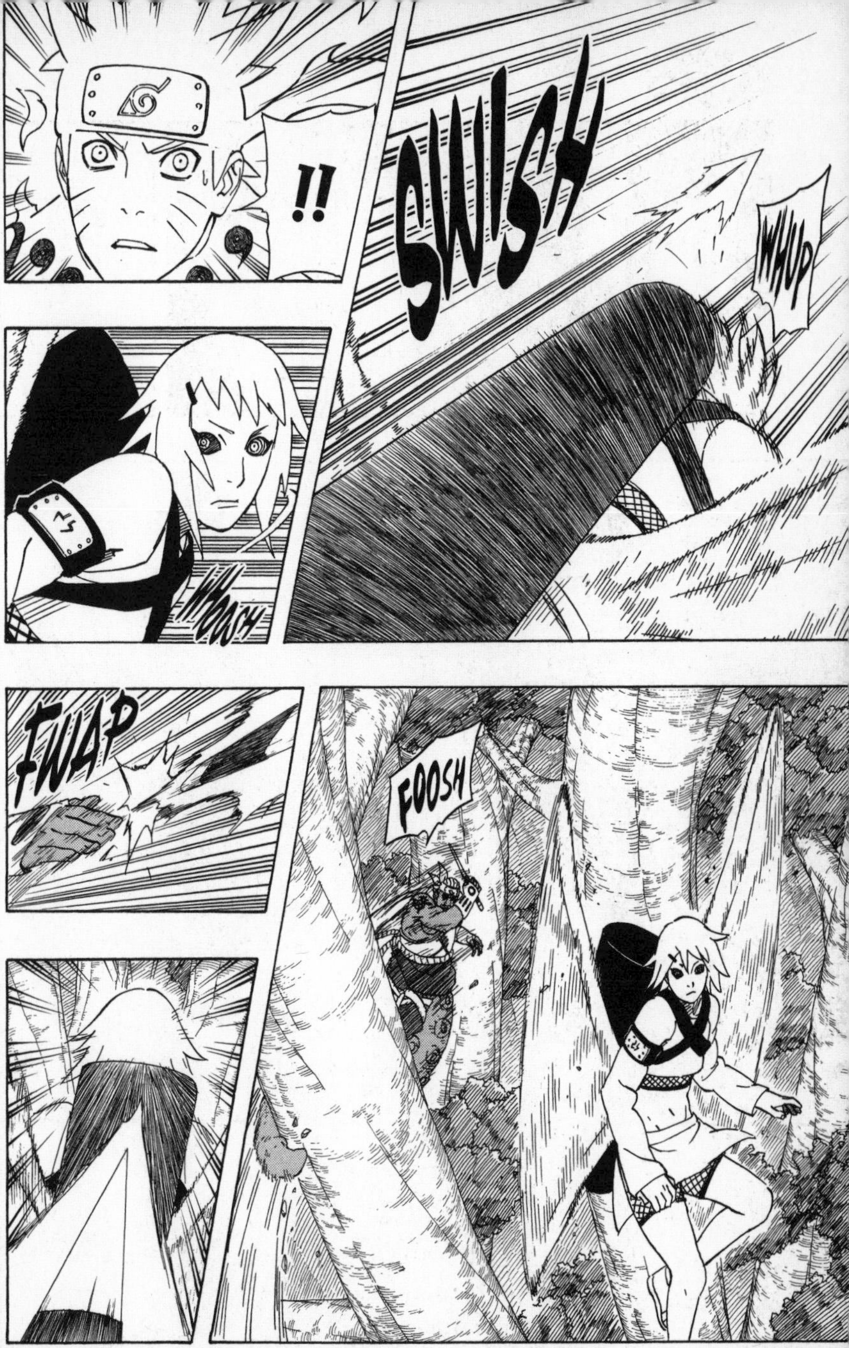
SWISH
WHUP
!!
WHOOSH
FOOSH
FWAP

READ THIS WAY

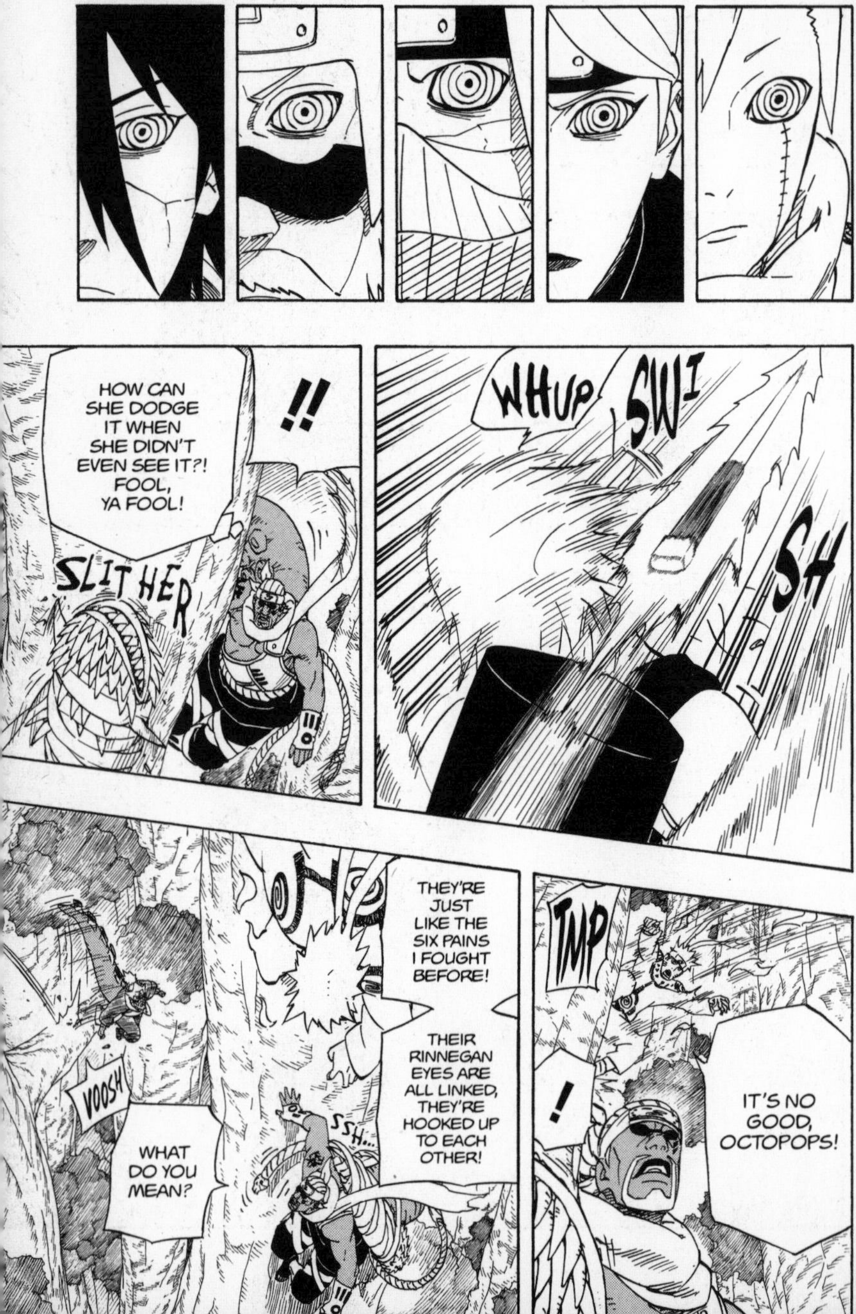
WHUP
SWI
SH
HOW CAN SHE DODGE IT WHEN SHE DIDN'T EVEN SEE IT?! FOOL, YA FOOL!
!!
SLITHER
TMP
IT'S NO GOOD, OCTOPOPS!
!
THEY'RE JUST LIKE THE SIX PAINS I FOUGHT BEFORE!
THEIR RINNEGAN EYES ARE ALL LINKED, THEY'RE HOOKED UP TO EACH OTHER!
SSH...
VOOSH
WHAT DO YOU MEAN?

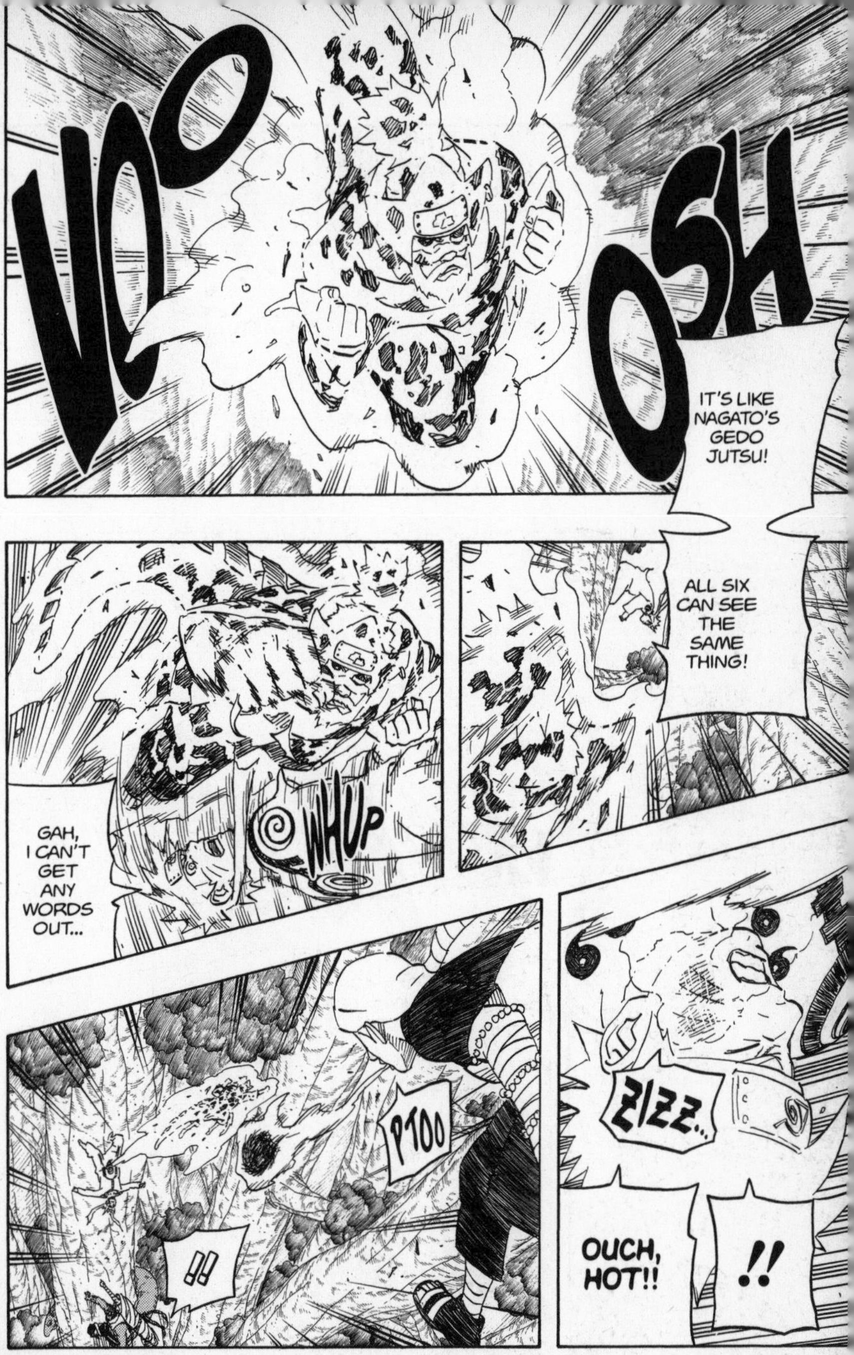
VOOOSH
IT'S LIKE NAGATO'S GEDO JUTSU!
ALL SIX CAN SEE THE SAME THING!
WHUP
GAH, I CAN'T GET ANY WORDS OUT...
ZIZZ..
!!
OUCH, HOT!!
PTOO
!!

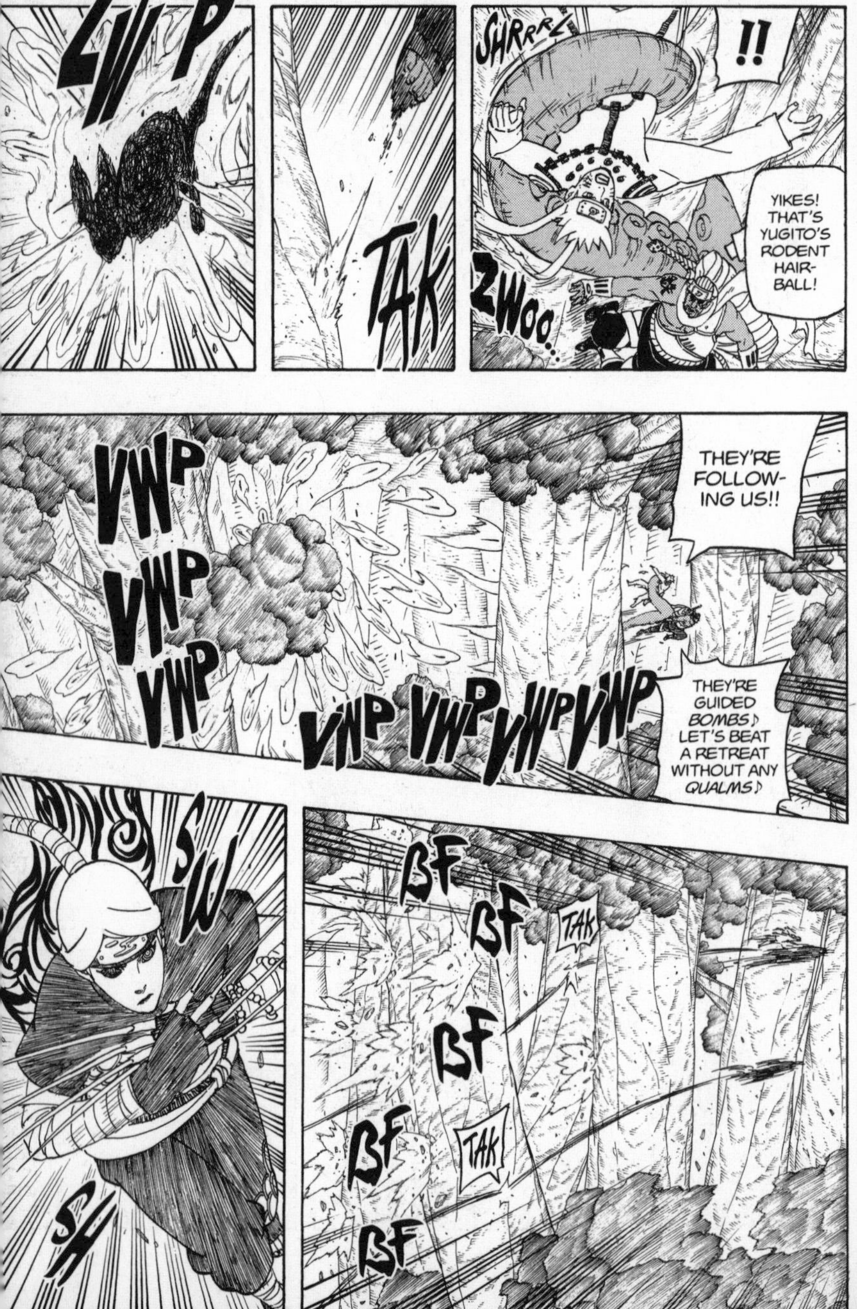
SHRRRL
!!
YIKES! THAT'S YUGITO'S RODENT HAIR-BALL!
ZWOO...
TAK
ZWIP
THEY'RE FOLLOW-ING US!!
THEY'RE GUIDED *BOMBS*♪ LET'S BEAT A RETREAT WITHOUT ANY *QUALMS*♪
VWP VWP VWP
VWP VWP VWP VWP
BF
BF
TAK
BF
BF
TAK
BF
SW
SH

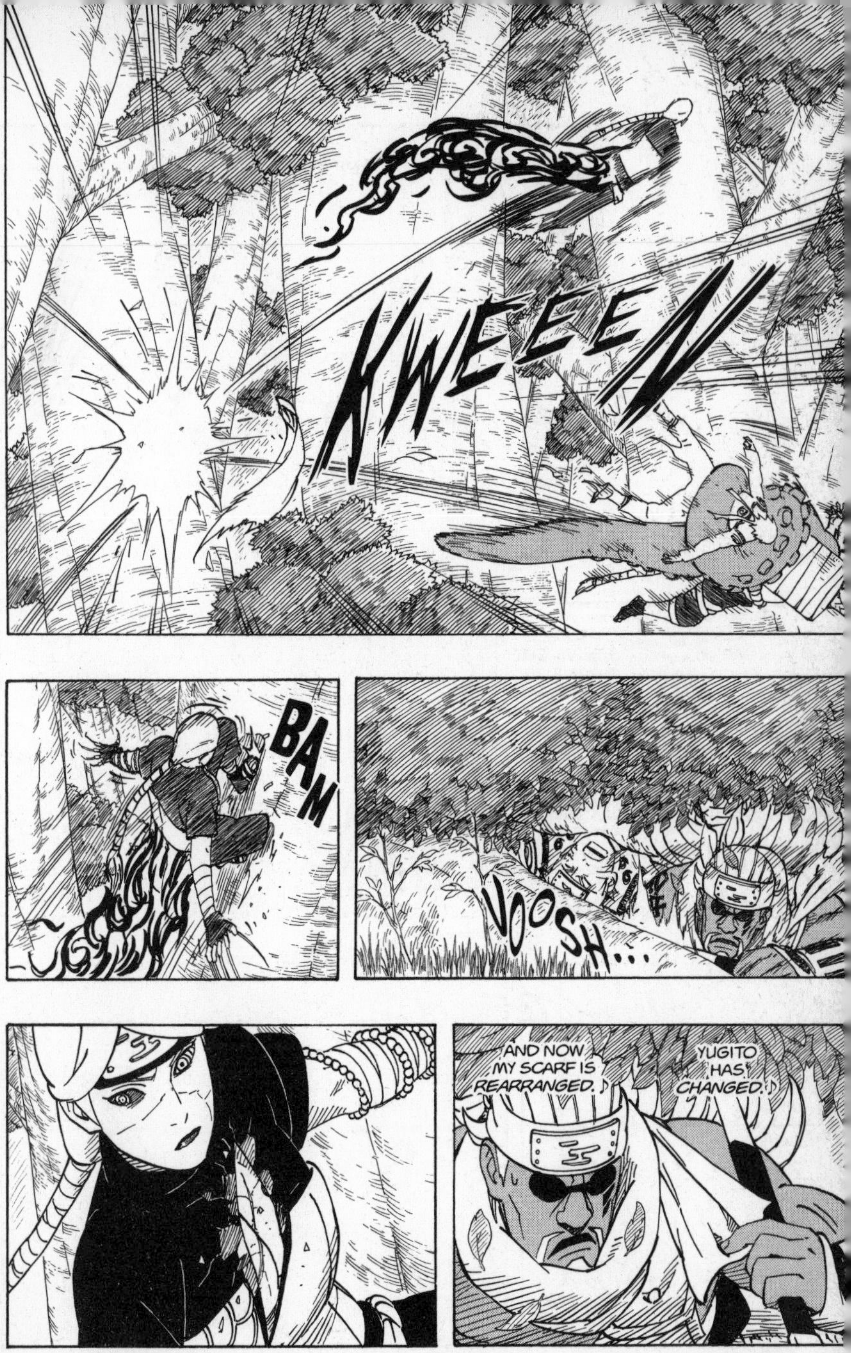
KWEEEN
VOOSH...
BAM
YUGITO HAS CHANGED.♪
AND NOW MY SCARF IS REARRANGED.♪

READ THIS WAY

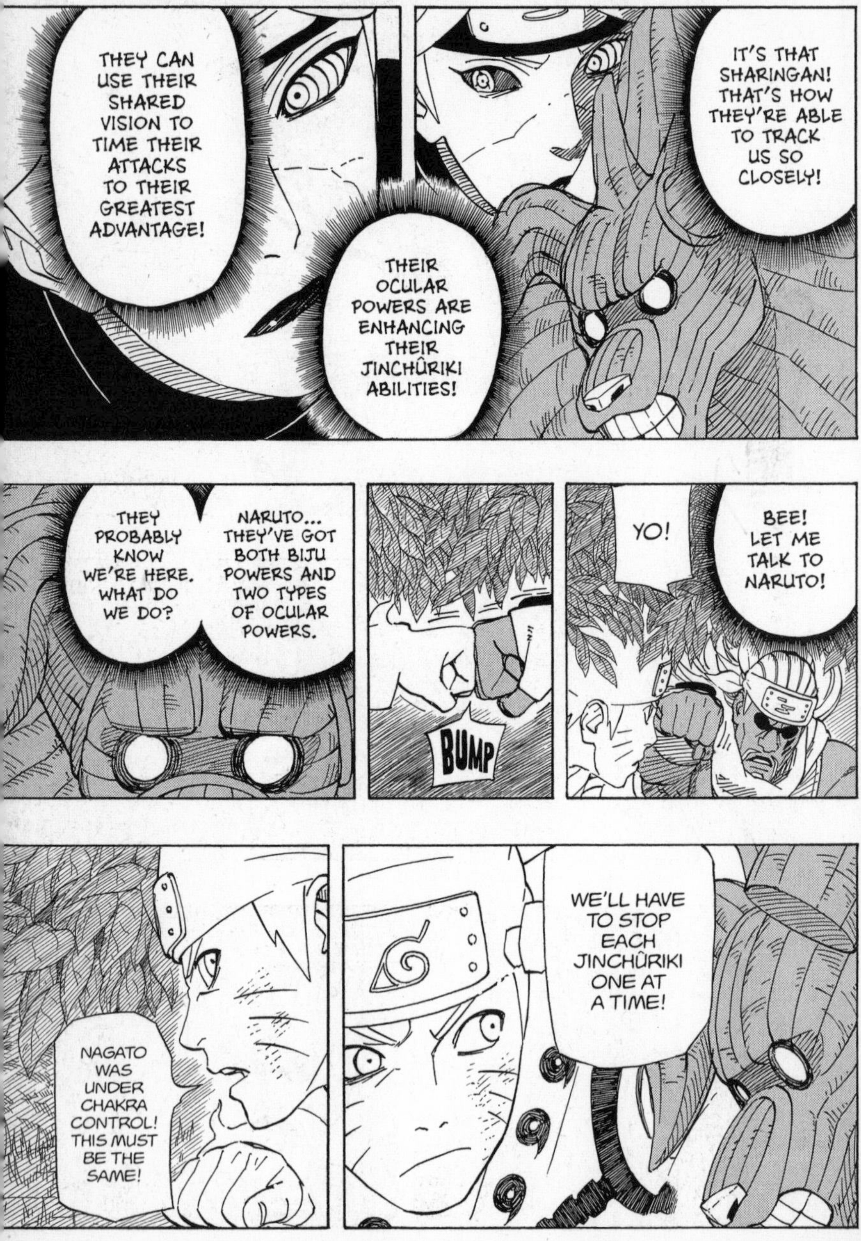
IT'S THAT SHARINGAN! THAT'S HOW THEY'RE ABLE TO TRACK US SO CLOSELY!
THEY CAN USE THEIR SHARED VISION TO TIME THEIR ATTACKS TO THEIR GREATEST ADVANTAGE!
THEIR OCULAR POWERS ARE ENHANCING THEIR JINCHÛRIKI ABILITIES!
BEE! LET ME TALK TO NARUTO!
YO!
BUMP
NARUTO... THEY'VE GOT BOTH BIJU POWERS AND TWO TYPES OF OCULAR POWERS.
THEY PROBABLY KNOW WE'RE HERE. WHAT DO WE DO?
WE'LL HAVE TO STOP EACH JINCHÛRIKI ONE AT A TIME!
NAGATO WAS UNDER CHAKRA CONTROL! THIS MUST BE THE SAME!

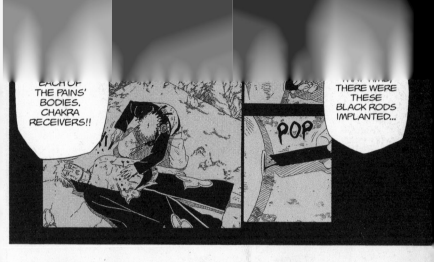

THERE WERE THESE BLACK RODS IMPLANTED...
POP
THE PAINS' BODIES. CHAKRA RECEIVERS!!
I SEE... SO IF WE CAN EXTRACT OR DESTROY THOSE, THIS GEDO JUTSU WOULD COME UNDONE...
...BUT THAT'S A BOTHER... IT'S HARD ENOUGH TO GET OUR ATTACKS TO HIT, PERIOD...
...MUCH LESS TO TARGET BLACK RECEIVERS THAT WE DON'T EVEN KNOW WHERE THEY ARE...
IS THAT IT?
?!
WHERE?!
?!
I WAS INSPECTING YUGITO, CHECKING HER OUT♪
WHEN I DISCOVERED SOMETHING STRANGE STICKING OUT♪
I WASN'T SURE WHAT I WAS SEEING!
BUT...!!
WHAP

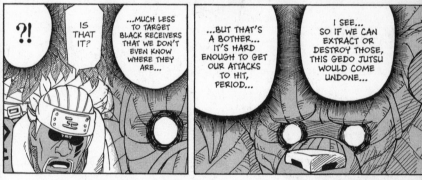

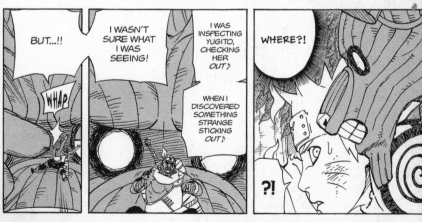

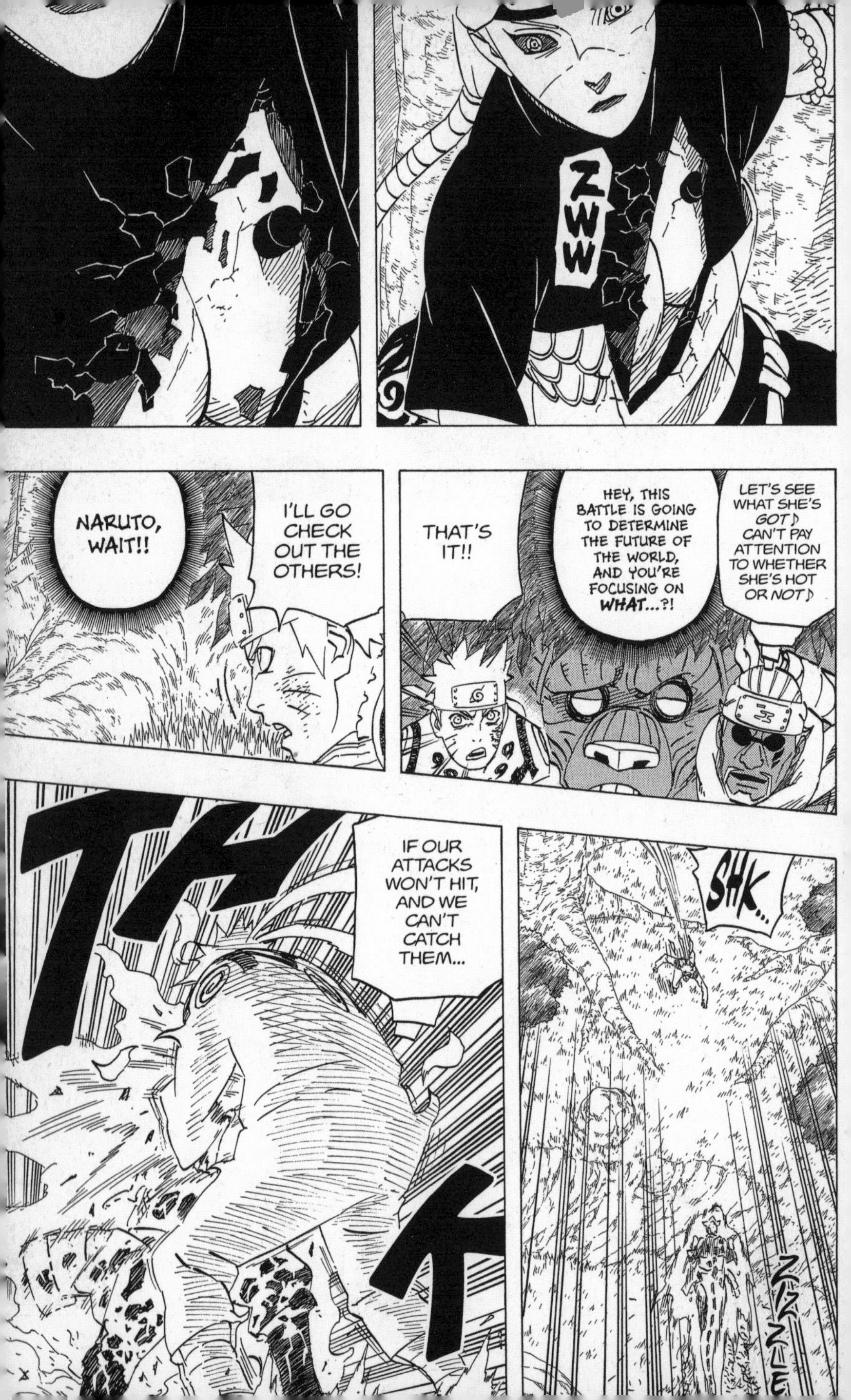
ZWW
LET'S SEE WHAT SHE'S GOT♪ CAN'T PAY ATTENTION TO WHETHER SHE'S HOT OR NOT♪
HEY, THIS BATTLE IS GOING TO DETERMINE THE FUTURE OF THE WORLD, AND YOU'RE FOCUSING ON **WHAT...?!**
THAT'S IT!!
I'LL GO CHECK OUT THE OTHERS!
NARUTO, WAIT!!
SHK...
ZZZLE
IF OUR ATTACKS WON'T HIT, AND WE CAN'T CATCH THEM...

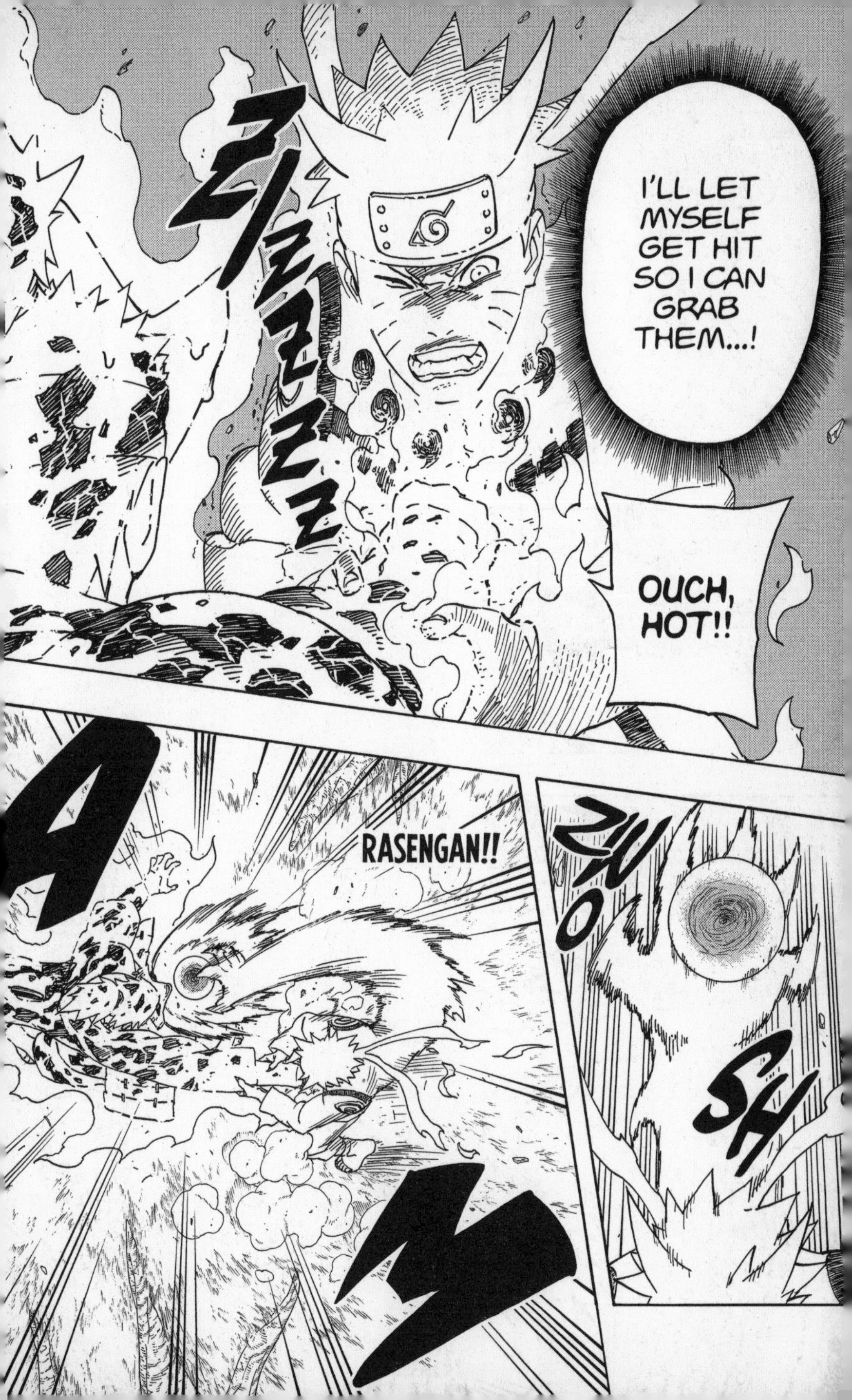

I'LL LET MYSELF GET HIT SO I CAN GRAB THEM...!
OUCH, HOT!!
SH
RASENGAN!!

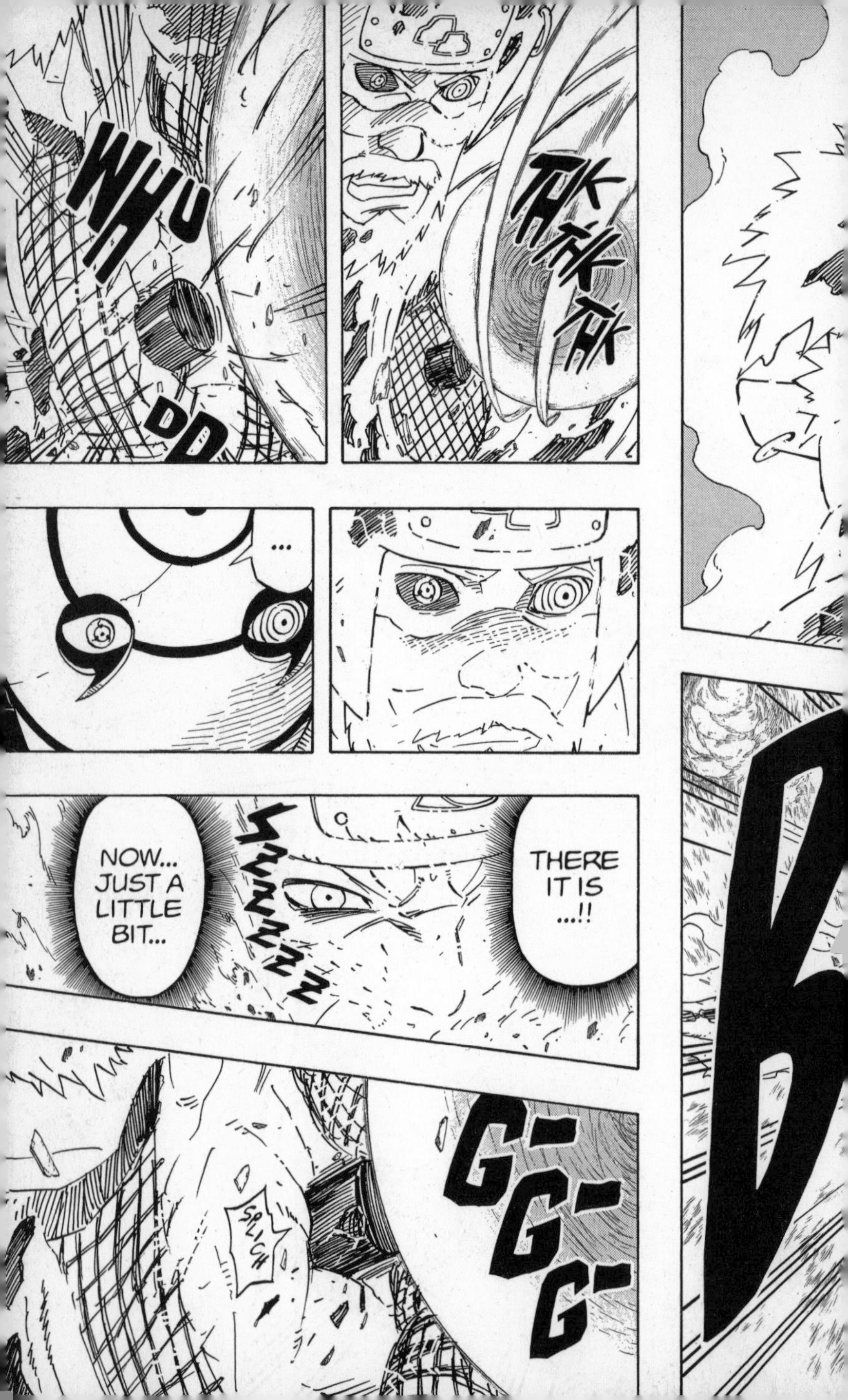

TAK TAK TAK TAK
WHUDD
...
B
THERE IT IS ...!!
SZZZZZZ
NOW... JUST A LITTLE BIT...
G-G-G-
SPLICH

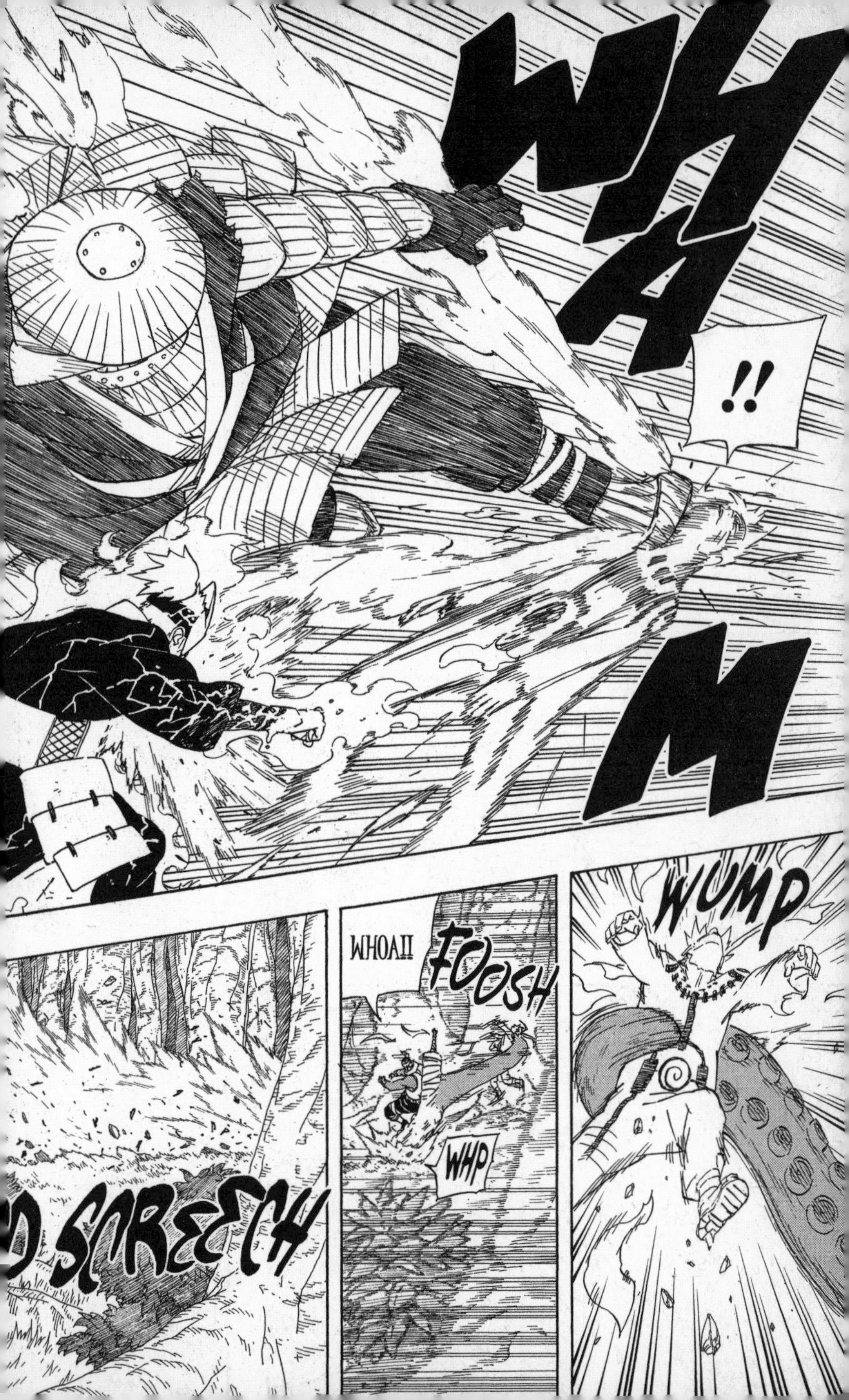

WHAM
!!
WUMP
WHOA!!
FOOSH
WHP
SCREECH

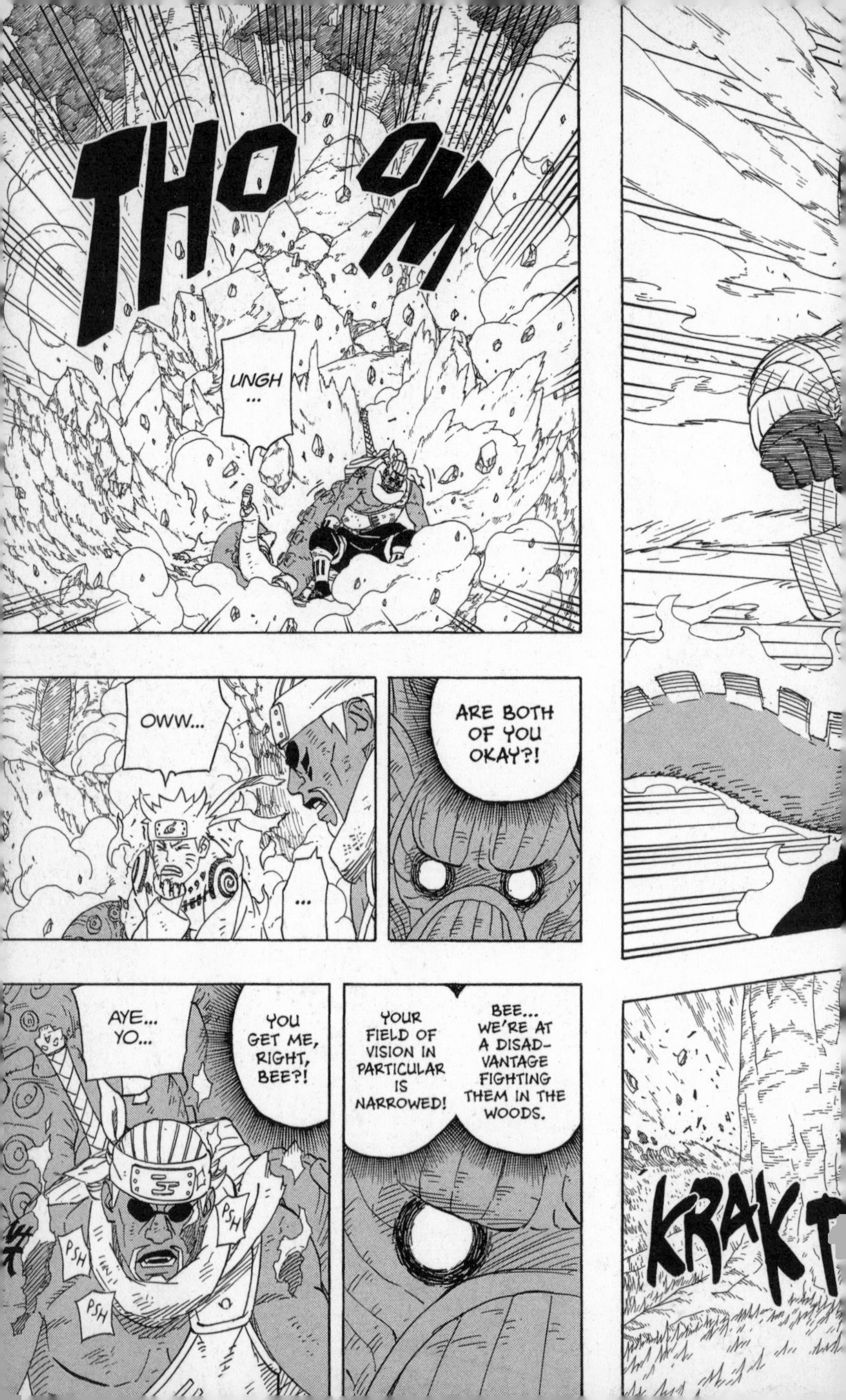
THOOM
UNGH...
ARE BOTH OF YOU OKAY?!
OWW...
...
KRAKT
BEE... WE'RE AT A DISADVANTAGE FIGHTING THEM IN THE WOODS.
YOUR FIELD OF VISION IN PARTICULAR IS NARROWED!
YOU GET ME, RIGHT, BEE?!
AYE... YO...
PSH
PSH
PSH

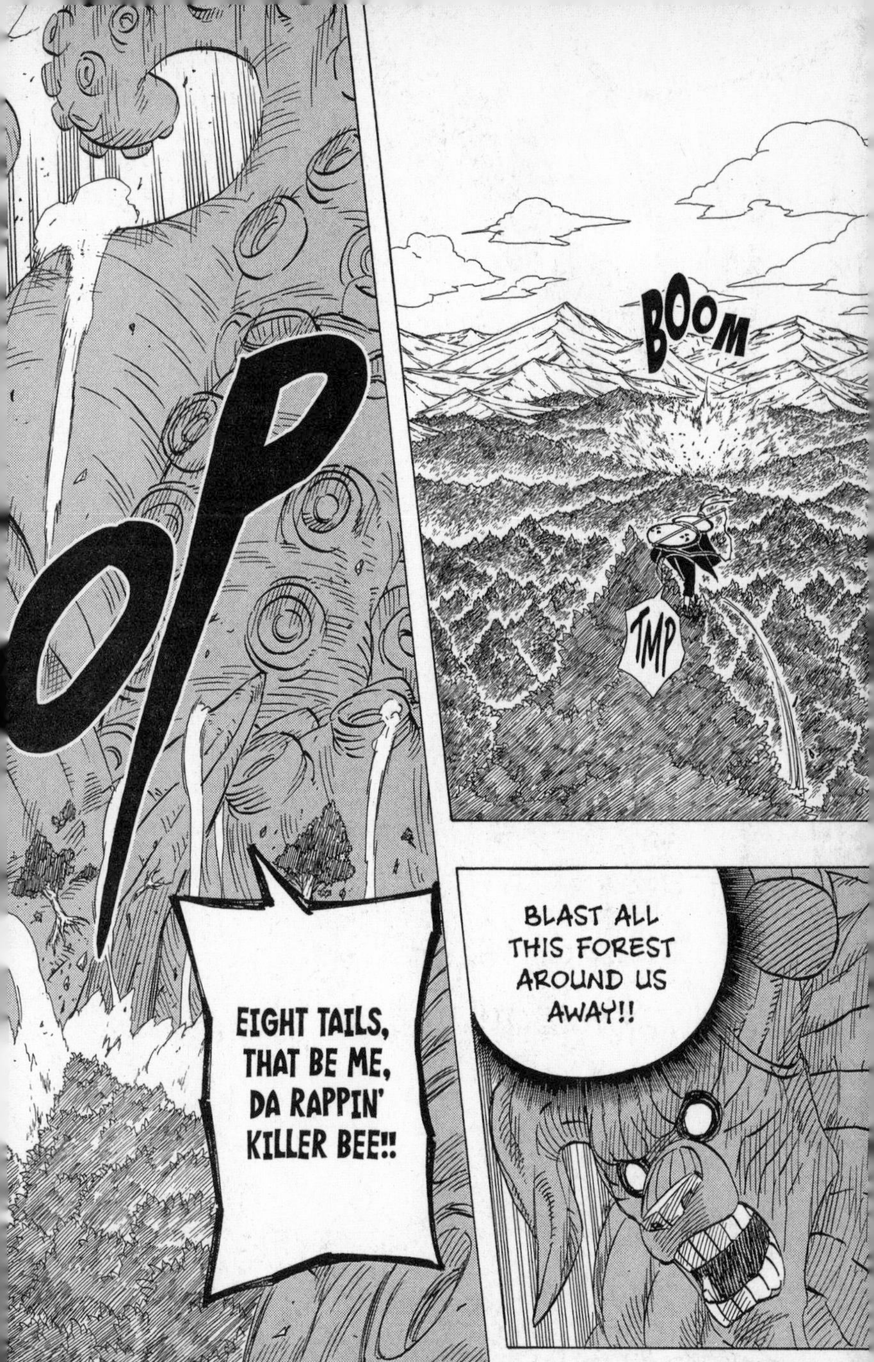
BOOM
TMP
BLAST ALL THIS FOREST AROUND US AWAY!!
OP
EIGHT TAILS, THAT BE ME, DA RAPPIN' KILLER BEE!!

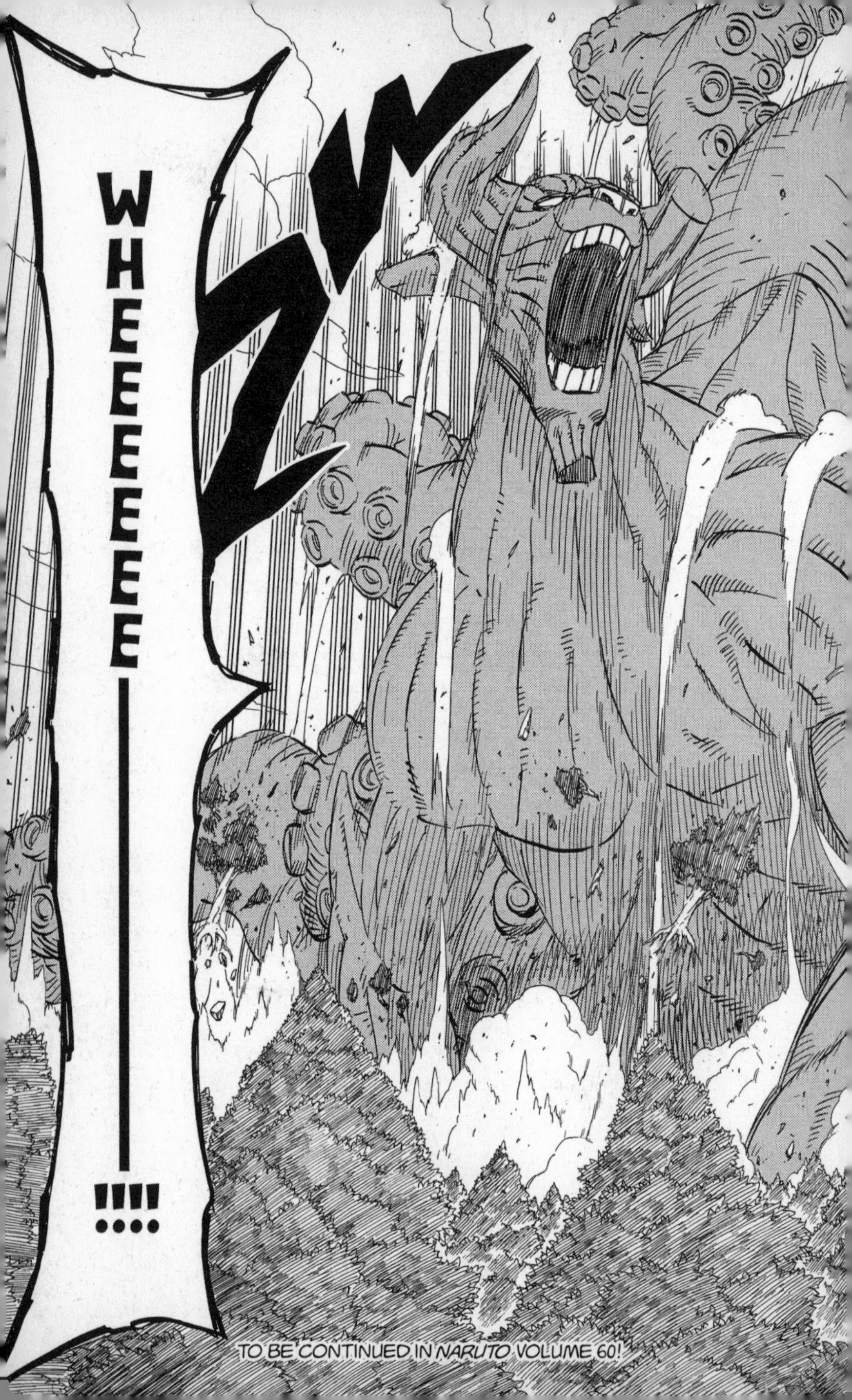
WHEEEEEE—!!!!
ZWW

TO BE CONTINUED IN *NARUTO* VOLUME 60!

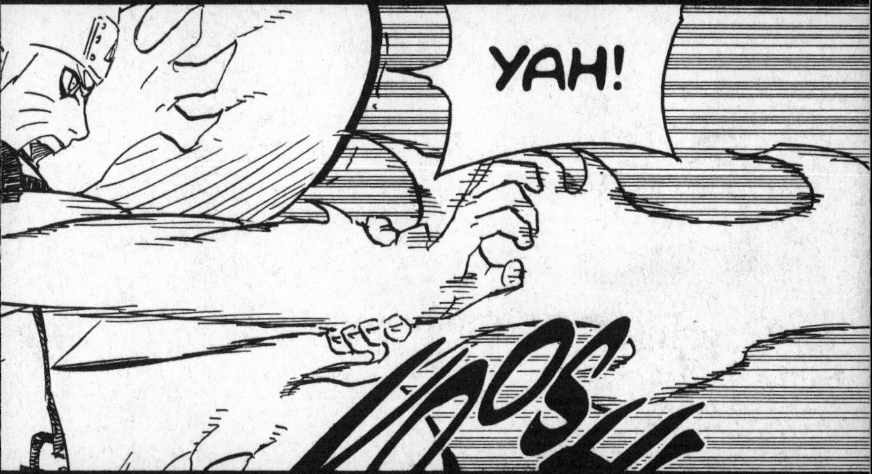
YAH!

IN THE NEXT VOLUME...

KURUMA

Naruto impresses the Allied Shinobi Forces with his newfound strengths, but his comrades are not going to leave this final battle with the forces of Tobi (aka Uchiha Madara) up to Naruto alone. As they rush to assist their friend, old pals like Sakura vow to stand by Naruto this time till the end. In the midst of all this... Sasuke returns. And this time, he's intent on taking out Naruto once and for all.

AVAILABLE FEBRUARY 2013!

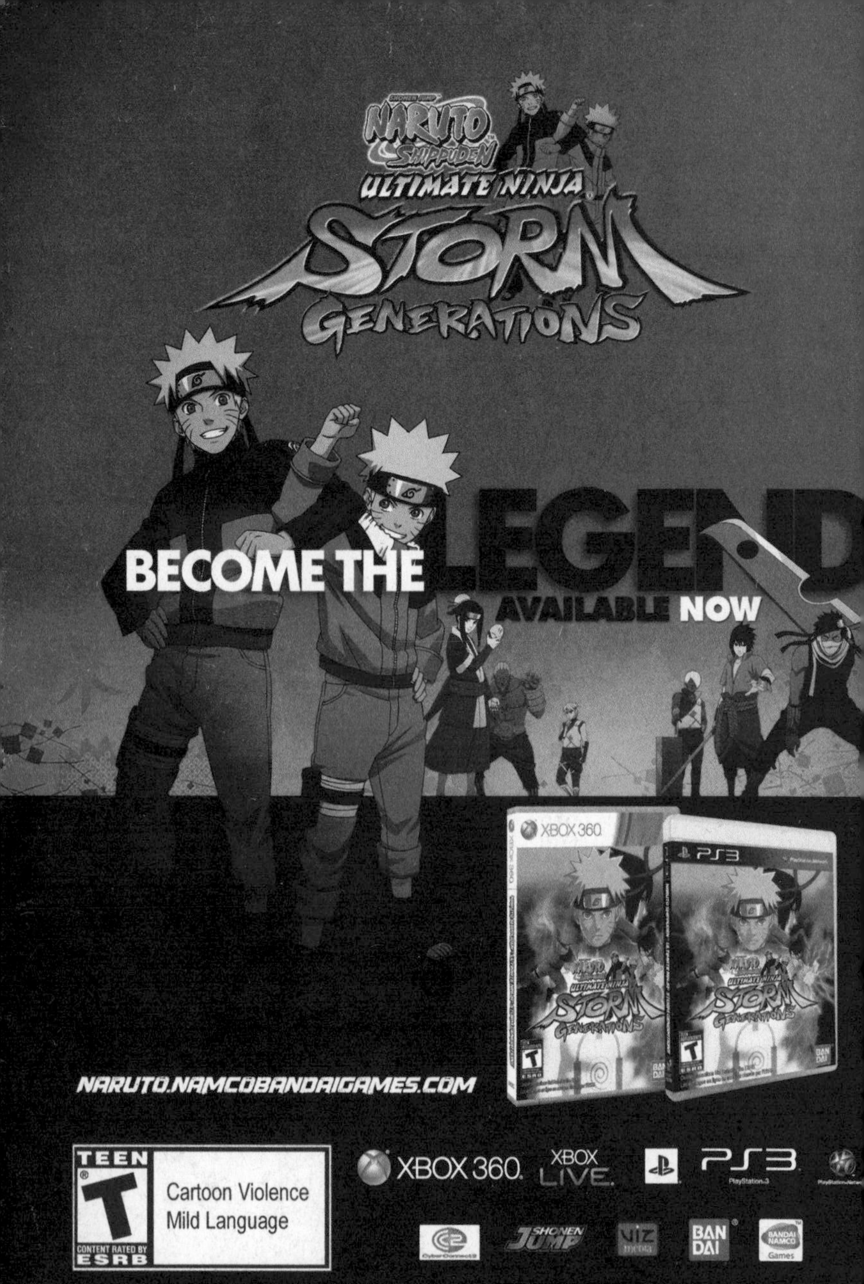
NARUTO SHIPPUDEN
ULTIMATE NINJA
STORM
GENERATIONS
BECOME THE LEGEND
AVAILABLE NOW
XBOX 360
PS3
NARUTO.NAMCOBANDAIGAMES.COM
TEEN
T
CONTENT RATED BY ESRB
Cartoon Violence
Mild Language
XBOX 360
XBOX LIVE
PlayStation 3
SHONEN JUMP
VIZ media
BANDAI
BANDAI NAMCO Games

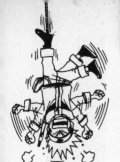

You're Reading in the Wrong Direction!!

Whoops! Guess what? You're starting at the wrong end of the comic!

...It's true! In keeping with the original Japanese format, **Naruto** is meant to be read from right to left, starting in the upper-right corner.

Unlike English, which is read from left to right, Japanese is read from right to left, meaning that action, sound effects and word-balloon order are completely reversed... something which can make readers unfamiliar with Japanese feel pretty backwards themselves. For this reason, manga or Japanese comics published in the U.S. in English have sometimes been published "flopped"—that is, printed in exact reverse order, as though seen from the other side of a mirror.

By flopping pages, U.S. publishers can avoid confusing readers, but the compromise is not without its downside. For one thing, a character in a flopped manga series who once wore in the original Japanese version a T-shirt emblazoned with "M A Y" (as in "the merry month of") now wears one which reads "Y A M"! Additionally, many manga creators in Japan are themselves unhappy with the process, as some feel the mirror-imaging of their art alters their original intentions.

We are proud to bring you Masashi Kishimoto's **Naruto** in the original unflopped format. For now, though, turn to the other side of the book and let the ninjutsu begin...!

—Editor

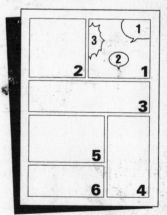